Preface

Welcome to the world of Mastering Cloud Computing With Best Practices! As you hold this book in your hands, you are embarking on a remarkable journey that will unravel the mysteries of cloud technologies and open up a universe of possibilities.

Cloud Computing has transformed the way we interact with technology, both in our personal lives and in the business world. It has revolutionized the landscape of IT infrastructure, enabling unprecedented scalability, flexibility, and cost-efficiency. From startups to global enterprises, from mobile apps to complex data analytics, the cloud has become an indispensable part of modern computing.

In "Mastering Cloud Computing", we have curated a comprehensive guide to help you master the cloud. Whether you are a seasoned IT professional seeking to enhance your cloud expertise or a curious enthusiast looking to explore the latest technological trends, this book is designed to cater to your learning needs.

What You Will Find in This Book

Our journey begins with an Introduction to Cloud Computing, where we lay the foundation by explaining what cloud computing is and the benefits it offers. You'll gain insights into different cloud service models - Infrastructure as a Service (IaaS), Platform as a Service (PaaS), and Software as a Service (SaaS) - to understand how they shape cloud solutions.

As we venture further, we delve into Cloud Infrastructure and explore the fascinating world of virtualization, data centers, server farms, networking, and storage technologies in the cloud. Understanding these essential components will empower you to build robust cloud environments.

Security is of utmost importance, and we dedicate an entire section to Cloud Security and Compliance. You'll learn about securing access, data encryption, and how to comply with regulatory standards, ensuring your cloud environment remains safe and compliant.

We then embark on a journey through the cloud landscapes of major Cloud Service Providers, such as Amazon Web Services (AWS), Microsoft Azure, Google Cloud Platform (GCP), and other key players. By the end of this section, you'll have a comprehensive understanding of the unique offerings and strengths of each provider.

Migrating to the cloud can be a daunting task, but our detailed exploration of Cloud Migration Strategies will equip you with the knowledge and confidence to plan and execute successful cloud migrations. We'll also dive into Cloud Cost Optimization, where you'll learn how to optimize expenses and maximize the value of your cloud investments.

Throughout this book, we've included practical exercises to reinforce your learning and apply the concepts in real-world scenarios. Whether you're an individual reader or part of a study group, these exercises will help solidify your understanding and practical skills.

As we move forward, we'll venture into Cloud Services and Architectures, Cloud Backup and Disaster Recovery, Future Trends in Cloud Computing, Cloud Monitoring and Performance Optimization, Cloud Governance and Management, and many other exciting topics.

Our goal is to empower you with the knowledge and expertise needed to navigate the cloud computing landscape confidently. This book is designed to be your companion, guiding you through the complexities and nuances of cloud technologies.

Thank you for choosing this book. We hope you find it a valuable resource in your quest to harness the full potential of the cloud. May this knowledge drive innovation, efficiency, and growth, transforming the way you interact with technology and revolutionizing your approach to IT.

Table of Contents

Chapter 1: Introduction to Cloud Computing

Cloud computing has changed the way businesses and individuals use computing resources. It provides a scalable, flexible and cost-effective solution for storing data, running applications and accessing services over the Internet. In this article, we will provide a comprehensive introduction to cloud computing, exploring its basic concepts, benefits and real-world applications. By the end of this article, you will have a clear understanding of what cloud computing is and how it can revolutionize your digital journey.

1.1 What is Cloud Computing: Uncovering the Power of Cloud

1.1.1. Defining Cloud Computing

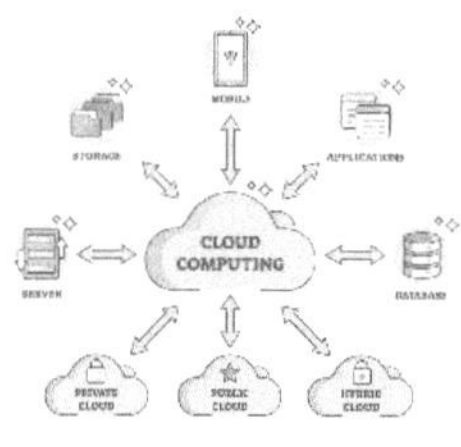

Cloud computing is a paradigm shift in the delivery of computing services over the Internet. Instead of relying on local servers or personal computers, cloud computing enables users to access a vast pool of shared resources placed in remote data centres. These resources include storage, processing power, applications and more. Cloud acts as a virtualized infrastructure, providing on-demand services to users, dynamically scaling to meet their needs.

1.1.2. Key Characteristics of Cloud Computing

- **Scalability and Elasticity:** One of the main features of cloud computing is the ability to scale resources up or down on a demand basis. This scalability ensures that businesses can easily adapt to fluctuating workloads and adjust growth without the need for significant hardware investments.

- **On-demand self-service:** Cloud computing empowers users to provision and manage on-demand computing resources, without the need for human interaction with service providers. This self-service aspect allows agility and flexibility to increase resource allocation.

- **Broad Network Access:** Cloud services are accessible on the Internet, allowing users to access their applications and data from anywhere using various devices such as laptops, smartphones, or tablets. This ubiquitous access promotes collaboration and increases productivity.

- **Resource Pooling:** Cloud providers consolidate resources from multiple users into a shared pool. This pooling enables efficient use of resources, optimizing costs and reducing wastage. Users benefit from accessing a vast pool of resources, while only paying for what they consume.

- **Rapid Elasticity:** Cloud systems can quickly or down resources to meet workload demands. This rapid elasticity ensures that businesses can handle sudden spikes in traffic or dynamically adjust resource allocation while improving performance and user experience Hub.

1.1.3. Benefits of Cloud Computing

- **Cost Savings:** By leveraging cloud resources, organizations can reduce capital expenditure on hardware and maintenance costs. Cloud computing works on pay-as-you-go models, helping businesses align their costs with actual usage and scale resources.

- **Scalability and Flexibility:** Cloud computing provides the ability to radically up or down resources. Whether it is accommodating sudden spikes in user demand or supporting business development, the cloud offers unmatched scalability and flexibility.

- **Enhanced Collaboration and Mobility:** Cloud facilitates collaboration between teams and remote workers at any time, by providing access to shared data and applications from anywhere. It promotes productivity and enables efficient remote working arrangements.

- **Better reliability and disaster recovery:** Cloud service providers employ robust infrastructure and backup mechanisms, ensuring high availability and data redundancy. It increases reliability and provides businesses with built-in disaster recovery capabilities.

- **Innovation and Time-to-Market:** Cloud computing allows businesses to rapidly experiment, innovate and launch new products and services. The agility and speed offered by the cloud enable shorter development cycles and faster time-to-market.

1.1.4. Real-World Applications

- **Infrastructure as service (IaaS):** IaaS provides virtualized computing resources, including servers, storage, and networking, enabling businesses to build and manage their IT infrastructure in the cloud. This flexibility and control are ideal for businesses with specific infrastructure requirements.

- **Platform as service (PaaS):** PaaS provides a development platform and tools for building, testing and deploying applications without the complexity of managing the underlying infrastructure. This application accelerates development, simplifies deployment, and supports scalability.

- **Software as service (SaaS):** SaaS distributes ready-to-use software applications over the Internet, eliminating the need for installation and maintenance. Users can easily access and use software applications such as customer relationship management (CRM) systems, productivity tools and collaboration platforms.

1.2 Uncovering the Benefits of Cloud Computing

1.2.1. Cost Savings:

Cloud computing provides significant cost savings compared to traditional IT infrastructure. Here's how:

- **Reduction in capital expenditure:** With cloud computing, businesses can avoid large investments in hardware, data centres, and infrastructure. Instead, they pay for cloud services on a subscription or pay-per-use basis, allowing for better cost management and allocation of resources.

- **Low Operating Cost:** Maintaining and managing in-house IT infrastructure requires ongoing expenses for maintenance, upgrades, security and skilled personnel. Cloud computing eliminates many of these costs, as the cloud service provider takes care of infrastructure management and maintenance. This allows businesses to focus on their core competencies.

- **Scalable Resource Consumption:** Cloud services enable businesses to up or down their computing resources as needed. This scalability ensures optimal resource utilization, eliminates dissipation and overprovisioning. Organizations can align their costs with real resource utilization, saving money during periods of low demand.

1.2.2. Agility and flexibility:

Cloud computing provides unique agility and flexibility, enabling businesses to react rapidly to changing market conditions:

- **Rapid Resource Provision:** Cloud services provide on-demand self-service, allowing businesses to quickly provision and deploy computing resources as needed. This agility facilitates rapid time-market for new products and services.

- **Elastic Scaling:** The cloud platform allows organizations to immediately scale their resources to accommodate fluctuating workloads. Whether it is handling peak traffic during seasonal sales or scaling during quiet periods, Cloud ensures that businesses can meet customer demands efficiently.

- **Global Access:** Cloud services provide extensive network access, enabling users to access data and applications from anywhere using any device with an Internet connection. This flexibility allows businesses to embrace remote work and collaborate geographically.

1.2.3. Increased data security and reliability:

Cloud computing provides robust security measures and ensures high levels of data reliability and availability:

- **Data redundancy and backup:** Cloud service providers employ advanced data replication and backup mechanisms, ensuring that data is stored unnecessarily at multiple geographic locations. This redundancy reduces the risk of data loss and provides inherent disaster recovery capabilities.

- **Security Expertise:** Cloud service providers invest heavily in security measures, employing teams of cyber security experts to protect data and infrastructure. These experts keep up to date with the latest security threats and implement industry best practices. Businesses provide a higher level of protection than traditional on-premises solutions.

- **Compliance and Regulatory Assistance:** Cloud providers often follow stringent compliance standards and certifications, ensuring that businesses can meet industry-specific regulations. This support simplifies compliance efforts and reduces the burden of managing regulatory requirements.

1.2.4. Innovation and collaboration:

Cloud computing fuel innovation and collaboration, empowering businesses to remain competitive in the digital landscape:

- **Rapid Prototype and Development:** Cloud platforms provide development tools, prefabricated environments, and managed services that accelerate application development and testing. This allows businesses to innovate and market new ideas faster.

- **Collaboration and Integration:** Cloud-based collaboration tools enable teams to work together natively, regardless of their physical locations. These tools facilitate real-time communication, document sharing and project management, promoting collaboration and improving productivity.

- **Access to advanced technologies**: Cloud providers often provide access to cutting-edge technologies such as artificial intelligence (AI), machine learning (ML) and big data analytics. It enables businesses to take advantage of these technologies without need comprehensive infrastructure investment or specialized expertise.

1.3 Cloud service model (IaaS, PaaS, SaaS)

1.3.1. Infrastructure as a service (IaaS):

Infrastructure as a service (IaaS) provides businesses with virtualized computing resources on the Internet. With IaaS, organizations can build and manage their IT infrastructure without the need for physical hardware. Key features of IaaS include:

Virtual Machines (VMs): IaaS allows businesses to create and manage virtual machines, which serve as the foundation for running applications and storing data.

Scalability and elasticity: IaaS platforms provide the ability to top or lower resources on a demand basis, ensuring optimal resource utilization and cost efficiency.

Storage and networking: IaaS providers provide storage solutions for data storage and management, as well as networking capabilities to establish secure connections between resources.

Infrastructure Management: Businesses have control over operating systems, middleware and applications running on virtual infrastructure.

1.3.2. Platform as service (PaaS):

The platform as a service (PaaS) provides a complete development and deployment environment in the cloud, which enables businesses to focus on application development rather than managing the underlying infrastructure. Key features of PaaS include:

Development tools and middleware: PaaS platforms provide a wide range of development tools, programming languages, and middleware to streamline the application development process.

Application Lifecycle Management: PaaS provides integrated tools and frameworks to build, test, deploy and manage applications, collaborate and promote efficient software development practices.

Scalability and Flexibility: PaaS platforms provide automated scaling and resource allocation, allowing applications to handle different workloads effectively.

Database Integration: PaaS solutions often include managed database services, simplifying data management and ensuring scalability and availability.

1.3.3. Software as service (SaaS):

Software as a service (SaaS) distributes applications over the Internet, eliminates the need for organizations to install and manage software on their own infrastructure. Key features of SaaS include:

Ready-to-use applications: SaaS providers provide a range of applications accessible through web browsers, allowing users to use software functionality without the need for local installations.

Multi-tenancy: SaaS applications are created to serve many customers, sharing a common infrastructure and resources while maintaining data isolation and security.

Automatic Updates and Maintenance: SaaS providers handle software updates, patches and maintenance, ensuring that users always have access to the latest features and enhancements.

Pay-as-you-go model: SaaS applications typically work on membership-based pricing models. This allows businesses to pay for software on a per-user or per-month basis.

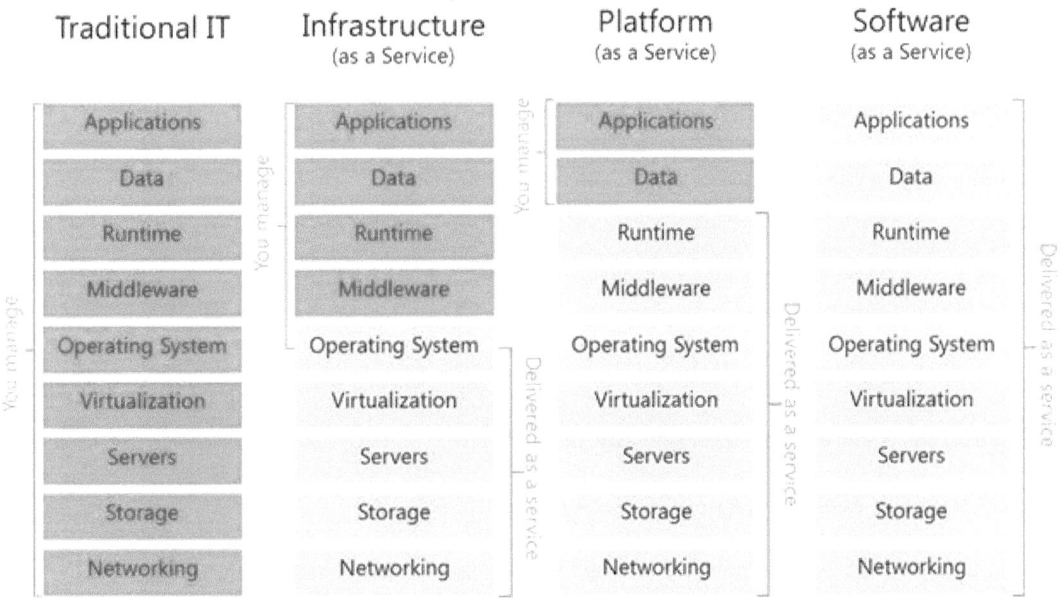

Exercise
Multiple Choice Questions

1. Cloud computing enables users to access computing resources from:

a. Local servers

b. Personal computers

c. Remote data centers

d. Dedicated hardware

2. Which of the following is not a key characteristic of cloud computing?

a. Scalability and elasticity

b. On-demand self-service

c. Limited network access

d. Resource pooling

3. Cloud computing offers cost savings by:

a. Increasing capital expenditure on hardware

b. Providing in-house IT infrastructure management costs

c. Aligning costs with actual usage through a pay-as-you-go model

d. Eliminating data redundancy and backup mechanisms

4. The ability to rapidly provision and deploy computing resources is a result of:

a. Cloud's broad network access

b. On-demand self-service

c. Resource pooling

d. Measured service model

5. Cloud computing promotes collaboration and mobility by:

a. Limiting access to shared data and applications

b. Providing access to applications only on personal computers

c. Allowing access from anywhere using various devices and Internet connection

d. Restricting collaboration to on-premises environments

6. Which of the following is a benefit of cloud computing in terms of data security and reliability?

a. Increased risk of data loss due to lack of redundancy

b. Lower level of protection compared to traditional on-premises solutions

c. Compliance with industry-specific regulations

d. Lack of backup mechanisms for data storage

7. Cloud computing facilitates innovation and collaboration by:

a. Slowing down the application development process

b. Restricting access to cutting-edge technologies

c. Enabling rapid prototyping and development

d. Limiting collaboration to on-site teams only

8. Infrastructure as a Service (IaaS) allows businesses to:

a. Build and manage their IT infrastructure in the cloud

b. Distribute ready-to-use software applications over the Internet

c. Develop and deploy applications without managing the underlying infrastructure

d. Access virtualized computing resources on personal computers

9. Platform as a Service (PaaS) accelerates application development and deployment by:

a. Providing virtualized computing resources on the Internet

b. Eliminating the need for installation and maintenance of software

c. Offering a complete development and deployment environment in the cloud

d. Enabling scalability and flexibility in resource consumption

10. Software as a Service (SaaS) eliminates the need for:

a. Collaboration between teams

b. Paying for software on a per-user or per-month basis

c. Accessing software applications via web browsers

d. Managing the underlying infrastructure and software maintenance

1. **What is cloud computing?**
2. **What are the key characteristics of cloud computing?**
3. **How does cloud computing provide cost savings?**
4. **How does cloud computing enhance collaboration and mobility?**
5. **What are the benefits of cloud computing in terms of data security and reliability?**
6. **How does cloud computing promote innovation and collaboration?**
7. **What are the different cloud service models?**
8. **How does cloud computing enable scalability and elasticity for businesses?**
9. **What is Infrastructure as a Service (IaaS)?**
10. **What is Software as a Service (SaaS)?**
11. **What are the advantages of using Infrastructure as a Service (IaaS) for businesses?**
12. **How does Platform as a Service (PaaS) accelerate application development and deployment?**
13. **What are the benefits of Software as a Service (SaaS) for users?**

Answer Section
Multiple Choice Questions

1. c) Remote data centers

2. c) Limited network access

3. c) Aligning costs with actual usage through a pay-as-you-go model

4. b) On-demand self-service

5. c) Allowing access from anywhere using various devices and Internet connection

6. c) Compliance with industry-specific regulations

7. c) Enabling rapid prototyping and development

8. a) Build and manage their IT infrastructure in the cloud

9. c) Offering a complete development and deployment environment in the cloud

10. d) Managing the underlying infrastructure and software maintenance

Review Questions

1. Cloud computing is a paradigm shift in the delivery of computing services over the Internet. It allows users to access shared resources, such as storage, processing power, and applications, from remote data centers instead of relying on local servers or personal computers

2. The key characteristics of cloud computing include scalability and elasticity, on-demand self-service, broad network access, resource pooling, rapid elasticity, and measured service.

3. Cloud computing provides cost savings by reducing capital expenditure on hardware and infrastructure, enabling businesses to align costs with actual usage through a pay-as-you-go model, and eliminating the need for in-house IT infrastructure maintenance and management costs

4. Cloud computing enables collaboration and mobility by providing ubiquitous access to shared data and applications over the Internet. This allows teams to work together and access resources from anywhere, promoting productivity and supporting remote work arrangements.

5. Cloud computing offers benefits in terms of data security and reliability through data redundancy and backup mechanisms, robust infrastructure, security expertise of cloud service providers, and compliance with industry-specific regulations.

6. Cloud computing promotes innovation and collaboration by providing rapid prototype and development environments, facilitating real-time communication and document sharing through cloud-based collaboration tools, and offering access to advanced technologies like AI and ML without extensive infrastructure investments.

7. The different cloud service models are Infrastructure as a Service (IaaS), Platform as a Service (PaaS), and Software as a Service (SaaS).

8. Cloud computing allows businesses to scale their resources up or down on-demand, ensuring optimal resource utilization and cost efficiency. This scalability and elasticity enable businesses to handle fluctuating workloads, accommodate sudden spikes in user demand, and dynamically adjust resource allocation.

9. Infrastructure as a Service (IaaS) provides virtualized computing resources over the Internet, allowing businesses to build and manage their IT infrastructure without physical hardware. It includes features like virtual machines, scalability, storage, networking, and infrastructure management.

10. Software as a Service (SaaS) distributes applications over the Internet, eliminating the need for organizations to install and manage software on their infrastructure. It offers ready-to-use applications, multi-tenancy, automatic updates and maintenance, and a pay-as-you-go pricing model.

11. Infrastructure as a Service (IaaS) provides virtualized computing resources, including servers, storage, and networking, allowing businesses to build and manage their IT infrastructure in the cloud. The advantages of IaaS include flexibility and control over infrastructure, scalability, cost savings by avoiding hardware investments, and efficient resource allocation..

12. Platform as a Service (PaaS) offers a development platform and tools for building, testing, and deploying applications without the complexity of managing the underlying infrastructure. PaaS accelerates application development by providing development tools, middleware, application lifecycle management, automated scaling, and integration with managed database services.

13. Software as a Service (SaaS) provides ready-to-use software applications over the Internet, eliminating the need for installation and maintenance. The benefits of SaaS for users include easy access to software functionality via web browsers, automatic updates and maintenance, multi-tenancy for efficient resource sharing, and a pay-as-you-go model for cost-effectiveness.

Chapter 2: Cloud Infrastructure

Cloud computing has revolutionized the way it provides scalable and flexible infrastructure to support the growing demands of the digital world. At the core of cloud computing is the concept of cloud infrastructure, which includes a vast network of servers, storage systems, networking components, and software applications. This infrastructure delivers cloud services and drives innovation. Servers as a foundation to enable organizations to harness the power of technology to increase productivity and achieve business objectives. In this article, we will explore the importance of cloud infrastructure, its key components.

Cloud infrastructure refers to physical and virtual resources that enable the delivery of cloud services. It includes both hardware and software components that work together to provide the computing power, storage capacity, and networking capabilities required for cloud-based applications and services. Cloud infrastructure is typically hosted and managed by cloud service providers, without requiring organizations to make significant upfront investment in physical infrastructure. On-demand computing provides the ability to access and use resources.

2.1 Virtualization in the cloud: exposing the power of efficient resource utilization

2.1.1. Understanding virtualization in the cloud:

Virtualization in the cloud refers to the practice of creating multiple virtual examples of servers, storage systems, networks, and other computing resources on a shared physical infrastructure. These virtual instances, known as virtual machines (VMs), operate independently, which provide the illusion of dedicated resources using built-in hardware efficiently.

2.1.2. Key aspects of virtualization in the cloud:

- **Hypervisor:** At the core of virtualization in the cloud is hypervisor, also known as virtual machine monitor (VMM). The hypervisor is responsible for managing and allocating physical resources to virtual machines, ensuring efficient use and isolation.

- **Resource pooling**: Virtualization in the cloud enables resource pooling, where physical resources, such as CPUs, memory, and storage, are collected in a shared pool. Virtual machines can then access and use resources from this pool, allowing efficient use across multiple workloads.

- **Scalability and elasticity**: Virtualization in the cloud provides organizations with the ability to up or down resources on a demand basis. Businesses can easily add or remove virtual machines as needed, ensuring optimal resource allocation and cost efficiency.

- **Isolation and Security**: Virtualization in the cloud ensures strong separation between virtual machines. Each virtual machine operates in its own isolated environment, prevents interference and provides a high degree of security and data security.

2.1.3. Benefits of virtualization in the cloud:

- **Efficient resource utilization**: Virtualization in the cloud allows better use of computing resources. By consolidating multiple workloads on a single physical server through virtualization. Businesses can achieve higher resource utilization rates, reducing costs and energy consumption.

- **Flexibility and Agility:** Virtualization in the cloud enables businesses to quickly provision and deploy virtual machines, reduces the time and effort required to establish infrastructure. This agility allows organizations to react rapidly to changing business needs and market demands.

- **Cost savings**: Virtualization in the cloud helps organizations optimize their IT infrastructure costs. By consolidating workloads on low physical servers, businesses can reduce hardware investment, maintenance costs, and physical space requirements.

- **High Availability and Disaster Recovery**: Virtualization in the cloud enables strong high availability and disaster recovery solutions. Virtual machines can be replicated or migrated between different physical servers, ensuring continuous operation and reducing downtime in case of hardware failures or disasters.

- **Testing and Development:** Virtualization in the cloud provides a scalable and cost-effective environment for testing and development purposes. Developers can easily create and deploy virtual machines with different configurations, enabling faster software development cycles and efficient testing environments.

2.2 Data Center in Cloud Computing: Powerhouses of Digital Infrastructure

Data centers are the backbone of cloud computing, providing the physical infrastructure needed to support the vast amount of digital services and data storage in the cloud. These features include a multitude of servers, networking equipment and storage systems, enabling delivery of cloud services to users worldwide. This article explores the role of data centers in cloud computing, their key components, and the benefits to be brought to the digital ecosystem.

1. Data Center: Heart of Cloud Computing:

- **Definition and purpose**: A data center is a centralized facility designed for computer systems and network infrastructure. Its primary purpose is to securely store, manage and distribute data and applications. In the context of cloud computing, data centers serve as the foundation for delivering cloud services to users on the Internet.

2.2.1.1 Infrastructure and components: Data centers include several key components, including:

- **Servers:** These are the workhorse of the data center, which is responsible for the processing and storage of data. They can be virtual machines running on physical servers or physical hardware.

- **Networking tools**: Data centers employ a robust network infrastructure, including switches, routers, and firewalls, to facilitate data transfer between servers and enable connectivity to the Internet.

- **Storage systems:** Data centers have various storage systems, such as hard disk drives (HDDs) and solid-state drives (SSDs), to store large amounts of data. These storage systems provide high performance, reliable and scalable storage solutions.

- **Cooling system:** Data centers generate sufficient heat due to the operation of servers and networking devices. Cooling systems, such as air conditioning and precision cooling units, are deployed to maintain optimal temperatures and prevent equipment from heating.

- **Power Infrastructure**: Seamless power supply is important for data centers. They are equipped with backup generators, power distribution units (PDUs), and battery systems to ensure continuous operation during power outages.

2.3 Server Farm: Powerhouse of Computing Power:

- **Definition and Functions**: Server farms, also known as server clusters or server racks, are collections of servers placed within data centers. They work together to deliver the high-performance computing capabilities required by cloud applications and services. Server farms provide the necessary processing power, storage capacity, and networking capability to handle large amounts of data and serve a large number of users simultaneously.

- **Scalability and Redundancy:** The server farm is designed for scalability and redundancy. They can scale horizontally by adding more servers to handle increased workloads and user demands. Redundancy is achieved through techniques such as load balancing, where workloads are distributed across multiple servers, and fault-tolerant architectures that ensure continuous operation even when individual servers fail.

- **Virtualization and resource optimization**: Server farms often take advantage of virtualization techniques to optimize resource utilization. Virtualization allows multiple virtual machines to run on a single physical server, maximize server capacity, and reduce energy consumption. This enables efficient use of resources and cost savings for cloud service providers.

2.3.1. Benefits of data centers and server farms in cloud computing:

- **High Availability and Reliability:** Data center and server farms are built keeping in mind redundancy and fault tolerance. They employ backup power systems, redundant network connections and redundant hardware configurations to ensure high availability and minimize service interruption.

- **Scalability and elasticity:** The infrastructure of data centers and server farms enables easy scalability and elasticity. Cloud service providers can quickly or below resources to meet fluctuating user demands, ensuring optimal performance and cost-efficiency.

- **Geographic Access and Performance**: By strategically locating data centers in different regions, cloud providers can provide services close to end users, can reduce latency and improve performance. This global presence enables users to access cloud resources from anywhere in the world with minimal delay.

- **Cost efficiency:** Data centers and server farms enable resource pooling and sharing, allowing many users to share the same physical infrastructure. This shared model results in cost savings for users, as they only pay for the resources they consume, while providers benefit from economies of scale.

2.4 Networking in the cloud: enabling seamless connectivity and collaboration

Networking is an important component of cloud computing that connects resources. The cloud plays an important role in facilitating data transfer and ensuring seamless communication between different components within the environment. As businesses increasingly adopt cloud solutions, it becomes necessary to understand the fundamentals of networking in the cloud. In this article, we will explore the concept of networking in the cloud, its key components, and its importance in supporting modern cloud-based applications and services.

2.4.1. Understanding Networking in the Cloud:

Networking in the cloud refers to infrastructure and technologies that enable communication and connectivity between various components, including servers, storage systems, virtual machines, and end-users. It incorporates hardware, software, protocols and services that work together to establish and maintain reliable and secure connections within a cloud environment

2.4.2. Key components of networking in the cloud:

- **Virtual networks**: Virtual networks in the cloud provide logical network segmentation, allowing businesses to create separate network environments for different purposes. They enable secure communication between virtual machines, containers and other cloud resources while maintaining isolation from other networks. Virtual networks provide flexibility, scalability and the ability to define network policies and access control.

- **Virtual Private Cloud (VPC):** A virtual private cloud is a private and isolated network space within the infrastructure of a public cloud provider. It enables businesses to build their own virtual network with a defined IP address range, subnet and routing table. VPCs provide enhanced security and control, allowing organizations to securely connect their on-premises infrastructure to the cloud.

- **Load balancing**: distributes network traffic across multiple servers or instances to optimize load balancing resource utilization and ensure high availability. In the cloud, load balancers can automatically scale up or down depending on demand, ensuring that traffic is evenly distributed and applications are responsive and accessible.

- **Firewalls and Security**: Firewalls and security measures are important in the cloud to protect resources from unauthorized access and potential threats. Cloud providers offer built-in security features, such as network access control lists (ACLs) and security groups, which enable organizations to define rules and policies to control inbound and outbound network traffic.

- **Virtual Private Network (VPN):** A VPN establishes a secure connection between a user's device and a private network, enabling secure remote access to cloud resources. VPNs use encryption protocols to ensure data privacy and integrity, allowing users to securely access cloud-based applications and services from anywhere.

2.4.3. Importance of networking in the cloud:

- **Connectivity and collaboration:** Networking in the cloud enables seamless connectivity and collaboration between geographically dispersed teams and users. It allows real-time communication, file sharing and resource access, boosting productivity and enabling efficient collaboration on cloud-based projects.

- **Scalability and elasticity**: Cloud networking provides the scalability and elasticity required to adjust fluctuating workloads. Organizations can easily up or down network resources on a demand basis, ensuring optimal performance and resource utilization.

- **High Availability and Redundancy**: Includes redundancy and failure mechanisms to ensure high availability of networking applications and services in the cloud. Multiple network paths, load balancing and redundant connections reduce the risk of downtime and provide flexibility for potential network failures.

- **Global Reach:** Cloud networking enables businesses to deploy applications and services globally to reach customers and users in various geographic locations. It leverages the cloud provider's global infrastructure and network points of presence (PoPs) to deliver content and services with low latency and high performance.

- **Cost Efficiency**: Provides cost efficiencies by eliminating the need for networking organizations in the cloud to invest in and manage their own networking infrastructure. Cloud providers provide pay-as-you-go pricing models, allowing businesses to pay for the networking resources they consume, Advance cost reduction and cost forecasting improve.

2.5 Storage Technologies in the Cloud: Empowering Data Management and Access

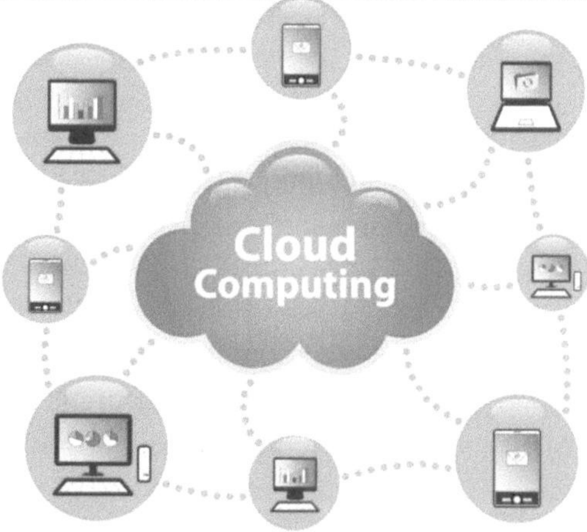

In the digital age, data is at the heart of every organization's operations, decision making and innovation. Cloud computing has revolutionized the way data is stored, managed and accessed, providing scalable and cost-effective storage solutions. Storage technologies in the cloud provide the ability to securely store and recover large amounts of data, enabling seamless collaboration, data analytics and disaster recovery. In this article, we will explore the various storage technologies used in the cloud, their benefits and their impact on data management and access

2.5.1. Understanding Storage Technologies in the Cloud:

Storage technologies in the cloud cover a wide range of solutions that meet various data storage and retrieval requirements. These technologies leverage cloud infrastructure to offer scalable, reliable and flexible storage options for businesses of all sizes. Let's explore some of the major storage techniques used in the cloud:

- **Object Storage:** Object storage is a popular storage technology in the cloud that stores data as objects, each identified by a unique key. It provides a highly scalable and durable storage environment where data is accessed via APIs. Object storage is ideal for storing unstructured data, such as documents, images, videos and backups. It provides high availability, data redundancy and seamless scalability.

- **Block storage:** Block storage is a storage technology that divides data into fixed-size blocks and stores them as separate entities. It provides direct access to data at the block level and is commonly used to host operating systems, databases and applications in the cloud. Block storage provides high performance, low latency and data stability, making it suitable for applications for which fast and frequent reading / Writing operations are required.

- **File Storage:** File storage in the cloud provides a distributed file system accessible through standard file protocols, such as network file system (NFS) or server message block (SMB). This allows many users and applications to access and share files concurrently. File storage is well suited for scenarios that require shared access to files such as content repositories, document management systems, and file sharing applications.

- **Archival Storage**: Archival storage is designed for long-term data retention and frequently accessed data. It provides cost-effective storage solutions for data that need to be stored for regulatory compliance, legal requirements, or historical analysis. Archival storage provides low-cost storage options with slower recovery times than other storage types. It is ideal for organizations that need to maintain large amounts of data while reducing storage costs.

2.5.2. Benefits of Storage Technologies in the Cloud:

- **Scalability:** Cloud storage technologies provide unique scalability, allowing businesses to scale their storage resources up or down depending on demand. Organizations can quickly adapt to change storage needs without the need for significant upfront investment or hardware upgrades.

- **Cost efficiency**: Cloud storage eliminates the need for organizations to invest in and manage their own physical storage infrastructure. Cloud providers provide flexible pricing models, where businesses only pay for the storage they consume, reduce capital expenditure and provide cost forecasts.

- **Data redundancy and sustainability**: Cloud storage technologies ensure high data redundancy and durability. Data is distributed across multiple storage devices and geographic locations, reducing the risk of data loss or corruption. Redundancy mechanisms, such as data replication and eraser coding, provide data durability and enable reliable data recovery.

- **Data Accessibility and Collaboration**: Cloud storage enables seamless data access and collaboration. Users can securely access and share data from anywhere using any device with an Internet connection. Cloud storage facilitates real-time collaboration, version control and file synchronization, increases productivity and streamlines workflows.

- **Disaster Recovery:** Cloud storage plays an important role in disaster recovery strategies. Organizations can replicate data in geographically scattered data centers, ensure data availability, and hardware failures, can reduce downtime in case of natural disasters or other disruptions. Cloud Storage providers provide robust backup and recovery solutions, enabling efficient data restoration.

Exercise
Multiple Choice Questions

1. Which of the following is a key characteristic of cloud computing?

a) Scalability and Elasticity
b) Physical infrastructure management
c) Limited network access
d) High capital expenditure

2. What is the primary purpose of data centers in cloud computing?

a) Processing and storing data
b) Managing cloud applications
c) Distributing cloud services
d) Maintaining network connectivity

3. Virtualization in the cloud refers to:

a) Creating multiple instances of physical servers
b) Consolidating workloads on physical servers
c) Sharing resources on a shared physical infrastructure
d) Using virtual machines for data storage

4. Which storage technology is suitable for storing unstructured data such as images and videos?

a) Object storage
b) Block storage
c) File storage
d) Archival storage

5. What is the purpose of load balancing in cloud networking?

a) Ensuring high availability
b) Reducing network latency
c) Managing storage resources
d) Providing data security

6. Which cloud service model provides a complete development and deployment environment?

a) Infrastructure as a Service (IaaS)
b) Platform as a Service (PaaS)
c) Software as a Service (SaaS)
d) Storage as a Service (STaaS)

7. What is the main benefit of virtualization in the cloud?

a) Cost savings
b) Enhanced collaboration
c) Improved data security
d) Increased network speed

8. Which networking component is responsible for establishing secure connections between user devices and private networks?

a) Virtual private cloud (VPC)
b) Load balancer

c) Firewall
d) Virtual private network (VPN)

Review Questions

1.What is cloud infrastructure?
2.What are the key components of cloud infrastructure?
3.What is virtualization in the context of cloud computing?
4.What is the role of a hypervisor in virtualization?
5.How does virtualization enable efficient resource utilization?
6.What are the benefits of virtualization in the cloud?
7.What is the purpose of data centers in cloud computing?
8.What are the key components of a data center?
9.How do data centers ensure high availability and reliability?
10.What is the role of server farms in cloud computing?
11.What is the significance of networking in the cloud?
12.What are the key components of networking in the cloud?
13.How does networking support connectivity and collaboration in cloud environments?
14.What is the role of storage technologies in the cloud?
15.What are the advantages of cloud storage in terms of data redundancy and accessibility?
16.Explain the concept of virtualization in the context of cloud computing and how it enables efficient resource utilization. Provide examples to support your explanation.
17.Discuss the significance of data centers in cloud computing and explain their role in delivering cloud services. Include a detailed description of the key components and their functions within a data center.

Answer Section

Multiple Choice Questions

1. a) Scalability And Elasticity
2. a) Processing And Storing Data
3. c) Sharing Resources On A Shared Physical Infrastructure
4. a) Object Storage
5. a) Ensuring High Availability
6. b) Platform As A Service (PaaS)
7. a) Cost Savings
8. d) Virtual Private Network (VPN)

Review Questions

1. Cloud infrastructure refers to the physical and virtual resources, including servers, storage systems, networking components, and software applications, that enable the delivery of cloud services.

2. The key components of cloud infrastructure include servers, storage systems, networking tools, cooling systems, and power infrastructure

3. Virtualization in the cloud refers to the practice of creating multiple virtual instances of servers, storage systems, networks, and other computing resources on a shared physical infrastructure.

4. The hypervisor, also known as a virtual machine monitor (VMM), is responsible for managing and allocating physical resources to virtual machines, ensuring efficient use and isolation.

5. Virtualization enables efficient resource utilization by consolidating multiple workloads on a single physical server, maximizing server capacity and reducing costs and energy consumption.

6. The benefits of virtualization in the cloud include efficient resource utilization, flexibility and agility in provisioning and deployment, cost savings, high availability and disaster recovery, and improved testing and development environments.

7. Data centers serve as the foundation for delivering cloud services to users on the Internet. They securely store, manage, and distribute data and applications required for cloud-based services.

8. The key components of a data center include servers, networking equipment, storage systems, cooling systems, and power infrastructure.

9. Data centers ensure high availability and reliability through redundancy mechanisms, such as backup power systems, redundant network connections, and redundant hardware configurations.

10. Server farms, also known as server clusters or server racks, provide the necessary processing power, storage capacity, and networking capability to handle large

11. amounts of data and serve a large number of users simultaneously

12. Networking in the cloud facilitates seamless connectivity and collaboration between various cloud components, enabling data transfer and communication.

13. The key components of networking in the cloud include virtual networks, virtual private clouds (VPCs), load balancing, firewalls and security measures, and virtual private networks (VPNs).

14. Networking in the cloud enables seamless connectivity and collaboration between geographically dispersed teams and users through real-time communication, file sharing, and resource acces

15. Storage technologies in the cloud provide scalable and cost-effective solutions for securely storing and retrieving large amounts of data, facilitating collaboration, data analytics, and disaster recovery.

16. Cloud storage provides high data redundancy and durability through data replication and distribution across multiple storage devices and geographic locations. It also enables seamless data access and collaboration from anywhere using any device with an Internet connection.

17. Virtualization in cloud computing involves creating multiple virtual instances of servers, storage systems, networks, et, on a shared physical infrastructure. This practice allows for efficient utilization of resources by consolidating workloads and maximizing server capacity. For example, a physical server can host multiple virtual machines, each running different applications or services. This consolidation reduces hardware costs, energy consumption, and physical space requirements. Virtualization also enables better resource allocation, as resources can be dynamically assigned or scaled up/down based on demand. This flexibility enhances scalability, agility, and cost efficiency within cloud environments. Overall, virtualization plays a crucial role in optimizing resource utilization and enabling organizations to leverage the benefits of cloud computing.

18. Data centers are essential to the functioning of cloud computing as they serve as the backbone for delivering cloud services to users. They provide the physical infrastructure necessary for storing, managing, and distributing data and applications. Key components of a data center include servers, networking equipment, storage systems, cooling systems, and power infrastructure. Servers act as the

workhorses of the data center, handling processing and storage tasks. Networking equipment enables data transfer and connectivity between servers and facilitates access to the Internet. Storage systems store large amounts of data securely, while cooling systems maintain optimal temperatures to prevent equipment overheating. Power infrastructure ensures uninterrupted power supply through backup generators and battery systems. Together, these components create a reliable and efficient environment for delivering cloud services.

Chapter 3: Cloud Security and Compliance

In today's interconnected and data-driven world, cloud computing has become an integral part of business operations, providing scalability, flexibility and cost efficiencies. However, strong security measures and compliance frameworks are significantly needed to ensure the security and regulatory adherence to sensitive data with increasing reliance on cloud services. Practices aimed at protecting cloud security and compliance data, reducing risks and maintaining the integrity and confidentiality of information stored and processed in the cloud, includes a range of technologies and standards. In this article, we will delve into the importance of cloud security and compliance, the challenges involved, and the strategies employed to ensure data security in the digital age.

3.1 Cloud Security Overview: Data Security in the Cloud

As businesses increasingly rely on cloud computing for their data storage, processing, and applications, ensuring that robust security measures are paramount. Cloud security refers to practices, technologies, and protocols designed to protect data, applications, and infrastructure within a cloud environment. It incorporates a number of measures aimed at securing sensitive information, reducing risks and ensuring the integrity and availability of data stored and processed in the cloud. In this article, we will provide an overview of cloud security, its key components and its importance in maintaining data security in the digital age.

3.1.1. Key components of cloud security:

- **Identification and Access Management (IAM):** IAM is a fundamental component of cloud security that controls access to cloud resources. This includes authentication, authorization, and access control mechanisms that ensure that only authorized individuals can access sensitive data and perform specific tasks within a cloud environment. IAM solutions manage user identities, credentials, and permissions, reducing the risk of unauthorized access or data breaches.

- **Data Encryption:** Data encryption plays an important role in protecting data privacy in the cloud. This involves converting data into an unreadable format using encryption algorithms, making it inaccessible to unauthorized parties. Encryption is applied during data transmission (in transit) and when data is at rest in storage. Encryption keys are used to encrypt and decrypt data, providing an additional layer of security.

- **Network Security:** Network security in the cloud focuses on network infrastructure, connection and security of communication channels. This includes firewalls, intrusion detection systems (IDS), virtual private networks (VPNs), and preventing unauthorized access, Other security measures are included to detect and mitigate threats, and ensure secure data transmission within the cloud environment.

- **Vulnerability Management:** Vulnerability management is the process of identifying, assessing and defending potential security vulnerabilities in cloud systems and applications. This includes regular scanning for vulnerabilities, patch management, and proactive monitoring to quickly detect and mitigate security risks. Vulnerability management ensures that the cloud environment is protected from known security vulnerabilities and emerging threats.

- **Security Incident Monitoring and Response:** Monitoring and response mechanisms are important in cloud security to quickly detect and respond to security incidents. Security information and incident management (SIEM) tools, log analysis and real-time monitoring help identify and investigate potential security breaches. The Incident Response Plan outlines the steps to be taken in case of security incidents, including prevention, elimination, recovery and post-incident analysis.

3.1.2. Importance of cloud security:

- **Data Security**: Cloud security measures protect sensitive data from unauthorized access, breaches and data loss. Protecting data privacy, integrity and availability is important to maintain customer confidence, meet regulatory requirements, and prevent financial and reputational damage.

- **Compliance:** Cloud security helps organizations comply with regulatory compliance frameworks, industry-specific requirements and data privacy laws. Compliance measures ensure that organizations meet legal obligations regarding data security, privacy and confidentiality.

- **Risk mitigation**: Cloud environments are susceptible to various security risks, including data breaches, malware attacks, and insider threats. Strong cloud security measures reduce these risks, protect against vulnerabilities, and reduce potential losses to businesses.

- **Business Continuity**: Cloud security plays an important role in business continuity and disaster recovery. Cloud service providers provide redundancy, backup and disaster recovery mechanisms that ensure data availability and reduce downtime in case of disruption or disasters.

- **Customer Trust:** Implementing robust cloud security measures boosts customer trust by demonstrating a commitment to protecting their data and maintaining the confidentiality and integrity of their information. Advanced security measures contribute to building a positive reputation and alienating businesses in the market.

3.2 Identification and Access Management (IAM): Ensuring safe and controlled access to cloud resources

In this digital age, where data is a valuable asset and cyber threats are widespread, it is necessary for organizations to implement strong security measures to protect their sensitive information. Identification and access management (IAM) is an important component of cyber security that focuses on managing and controlling access to resources within the organization's IT infrastructure. In the context of cloud computing, IAM plays an important role in ensuring secure and

controlled access to cloud resources, protecting data and maintaining regulatory compliance. This article provides an overview of IAM, its key components and its importance in protecting cloud environments.

3.2.1. Understanding IAM:

IAM refers to policies, technologies and processes that govern digital identity and access to privileges of individuals within an organization. This includes managing user authentication, authorization, and access control to ensure that only authorized individuals can access specific resources, applications or data.

3.2.2 Key components of IAM:

- **User Identification Management:** IAM begins with creating and managing digital identities for each user within the organization. This includes specific identifiers, such as usernames or email addresses, and related credentials, such as passwords or multi-factor authentication methods. User identification management includes processes such as role change or account termination such as user provision, deprovisioning, and management of lifecycle events.

- **Authentication**: Authentication is the process of verifying the identities of users attempting to access cloud resources. The IAM system employs various authentication methods, including passwords, biometrics, smart cards, or one-time passwords (OTPs). Strong authentication mechanisms, such as multi-factor authentication (MFA), provide an additional layer of security to provide users with multiple forms of verification.

- **Authority:** The authority determines the level of access and privileges granted to certified users. The IAM system implements access control based on user roles, responsibilities and permissions. Role-based access control (RBAC) is a general authorization framework in which access is granted based on predefined roles associated with specific sets of permissions.

- **Access Control:** The IAM system implements granular access control to control user access to specific cloud resources. Access control lists (ACLs) or access policies are defined to specify which resources and functions they may allow to perform. Access controls help prevent unauthorized access, limit privilege enhancement, and reduce the risk of data breaches.

- **User Governance and Administration:** IAM incorporates procedures and tools for the operation and administration of user accounts, roles and access privileges. User governance ensures that user accounts and permissions are regularly reviewed, updated and revoked as needed. This includes periodic access reviews, user activity monitoring and audit trails to detect and mitigate potential security risks.

3.2.3. Importance of IAM in the cloud:

- **Enhanced Security:** IAM provides a robust security framework by ensuring that only authorized users have access to cloud resources. It helps prevent unauthorized access, data breaches and insider threats, thereby protecting sensitive data and protecting the organization's digital assets.

- **Regulatory compliance:** IAM is critical to regulatory compliance because it helps organizations meet the requirements of data protection regulations, industry-specific standards, and privacy laws. IAM systems enable organizations to implement access control, maintain audit trails, and demonstrate accountability in data handling.

- **Centralized Access Management:** IAM provides a centralized approach to access management, making it easier to manage user identification and access privileges across various cloud resources and services. It simplifies user provision, streamlines access requests and approvals, and enables organizations to implement consistent security policies.

- **Improved productivity and efficiency:** The IAM system automates user onboarding and offboarding processes, reduces administrative overhead and employees, ensures timely access provision for contractors and partners. IAM also enables self-service access management, allowing users to reset passwords, can manage profiles and request access to resources independently by freeing IT resources.

- **Audit and Accountability:** IAM Systems Generate audit logs and provide visibility into user activity, allowing organizations to monitor and track user access, enables detection of heterogeneous behavior and investigation of security incidents. The IAM facilitates compliance audits and supports forensic analysis in the event of a security breach.

3.3 Data encryption and privacy in cloud computing: ensuring data security in the cloud

Cloud computing has revolutionized the way businesses store, process and access data. However, with the convenience and benefits of cloud computing, there are concerns about data security and privacy. Data encryption plays an important role in addressing these concerns by securing sensitive information stored in the cloud. This article explores the importance of data encryption and privacy in cloud computing, the challenges involved, and the measures implemented to ensure data security in the cloud.

3.3.1. Data Encryption and Privacy Requirement in Cloud Computing:

- **Protection against unauthorized access:** Cloud computing involves storing data on shared infrastructure, making it susceptible to unauthorized access. Data encryption provides an additional layer of security by providing unreadable data to unauthorized parties. Even if there is a breach, the encrypted data remains secure and confidential.

- **Compliance with data protection regulations:** Cloud users are often subject to data protection regulations and privacy laws, such as GDPR, HIPAA, or CCP. These rules mandate the protection of personal and sensitive data through encryption or other security measures. By encrypting data in the cloud, organizations can meet regulatory requirements and avoid penalties.

- **Trust and Customer Confidence:** Data breaches can damage customer trust and reputation. By implementing strong encryption measures, cloud service providers can assure their customers that their data is secure and in still confidence in the security of the cloud platform. This belief is important for businesses to adopt cloud services and hand over their sensitive information to cloud providers.

3.3.2. Data Encryption in Cloud Computing:

- **Encryption of data in transit:** Data transmitted between the user and the cloud provider must be encrypted to prevent eavesdropping and interception. Secure protocols such as HTTPS and VPN are used to establish encrypted connections, which ensure data confidentiality during transmission.

- **Encryption of data on rest:** Data stored in the cloud must be encrypted to protect it from unauthorized access. Encryption keys and algorithms are employed to encrypt data before being stored on a cloud server. Only authorized users with related decryption keys can access and decrypt data.

- **Key Management:** Proper key management is important for data encryption in the cloud. Cloud providers must implement secure key storage, rotation and access controls to ensure the confidentiality and integrity of encryption keys. Strong key management practices are necessary to prevent unauthorized access to the key and to avoid major agreements.

3.3.3. Challenges in data encryption and privacy in cloud computing:

- **Performance effects**: Data encryption introduces additional processing overhead, which can affect the performance of cloud services. It is necessary to strike a balance between data security and performance to ensure a seamless user experience.

- Key management complexity: Managing encryption keys for large-scale cloud environments can be complex. Cloud providers must implement robust key management systems to effectively handle generation, storage, rotation, and revocation of encryption keys.

- Regulatory compliance: There are specific data protection regulations and compliance requirements in various industries and sectors. Cloud providers must ensure that their encryption practices align with these regulations and provide the necessary tools and documentation to assist their customers in meeting compliance obligations do it.

3.4 Regulatory compliance in the cloud: ensuring data security and privacy

The adoption of cloud computing has led to many benefits for organizations, such as cost savings, scalability, and increased flexibility. However, the use of cloud services also raises concerns about regulatory compliance, especially when it comes to data security and privacy. This article explores the importance of regulatory compliance in the cloud, challenges it faces, and measures they can take to ensure compliance with relevant regulations and standards.

3.4.1. Importance of regulatory compliance in the cloud:

- Data Security and Privacy: Regulatory compliance in the cloud is critical to protecting sensitive data and maintaining the privacy of individuals. Regulations such as the General Data Protection Regulation (GDPR), Health Insurance Portability and Accountability Act (HIPAA), and the payment card industry data protection standard (PCI DSS) imposes strict requirements on how organizations handle and protect personal and sensitive data. Failure to follow these rules can result in severe financial penalties and reputational damage.

- Legal and Ethical Obligations: Regulatory compliance helps organizations fulfill their legal and ethical obligations. Compliance with industry-specific regulations ensures the protection of customer data, safeguards against data breaches, and promotes trust and transparency in business functions. Adhering to the rules reflects an organization's commitment to maintaining high standards of data security and privacy.

- International Business Operations: Cloud computing enables organizations to operate globally. However, data protection laws and regulations differ in different countries. Compliance with international regulations is important for organizations that store and process data in various jurisdictions. By ensuring regulatory compliance, organizations can navigate legal complexities and build trust with clients worldwide.

3.4.2. Challenges in achieving regulatory compliance in the cloud:

- Data Location and Sovereignty: Cloud computing involves the storage and processing of data in many data centers, often located in different regions or countries. Ensuring compliance with the rules governing data space and sovereignty can be challenging. Organizations need visibility and control where their data is stored, processed and transmitted, especially when dealing with cross-border data transfer.

- Data Access and Control: Regulatory compliance requires strict control of organizations that have access to sensitive data. In the cloud, data can be stored and processed by cloud service providers, presenting complications in managing access controls and ensuring compliance with regulatory requirements. Organizations need to establish strong identity and access management (IAM) practices to implement appropriate access controls and monitor data access activities.

- Cloud service provider accountability: When using cloud services, organizations often rely on third-party cloud service providers (CSPs) to manage their data and infrastructure. It is important to ensure compliance of these CSPs with relevant regulations. Organizations need to carefully evaluate the safety and compliance measures of their CSPs, including contractual agreements, Service-level agreements (SLAs) and regular audits to verify compliance are included.

3.4.3. Measures to ensure regulatory compliance in the cloud:

- **Conduct a regulatory compliance assessment:** Organizations must deeply evaluate regulatory requirements applicable to their industry and geographic locations. This assessment helps identify specific compliance obligations and provides a basis for implementing appropriate controls.

- **Implement security controls and data security measures**: Organizations must implement robust security controls and data security measures to meet regulatory requirements. This includes encryption of sensitive data, implementing access control and authentication mechanisms, routine security assessments and audits, and maintaining appropriate incident response and data breech notification procedures.

- **Establish data governance and data lifecycle management**: Effective data governance practices are essential for regulatory compliance. Organizations should define data ownership, establish data classification policies, and implement data lifecycle management practices, including data retention and deletion policies.

- **Contractual agreements with cloud service providers**: When engaging with cloud service providers, organizations must ensure that contractual agreements address regulatory compliance obligations. This includes clearly defining the responsibilities of both parties, data security requirements, data access and ownership rights and mechanisms to conduct compliance audits.

- **Regular Compliance Audit and Evaluation:** Organizations must conduct regular compliance audits and assessments to ensure ongoing adherence to regulatory requirements. This includes reviewing security controls, data security practices, and the effectiveness of internal processes and procedures.

Exercise
Multiple Choice Questions

1. What is the primary focus of cloud security?

a. Ensuring data availability

b. Reducing cloud infrastructure costs

c. Protecting data, applications, and infrastructure in the cloud

d. Enhancing cloud service scalability

2. Which component of cloud security manages user identities and permissions?

a. Data Encryption

b. Network Security

c. Vulnerability Management

d. Identification and Access Management (IAM)

3. What does data encryption in cloud computing achieve?

a. Faster data transmission

b. Reduction of cloud service performance overhead

c. Prevention of unauthorized access to data

d. Elimination of the need for access control mechanisms

4. Which of the following is a key challenge in implementing data encryption in the cloud?

a. Complexity of key management

b. Improved data availability

c. Reduced data storage costs

d. Simplified data access control

5. What does IAM stand for in cloud security?

a. Identity and Access Management

b. Information and Asset Management

c. Internet and Application Monitoring

d. Infrastructure and Authorization Management

6. Why is regulatory compliance crucial in the cloud?

a. It enhances cloud service scalability

b. It reduces the need for data encryption

c. It ensures data security and privacy

d. It eliminates the need for vulnerability management

7. What is the importance of vulnerability management in cloud security?

a. It ensures data privacy during data transmission

b. It protects against unauthorized access to cloud resources

c. It mitigates potential security risks in cloud systems

d. It provides real-time monitoring of security incidents

8. What is the primary purpose of data encryption during data transmission?

a. To ensure data availability

b. To reduce data storage costs

c. To simplify access control

d. To protect data confidentiality during transmission

9. What does IAM help organizations achieve in the cloud?

a. Enhanced data availability

b. Simplified data governance

c. Improved cloud service performance

d. Secure and controlled access to cloud resources

Review Questions

1. What is the significance of cloud security in today's interconnected and data-driven world?

2. What are the key components of cloud security?

3. Why is Identification and Access Management (IAM) crucial in cloud security?

4. How does data encryption contribute to cloud security and privacy?

5. What is the importance of network security in cloud environments?

6. How does vulnerability management contribute to cloud security?

7. What role does security incident monitoring and response play in cloud security?

8. How does cloud security contribute to data protection and compliance?

9. What benefits does cloud security offer in terms of business continuity?

10. How does cloud security contribute to building customer trust?

Answer Section

Multiple Choice Questions

1. c) Protecting data, applications, and infrastructure in the cloud

2. d) Identification and Access Management (IAM)

3. c) Prevention of unauthorized access to data

4. a) Complexity of key management

5. a) Identity and Access Management

6. c) It ensures data security and privacy

7. c) It mitigates potential security risks in cloud systems

8. d) To protect data confidentiality during transmission

9. d) Secure and controlled access to cloud resources

Review Questions

1. Cloud security is of paramount importance in the digital age as it protects sensitive data, applications, and infrastructure in cloud environments. With businesses increasingly relying on cloud computing for storage and processing, robust security measures are necessary to prevent unauthorized access and data breaches. Cloud security ensures data privacy, maintains regulatory compliance, and mitigates risks, safeguarding the integrity and confidentiality of information stored and processed in the cloud.

2. The key components of cloud security include Identification and Access Management (IAM), data encryption, network security, vulnerability management, and security incident monitoring and response. IAM controls access to cloud resources, while data encryption protects data privacy. Network security ensures secure communication channels, and vulnerability management identifies and mitigates security risks. Security incident monitoring and response help detect and respond to security breaches promptly.

3. IAM is crucial in cloud security as it controls access to cloud resources, ensuring that only authorized users can access sensitive data and perform specific tasks. It manages user identities, credentials, and permissions, reducing the risk of unauthorized access or data breaches. IAM helps organizations enforce access control policies, maintain data privacy, and meet regulatory compliance requirements.

4. Data encryption plays a critical role in cloud security by ensuring data privacy and protection against unauthorized access. It involves converting data into an unreadable format using encryption algorithms, making it inaccessible to unauthorized parties. Encryption is applied during data transmission (in transit) and when data is at rest in storage. Proper key management ensures the confidentiality and integrity of encryption keys, adding an additional layer of security.

5. Network security is crucial in cloud environments as it focuses on securing network infrastructure, connections, and communication channels. It involves implementing firewalls, intrusion detection systems (IDS), and virtual private networks (VPNs) to prevent unauthorized access and detect and mitigate threats. Network security ensures data transmitted between cloud resources and users remains confidential and protected from potential cyberattacks.

6. Vulnerability management is essential in cloud security as it involves identifying, assessing, and defending against potential security vulnerabilities in cloud systems and applications. Regular scanning for vulnerabilities, patch management, and proactive monitoring help organizations quickly detect and

mitigate security risks. By addressing vulnerabilities promptly, organizations reduce the likelihood of data breaches and enhance the overall security of their cloud environment.

7. Security incident monitoring and response are crucial in cloud security to quickly detect and respond to security incidents. Tools like Security Information and Event Management (SIEM) and real-time monitoring help identify and investigate potential security breaches. An Incident Response Plan outlines the steps to be taken in case of security incidents, including prevention, elimination, recovery, and post-incident analysis.

8. Cloud security measures contribute significantly to data protection and compliance by safeguarding sensitive data from unauthorized access, breaches, and data loss. Compliance with data protection regulations and industry-specific requirements is ensured through the implementation of robust security controls and data security measures. Cloud security enables organizations to meet legal obligations regarding data security, privacy, and confidentiality, reducing the risk of financial penalties and reputational damage.

9. Cloud security plays an important role in business continuity and disaster recovery. Cloud service providers provide redundancy, backup, and disaster recovery mechanisms that ensure data availability and reduce downtime in case of disruption or disasters. By ensuring data integrity and availability, cloud security helps organizations maintain uninterrupted operations and recover quickly from potential incidents.

10. Implementing robust cloud security measures boosts customer trust by demonstrating a commitment to protecting their data and maintaining the confidentiality and integrity of their information. Advanced security measures contribute to building a positive reputation and aligning businesses as trustworthy and reliable in the market. Customer trust is essential for businesses to gain a competitive edge and establish long-term relationships with their clients.

Chapter 4: Cloud Service Providers

In today's rapidly evolving digital landscape, organizations are increasingly transforming cloud service providers (CSPs) to leverage the power of cloud computing. Cloud service providers provide a wide range of services, infrastructure and expertise to help businesses transform innovation, scale and their operations.

4.1 Services (AWS): Empowering the Cloud Revolution

In the realm of cloud computing, Amazon Web Services (AWS) has emerged as a major force, providing a comprehensive suite of cloud services to organizations around the world. AWS offers a vast array of infrastructure, platforms and software solutions, enabling businesses to innovate, scale
and transform their operations in the digital age.

4.1.1. Amazon Web Services Overview (AWS):

- **Definition and Scope:** Amazon Web Services (AWS) is a cloud computing platform offered by Amazon.com. Launched in 2006. AWS has become one of the world's most comprehensive and widely adopted cloud service providers. AWS offers a wide range of cloud services, including compute power, storage, databases, networking, analytics, machine learning, artificial intelligence (AI), Internet of Things (IoT), Security and more are included.

- **Infrastructure and Global Presence:** AWS operates a large and highly scalable infrastructure worldwide, including data centers, networking and edge locations. With data centers strategically located in various fields, AWS organizations need to deploy their applications and services closer to end users, enables reducing latency and enhancing performance. This global presence allows businesses to reach a broad customer base with minimal geographic constraints.

4.1.2. Key services and features of AWS:

- **Compute Services:** AWS provides a variety of computation services, including the Elastic Compute Cloud (EC2), which provides virtual servers in the cloud. EC2 allows organizations to calculate resources based on demand, providing flexibility and cost efficiency. AWS Lambda provides serverless computing capability, allowing developers to run code without provision or server.

- **Storage and database services:** AWS provides scalable and durable storage options, such as Amazon Simple Storage Service (S3), Which provides secure object storage for different data types. AWS also provides managed database services, including Amazon Relational Database Service (RDS) for relational databases, includes Amazon DynamoDB for NoSQL database and Amazon Aurora for high performance and scalable relational database.

- **Networking and content delivery**: AWS provides networking services, such as Amazon Virtual Private Cloud (VPC), which enables organizations to create separate virtual networks in the cloud. AWS also Amazon CloudFront, Provides content delivery services through a global content delivery network (CDN) that distributes web content with low latency and high data transfer speeds.

- **Analytics and Machine Learning**: AWS provides a comprehensive suite of analytics and machine learning services. Amazon Redshift allows organizations to analyze large datasets with data warehousing solutions. Amazon Kinesis enables real-time streaming and analysis of data from various sources. Additionally, AWS provides AI and machine learning services including Amazon SageMaker, which simplifies the development and deployment of machine learning models.

- **Security and Compliance**: AWS prioritizes the security and privacy of customer data. It provides a wide range of security services and facilities, such as AWS Identification and Access Management (IAM) for managing user access, AWS Key Management Service (KMS) for data encryption, and AWS Shield to protect against DDoS attacks. AWS assists organizations in achieving compliance with various regulatory frameworks, such as GDPR, HIPAA, and PCI DSS.

4.1.3. Benefits of using AWS:

- **Scalability and elasticity**: AWS allows organizations to quickly scale their infrastructure and services to meet changing business needs. With AWS, businesses can handle increased workloads, up or down resources, and only pay for used resources, can provide cost efficiency and flexibility.

- **Global Infrastructure: AWS's** extensive global infrastructure enables organizations to expand their operations and reach customers worldwide. With data centers in many areas, businesses can deliver their applications and services with low latency and high availability.

- **Extensive service portfolio**: AWS offers a vast selection of cloud services,

- Catering to various business needs. Organizations can easily leverage AWS's diverse range of services to build, deploy and manage applications and services.

- **Reliability and flexibility**: AWS has a strong infrastructure that ensures high availability and reliability of services. Its data centers are designed with redundancy and fault tolerance, reducing the risk of service disruptions and providing a reliable environment for businesses.

- **Cost efficiency:** AWS follows a pay-as-you-go pricing model, allowing organizations to pay for the resources they consume. This cost-effective approach eliminates the need for advance capital investment and enables businesses to optimize their IT budgets.

4.2 Microsoft Azure: Empowering Businesses with Scalable Cloud Solutions

In the dynamic world of cloud computing, Microsoft Azure has emerged as a leading cloud service provider, which offers a comprehensive suite of services and solutions to empower businesses of all sizes. Azure provides a scalable and flexible cloud platform that enables organizations to build, deploy and manage a wide range of applications and services.

4.2.1. Overview of Microsoft Azure:

Definition and Scope: Microsoft Azure is a cloud computing platform and service offered by Microsoft. Launched in 2010, Azure provides a robust infrastructure that allows businesses to deploy and manage applications, allows to store and analyze data and integrate various services. Azure offers a wide range of cloud-based solutions, including computing power, storage, databases, networking, AI, machine learning, and the Internet of Things (IoT) capabilities.

4.2.1.1 Extensive service portfolio

Microsoft provides a broad portfolio of Azure services, enabling organizations to meet their diverse computing needs. These services include:

- **Compute Services**: Azure Virtual Machine provides scalable virtual servers, allowing businesses to run applications and workloads in the cloud. Azure functions offer serverless computation capabilities, allowing developers to execute code in a pay-per-use manner.

- **Storage Services**: Azure Blob Storage provides scalable object storage for unstructured data, while Azure Files provides fully managed file shares in the cloud. Azure Disk Storage provides durable and high performance block storage for virtual machines and applications.

- **Database Services**: Azure offers various database options, including Azure SQL Database for relational databases, Azure Cosmos DB for globally distributed NoSQL databases, and Azure databases for MySQL and Azure databases for PostgreSQL for open-source databases.

- **Networking Services**: Azure virtual networks enable organizations to create separate networks in the cloud, while Azure load balancers and application gateways provide load balancing and traffic management capability. Azure VPN Gateway provides secure connectivity to on-premises networks.

- **AI and Machine Learning Services**: Azure provides a suite of services for AI and machine learning, including Azure Machine Learning for model making, training and deployment. Azure Cognitive Services to add pre-built AI capabilities, and Azure Bot Services to create intelligent chat bots.

- **Internet of Things (IoT) Services**: Azure IoT Hub allows organizations to connect, monitor and manage large-scale IoT devices. Azure IoT Central provides a fully managed platform for building and deploying IoT solutions.

- **DevOps and Developer Tools**: Azure DevOps provides a set of services for efficient application development and deployment, including version control, continuous integration and continuous deployment. Azure Dev Test Labs provides an environment for developing and testing applications.

- **Security and Compliance Services**: Azure provides robust security features, including Azure Active Directory for Identification and Access Management, Azure Security Center for Hazard Detection and Monitoring and Azure Policy for Implementing Compliance.

4.2.2. Benefits of using Microsoft Azure:

- **Scalability and Flexibility**: Azure allows organizations to quickly scale their applications and services to meet changing business demands. With Azure's elastic infrastructure, businesses can easily up or down resources, ensuring optimal performance and cost efficiency.

- **Hybrid Cloud Capabilities**: Azure provides seamless integration with on-premises environments, offering hybrid cloud capabilities. This allows organizations to build hybrid architectures, leverage existing infrastructure investments, and create an integrated and flexible environment.

- **Global Presence**: Azure operates a global network of data centers, enabling businesses to deploy their applications and services close to their customers. This ensures low latency, improved performance and compliance with data residency requirements in various fields.

- **Comprehensive security**: Azure prioritizes the security and privacy of customer data. It provides robust security measures, including inherent threat detection, identity management, encryption and compliance frameworks. Azure's compliance certificates cover one wide range of industry standards and regulations.

- **Comprehensive partner ecosystem**: Azure has a large partner ecosystem, including technology partners, solution providers and independent software vendors (ISVs). This ecosystem offers a wide range of pre-built solutions, integration options and expert support, allowing organizations to accelerate their cloud adoption journey.

4.3 Google Cloud Platform (GCP)

Google Cloud Platform is a suite of cloud computing services provided by Google, encompassing computing power, storage, machine learning, networking, and more. GCP operates on the same infrastructure that powers Google's products and services, ensuring reliability, scalability, and global reach. By leveraging Google's vast experience and expertise, GCP offers a competitive edge to businesses of all sizes.

4.3.1. Key Services and Features of GCP:

Google Cloud Platform offers an extensive array of services across various domains. Here are some notable ones:

- **Compute Services:** GCP provides flexible and scalable compute options with services like Google Compute Engine, enabling users to launch virtual machines in the cloud quickly. Additionally, Google Kubernetes Engine offers managed Kubernetes clusters for containerized applications.

- **Storage Services:** GCP offers various storage solutions, such as Google Cloud Storage, which provides object storage with high availability, durability, and low latency access. Google Cloud SQL and Cloud Bigtable are managed database solutions available on GCP.

- **Networking Services:** GCP provides a robust network infrastructure, including Virtual Private Cloud (VPC), which enables users to create isolated networks for their applications. Google Cloud Load Balancing ensures high availability and scalability for applications.

- **Big Data and Machine Learning:** GCP offers powerful tools for big data processing and analysis. Google BigQuery allows businesses to run fast and SQL-like queries on massive datasets, while Google Cloud AI provides pre-trained models and APIs for machine learning tasks.

- **Identity and Security:** GCP incorporates advanced security measures to protect data and applications. Google Cloud IAM manages access control, while Cloud Identity offers identity and access management solutions for users and devices.

- Developer Tools: GCP provides a range of developer-friendly tools, such as Google Cloud SDK and Cloud Source Repositories, which streamline development workflows. Cloud Build and Cloud Deployment Manager automate building and deploying applications.

4.3.2. Advantages of GCP:

GCP offers several key advantages that make it a compelling choice for businesses:

- Scalability and Performance: With Google's global infrastructure, GCP provides virtually limitless scalability, allowing businesses to handle any level of demand efficiently. The platform also offers high-performance computing resources for demanding workloads.

- Cutting-Edge Technologies: Google's continuous innovation ensures that GCP stays at the forefront of technology advancements. From machine learning and artificial intelligence to data analytics and serverless computing, GCP offers access to the latest tools and capabilities.

- Cost-Effective Pricing: GCP provides flexible pricing options, including pay-as-you-go models and sustained use discounts, allowing businesses to optimize costs based on their usage patterns. Additionally, Google offers cost management tools to monitor and control spending.

- Data Insights and Analytics: GCP's robust data analytics tools enable businesses to derive valuable insights from vast amounts of data. With offerings like BigQuery and Dataflow, organizations can process and analyze data efficiently to make data-driven decisions.

- Collaboration and Integration: GCP seamlessly integrates with other Google services, such as Google Workspace (formerly G Suite), enabling easy collaboration and data sharing. The platform also supports interoperability with various third-party tools and technologies.

4.3.3. Use Cases for GCP:

Google Cloud Platform caters to a broad range of use cases across industries:

- Web and Mobile Applications: GCP provides a scalable and reliable infrastructure for hosting web and mobile applications, handling high traffic volumes seamlessly.

- Data Analytics and Business Intelligence: GCP's powerful data analytics tools empower organizations to gain insights from large datasets, enabling informed business decisions and strategic planning.

- Machine Learning and AI: GCP's machine learning services support the development and deployment of intelligent applications, including image and speech recognition, natural language processing, and recommendation systems.

- IoT (Internet of Things): GCP offers robust services for managing and processing data from IoT devices, enabling organizations to leverage IoT data for monitoring, analysis, and automation.

- Digital Transformation: GCP provides the necessary infrastructure and tools to drive digital transformation initiatives, helping businesses modernize their operations, optimize processes, and enhance customer experiences.

4.4 Exploring Other Leading Cloud Service Providers

While Amazon Web Services (AWS), Microsoft Azure and Google Cloud Platform (GCP) dominate the cloud computing market, there are several other notable cloud service providers that offer unique features and capabilities.

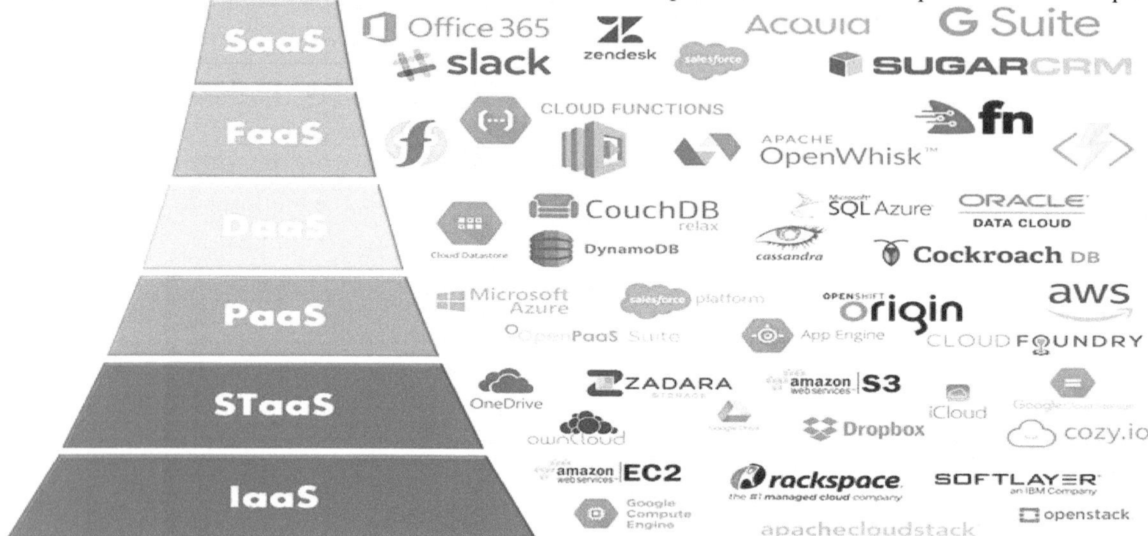

4.4.1. IBM Cloud:

IBM Cloud is a robust and secure cloud computing platform that combines infrastructure, platform, and software-as-a-service offerings. It provides a comprehensive suite of services, including compute, storage, networking, AI, blockchain, and IoT, catering to various industries and enterprise needs. IBM Cloud stands out for its focus on data security, compliance, and privacy, making it an excellent choice for businesses operating in highly regulated sectors such as finance and healthcare. Moreover, IBM's expertise in enterprise solutions and its strong support for open-source technologies make it a preferred option for organizations seeking hybrid or multi-cloud environments.

4.4.2. Alibaba Cloud:

Alibaba Cloud, the cloud computing arm of Alibaba Group, is one of the leading cloud service providers in the Asia-Pacific region. With a comprehensive suite of services that covers compute, storage, networking, databases, and AI, Alibaba Cloud caters to a wide range of industries and use cases. It offers extensive support for businesses entering or expanding into the Chinese market, thanks to its strong presence in China and compliance with local regulations. Alibaba Cloud's global network, high scalability, and competitive pricing make it an attractive option for businesses looking to expand their operations in the Asia-Pacific region or seeking a global cloud presence.

4.4.3. Oracle Cloud Infrastructure (OCI):

Oracle Cloud Infrastructure (OCI) provides a set of cloud services designed for enterprise workloads, including compute, storage, networking, database, and application development. OCI differentiates itself with its focus on high-performance computing, advanced networking capabilities, and strong support for Oracle Database workloads. It also offers specialized services for AI and machine learning, data management, and application development. OCI's hybrid cloud capabilities, along with its close integration with Oracle's on-premises technologies, make it a suitable choice for organizations seeking a seamless hybrid cloud environment.

4.4.4. DigitalOcean:

DigitalOcean is a cloud infrastructure provider known for its simplicity and developer-friendly approach. It offers scalable compute resources, storage, networking, and databases, targeting developers and small to medium-sized businesses. DigitalOcean's user-friendly interface, affordable pricing, and focus on simplicity make it a popular choice for developers and startups. It provides pre-configured application stacks and development environments, along with an active community and extensive documentation, making it easy for developers to get started quickly and deploy applications effortlessly.

Exercise

Multiple Choice Questions

1. Which term refers to the practice of leveraging cloud service providers for data storage and processing?

a. Cloud computing

b. Cloud service utilization

c. Cloud management

d. Cloud virtualization

2. Amazon Web Services (AWS) is a cloud computing platform provided by:

a. Google

b. Microsoft

c. Amazon.com

d. IBM

3. Which cloud service provider offers Azure Virtual Machine for scalable virtual servers?

a. Google Cloud Platform (GCP)

b. Microsoft Azure

c. Amazon Web Services (AWS)

d. Oracle Cloud Infrastructure (OCI)

4. Google Cloud Platform (GCP) offers a suite of services for:

a. Enterprise resource planning

b. Content management

c. Human resources management

d. Cloud computing

5. IBM Cloud is known for its focus on:

a. Cutting-edge technologies

b. Data security and compliance

c. Hybrid cloud capabilities

d. Developer-friendly tools

6. Which cloud service provider caters to businesses in the Asia-Pacific region and provides support for entering the Chinese market?

a. Microsoft Azure

b. Alibaba Cloud

c. Google Cloud Platform (GCP)

d. DigitalOcean

7. Oracle Cloud Infrastructure (OCI) is distinguished by its strong support for which type of workloads?

a. Artificial intelligence

b. Machine learning

c. High-performance computing

d. Data analytics

8. DigitalOcean is known for its popularity among:

a. Large enterprises

b. Government organizations

c. Developers and startups

d. Healthcare institutions

9. Which cloud service provider offers AWS Lambda for serverless computing?

a. Microsoft Azure

b. Alibaba Cloud

c. Amazon Web Services (AWS)

d. IBM Cloud

10. GCP's data analytics tool that allows businesses to run fast and SQL-like queries on massive datasets is called:

a. Google Cloud SQL

b. Google BigQuery

c. Google Cloud Storage

d. Google Cloud Dataflow

11. Which cloud service provider offers managed database solutions like Azure SQL Database and Azure Cosmos DB?

a. Microsoft Azure

b. Oracle Cloud Infrastructure (OCI)

c. Google Cloud Platform (GCP)

d. Alibaba Cloud

Review Questions

1. What role do cloud service providers (CSPs) play in the digital landscape?
2. What are some key services offered by Amazon Web Services (AWS)?
3. How does Microsoft Azure support hybrid cloud capabilities?
4. What are the key advantages of using Google Cloud Platform (GCP)?
5. How does IBM Cloud stand out among other cloud service providers?
6. What makes Alibaba Cloud a compelling option for businesses in the Asia-Pacific region?
7. How does Oracle Cloud Infrastructure (OCI) cater to enterprise workloads?
8. What makes DigitalOcean a popular choice for developers and startups?
9. How does AWS ensure security and compliance for its customers?
10. What are some common use cases for Google Cloud Platform (GCP)?

Answer Secton

Multiple Choice Questions

1. a) Cloud computing

2. c) Amazon.com

3. b) Microsoft Azure

4. d) Cloud computing

5. b) Data security and compliance

6. b) Alibaba Cloud

7. c) High-performance computing

8. c) Developers and startups

9. c) Amazon Web Services (AWS)

10. b) Google BigQuery

11. a) Microsoft Azure

Review Questions

1. Cloud service providers (CSPs) offer a comprehensive range of cloud services, infrastructure, and expertise to help businesses innovate, scale, and transform their operations in the digital age. They enable organizations to leverage the power of cloud computing, providing on-demand resources and services to meet changing business needs.

2. Amazon Web Services (AWS) provides a vast array of cloud services, including compute power through Elastic Compute Cloud (EC2), scalable storage with Amazon Simple Storage Service (S3), managed databases like Amazon RDS, networking capabilities with Amazon VPC, and AI/ML services through Amazon SageMaker.

3. Microsoft Azure enables hybrid cloud capabilities by seamlessly integrating with on-premises environments. Organizations can build hybrid architectures, leverage existing infrastructure, and create an integrated environment for data sharing and collaboration between cloud and on-premises resources.

4. Google Cloud Platform (GCP) offers virtually limitless scalability, cutting-edge technologies, cost-effective pricing options, a global network of data centers for low-latency access, and robust data analytics tools for valuable insights.

5. IBM Cloud stands out for its focus on data security, compliance, and privacy, making it an excellent choice for businesses in highly regulated sectors. Its expertise in enterprise solutions and support for open-source technologies are ideal for organizations seeking hybrid or multi-cloud environments.

6. Alibaba Cloud's extensive support for businesses entering or expanding into the Chinese market, combined with its global network, high scalability, and competitive pricing, makes it an attractive choice for organizations looking to expand operations in the Asia-Pacific region.

7. Oracle Cloud Infrastructure (OCI) provides a set of cloud services designed for enterprise workloads, including high-performance computing, advanced networking capabilities, and strong support for Oracle Database workloads, making it suitable for seamless hybrid cloud environments.

8. DigitalOcean's user-friendly interface, affordable pricing, pre-configured application stacks, and extensive documentation make it a preferred choice for developers and startups to quickly get started and deploy applications effortlessly.

9. AWS prioritizes data security and privacy, offering a range of security services like AWS IAM, KMS, and Shield to protect against potential threats and ensure compliance with industry-specific regulations like GDPR, HIPAA, and PCI DSS.

10. GCP caters to various use cases, including hosting web and mobile applications, data analytics and business intelligence, implementing machine learning and AI solutions, managing IoT devices, and driving digital transformation initiatives for businesses.

Chapter 5: Cloud Migration Strategies

5.1 Assessing On-Premises Infrastructure: A Comprehensive Guide

In the era of cloud computing, assessing the state of your on-premises infrastructure is a critical step in determining your organization's IT strategy. Understanding the strengths, weaknesses, and potential improvements of your existing infrastructure enables you to make informed decisions about modernization, migration to the cloud, or optimizing your on-premises setup.

5.1.1. Defining the Assessment Goals:

Before diving into the assessment process, it is essential to define clear goals and objectives. These goals may include:

- **Performance and Scalability:** Assessing the current infrastructure's performance, identifying bottlenecks, and evaluating scalability options.

- **Security and Compliance:** Evaluating security measures, identifying vulnerabilities, and ensuring compliance with industry regulations and standards.

- **Cost Optimization:** Analyzing the total cost of ownership (TCO), identifying areas of inefficiency, and exploring opportunities for cost optimization.

- **Reliability and Availability:** Assessing the reliability and availability of critical systems, identifying single points of failure, and exploring high availability solutions.

5.1.2. Gathering Information:

To assess your on-premises infrastructure effectively, gather the following information:

- **Inventory:** Document a comprehensive inventory of hardware, software, and network components.

- **Performance Data:** Collect performance metrics such as CPU utilization, memory usage, network throughput, and storage performance.

- **Configuration Details:** Capture information on network configurations, security settings, and system architecture.

- **Business Requirements:** Understand the current and future business needs to align the assessment with organizational goals.

5.1.3. Evaluating Infrastructure Components:

Assess the following key components of your on-premises infrastructure:

- **Hardware:** Evaluate the age, performance, and capacity of servers, storage devices, networking equipment, and other hardware components.

- **Software:** Review the software stack, including operating systems, databases, virtualization technologies, and middleware, for compatibility, security patches, and updates.

- **Network Infrastructure:** Assess network architecture, bandwidth requirements, routing, switching, and firewall configurations.

- **Security Measures:** Evaluate security protocols, access controls, authentication mechanisms, encryption practices, and disaster recovery plans.

- **Storage and Backup:** Review data storage mechanisms, backup strategies, disaster recovery capabilities, and data retention policies.

5.1.4. Analyzing Performance and Workloads:
Examine the performance and workloads running on your infrastructure:
- **Performance Analysis:** Analyze performance metrics and identify performance bottlenecks, resource utilization patterns, and areas for improvement.

- **Workload Assessment:** Understand the types of workloads running on the infrastructure, their resource requirements, and any limitations or constraints.

- **Capacity Planning:** Forecast future capacity requirements based on growth projections, seasonal variations, and anticipated workload changes.

5.1.5. Identifying Risks and Opportunities:
Based on the assessment, identify risks, challenges, and opportunities for improvement:
- **Risk Identification:** Identify potential risks, such as hardware or software obsolescence, security vulnerabilities, single points of failure, or scalability limitations.

- **Cost Optimization**: Identify areas of cost inefficiency, such as underutilized resources, license optimization opportunities, or energy consumption optimization.

- **Modernization Opportunities:** Assess the feasibility and benefits of modernization initiatives, such as server virtualization, containerization, or software-defined infrastructure.

- **Cloud Readiness:** Determine the suitability of workloads for migration to the cloud, considering factors like data sensitivity, regulatory compliance, and cost implications.

5.1.6. Developing an Action Plan:
Based on the assessment findings, develop a comprehensive action plan:
- **Prioritize Initiatives:** Rank identified risks, opportunities, and improvement areas based on their impact and urgency.

- **Budget and Timeline:** Define a realistic budget and timeline for implementing recommended changes and improvements.

- **Collaboration and Support:** Engage stakeholders, IT teams, and external experts, as needed, to gain support and expertise in executing the action plan effectively.

- **Monitoring and Review:** Establish mechanisms to monitor progress, measure success, and regularly review and update the action plan as needed.

5.2 Planning a Successful Cloud Migration

Cloud migration has become a strategic imperative for organizations looking to leverage the benefits of scalability, flexibility, and cost-efficiency offered by cloud computing. However, a successful cloud migration requires careful planning and execution to ensure a smooth transition.

5.2.1. Define Migration Goals and Objectives:

Before embarking on a cloud migration journey, establish clear goals and objectives that align with your organization's overall strategy. These goals may include:

- **Cost Optimization:** Reduce infrastructure costs and achieve better cost predictability by leveraging cloud services.

- **Scalability and Flexibility:** Improve the ability to scale resources up or down based on demand and adapt to changing business needs.

- **Performance and Availability:** Enhance application performance, achieve high availability, and ensure business continuity.

- **Security and Compliance:** Strengthen security measures and ensure compliance with industry regulations and data protection standards.

5.2.2. Assess Current Environment:

Evaluate your existing IT environment to gather critical information and insights that will inform your migration strategy:

- **Application Inventory:** Identify and document all applications and their dependencies, including infrastructure, software, and data requirements.

- **Performance Analysis:** Analyze the performance and utilization of your current infrastructure to understand resource requirements and potential bottlenecks.

- **Data Classification:** Categorize your data based on its sensitivity, regulatory requirements, and any compliance considerations.

- **Interdependencies:** Identify any interdependencies among applications, databases, and systems to plan for their migration sequence.

5.2.3. Select a Cloud Service Provider:

Evaluate different cloud service providers based on your organization's specific needs, considering factors such as pricing, service offerings, reliability, security, compliance, and geographical presence.

5.2.4. Define Migration Strategy:

Develop a comprehensive migration strategy that outlines the approach, timeline, and key milestones:

- **Migration Phases:** Break down the migration into logical phases or waves based on application criticality, complexity, and interdependencies.

- **Lift-and-Shift vs. Refactoring:** Determine whether a lift-and-shift approach (rehosting) or refactoring (re-architecting) is appropriate for each application or workload.

- **Data Migration:** Plan the migration of your data, ensuring minimal downtime and data integrity during the transition.

- **Testing and Validation:** Define testing strategies to validate application functionality, performance, and security in the cloud environment.

5.2.5. Establish Security and Compliance Measures:

Develop robust security and compliance measures to protect data and meet regulatory requirements:

- **Identity and Access Management:** Implement proper access controls, authentication mechanisms, and encryption practices.

- **Data Protection:** Define data encryption, backup, and disaster recovery strategies to ensure data integrity and availability.

- **Compliance:** Understand and adhere to relevant industry-specific compliance standards and regulations.

5.1.6. Develop a Migration Plan:

Create a detailed migration plan that outlines the tasks, dependencies, timelines, and responsible stakeholders:

- **Application Priority:** Prioritize applications based on their criticality, complexity, and business impact.

- **Resource Provisioning:** Determine the required cloud resources (compute, storage, networking) for each application or workload.

- **Data Migration Strategy:** Define the approach and tools for data migration, considering factors such as data volume, synchronization, and transfer methods.

- **Testing and Validation:** Incorporate testing and validation activities to ensure proper functionality, performance, and security in the cloud environment.

5.1.7. Execute and Monitor the Migration:

Execute the migration plan, closely monitoring the progress and addressing any issues or challenges that arise:

- **Communication and Change Management:** Maintain clear communication channels with stakeholders and users, managing expectations and providing regular updates.

- **Training and Support:** Provide training and support to users and IT teams to ensure a smooth transition and adoption of the cloud environment.

- **Performance Optimization:** Continuously monitor application performance, identify optimization opportunities, and fine-tune resource allocation as needed.

5.1.8. Post-Migration Validation and Optimization:

Once the migration is complete, validate the functionality, performance, and security of your applications in the cloud environment. Optimize and fine-tune the cloud infrastructure based on real-world usage patterns and feedback from users.

5.2 Lift and Shift vs. Cloud-Native Development: Choosing the Right Approach

When migrating applications to the cloud, organizations often face a critical decision: whether to lift and shift their existing applications or embrace cloud-native development. Both approaches have their merits and considerations. In this article, we will explore the differences between lift and shift and cloud-native development, discuss their advantages and challenges, and provide guidance on choosing the right approach for your specific requirements.

5.2.1. Lift and Shift Approach:

The lift and shift approach, also known as rehosting, involves migrating applications from on-premises infrastructure to the cloud with minimal changes. Here are key aspects of this approach:

1. Migration Speed: Lift and shift allows for a faster migration process since it focuses on moving existing applications without extensive modifications.

2. Infrastructure Compatibility: Applications remain largely unchanged, leveraging existing configurations and dependencies, making the migration process smoother.

3. Immediate Benefits: Lift and shift enables organizations to quickly leverage cloud benefits such as scalability, high availability, and cost optimization without significant upfront investment or development effort.

4. Limited Cloud-Native Features: This approach may not take full advantage of cloud-native services and capabilities, potentially missing out on some benefits and optimizations.

5.2.2. Cloud-Native Development:

Cloud-native development involves rearchitecting applications to fully leverage cloud-native services and principles. Key aspects of this approach include:

1. Scalability and Resilience: Cloud-native development allows applications to scale horizontally, leveraging auto-scaling and containerization to meet varying demand. Resilience is achieved through distributed architectures and redundancy.

2. Microservices Architecture: Cloud-native applications often follow a microservices architecture, where applications are decomposed into smaller, loosely coupled services, enabling agility, independent scaling, and ease of deployment.

3. DevOps and Automation: Cloud-native development embraces DevOps practices and automation, enabling continuous integration, continuous delivery, and infrastructure-as-code to achieve faster deployments and more efficient operations.

4. Utilizing Cloud-Native Services: Cloud-native development fully leverages the native services provided by cloud platforms, such as serverless computing, managed databases, messaging queues, and AI/ML services, to enhance application functionality and performance.

5.2.3. Choosing the Right Approach:

When deciding between lift and shift and cloud-native development, consider the following factors:

- Application Complexity: Lift and shift may be more suitable for legacy applications with complex dependencies, tightly coupled components, or limited resources for extensive rearchitecting. Cloud-native development is advantageous for new or greenfield applications where flexibility and scalability are critical.

- Time and Resource Constraints: If time is of the essence or if resource constraints limit the ability to undertake extensive redevelopment, lift and shift can be a pragmatic approach to quickly migrate applications to the cloud.

- Long-Term Goals: Evaluate your long-term goals and strategic vision. If the organization aims to take full advantage of cloud-native features, scalability, and agility, investing in cloud-native development may provide greater benefits in the long run.

- Cost Considerations: Assess the cost implications of both approaches. While lift and shift may offer immediate cost benefits by moving to the cloud, cloud-native development can optimize costs through finer-grained resource allocation and scaling.

5.2.4. Hybrid Approaches:

Organizations can also consider hybrid approaches that combine elements of both lift and shift and cloud-native development. For instance, lift and shift can be initially performed for time-sensitive migrations, followed by incremental rearchitecting of specific application components to embrace cloud-native principles.

5.3 Best Practices for a Successful Cloud Migration

Cloud migration is a complex process that requires careful planning, execution, and management to ensure a smooth transition and maximize the benefits of cloud computing.

5.3.1. Develop a Comprehensive Migration Strategy:

Creating a well-defined migration strategy is crucial for a successful cloud migration. Consider the following key elements:

- Set Clear Goals: Define clear objectives and align them with the organization's overall strategy, such as cost optimization, scalability, or improved security.

- Assess Readiness: Evaluate your existing infrastructure, applications, and data to identify potential challenges, dependencies, and migration priorities.

- Prioritize Applications: Determine the order in which applications will be migrated based on criticality, complexity, and business impact.

- Plan for Data Migration: Develop a robust data migration strategy, including data classification, transfer methods, and ensuring data integrity during the transition.

- Test and Validation: Incorporate testing and validation activities to ensure proper functionality, performance, and security in the cloud environment.

5.3.2. Consider Cloud Provider Selection:

Choosing the right cloud service provider is crucial for a successful migration. Consider the following factors:

- Compatibility and Interoperability: Assess how well your applications and infrastructure align with the cloud provider's services, APIs, and compatibility requirements.

- Security and Compliance: Evaluate the cloud provider's security measures, data protection capabilities, and adherence to industry regulations and compliance standards.

- Scalability and Performance: Consider the cloud provider's infrastructure capabilities, including scalability, availability, and network performance, to meet your application requirements.

- Cost Optimization: Understand the cloud provider's pricing models, cost management tools, and options for optimizing costs based on your usage patterns.

5.3.3. Optimize Applications for the Cloud:

To maximize the benefits of the cloud, consider optimizing your applications for the cloud environment:

- Cloud-Native Architecture: Refactor or rearchitect applications to leverage cloud-native principles, such as microservices, scalability, and serverless computing.

- **Performance Optimization:** Fine-tune applications for optimal performance in the cloud environment, considering factors like resource utilization, caching, and network latency.

- **Security and Compliance:** Enhance security measures by adopting cloud-native security services, implementing secure coding practices, and ensuring compliance with data protection regulations.

- **Data Management:** Consider data storage and database optimization techniques, such as data partitioning, indexing, and replication, to improve data access and reliability.

5.3.4. Implement Robust Security Measures:

Maintaining robust security during the migration process is crucial. Consider the following security best practices:

- **Identity and Access Management:** Implement strong authentication mechanisms, access controls, and role-based access management to secure cloud resources.

- **Data Encryption:** Encrypt sensitive data at rest and in transit to ensure confidentiality and protect against unauthorized access.

- **Network Security**: Configure firewalls, network segmentation, and secure connectivity to protect cloud resources from external threats.

- **Incident Response and Monitoring:** Establish monitoring and logging mechanisms to detect and respond to security incidents promptly.

5.3.5 Plan for Change Management and Communication:

- Smoothly managing the organizational impact of cloud migration is essential for success. Consider the following practices:

- **Stakeholder Engagement:** Involve key stakeholders from different departments to ensure their buy-in, support, and understanding of the migration process.

- **Training and Knowledge Transfer:** Provide training to employees to familiarize them with the new cloud environment and technologies.

- **Change Communication:** Regularly communicate updates, progress, and expected changes to employees and stakeholders to manage expectations and minimize disruptions.

- **Establish Support Channels:** Set up support channels and help desk services to address user questions, concerns, and issues during and after the migration.

5.3.6. Monitor, Optimize, and Iterate:

Once the migration is complete, continuously monitor and optimize your cloud infrastructure to ensure its optimal performance and cost-effectiveness:

- **Performance Monitoring:** Establish monitoring tools and practices to track application performance, resource utilization, and user experience.

- **Cost Optimization:** Regularly review and optimize your cloud resources, rightsizing instances, leveraging automation, and monitoring spending patterns.

- **Continuous Improvement:** Embrace the DevOps culture by implementing continuous integration and delivery practices, enabling rapid iteration and improvement of applications and infrastructure.

Exercise
Multiple Choice Questions

1. What is the primary purpose of assessing on-premises infrastructure before cloud migration?

a. To determine the compatibility of existing applications with cloud platforms

b. To identify potential risks and vulnerabilities in the current infrastructure

c. To estimate the cost of cloud migration

d. To prioritize applications for migration based on their criticality

2. Which of the following is NOT a key component of on-premises infrastructure assessment for cloud migration?

a. Hardware evaluation

b. Network architecture analysis

c. Application code optimization

d. Security protocol review

3. What is one of the primary benefits of the lift and shift approach in cloud migration?

a. It allows applications to fully leverage cloud-native services

b. It requires minimal changes to existing applications for migration

c. It provides better cost optimization than cloud-native development

d. It involves rearchitecting applications into microservices

4. In cloud-native development, what architectural style is often followed for applications?

a. Monolithic architecture

b. Service-Oriented Architecture (SOA)

c. Microservices architecture

d. Distributed architecture

5. What is the primary reason for choosing the lift and shift approach in cloud migration?

a. To fully utilize cloud-native services

b. To achieve immediate cost optimization

c. To ensure better application performance in the cloud

d. To enable horizontal scalability of applications

6. Which factor should NOT be considered when selecting a cloud service provider for migration?

a. Security measures

b. Scalability

c. Application code complexity

d. Service offerings

7. What is a key advantage of cloud-native development in cloud migration?

a. Faster migration process

b. Minimal upfront investment

c. Leveraging existing infrastructure configurations

d. Full utilization of cloud-native services and capabilities

8. What should organizations prioritize when developing a migration action plan based on assessment findings?

a. Budget and timeline

b. Application complexity

c. Hardware inventory

d. Network throughput

9. What is the primary purpose of establishing monitoring and review mechanisms after cloud migration?

a. To assess the compatibility of applications with the cloud platform

b. To measure the success of the migration process

c. To identify potential risks and vulnerabilities in the cloud environment

d. To prioritize applications for future migrations

10. Why is it essential to plan for change management and communication during cloud migration?

a. To minimize cloud migration costs

b. To prevent data loss during the migration process

c. To ensure data integrity and availability in the cloud

d. To manage the organizational impact and user expectations

Review Questions

1. Why is assessing on-premises infrastructure crucial for an organization's IT strategy in the era of cloud computing?

2. What are the main goals of the assessment process when evaluating on-premises infrastructure for cloud migration?

3. What information should be gathered to effectively assess the on-premises infrastructure?

4. When evaluating on-premises infrastructure, what key components should be assessed?

5. Why is it important to identify risks and opportunities during the infrastructure assessment?

6. What elements should be included in the action plan developed based on the assessment findings?

7. Why is careful planning necessary for a successful cloud migration?

8. What are the goals and objectives that should be defined before starting a cloud migration?

9. Why is assessing the current environment crucial in the cloud migration planning process?

10. What factors should be considered when selecting a cloud service provider for migration?

11. What are some best practices to ensure a successful cloud migration?

Answer Section

Multiple Choice Questions

1. b) To identify potential risks and vulnerabilities in the current infrastructure

2. c) Application code optimization

3. b) It requires minimal changes to existing applications for migration

4. c) Microservices architecture

5. b) To achieve immediate cost optimization

6. c) Application code complexity

7. d) Full utilization of cloud-native services and capabilities

8. a) Budget and timeline

9. b) To measure the success of the migration process

10. d) To manage the organizational impact and user expectations

Review Questions

1. Assessing on-premises infrastructure is vital because it provides insights into existing strengths, weaknesses, and potential improvements. This information helps organizations make informed decisions about modernization, cloud migration, or optimizing their current setup, ensuring alignment with their overall IT strategy and business goals.

2. The main goals of the assessment process are to evaluate performance and scalability, security and compliance measures, cost optimization opportunities, and the reliability and availability of critical systems. This evaluation aids in identifying areas for improvement and planning a successful migration strategy.

3. To effectively assess the on-premises infrastructure, organizations should gather a comprehensive inventory of hardware, software, and network components, along with performance metrics, configuration details, and an understanding of current and future business requirements.

4. Key components to assess include hardware, such as servers, storage devices, and networking equipment, the software stack, network infrastructure, security measures, and storage and backup mechanisms. Evaluating these components helps identify areas for improvement and potential migration opportunities.

5. Identifying risks helps organizations address potential issues, such as hardware obsolescence or security vulnerabilities, while identifying opportunities allows for cost optimization, modernization initiatives, and effective cloud migration planning, ensuring a successful and efficient migration process.

6. The action plan should prioritize initiatives based on their impact and urgency, define a realistic budget and timeline for implementation, involve collaboration and support from stakeholders and IT teams, and establish monitoring and review mechanisms to track progress and measure success.

7. Careful planning is essential to ensure a smooth transition and minimize disruptions during the cloud migration process. Proper planning helps identify potential challenges, define migration goals, and align the migration strategy with organizational objectives, leading to a successful and efficient migration.

8. The goals and objectives should align with the organization's overall strategy and may include cost optimization, scalability, flexibility, improved performance and availability, strengthened security and compliance measures, and enhanced business agility.

9. Assessing the current environment is crucial because it provides critical information about existing applications, infrastructure, and data dependencies. This assessment is necessary to plan the migration strategy, prioritize applications, and anticipate potential challenges, ensuring a seamless and successful cloud migration.

10. Factors such as compatibility with existing infrastructure and applications, security measures, scalability, cost, service offerings, and geographical presence should be considered when selecting a cloud service provider. The right choice ensures a suitable cloud environment that meets the organization's specific needs.

11. Best practices include developing a comprehensive migration strategy, optimizing applications for the cloud environment, implementing robust security measures, planning for change management and communication, and continuously monitoring and optimizing the cloud infrastructure post-migration. These practices ensure a smooth and successful cloud migration with maximum benefits.

Chapter 6: Cloud Cost Optimization

6.1 Understanding Cloud Cost Components

Cloud computing offers flexibility and scalability, but it's crucial to understand the cost components associated with cloud services to effectively manage expenses. Understanding the cost components of cloud computing is crucial for effective cost management and budget planning. Compute instances, storage, data transfer, network services, databases, additional services, support, and security measures all contribute to cloud costs. By gaining a comprehensive understanding of these cost components and utilizing cost optimization tools and strategies, businesses can make informed decisions, optimize their cloud spending, and maximize the value they derive from cloud services. we will explore the key cost components of cloud computing to help you gain a better understanding of how cloud costs are structured.

6.1.1 Compute Instances:

Compute instances, such as virtual machines (VMs) or containers, form the foundation of cloud computing. The cost of compute instances typically depends on factors such as the instance type, CPU, memory, and storage capacity. Different cloud service providers offer various pricing models, including on-demand pricing (pay-as-you-go), reserved instances (long-term commitments with lower rates), and spot instances (bid-based pricing for spare capacity).

6.1.2. Storage:

Cloud storage provides scalable and durable data storage solutions. Cloud storage costs are based on factors such as storage capacity, data transfer (both ingress and egress), and storage class (e.g., standard, infrequent access, archival). Additionally, cloud providers may charge for data management services like snapshots, backups, and object lifecycle management.

6.1.3. Data Transfer and Bandwidth:

Cloud providers charge for data transfer between different regions, availability zones, or the internet. Ingress refers to data coming into the cloud, while egress refers to data leaving the cloud. Bandwidth costs may vary depending on the volume of data transferred and the geographical regions involved. It's essential to be aware of these costs, especially when dealing with large-scale data movement.

6.1.4. Network and Load Balancing:

Networking costs may include charges for virtual networks, subnets, IP addresses, and network traffic within or outside the cloud environment. Load balancing services, which distribute traffic across multiple instances, can also have associated costs, such as per-hour or per-GB charges.

6.1.5. Database Services:

Cloud database services, such as managed relational databases or NoSQL databases, come with their own pricing models. Costs may be based on factors like the database size, I/O operations, backups, and data transfer. It's important to consider the specific pricing details and options for the chosen database service.

6.1.6. Additional Services and Features:

Cloud providers offer a wide range of additional services, such as analytics, machine learning, monitoring, security, and identity and access management. These services may have their own cost structures based on usage, API requests, data processed, or the number of resources managed. Understanding the pricing models for these services is important when considering their inclusion in your cloud architecture.

6.1.7. Support and Service Level Agreements (SLAs):

Cloud providers often offer different support tiers with varying response times and access to technical support. Premium support packages typically involve additional costs. It's crucial to evaluate the support options and associated costs, especially if your business requires high availability and timely technical assistance.

6.1.8. Data Compliance and Security:

Depending on your industry and regulatory requirements, you may need to invest in additional security and compliance measures. For example, encryption services, dedicated private network connections, or compliance certifications may involve extra costs to meet specific data protection and regulatory standards.

6.1.9. Cost Optimization Tools and Strategies:

Cloud providers offer various tools and services to help optimize costs. These include cost management dashboards, budget alerts, resource tagging, rightsizing recommendations, and reserved instance planning. Leveraging these tools and implementing cost optimization strategies can help optimize spending and prevent unexpected cost overruns.

6.2 Cost Monitoring and Management

Cost monitoring and management in the context of cloud computing refer to the practices and strategies implemented by organizations to effectively control and optimize their cloud expenses. As cloud usage grows and becomes more complex, it's crucial for businesses to have a comprehensive approach to managing their cloud spending. Below is a deeper explanation of the key aspects mentioned in the provided text:

6.2.1. Establish a Cost Monitoring Framework:

Creating a cost monitoring framework involves setting up processes and tools that allow organizations to gain better visibility into their cloud spending. This is achieved through various steps, such as:

- **Cost Allocation Tags:** These are labels applied to cloud resources, services, and deployments. By consistently tagging resources, organizations can categorize their expenses and gain insights into spending patterns based on tags like departments, projects, or environments.

- **Cloud Provider Cost Management Tools:** Cloud service providers offer built-in cost management tools and dashboards that provide valuable information about cloud usage, costs, and trends. Organizations can use these tools to track their spending, understand resource utilization, and receive optimization suggestions.

- **Third-Party Cost Monitoring Solutions:** Beyond native cloud provider tools, there are third-party tools available that offer more advanced cost monitoring and optimization features. These tools often provide deeper analytics, forecasting capabilities, and customizable reports for better cost management.

6.2.2. Set Budgets and Alerts:

Organizations should define financial budgets and thresholds for cloud spending. By setting up budget alerts, they can be promptly notified when spending exceeds the predefined limits. This allows businesses to take corrective actions early on and avoid unexpected cost overruns.

6.2.3. Optimize Resource Utilization:

Efficiently using cloud resources is essential for cost optimization. Key practices include:

- **Rightsizing:** Continuously evaluating resource usage and adjusting instances to match actual workload requirements. This ensures that resources are neither underutilized (wasting money) nor overprovisioned (incurring unnecessary costs).

- **Scheduled Shutdowns:** Automating the shutdown of non-production resources during periods of inactivity to save on costs.

- **Auto-Scaling:** Utilizing auto-scaling capabilities to automatically adjust resources based on demand. This ensures that the infrastructure scales up during peak usage and scales down during low activity, preventing overpayment for unused resources.

6.2.4. Reserved Instances and Savings Plans:

Cloud providers often offer options like Reserved Instances or Savings Plans, allowing organizations to commit to longer-term contracts in exchange for discounted rates. This approach is particularly beneficial for predictable workloads, as it can result in significant cost savings.

6.2.5. Monitor Data Transfer and Bandwidth:

Data transfer and bandwidth usage can contribute significantly to cloud costs. Organizations should optimize data transfer by employing techniques such as compression, caching, and using content delivery networks (CDNs). Monitoring network traffic patterns helps identify areas of high data transfer and allows for better resource allocation.

6.2.6. Cost-Aware Architecture and Design:

When designing cloud architectures and applications, organizations should be mindful of cost implications. Emphasizing cost-aware design principles involves choosing cost-effective services, adopting serverless computing for fine-grained scaling, utilizing managed services to minimize administrative overhead, and optimizing data storage strategies for cost efficiency.

6.2.7. Regularly Review and Optimize:

Cost monitoring and management are continuous processes. Organizations should regularly review their cloud spending, analyze cost reports, and identify optimization opportunities. Staying informed about new pricing models and cost-saving options from the cloud provider helps ensure ongoing cost optimization.

6.2.8. Foster Cost-Conscious Culture:

Building a cost-conscious culture involves encouraging all stakeholders to prioritize cost optimization. This includes educating employees about cost implications, promoting responsible cloud resource usage, and establishing policies and guidelines to enforce cost efficiency.

By implementing these best practices, organizations can effectively manage cloud costs, optimize spending, and maximize the value derived from their cloud investments.

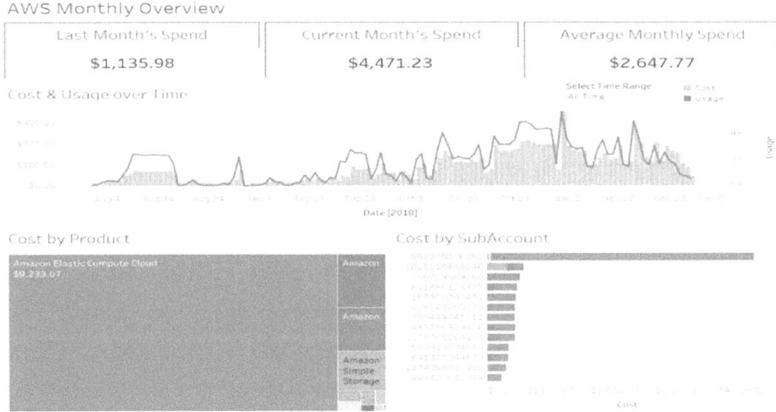

6.3 Strategies for Cost Optimization in the Cloud

As businesses increasingly adopt cloud computing, optimizing costs becomes a critical priority to leverage the scalability and flexibility that the cloud offers. By implementing effective cost optimization strategies, organizations can achieve significant savings while ensuring the performance and functionality of their cloud infrastructure remain intact. This article explores various strategies to optimize costs in the cloud.

6.3.1. Monitor and Analyze Resource Utilization:

Regularly monitoring and analyzing resource utilization is the foundation of effective cost optimization. By identifying underutilized or idle resources, organizations can take appropriate actions to minimize unnecessary expenses. Key practices include:

- **Rightsizing Instances:** Continuously assess the resource requirements of applications and adjust instance sizes accordingly. Downsizing or upsizing instances based on workload demands can lead to substantial cost savings.

- **Implement Auto-Scaling:** Leveraging auto-scaling capabilities ensures resources automatically adjust to meet demand fluctuations. Scaling up during peak periods and scaling down during low-usage periods optimize resource allocation and cost efficiency.

- **Schedule Shutdowns:** Setting up automated schedules to shut down non-production resources during periods of inactivity helps avoid unnecessary costs associated with running idle resources.

6.3.2. Leverage Cost Optimization Tools:

Cloud service providers offer a range of tools and services to support cost optimization efforts. Leveraging these offerings provides valuable insights into cost patterns, optimization opportunities, and efficient resource management. Examples include:

- **Cost Management Dashboards:** Utilize built-in cost management dashboards provided by cloud providers to monitor spending, track usage, and identify cost trends in real-time.

- **Cost Explorer and Reporting:** Utilize cost explorer tools to generate reports and perform in-depth analysis of cost data. This enables identifying cost drivers and optimizing spending based on various dimensions such as tags, regions, or services.

- **Recommendations and Alerts:** Take advantage of cost optimization recommendations and alerts provided by cloud providers. These features suggest potential cost-saving opportunities and notify you of any unusual spending patterns.

6.3.3. Utilize Reserved Instances and Savings Plans:

Reserved instances and savings plans are cost-saving options offered by cloud service providers. They provide discounted pricing in exchange for committing to longer-term contracts. Consider the following:

- **Reserved Instances:** Evaluate workload stability and predictability to determine the suitability of purchasing reserved instances. Reserved instances offer significant cost savings for steady-state workloads with predictable resource requirements.

- **Savings Plans:** Savings plans offer flexibility by providing discounts across different instance families, sizes, or regions. Evaluate workload patterns to select the most appropriate savings plan that aligns with your usage.

6.3.4. Optimize Data Transfer and Bandwidth:

Data transfer and bandwidth costs can accumulate if not monitored and optimized effectively. Consider the following approaches:

- **Minimize Unnecessary Data Transfers:** Review and optimize data transfer patterns to minimize unnecessary movement of data between regions or services.

- **Use Content Delivery Networks (CDNs):** Leveraging CDNs helps cache and deliver content closer to end-users, reducing data transfer costs and improving performance.

- **Implement Compression and Caching:** Utilize compression techniques and caching strategies to reduce bandwidth requirements and enhance data delivery efficiency.

6.3.5. Cloud-Native Architecture and Serverless Computing:

Embracing cloud-native architecture and serverless computing can lead to substantial cost optimization and improved scalability. Key considerations include:

- **Microservices and Containerization:** Decompose monolithic applications into microservices and containerize them. This approach enables efficient resource allocation, scalability, and cost optimization by allowing independent scaling of individual components.

- **Serverless Computing:** Adopt serverless computing models, such as AWS Lambda or Azure Functions, to optimize costs by paying only for the actual execution time of functions without the need to manage underlying infrastructure.

6.3.6. Implement Tagging and Resource Organization:

Effective tagging and resource organization practices provide better visibility and control over cloud resources. This allows for more accurate cost allocation and targeted optimization efforts. Key steps include:

- **Consistent Tagging:** Implement consistent tagging practices to label resources, enabling easier identification, grouping, and cost allocation across services, projects, or departments.

- **Resource Grouping:** Organize resources into logical groups or hierarchies based on functional or business-related criteria. This facilitates centralized monitoring and cost analysis.

6.3.7. Continuous Improvement and Cost-Aware Culture:

Adopting a continuous improvement mindset and fostering a cost-aware culture within the organization are vital for sustainable cost optimization. Key steps include:

- **Regular Review and Optimization:** Continuously review cost reports, performance metrics, and cloud architecture to identify optimization opportunities and implement cost-saving measures.

- **Employee Education:** Provide training and awareness programs to educate employees about cloud cost implications, resource management best practices, and the importance of cost optimization.

- **Collaboration and Knowledge Sharing:** Encourage collaboration among teams and facilitate knowledge sharing of cost optimization techniques and success stories.

- By incorporating these strategies into their cloud management practices, organizations can effectively optimize their cloud costs, improve overall efficiency, and maximize the benefits of cloud computing.

6.4 Understanding Reserved Instances and Spot Instances in Cloud Computing

Cloud service providers offer diverse pricing models to enable organizations to optimize costs and efficiently manage their workloads. Reserved Instances and Spot Instances are two pricing options that can provide significant cost savings for cloud infrastructure.

6.4.1. Reserved Instances (RIs):

Reserved Instances allow organizations to reserve cloud computing capacity for a specified period, typically ranging from one to three years. Here are key aspects of Reserved Instances:

- **Cost Savings:** One of the main benefits of RIs is the substantial cost savings they offer compared to on-demand pricing. By committing to a specific usage plan, organizations receive discounted rates based on the term and payment option chosen. This predictability in pricing can result in significant cost reductions for long-term workloads.

- **Instance Flexibility:** RIs provide flexibility within the selected instance family. Users can match instance attributes, such as instance type, operating system, and tenancy, to their workload requirements. This allows businesses to optimize resource allocation while benefiting from reduced costs.

- **Reservation Scopes:** RIs can be scoped to a specific availability zone or region, providing organizations with more control over resource allocation and availability. This enables fine-tuning of infrastructure planning based on workload distribution and redundancy needs.

- **Usage Commitment:** With RIs, organizations commit to using a specific instance type for a given term. While this ensures cost savings, it requires careful planning and assessment of long-term workload requirements. Organizations should analyze their usage patterns and select the most appropriate RIs to avoid underutilization or overprovisioning.

- **Convertibility and Marketplace:** Some cloud providers offer convertible RIs, allowing users to modify instance attributes during the reservation period. Additionally, there may be a marketplace where users can sell or exchange their unused RIs, providing more flexibility in managing reserved capacity.

6.4.2. Spot Instances:

Spot Instances provide access to spare compute capacity at significantly discounted prices. However, they are subject to availability and fluctuating market prices based on supply and demand. Consider the following aspects of Spot Instances:

- **Cost Efficiency:** Spot Instances offer the lowest pricing among cloud pricing options. Prices can vary greatly depending on demand, and users bid on available capacity. Spot Instances can deliver cost savings of up to 90% compared to on-demand pricing, making them highly attractive for certain workloads.

- **Flexible Workloads:** Spot Instances are ideal for workloads with flexible start and end times or those that can tolerate interruptions. They are well-suited for tasks like data analysis, batch processing, and fault-tolerant workloads, where occasional interruptions can be accommodated without disrupting the overall operation.

- **Instance Interruption:** Spot Instances can be interrupted by the cloud provider with a two-minute notification when demand exceeds the available capacity or if the user's bid price is lower than the current market price. Interruptions should be factored into workload design and application architecture to ensure they can handle such interruptions gracefully.

- **Spot Block:** Some cloud providers offer Spot Blocks, which allow users to specify a duration (1 to 6 hours) for uninterrupted Spot Instance usage. Spot Blocks provide predictability and stability at a slightly higher price than regular Spot Instances, making them suitable for longer-running tasks.

- **Instance Termination Policies:** To handle Spot Instance interruptions, organizations can utilize instance termination policies to automate tasks like checkpointing, saving state, or rescheduling workloads. This helps maintain data integrity and minimize any disruptions caused by Spot Instance terminations.

6.4.3. Leveraging Reserved Instances and Spot Instances:

Effectively utilizing Reserved Instances and Spot Instances requires careful consideration of the following factors:

- **Workload Analysis:** Assess workload characteristics, utilization patterns, and availability requirements. Reserved Instances are suitable for steady-state workloads with predictable usage, while Spot Instances are well-suited for flexible, fault-tolerant, or time-constrained workloads.

- **Cost Optimization:** Analyze the cost savings potential by comparing on-demand pricing with Reserved Instance pricing or bidding for Spot Instances. Consider factors such as utilization, workload duration, and cost fluctuations to determine the best pricing model for each workload.

- **Instance Planning:** Understand the resource requirements of your workloads to select the appropriate instance types, sizes, and configurations for Reserved Instances or Spot Instances. Ensuring the right resource fit optimizes performance and cost efficiency.

- **Resource Flexibility:** Evaluate the level of flexibility required for your workloads. Reserved Instances offer flexibility within the selected instance family, while Spot Instances require workload architectures that can tolerate interruptions and potential termination.

- **Automation and Monitoring:** Implement automation and monitoring practices to manage and optimize the usage of Reserved Instances and Spot Instances effectively. This includes scheduling, bidding strategies, instance termination policies, and resource allocation management.

- By strategically leveraging Reserved Instances and Spot Instances based on workload characteristics and cost considerations, organizations can achieve significant cost savings while maintaining the required level of performance and reliability in their cloud infrastructure. savings while maintaining the required level of performance and reliability in their cloud Infrastructure.

Exercise
Multiple Choice Questions

1. Which of the following are key cost components associated with cloud services?

a. Compute instances, storage, and data transfer

b. Compute instances, storage, data transfer, and databases

c. Compute instances, storage, data transfer, and network services

d. Compute instances, storage, data transfer, and additional services

2. What is the primary factor that influences the cost of compute instances in cloud computing?

a. Storage capacity

b. Instance type

c. Data transfer

d. Number of CPU cores

3. Which pricing model allows organizations to reserve cloud computing capacity for a specified period?

a. Spot Instances

b. Pay-as-you-go

c. On-demand Instances

d. Reserved Instances

4. Which cloud service is suitable for workloads with flexible start and end times, or those that can tolerate interruptions?

a. Reserved Instances

b. On-demand Instances

c. Spot Instances

d. Serverless Instances

5. What cost optimization strategy involves automatically adjusting resources based on demand fluctuations?

a. Scheduled Shutdowns

b. Reserved Instances

c. Auto-scaling

d. Instance Flexibility

6. Which cloud storage class is designed for long-term data archiving?

a. Standard

b. Infrequent Access

c. Archive

d. Glacier

7. What aspect of cloud services may involve charges for virtual networks and network traffic within or outside the cloud environment?

a. Support and Service Level Agreements (SLAs)

b. Database Services

c. Network and Load Balancing

d. Cost Optimization Tools

8. What cloud pricing model provides discounted rates in exchange for longer-term commitments?

a. Reserved Instances

b. Pay-as-you-go

c. Spot Instances

d. On-demand Instances

9. Which cost optimization practice involves labeling resources to gain insights into spending patterns based on departments, projects, or environments?

a. Cost monitoring

b. Reserved Instances

c. Resource tagging

d. Auto-scaling

10. What cloud-native computing model allows users to pay only for the actual execution time of functions?

a. Reserved Instances

b. Spot Instances

c. On-demand Instances

d. Serverless computing (e.g., AWS Lambda)

11. Spot Blocks in cloud computing allow users to specify a duration for uninterrupted usage of:

a. Reserved Instances

b. Spot Instances

c. Pay-as-you-go Instances

d. On-demand Instances

Review Questions

1. What are the key cost components associated with cloud services?

2. How does the cost of compute instances typically vary in cloud computing?

3. What factors contribute to cloud storage costs?

4. How are data transfer and bandwidth costs determined in cloud services?

5. What services may have their own cost structures in addition to compute and storage in the cloud?

6. What are some considerations when evaluating support and service level agreements (SLAs) from cloud providers?

7. What are some additional costs organizations might need to consider for data compliance and security in the cloud?

8. How can organizations optimize cloud costs using cost optimization tools and strategies?

9. What does cost monitoring and management in cloud computing refer to?

10. How can organizations optimize resource utilization to reduce unnecessary expenses in the cloud?

11. What are some benefits of using Reserved Instances in cloud computing?

12. When are Spot Instances most suitable for cloud workloads?

Answers Section

Multiple Choice Questions

1. c) Compute instances, storage, data transfer, and network services

2. b) Instance type

3. d) Reserved Instances

4. c) Spot Instances

5. c) Auto-scaling

6. c) Archive

7. c) Network and Load Balancing

8. a) Reserved Instances

9. c) Resource tagging

10. d) Serverless computing (e.g., AWS Lambda)

11. b) Spot Instances

Review Questions

1. The key cost components of cloud services include compute instances (VMs/containers), storage, data transfer, network services, databases, additional services, support, and security measures.

2. The cost of compute instances in cloud computing depends on factors such as instance type, CPU, memory, and storage capacity. Cloud providers offer various pricing models, including on-demand, reserved instances, and spot instances.

3. Cloud storage costs are influenced by factors such as storage capacity, data transfer (ingress/egress), storage class, and data management services like snapshots and backups.

4. Cloud providers charge for data transfer between regions, availability zones, and the internet. Ingress refers to data coming into the cloud, while egress refers to data leaving the cloud.

5. Additional services like analytics, machine learning, monitoring, security, and identity management may have their own cost structures based on usage, API requests, data processed, or resource management.

6. Considerations for support and SLAs include response times, technical support access, and the costs associated with different support tiers, especially if high availability and timely assistance are essential for your business.

7. Organizations might need to invest in additional security and compliance measures, such as encryption services, dedicated private network connections, or certifications to meet specific data protection and regulatory standards.

8. Organizations can optimize cloud costs by leveraging cost management dashboards, budget alerts, resource tagging, rightsizing recommendations, and reserved instance planning provided by cloud providers.

9. Cost monitoring and management in cloud computing involve practices and strategies implemented by organizations to control and optimize their cloud expenses effectively.

10. Organizations can optimize resource utilization by rightsizing instances, implementing auto-scaling, and scheduling shutdowns for non-production resources during periods of inactivity.

11. Reserved Instances offer substantial cost savings compared to on-demand pricing, instance flexibility, and the ability to scope reservations to specific availability zones or regions.

12. Spot Instances are best suited for workloads with flexible start and end times or those that can tolerate interruptions. They are ideal for tasks like data analysis, batch processing, and fault-tolerant workloads with occasional interruptions.

Chapter 7: Cloud Performance and Scalability

7.1 Scalability in the Cloud: Unlocking Growth Potential : Scalability in the cloud is a fundamental capability that empowers organizations to handle increasing workloads, achieve cost-efficiency, and deliver optimal performance. By understanding the benefits of scalability, adopting the right types of scalability (vertical and horizontal), and implementing best practices for scalable architectures, businesses can unlock their growth potential and leverage the full benefits of cloud computing. Scalability allows organizations to scale their resources dynamically, respond to changing demands, and ensure an exceptional user experience in the face of evolving business requirements.

7.1.1. Understanding Scalability in the Cloud:

Scalability refers to the ability of a system to handle increased workloads or accommodate growth without sacrificing performance or reliability. In the context of cloud computing, scalability is achieved through the dynamic allocation of resources based on demand. This means that as the workload increases, the cloud infrastructure automatically provisions additional resources to meet the increased demand, and when the demand decreases, excess resources are deprovisioned to avoid unnecessary costs.

7.2.2. Benefits of Scalability in the Cloud:

Scalability in the cloud offers several significant benefits:

- **Elastic Resource Provisioning:** Cloud platforms enable the provisioning of computing resources, such as virtual machines, storage, and network capacity, on-demand. This flexibility allows organizations to quickly scale their resources up or down based on changing requirements, providing agility and responsiveness to varying workloads.

- **Cost Efficiency:** With cloud scalability, businesses can avoid overprovisioning and pay only for the resources they actually use. This cost-effective approach eliminates the need for upfront investments in infrastructure and enables organizations to align their expenses with actual demand. Scaling down during periods of low activity ensures that resources are not wasted and costs are optimized.

- **Improved Performance:** Scalable architectures ensure that applications can handle increasing workloads without experiencing performance degradation. By dynamically adjusting resource allocation, organizations can maintain optimal performance levels even during peak usage periods. Users experience consistent performance, and response times remain steady regardless of varying loads.

- **Enhanced Availability and Resilience:** Scalable cloud architectures leverage distributed systems and redundancy to improve availability and fault tolerance. Scaling across multiple servers or regions ensures that applications remain operational even in the event of failures or high traffic. This high availability enhances the reliability of services and minimizes the risk of downtime.

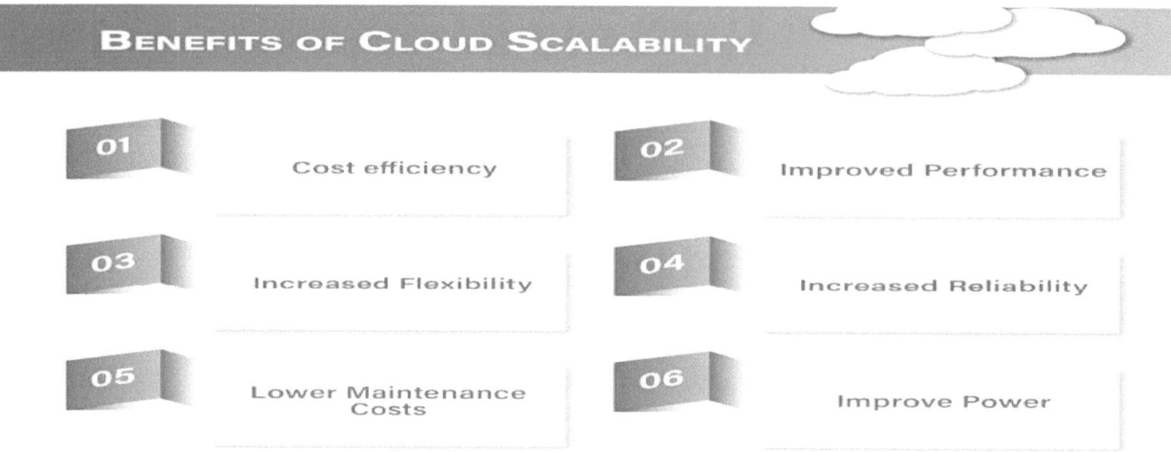

7.2.3. Types of Scalability in the Cloud:

Scalability can be categorized into two primary types:

- **Vertical Scalability (Scaling Up):** Vertical scalability involves increasing the capacity of individual resources within a system. It typically involves upgrading the size or power of a single server or virtual machine, such as adding more CPU cores or increasing memory. Vertical scalability is suitable for applications with a single point of contention or resource bottleneck. However, it may have limitations in terms of maximum capacity.

- **Horizontal Scalability (Scaling Out):** Horizontal scalability involves adding more resources to a system by distributing the workload across multiple servers or instances. It involves adding more virtual machines, containers, or servers to handle increased demand. Horizontal scalability is well-suited for distributed systems and applications that can be divided into smaller, independent components. It allows for virtually limitless expansion as more resources can be added as needed.

7.2.4. Best Practices for Achieving Scalable Architectures:

To effectively achieve scalability in the cloud, consider the following best practices:

- **Design for Failure:** Assume that failures can occur at any level of the system and design architectures that can tolerate and recover from failures automatically. This includes leveraging redundancy, fault-tolerant design patterns, and distributed systems. By designing for failure, organizations can ensure high availability and resiliency.

- **Decouple Components:** Decouple application components and services to allow for independent scaling. This approach enables organizations to scale specific components without affecting others and facilitates agility and flexibility in resource management. Microservices architecture is an excellent example of decoupling, where individual services can scale independently.

- **Leverage Auto-Scaling:** Utilize auto-scaling capabilities provided by cloud platforms to automatically adjust resources based on demand. Define scaling policies and triggers based on metrics such as CPU utilization, network traffic, or queue length. Auto-scaling ensures that resources are dynamically adjusted to meet changing requirements while minimizing manual intervention.

- **Use Managed Services:** Leverage managed services provided by cloud providers, such as load balancers, databases, and message queues. These services are designed for scalability and provide built-in auto-scaling and load distribution capabilities. By utilizing managed services, organizations can offload operational complexity and focus on core application development.

- **Embrace Microservices** Architecture: Adopt a microservices architecture that decomposes applications into smaller, loosely coupled services. This approach allows for independent scaling of individual services based on their specific resource requirements. Microservices enable organizations to scale only the components that experience increased demand, promoting efficient resource utilization.

- **Implement Caching and Content Delivery Networks (CDNs):** Utilize caching mechanisms and CDNs to reduce the load on backend resources. Caching frequently accessed data or static content at the edge locations can improve performance and reduce the load on the backend infrastructure, leading to better scalability.

- **Continuous Performance Monitoring:** Implement robust monitoring and performance measurement practices to gain insights into application performance and resource utilization. Use these insights to optimize resource allocation, detect bottlenecks, and identify areas for improvement. Continuous monitoring ensures that the system can adapt to changing conditions promptly.

- **Test and Validate:** Regularly test and validate the scalability of your architectures using performance testing and load testing. This helps identify potential limitations, bottlenecks, and areas requiring optimization before deployment. Testing also provides confidence that the system can handle expected workloads.

7.2 Performance Monitoring and Optimization in the Cloud

Performance monitoring and optimization are essential for delivering excellent user experiences, optimizing resource utilization, and driving business success in the cloud. By tracking key performance metrics, leveraging performance monitoring tools, conducting load testing, optimizing resource allocation, and implementing best practices, organizations can achieve optimal performance and scalability. Regular performance monitoring, analysis, and optimization enable businesses to proactively address issues, meet growing demands, and ensure their cloud-based applications and infrastructure operate at peak efficiency. A well-optimized and monitored cloud environment lays the foundation for high-performing applications, satisfied users, and a competitive edge in the market.

7.2.1. Importance of Performance Monitoring and Optimization in the Cloud:

Performance monitoring and optimization play a vital role in delivering a seamless user experience and optimizing resource utilization. Key reasons why it is important include:

- **User Satisfaction:** Monitoring performance allows organizations to identify and resolve issues that can impact user experience, ensuring high levels of customer satisfaction and retention. A positive user experience is crucial for customer loyalty and brand reputation.

- **Efficient Resource Utilization:** Optimizing performance helps minimize resource waste and ensures efficient utilization of cloud resources, resulting in cost savings and improved scalability. Properly allocated resources prevent overprovisioning and reduce unnecessary expenses.

- **Proactive Issue Detection:** Performance monitoring enables early detection of bottlenecks, failures, or performance degradation, allowing organizations to take proactive measures before they impact critical operations. Proactive monitoring minimizes downtime and ensures continuous service availability.

- **Capacity Planning:** By monitoring performance metrics, organizations can gain insights into resource utilization trends, enabling effective capacity planning and scalability to handle increased workloads. This enables businesses to be prepared for future growth and prevents performance bottlenecks.

7.2.2. Key Performance Metrics to Monitor:

Monitoring the right performance metrics helps identify areas for improvement and ensure optimal performance. Consider tracking the following metrics:

- **Response Time:** Measure the time taken for a system to respond to a request. Low response times contribute to a better user experience, as users receive faster results and interactions.

- **Throughput:** Measure the number of requests or transactions processed per unit of time. Monitoring throughput helps ensure the system can handle the expected load efficiently and avoids performance degradation under high demand.

- **Error Rates:** Track the percentage of errors encountered during application execution or data processing. High error rates may indicate issues requiring investigation and resolution, allowing for a more stable and reliable application.

- **Latency:** Monitor the time it takes for data to travel from the source to the destination. Low latency is crucial for real-time applications and improved user experience, as it reduces delays in data processing and transmission.

- **CPU and Memory Utilization:** Monitor CPU and memory utilization to identify potential bottlenecks and optimize resource allocation. Overloaded CPU or memory can lead to performance issues and affect application responsiveness.

- **Network Traffic:** Track network traffic patterns, including inbound and outbound data transfer rates, to identify any congestion or performance issues. Network bottlenecks can impact application performance and user experience.

- **Database Performance:** Monitor database performance metrics such as query response times, throughput, and resource utilization to ensure efficient data access and processing. Database performance is critical for applications that rely heavily on data processing.

- **Application-specific Metrics:** Depending on the nature of your application, monitor metrics specific to its functionality, such as transaction processing times, conversion rates, or user engagement metrics. Application-specific metrics provide valuable insights into the application's performance and user behavior.

7.2.3. Best Practices for Performance Optimization:

To optimize performance in the cloud, consider implementing the following best practices:

- **Establish Baselines:** Capture performance metrics under normal operating conditions to establish baselines. Baselines provide reference points for identifying anomalies and measuring performance improvements. They help organizations understand typical performance patterns and detect deviations.

- **Utilize Performance Monitoring Tools:** Leverage performance monitoring tools and services provided by cloud providers or third-party vendors. These tools offer real-time visibility into system performance, enabling efficient monitoring and diagnostics. Automated monitoring tools can alert teams to potential issues before they escalate.

- **Distributed Tracing and Logging:** Implement distributed tracing and logging mechanisms to track performance across distributed systems and identify bottlenecks or latency issues. Distributed tracing helps understand the flow of requests through various services and identify potential performance bottlenecks.

- **Load Testing and Performance Testing:** Conduct regular load and performance testing to simulate real-world scenarios and identify performance bottlenecks. This helps validate the system's performance under different levels of stress and workload, ensuring it can handle peak demand.

- **Horizontal Scaling:** Leverage horizontal scaling by adding more resources to distribute the workload. Autoscaling capabilities provided by cloud platforms enable automatic adjustment of resources based on demand, ensuring optimal performance during fluctuating workloads.

- **Caching and Content Delivery Networks (CDNs):** Implement caching mechanisms to reduce data retrieval and processing overhead. Utilize CDNs to deliver static content from edge locations, reducing latency and improving user experience. Caching and CDNs improve application responsiveness and reduce server load.

- **Optimize Database Performance:** Optimize database performance through techniques such as indexing, query optimization, and proper data modeling. Leverage managed database services offered by cloud providers to benefit from built-in optimizations and automated maintenance tasks.

- **Continuous Performance Monitoring and Analysis:** Implement continuous performance monitoring and analysis to detect anomalies, track trends, and identify areas for optimization. Use the insights gained to make informed decisions and iterate on performance improvements. Regular monitoring ensures that performance issues are promptly addressed.

- **Security Considerations:** Ensure that performance optimizations do not compromise security measures. Perform thorough security testing and implement appropriate measures to safeguard data and resources. Security should be a priority when making performance enhancements.

7.3 Load Balancing and Auto Scaling: Achieving Scalability and High Availability in the Cloud

Load balancing and auto scaling are fundamental techniques for achieving scalability, optimizing resource utilization, and ensuring high availability in cloud computing. By effectively implementing load balancing and auto scaling strategies, organizations can distribute workloads efficiently, maintain optimal performance, and respond to changing demands seamlessly. Best practices such as strategic traffic distribution, health checks, policy-based scaling, and continuous monitoring and adjustment contribute to a robust and scalable cloud infrastructure.

7.3.1. Load Balancing: Load balancing is a technique that distributes incoming network traffic across multiple servers or resources to optimize performance, enhance scalability, and improve fault tolerance. Key aspects of load balancing include:

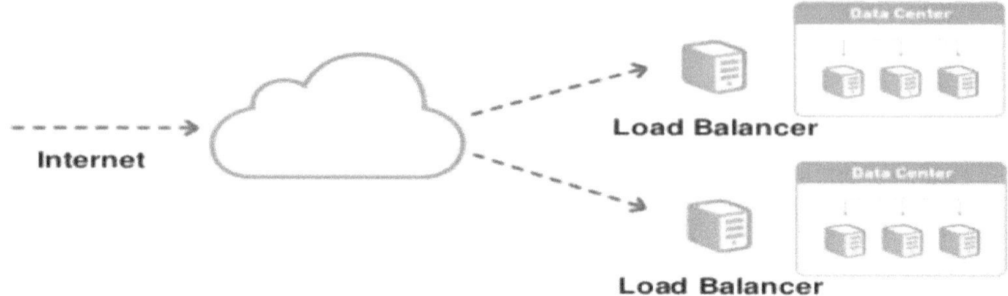

- **Scalability:** Load balancers enable horizontal scaling by distributing incoming traffic across multiple backend resources, ensuring efficient resource utilization and the ability to handle increased workloads. By dynamically allocating requests to available resources, load balancing allows organizations to scale their applications to meet growing demands without overburdening individual servers.

- **Performance Optimization:** By evenly distributing traffic, load balancers prevent overloading of individual resources, ensuring optimal performance and response times for users. This contributes to a seamless user experience and reduces the risk of bottlenecks that can lead to application slowdowns or failures.

- **High Availability:** Load balancing enhances availability by continuously monitoring backend resources and automatically routing traffic away from failed or unhealthy resources. In the event of a server failure, the load balancer redirects requests to healthy servers, minimizing downtime and improving reliability.

- **Session Persistence:** Load balancers can maintain session persistence by ensuring that subsequent requests from the same user are directed to the same backend resource, maintaining continuity for stateful applications. This ensures that user sessions are not disrupted during a load balancing event.

- **Health Checks:** Load balancers perform regular health checks to monitor the availability and responsiveness of backend resources. By automatically removing or redirecting traffic from unhealthy or failed resources, load balancers ensure that only healthy resources are handling incoming requests.

7.3.2. Auto Scaling:

Auto scaling is a mechanism that automatically adjusts the number of resources, such as virtual machines or containers, based on predefined policies or metrics. Auto scaling provides the following benefits:

- **Elasticity:** Auto scaling enables dynamic resource allocation, automatically scaling resources up or down based on demand. This elasticity ensures that organizations only pay for resources needed to handle current workloads, optimizing cost efficiency. During peak periods, additional resources are added to meet demand, and during off-peak times, unnecessary resources are removed, leading to cost savings.

- **Load Management:** Auto scaling monitors predefined metrics, such as CPU utilization or network traffic, and adds or removes resources as required to maintain optimal performance and prevent bottlenecks. This ensures that applications can efficiently handle varying workloads without manual intervention.

- **Fault Tolerance:** Auto scaling enhances fault tolerance by automatically replacing failed resources or instances, minimizing the impact of failures on application availability and user experience. When a resource becomes unhealthy or fails, the auto scaling group automatically replaces it, ensuring continuous service availability.

- **Event-Driven Scaling:** Auto scaling can be triggered by events such as increased traffic, scheduled times, or specific time-based patterns, ensuring resources scale in response to workload fluctuations. This dynamic scaling helps applications adapt to changing demands effectively.

- **Policy-Based Scaling:** Auto scaling policies define rules and thresholds based on metrics and conditions, enabling organizations to customize scaling behavior according to their specific needs and business requirements. Policies can be tailored to scale resources based on specific criteria, such as response time or queue length.

7.3.3. Best Practices for Load Balancing and Auto Scaling:

To effectively implement load balancing and auto scaling in the cloud, consider the following best practices:

- **Distribute Traffic Strategically:** Utilize load balancers to distribute traffic evenly across backend resources, considering factors such as resource capacity, response time, and geographical proximity. A well-balanced distribution ensures efficient utilization of resources and prevents overloading of specific servers.

- **Employ Health Checks:** Configure regular health checks to monitor the availability and performance of backend resources. By automatically removing or redirecting traffic from unhealthy resources, load balancers contribute to high availability and optimal performance.

- **Scaling Policies:** Define scaling policies based on relevant metrics and thresholds, ensuring resource allocation matches demand. Consider factors such as CPU utilization, network traffic, or queue length to trigger scaling actions. Define policies that are tailored to the specific workload patterns of your applications.

- **Monitor and Adjust:** Continuously monitor the performance, resource utilization, and scaling behavior of your applications and infrastructure. Regular monitoring provides valuable insights into application performance and scalability. Use the data obtained to fine-tune scaling policies and resource allocations for better efficiency.

- **Horizontal Scaling:** Leverage auto scaling to horizontally scale resources by adding or removing instances based on demand. Design applications and architectures that can seamlessly handle the addition or removal of resources without disruptions. Horizontal scaling is particularly effective for distributed systems.

- **Implement Scaling Limits:** Set upper and lower scaling limits to prevent excessive scaling and unexpected costs. Define sensible limits based on your application requirements, workload patterns, and resource availability. This ensures that auto scaling stays within the desired operational bounds.

- **Use Load Balancer Features:** Leverage advanced features provided by load balancers, such as SSL termination, content-based routing, or session persistence, to enhance security, routing flexibility, and user experience. These features enable load balancers to cater to diverse application needs.

- **Testing and Validation:** Regularly conduct load testing and performance testing to validate the effectiveness of load balancing and auto scaling configurations. Simulate real-world scenarios to identify bottlenecks, assess scalability, and fine-tune scaling policies. Testing helps ensure that your system can handle expected traffic spikes and workload changes.

- **Application Readiness:** Ensure that your applications are designed to be stateless or have mechanisms in place to handle session persistence across multiple backend resources. Consider factors like data consistency, caching, or session management during scaling events. State management is crucial to avoid data loss during auto scaling events.

Exercise
Multiple Choice Questions

1. What is the primary goal of scalability in cloud computing?

a. Minimizing resource utilization

b. Handling increased workloads without performance degradation

c. Reducing data storage costs

d. Achieving high network bandwidth

2. Which type of scalability involves increasing the capacity of individual resources within a system?

a. Horizontal scalability

b. Elastic scalability

c. Vertical scalability

d. Dynamic scalability

3. What benefit does load balancing provide in cloud computing?

a. Reducing security risks

b. Improving data encryption

c. Enhancing application responsiveness

d. Reducing cloud service costs

4. Which performance metric measures the number of requests or transactions processed per unit of time?

a. Response Time

b. Throughput

c. Latency

d. Error Rate

5. What does auto scaling help organizations achieve in the cloud?

a. Efficient resource waste

b. Static resource allocation

c. Dynamic resource allocation based on demand

d. Continuous monitoring of resources

6. What is the primary benefit of utilizing managed services in the cloud for load balancing?

a. Reduced data storage costs

b. Improved application performance

c. Enhanced fault tolerance

d. Offloading operational complexity

7. Which type of scalability is well-suited for distributed systems and applications that can be divided into smaller, independent components?

a. Vertical scalability

b. Dynamic scalability

c. Elastic scalability

d. Horizontal scalability (Scaling Out)

8. What is the purpose of conducting load testing in cloud environments?

a. To ensure data consistency

b. To validate security measures

c. To simulate real-world scenarios and identify bottlenecks

d. To monitor network traffic patterns

9. How does load balancing contribute to high availability in cloud applications?

a. It reduces the need for security measures

b. It distributes network traffic unevenly

c. It minimizes resource utilization

d. It automatically redirects traffic away from failed resources

Review Questions

1. What is the definition of scalability in the context of cloud computing, and how is it achieved?

2. What are the benefits of scalability in the cloud?

3. What are the two primary types of scalability in the cloud, and how do they differ?

4. What are the best practices for achieving scalable architectures in the cloud?

5. Why is performance monitoring and optimization crucial in the cloud?

6. What are the key performance metrics that organizations should track for optimal performance?

7. What are the benefits of load balancing in cloud computing?

8. How does auto scaling contribute to scalability and fault tolerance in the cloud?

9. What are the best practices for load balancing and auto scaling implementation in the cloud?

10. How does load balancing enhance high availability in cloud applications?

11. Why is event-driven scaling valuable in auto scaling implementations?

12. How can organizations ensure application readiness during auto scaling events?

Answer Section

Multiple Choice Questions

1. b) Handling increased workloads without performance degradation
2. c) Vertical scalability (Scaling Up)
3. c) Enhancing application responsiveness
4. b) Throughput
5. c) Dynamic resource allocation based on demand
6. d) Offloading operational complexity
7. d) Horizontal scalability (Scaling Out)
8. c) To simulate real-world scenarios and identify bottlenecks
9. d) It automatically redirects traffic away from failed resources

Review Questions

1. Scalability in cloud computing refers to a system's ability to handle increased workloads or growth without sacrificing performance or reliability. It is achieved through dynamic allocation of resources based on demand. As the workload increases, the cloud infrastructure automatically provisions additional resources, and when the demand decreases, excess resources are deprovisioned to avoid unnecessary costs.

2. Scalability in the cloud offers several significant benefits, including elastic resource provisioning, cost efficiency, improved performance, and enhanced availability and resilience. It allows businesses to quickly scale resources up or down based on changing requirements, optimize expenses, handle increasing workloads without performance degradation, and maintain service availability even in the face of failures or high traffic.

3. The two primary types of scalability in the cloud are vertical scalability (scaling up) and horizontal scalability (scaling out). Vertical scalability involves increasing the capacity of individual resources, like adding more CPU cores or memory to a single server. Horizontal scalability involves adding more resources to the system, distributing the workload across multiple servers or instances, such as adding more virtual machines or containers.

4. To achieve scalability in the cloud, consider designing for failure, decoupling components, leveraging auto-scaling, using managed services, embracing microservices architecture, implementing caching and CDNs, continuous performance monitoring, and regular testing and validation.

5. Performance monitoring and optimization are essential to deliver a seamless user experience, optimize resource utilization, and ensure business success. It helps identify and resolve issues impacting user satisfaction, avoid resource waste, detect bottlenecks proactively, and plan for future growth.

6. Key performance metrics to monitor include response time, throughput, error rates, latency, CPU and memory utilization, network traffic, database performance metrics, and application-specific metrics like transaction processing times or user engagement metrics.

7. Load balancing optimizes performance, enhances scalability, and improves fault tolerance by evenly distributing incoming network traffic across multiple backend resources. It enables organizations to handle increased workloads efficiently, achieve high availability, and prevent overloading of individual servers.

8. Auto scaling automatically adjusts the number of resources based on demand, ensuring elasticity and efficient resource allocation. It helps handle varying workloads, maintains optimal performance, and enhances fault tolerance by replacing failed resources or instances automatically.

9. Best practices include distributing traffic strategically, employing health checks, defining scaling policies based on relevant metrics, continuous monitoring and adjustment, horizontal scaling, setting scaling limits, and testing and validation of configurations.

10. Load balancing enhances high availability by continuously monitoring backend resources and automatically routing traffic away from failed or unhealthy resources. In case of a server failure, requests are redirected to healthy servers, minimizing downtime and improving reliability.

11. Event-driven scaling allows resources to scale in response to specific events, such as increased traffic or scheduled times. This dynamic scaling helps applications adapt effectively to changing demands and ensures resources match workload fluctuations.

12. To ensure application readiness during auto scaling events, organizations should design applications to be stateless or have mechanisms to handle session persistence across multiple backend resources. Factors like data consistency, caching, and session management are crucial to avoid data loss during scaling events.

Chapter 8: Cloud Services and Architectures

8.1 Exploring the Power of Serverless Computing

Serverless computing represents a revolutionary approach to developing, deploying, and scaling applications in the cloud. By capitalizing on its cost efficiency, automatic scaling, simplified operations, and rapid development cycles, organizations can empower their developers to concentrate on core business logic while leaving the complexities of infrastructure management to cloud providers. The versatility of serverless computing enables its application in diverse use cases, ranging from web applications to IoT processing and chatbots. Embracing serverless computing allows organizations to harness the power of event-driven architectures, enhance agility, and unlock new possibilities for innovation and growth in the cloud computing landscape.

8.1.1. Understanding Serverless Computing:

Serverless computing, also known as Function as a Service (FaaS), completely abstracts away the complexity of server infrastructure management. This allows developers to focus solely on writing and deploying code. In a serverless architecture, developers create individual functions that are designed to respond to specific events, while the cloud provider takes charge of provisioning and scaling the necessary resources to execute those functions.

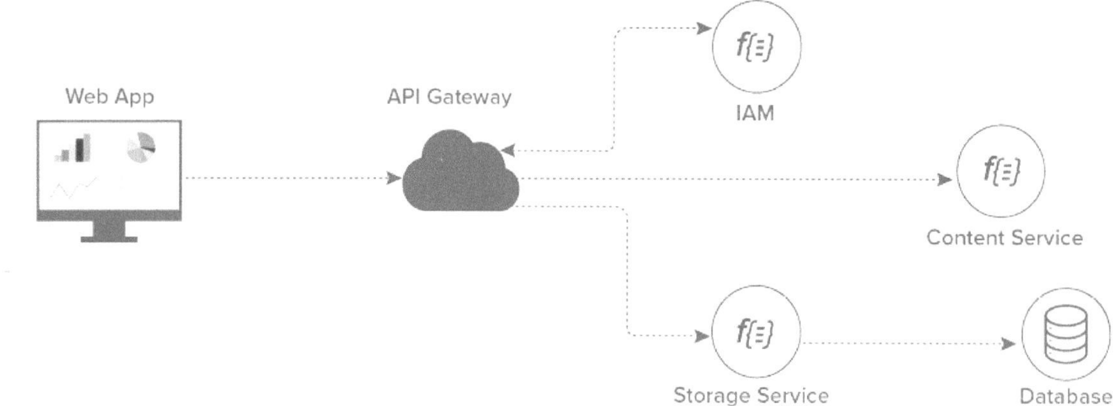

8.1.2. Benefits of Serverless Computing:

The adoption of serverless computing provides several significant benefits to organizations:

- **Cost Efficiency:** Serverless computing operates on a pay-per-invocation model, where organizations are billed solely for the actual execution time of functions. This eliminates the need to pay for idle resources, resulting in cost savings and a more cost-efficient usage of cloud resources.

- **Scalability and Elasticity:** Serverless architectures automatically adjust resources based on the incoming workload, ensuring optimal performance even during peak demand without requiring manual intervention. This elastic scaling capability allows applications to handle varying levels of traffic effectively.

- **Simplified Operations:** Serverless computing alleviates organizations from managing servers, operating systems, and runtime environments. This allows developers to concentrate exclusively on writing business logic, thus simplifying the development process and reducing operational overhead.

- **Rapid Development and Deployment:** Serverless architectures enable faster development cycles as developers can concentrate solely on writing code without the burden of infrastructure setup. Deployment is streamlined, and updates can be rolled out quickly, fostering agility and continuous innovation.

- **Event-Driven Architecture:** Serverless computing is ideally suited for event-driven applications, enabling functions to be triggered by specific events such as API calls, database changes, or message queue notifications. This enables developers to build highly responsive and dynamic applications.

8.1.3. Key Components of Serverless Computing:

Serverless computing comprises several essential components, each playing a crucial role in its operation:

- **Functions:** Functions are the core building blocks of serverless architectures. They represent individual pieces of code that perform specific tasks or respond to events. These functions can be written in various programming languages and are executed on-demand in response to specific triggers.

- **Event Triggers:** Serverless functions are triggered by events, such as HTTP requests, database changes, or timer-based events. These triggers initiate the execution of functions, allowing them to respond to specific events as defined by the developers.

- **Execution Environment:** Cloud providers manage the execution environment required to run serverless functions. This includes the underlying infrastructure, runtime environment, and resource provisioning, which are all handled transparently to the developers.

- **Cloud Services Integration:** Serverless functions can seamlessly interact with various cloud services, such as storage, databases, messaging queues, or authentication services. This integration enables developers to leverage existing cloud capabilities and build complex applications more efficiently.

8.1.4. Use Cases for Serverless Computing:

The versatility of serverless computing allows it to be effectively applied to a wide range of use cases, including:

- **Web Applications:** Serverless architectures are well-suited for building lightweight web applications, APIs, or microservices that require auto-scaling capabilities and cost efficiency, particularly for applications with unpredictable or fluctuating traffic patterns.

- **Real-time Data Processing:** Serverless functions can process and analyze real-time data streams, making them ideal for applications such as real-time analytics, data transformation, or event-driven processing.

- **IoT Applications:** Serverless computing is a natural fit for IoT applications that require processing and analyzing data from a large number of connected devices, triggering events based on sensor data, or sending notifications to users or devices.

- **Backend Processes:** Serverless functions excel at handling backend processes, such as data validation, file processing, image resizing, or email notifications, providing an efficient and cost-effective way to manage various routine tasks.

- **Chatbots and Voice Assistants:** Serverless computing powers chatbots and voice assistants by executing functions to process natural language queries, retrieve information from databases or APIs, and trigger appropriate responses, ensuring a seamless user experience.

- **DevOps Automation:** Serverless functions are well-suited for automating various DevOps tasks, such as continuous integration/continuous deployment (CI/CD) pipelines, infrastructure provisioning, or log aggregation, streamlining the software development and deployment process.

8.2 Embracing the Benefits of Microservices Architecture

Microservices architecture offers organizations a flexible, scalable, and modular approach to building applications. By embracing the principles of single responsibility, loose coupling, independent development and deployment, and decentralized data management, organizations can achieve benefits such as scalability, agility, fault isolation, and continuous deployment. However, adopting microservices architecture requires careful consideration of organizational alignment, service boundaries, communication mechanisms, data management strategies, and monitoring practices. With the right planning and implementation, organizations can leverage the power of microservices to drive innovation, enhance scalability, and meet the evolving needs of modern software applications.

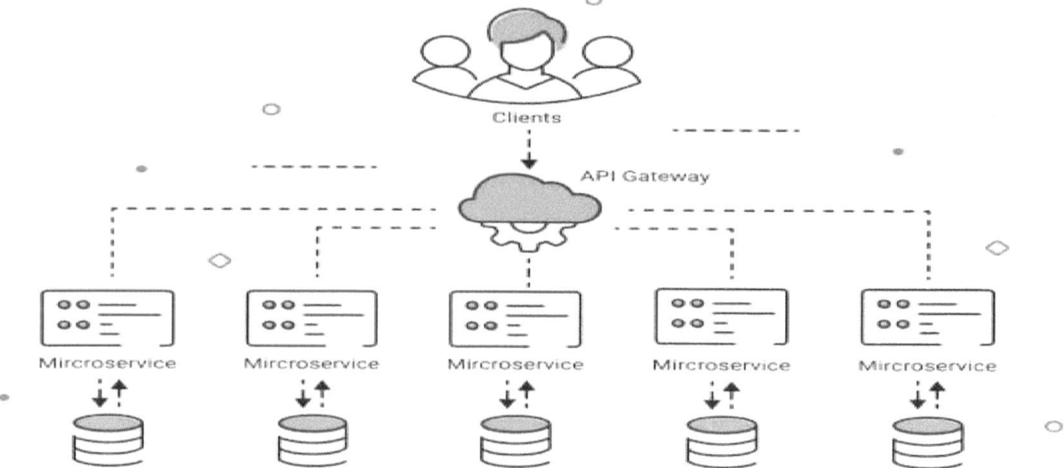

8.2.1. Understanding Microservices Architecture:

Microservices architecture is an architectural style that organizes an application as a collection of small, self-contained services, each responsible for handling a specific business capability. These services communicate with each other through well-defined APIs, facilitating flexibility, scalability, and independent development and deployment.

8.2.2. Benefits of Microservices Architecture:

Microservices architecture offers numerous advantages for organizations:

- **Scalability and Flexibility:** Microservices allow individual services to be independently scaled based on their resource requirements. This empowers applications to handle varying workloads and adapt seamlessly to changing demands.

- **Modularity and Agility:** Services within a microservices architecture are decoupled, enabling development teams to work on, test, and deploy services independently. This modularity enhances agility, accelerates development cycles, and enables faster time-to-market.

- **Fault Isolation and Resilience:** Isolating services in a microservices architecture helps contain failures and prevents cascading effects. When a service fails, other services can continue to function, ensuring overall system resilience.

- **Technology Diversity:** Microservices architecture allows organizations to use different technologies and programming languages for each service. This flexibility enables the selection of the most suitable tools and technologies for specific business requirements.

- **Continuous Deployment:** Independent services in a microservices architecture can be deployed and updated individually, allowing for continuous deployment without disrupting the entire system.

- **Scalable Development Teams:** Microservices architecture encourages small, cross-functional teams responsible for individual services. This allows for better ownership, autonomy, and faster decision-making within development teams.

8.2.3. Key Principles of Microservices Architecture:

Microservices architecture is guided by several key principles:

- **Single Responsibility:** Each microservice should have a single responsibility or business capability, allowing it to evolve independently without impacting other services. This ensures that services remain focused and manageable.

- **Independent Development and Deployment:** Services should be developed, tested, and deployed independently, enabling faster iteration and reducing dependencies, which promotes faster development cycles.

- **Loose Coupling:** Services should communicate through well-defined APIs and should not have strong dependencies on each other, promoting modularity and flexibility. This reduces the risk of system-wide failures due to changes in individual services.

- **Decentralized Data Management:** Each microservice should have its own data store, optimized for its specific needs. This promotes autonomy and reduces the impact of changes in data models across the system.

- **Infrastructure Automation:** Automation tools and techniques should be utilized for provisioning, deployment, and monitoring of microservices, ensuring consistency, scalability, and rapid response to changes.

- **Resilience and Fault Tolerance:** Services should be designed with resilience in mind, incorporating mechanisms for fault tolerance, circuit breaking, and graceful degradation. This ensures the overall system remains stable under adverse conditions.

8.2.4. Considerations for Adopting Microservices Architecture:

When adopting microservices architecture, organizations should consider the following:

- **Organizational Alignment:** Microservices architecture requires a significant shift in organizational culture and structure to enable small, autonomous teams and promote ownership of services. Collaboration and communication across teams become essential.

- **Service Boundaries:** Clearly defining service boundaries based on business capabilities is crucial. Factors such as communication patterns, data consistency, and transactional requirements must be taken into account to avoid potential issues with service interactions.

- **Service Discovery and Communication:** Establishing efficient mechanisms for service discovery and communication is vital. Implementing tools like service registries, API gateways, or messaging systems ensures seamless interaction between services.

- **Data Management:** Planning strategies for data consistency, synchronization, and data governance across multiple microservices is essential. Eventual consistency patterns and event-driven architectures can help manage data effectively.

- **Monitoring and Observability:** Implementing comprehensive monitoring and observability practices is critical to gain insights into the health, performance, and interactions of microservices. This helps identify and resolve issues promptly.

- **Testing and Deployment Strategies:** Defining testing strategies that focus on individual services, as well as integration and end-to-end testing, is vital to ensure the reliability and functionality of the entire system. Implementing deployment pipelines and strategies for independent deployment and continuous integration of services helps maintain a smooth development process.

8.3 Unleashing the Power of Containers and Container Orchestration with Kubernetes

Containers and container orchestration with Kubernetes have revolutionized the way organizations build, deploy, and manage applications. By harnessing the benefits of containers' portability, efficiency, and isolation, and leveraging the power of Kubernetes' scalability, high availability, and automation, organizations can achieve efficient application deployments, resource optimization, and enhanced resilience. Kubernetes, as the industry-leading container orchestration platform, provides a robust and extensible solution, empowering organizations to embrace cloud-native architectures, enhance DevOps practices, and unlock the full potential of containerized applications. The seamless integration of containers and Kubernetes ushers in a new era of efficient, scalable, and agile software development and deployment practices.

8.3.1. Containers:

Containers have emerged as a game-changer in software development and deployment, offering several key attributes:

- **Portability:** Containers encapsulate applications and their dependencies in a consistent environment, enabling seamless deployment across diverse computing environments. This reduces compatibility issues and facilitates easy migration between cloud platforms and on-premises infrastructure.

- **Efficiency:** One of the major advantages of containers is their efficient resource utilization. They share the host operating system kernel and run in isolated environments, avoiding the overhead associated with running multiple virtual machines.

- **Isolation:** Each container operates within its isolated environment, ensuring that applications and their dependencies do not interfere with one another. This enhances security, stability, and the reliability of the entire system.

- **Fast Deployment:** Containers can be rapidly provisioned and deployed, which expedites application delivery and allows organizations to adopt efficient DevOps practices.

8.3.2. Container Orchestration:

Container orchestration takes container technology to the next level, automating the management, deployment, scaling, and networking of containers in distributed environments. Key aspects of container orchestration include:

- **Automated Deployment:** Orchestration tools automate the deployment of containers across multiple hosts or nodes, streamlining the process and ensuring consistent application deployments with minimal manual intervention.

- **Scaling and Load Balancing:** Orchestration platforms facilitate automatic scaling of containerized applications based on demand, distributing the workload across multiple containers and load balancing incoming traffic. This allows applications to handle varying workloads with ease.

- **Service Discovery and Networking:** Container orchestration tools provide mechanisms for service discovery, enabling containers to discover and communicate with one another effortlessly. Networking features ensure secure and efficient communication between containers.

- **High Availability and Resilience:** Orchestration platforms are designed to ensure application availability by automatically restarting failed containers, rescheduling containers on healthy nodes, and managing application health checks.

- Configuration and Secrets Management: Orchestration tools offer capabilities to manage configuration parameters and secrets securely, ensuring sensitive information is stored and distributed safely to containers.

8.3.3. Kubernetes:

Kubernetes, often referred to as K8s, has become the industry standard for container orchestration due to its rich feature set, scalability, and extensibility. Key features of Kubernetes include:

- Pod and Deployment Management: Kubernetes manages containers in units called pods, representing one or more containers running together. Deployments define the desired state of pods and handle their creation, scaling, and rolling updates to ensure smooth deployments.

- Scalability and Load Balancing: Kubernetes allows automatic scaling of pods based on resource usage or custom metrics. Load balancing features distribute incoming traffic across multiple pods, optimizing resource utilization and ensuring high availability.

- Service Discovery and Networking: Kubernetes provides a built-in service discovery mechanism, enabling containers to communicate with each other using stable DNS names. Networking features, such as the Kubernetes Service abstraction, ensure secure and reliable networking between services.

- Self-Healing and Rolling Updates: Kubernetes continuously monitors the health of pods and automatically restarts or reschedules failed containers. Rolling updates enable the seamless deployment of new application versions without causing downtime.

- Configuration Management: Kubernetes offers features for managing configuration parameters and secrets through ConfigMaps and Secrets, ensuring secure storage and distribution of application-specific settings.

- Extensibility and Ecosystem: Kubernetes boasts an extensible architecture, allowing seamless integration of various extensions and plugins. This extensibility enables customization and integration with other tools and platforms.

4. Benefits of Containers and Kubernetes:

The combination of containers and Kubernetes offers a plethora of benefits for organizations:

- Scalability and Flexibility: Leveraging containers and Kubernetes empowers organizations to scale applications efficiently, handle variable workloads, and adapt seamlessly to changing demands, ensuring optimal resource utilization.

- High Availability and Resilience: Kubernetes' built-in features for automatic container restarts, node failover, and load balancing ensure high availability and fault tolerance for applications, minimizing downtime and maximizing application reliability.

- DevOps Enablement: Containers and Kubernetes promote DevOps practices by fostering efficient collaboration, continuous integration/continuous deployment (CI/CD), and rapid application delivery.

- Resource Efficiency: Containers and Kubernetes optimize resource usage by providing a lightweight and isolated runtime environment, reducing infrastructure costs and improving overall efficiency.

- Portability and Vendor-Neutrality: Containers and Kubernetes offer portability across various cloud providers and on-premises environments, avoiding vendor lock-in and providing flexibility in deployment choices.

- Ecosystem and Community Support: Kubernetes boasts a large and active community, contributing to a rich ecosystem of tools, libraries, and extensions. This ensures ongoing development, support, and innovation in the container orchestration domain.

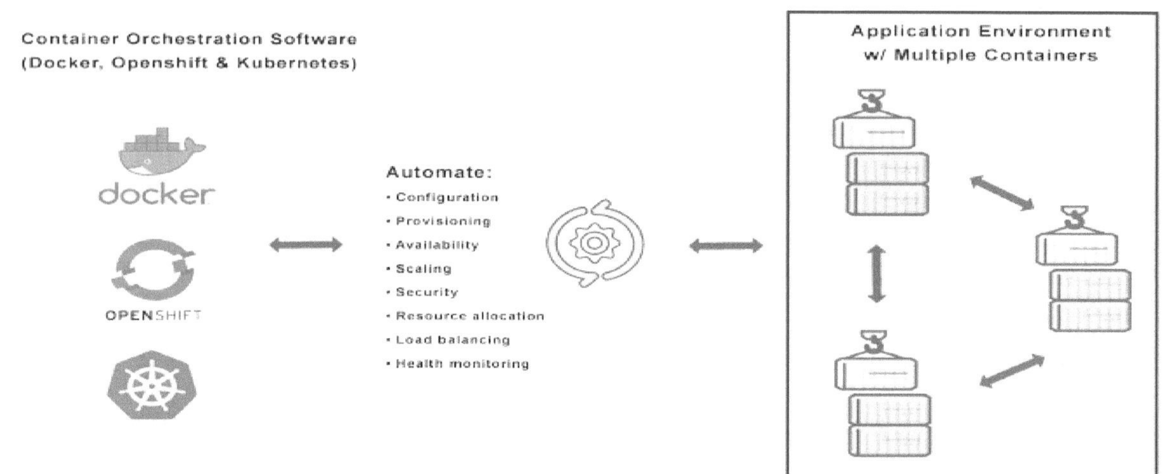

8.4 Harnessing the Power of Big Data and Analytics in the Cloud

The integration of Big Data and analytics in the cloud empowers organizations to leverage vast amounts of data for gaining valuable insights and making informed business decisions. The cloud's scalability, cost efficiency, and advanced analytics capabilities provide a robust foundation for processing, analyzing, and deriving meaningful insights from Big Data. By following best practices in data governance, integration, scalability, and performance optimization, organizations can unlock the true potential of their data, drive innovation, and gain a competitive edge in the digital era. The seamless integration of Big Data and analytics in the cloud paves the way for efficient, scalable, and agile data-driven strategies, propelling organizations towards success and growth in the dynamic and data-rich business landscape.

8.4.1. Big Data in the Cloud:

Big Data refers to the collection, storage, and processing of massive and intricate data sets that surpass the capabilities of traditional data processing systems. Cloud computing offers an optimal environment for Big Data processing and analysis due to several key factors:

- Scalability: Cloud platforms provide the flexibility to scale resources up or down according to the requirements of data processing and analysis. This scalability ensures efficient utilization of computing resources and facilitates accommodating growing data volumes.

- Cost Efficiency: Cloud-based Big Data solutions present a cost-effective approach by eliminating the need for substantial upfront investments in infrastructure. Organizations can pay for the resources they use, reducing capital expenditures, and optimizing overall costs.

- Agility and Flexibility: Cloud platforms empower organizations to quickly provision computing resources and experiment, iterate, and adapt their Big Data solutions rapidly. This agility translates into faster time-to-insights and better business decision-making.

- Advanced Analytics Capabilities: Cloud-based Big Data tools often come with built-in analytics capabilities, such as machine learning, artificial intelligence, and real-time analytics. These advanced features enable organizations to uncover hidden patterns, derive meaningful insights, and drive innovation.

- Data Integration and Accessibility: The cloud provides a centralized platform for integrating data from various sources and making it easily accessible for analysis. This enables comprehensive data exploration and enhances the effectiveness of analytics initiatives.

8.4.2. Benefits of Big Data and Analytics in the Cloud:

Integrating Big Data and analytics in the cloud offers several benefits for organizations:

- Scalability and Flexibility: The cloud's scalability allows organizations to handle varying workloads efficiently and adapt to changing data processing demands. This flexibility ensures that resources are used optimally and dynamically adjusted as needed.

- Cost Efficiency: By adopting cloud-based solutions, organizations avoid the need for large upfront investments in hardware and infrastructure. They can optimize costs by paying only for the computing resources they consume.

- Agility and Rapid Iteration: Cloud platforms enable organizations to provision resources quickly, experiment with different analytical models, and iterate on their data-driven strategies, leading to faster insights and improved decision-making.

- Advanced Analytics Capabilities: Cloud-based Big Data tools often come with built-in advanced analytics capabilities, such as machine learning and AI, allowing organizations to gain deeper insights and uncover valuable patterns in their data.

- Data Integration and Centralization: The cloud's centralized nature facilitates the integration of data from multiple sources, enabling comprehensive data analysis and fostering a more holistic understanding of business operations.

8.43. Popular Cloud-based Big Data Tools:

Several cloud providers offer specialized services and tools for Big Data processing and analytics. Here are some popular ones:

- Amazon Web Services (AWS): AWS offers services like Amazon EMR (Elastic MapReduce) for distributed processing of large datasets using Apache Hadoop and Spark, Amazon Redshift for data warehousing, and Amazon Athena for interactive query analysis on data stored in Amazon S3.

- Google Cloud Platform (GCP): GCP provides services like Google BigQuery for fast and scalable analytics, Google Cloud Dataproc for managed Hadoop and Spark clusters, and Google Cloud Pub/Sub for real-time messaging and data ingestion.

- Microsoft Azure: Azure offers services like Azure HDInsight for Hadoop and Spark analytics, Azure Data Lake Storage for scalable data storage, and Azure Databricks for collaborative and advanced analytics.

- **IBM Cloud:** IBM Cloud provides services like IBM Watson Studio for data exploration and machine learning, IBM Db2 Warehouse on Cloud for data warehousing, and IBM Cloud Object Storage for scalable data storage and retrieval.

8.4.4. Best Practices for Big Data and Analytics in the Cloud:
To ensure successful implementation of Big Data and analytics in the cloud, consider the following best practices:

- **Data Governance and Security:** Implement robust data governance practices to ensure data integrity, compliance, and privacy. Apply appropriate security measures, such as encryption and access controls, to protect sensitive data from unauthorized access.

- **Data Integration and Preparation:** Develop efficient data integration pipelines to consolidate data from various sources. Cleanse, transform, and prepare the data for analysis to ensure data quality and reliability.

- **Scalable Data Storage:** Utilize scalable and cost-effective storage solutions, such as cloud object storage or distributed file systems, to accommodate large volumes of data. Leverage data partitioning and indexing techniques for efficient data retrieval.

- **Distributed Processing and Parallelism:** Leverage distributed processing frameworks, such as Apache Hadoop or Apache Spark, to parallelize data processing tasks across a cluster of machines. Design jobs that can be executed in parallel to optimize performance.

- **Monitoring and Performance Optimization:** Implement comprehensive monitoring and logging practices to gain visibility into data processing workflows. Continuously optimize query performance, resource utilization, and data pipeline efficiency to ensure smooth operations.

- **Experimentation and Iteration:** Take advantage of the cloud's agility to experiment with different analytics approaches, models, or algorithms. Iteratively refine your analytics initiatives based on insights gained from experimentation.

- **Skillset and Training:** Invest in training and upskilling your team in cloud-based Big Data tools and analytics techniques. Develop expertise in areas like data engineering, data science, and machine learning to maximize the value of your Big Data initiatives.

Exercise
Multiple Choice Questions

1. What is serverless computing also known as?

a. Infrastructure as a Service (IaaS)

b. Platform as a Service (PaaS)

c. Function as a Service (FaaS)

d. Software as a Service (SaaS)

2. What is the billing model used in serverless computing?

a. Pay-as-you-go

b. Flat-rate monthly

c. Pay-per-hour

d. Pay-per-resource

3. What advantage does serverless computing offer for web applications with fluctuating traffic patterns?

a. Improved security

b. Faster response times

c. Automatic scaling and cost efficiency

d. Easier infrastructure management

4. In serverless computing, what initiates the execution of functions?

a. API calls

b. User login events

c. Manual deployment

d. Server provisioning

5. Which component of serverless computing handles the underlying infrastructure and runtime environment?

a. Functions

b. Event Triggers

c. Execution Environment

d. Cloud Services Integration

6. What type of applications is serverless computing ideally suited for?

a. Games and graphics-intensive applications

b. Machine learning algorithms

c. Event-driven applications with varying workloads

d. Complex database management systems

7. Which principle of microservices architecture ensures each microservice has a specific business capability?

a. Scalable Development Teams

b. Loose Coupling

c. Single Responsibility

d. Independent Development and Deployment

8. What benefit does microservices architecture offer in terms of fault isolation?

a. Automatic scaling

b. Resilience and fault tolerance

c. Continuous deployment

d. Isolating service failures

9. What is a key advantage of using containers in software development and deployment?

a. Cost efficiency through reduced resource sharing

b. Automatic scaling based on traffic patterns

c. Faster deployment and application delivery

d. Tight integration with physical hardware

10. Which container orchestration platform has become the industry standard for its scalability and extensibility?

a. Docker Swarm

b. Apache Mesos

c. Kubernetes

d. Amazon ECS

11. How do containers achieve isolation between applications and their dependencies?

a. By running each container in a virtual machineb. By using separate hardware for each container

b. By sharing the host operating system kernel

c. By using a specialized isolation layer

Review Questions

1. How does serverless computing abstract away the complexity of managing server infrastructure?

2. What are the benefits of adopting serverless computing, and how does it lead to cost efficiency?

3. Explain the concept of event-driven architecture in serverless computing and its significance for application development.

4. What are the key components of serverless computing, and how do they work together to execute functions?

5. Provide examples of use cases where serverless computing can be effectively applied in various applications.

6. How does serverless computing promote rapid development and deployment, and what advantages does it offer to developers?

7. What are the main principles that guide microservices architecture, and how do they contribute to scalability and agility?

8. How can microservices architecture enhance fault isolation and resilience in complex systems?

9. Describe the advantages of technology diversity in microservices architecture and how it enables organizations to choose suitable tools for specific business requirements.

Answer Section
Multiple Choice Questions

1. c) Function as a Service (FaaS)

2. a) Pay-as-you-go

3. c) Automatic scaling and cost efficiency

4. a) API calls

5. c) Execution Environment

6. c) Event-driven applications with varying workloads

7. c) Single Responsibility

8. d) Isolating service failures

9. c) Faster deployment and application delivery

10. c) Kubernetes

11. c) By sharing the host operating system kernel

Review Questions

1. Serverless computing abstracts away the complexity of managing server infrastructure by providing a higher-level abstraction for developers. In this architecture, developers create individual functions that respond to specific events. These functions are designed to execute specific tasks and handle particular events. When an event occurs, the cloud provider automatically provisions the necessary resources, executes the function, and scales resources as needed. This approach eliminates the need for developers to manage servers, operating systems, and runtime environments, allowing them to focus solely on writing and deploying code. As a result, developers can concentrate on business logic and application development, reducing operational overhead and speeding up the development process.

2. The adoption of serverless computing offers several benefits to organizations, leading to cost efficiency. One key advantage is the pay-per-invocation model, where organizations are billed solely for the actual execution time of functions. This eliminates the need to pay for idle resources, resulting in cost savings and more efficient usage of cloud resources. Serverless architectures also provide automatic scalability and elasticity. Resources are adjusted based on the incoming workload, ensuring optimal performance even during peak demand without manual intervention. This elastic scaling capability enables applications to handle varying levels of traffic effectively, eliminating the need to over-provision resources and saving costs.

3. Event-driven architecture is a fundamental aspect of serverless computing. It allows functions to be triggered by specific events, such as API calls, database changes, or message queue notifications. By leveraging event-driven design, developers can build highly responsive and dynamic applications. For example, an e-commerce application can trigger a function to process a purchase when a user makes an order through an API call. This event-driven approach allows organizations to create modular, loosely-coupled systems that respond instantly to user actions or other external events. By effectively responding to events, organizations can build more efficient and real-time applications.

4. The key components of serverless computing are functions, event triggers, execution environment, and cloud services integration. Functions represent individual pieces of code that perform specific tasks or respond to events. They can be written in various programming languages and are executed on-demand in response to specific triggers. Event triggers initiate the execution of functions, enabling them to respond to specific events as defined by developers. The cloud provider manages the execution environment, which includes underlying infrastructure, runtime environment, and resource provisioning transparently to developers. Lastly, serverless functions can seamlessly interact with various cloud services like storage, databases, messaging queues, or authentication services, allowing developers to leverage existing capabilities and build complex applications more efficiently.

5. Serverless computing is highly versatile, making it applicable to various use cases. It is well-suited for building lightweight web applications, APIs, or microservices that require auto-scaling capabilities and

cost efficiency, especially for applications with unpredictable or fluctuating traffic patterns. Additionally, serverless functions can process and analyze real-time data streams, making them ideal for applications like real-time analytics, data transformation, or event-driven processing. IoT applications that require processing and analyzing data from a large number of connected devices, triggering events based on sensor data, or sending notifications to users or devices can benefit from serverless computing. It also excels at handling backend processes such as data validation, file processing, image resizing, or email notifications, providing an efficient and cost-effective way to manage routine tasks. Furthermore, serverless computing powers chatbots and voice assistants by executing functions to process natural language queries, retrieve information from databases or APIs, and trigger appropriate responses, ensuring a seamless user experience. Finally, it can be effectively used for DevOps automation, automating tasks like continuous integration/continuous deployment (CI/CD) pipelines, infrastructure provisioning, or log aggregation, streamlining the software development and deployment process.

6. Serverless architectures enable faster development cycles by allowing developers to concentrate solely on writing code without the burden of infrastructure setup. With serverless computing, developers can rapidly deploy new functions or updates, fostering agility and continuous innovation. The serverless model abstracts away server management, which simplifies the development process, reduces operational overhead, and allows developers to focus on core business logic. By not worrying about server provisioning, monitoring, and maintenance, developers can allocate more time and resources to building and improving application features, resulting in faster time-to-market. The pay-per-invocation model ensures that costs are directly related to actual usage, providing cost predictability and facilitating efficient resource allocation. This encourages developers to experiment and iterate more freely, further enhancing the development process.

7. Microservices architecture is guided by several key principles that contribute to scalability and agility. The first principle is single responsibility, which means each microservice should have a single responsibility or business capability. This ensures that services remain focused, manageable, and easily replaceable without affecting other services. Independent development and deployment is another crucial principle, where microservices are developed, tested, and deployed independently. This allows faster iteration, reduces dependencies, and enables individual teams to work autonomously, fostering agility. Loose coupling is another essential principle that promotes modularity and flexibility. Microservices communicate through well-defined APIs and avoid strong dependencies on each other, reducing the risk of system-wide failures due to changes in individual services. Lastly, decentralized data management dictates that each microservice should have its own data store optimized for its specific needs. This promotes autonomy and minimizes the impact of changes in data models across the system, ensuring scalability and resilience.

8. Microservices architecture enhances fault isolation and resilience by isolating services from each other. When a microservice fails, it doesn't affect other services, reducing the chances of cascading failures in the system. This isolation helps contain failures within a specific service, preventing them from spreading to the entire application and ensuring overall system resilience. Microservices are independently deployable, so if a service requires updates or bug fixes, it can be deployed without disrupting the entire system. This enables organizations to maintain a high level of service availability and uptime even during updates and deployments. Additionally, by separating responsibilities into smaller, focused services,

organizations can better manage and monitor individual components. This enables them to identify issues more quickly, isolate problematic services, and apply targeted fixes, improving overall system reliability.

9. Technology diversity in microservices architecture allows organizations to use different technologies and programming languages for each service. This flexibility empowers teams to choose the most suitable tools and technologies for specific business requirements, rather than being limited to a single technology stack. For instance, a microservice responsible for real-time data processing may be written in Python, while a service handling complex calculations may use Java. This diversity enables teams to leverage their expertise and use the best tools for the job, resulting in more efficient and effective development. Furthermore, technology diversity fosters innovation within development teams, as they can explore new languages, frameworks, and libraries that align with their service's specific needs. By encouraging innovation and flexibility, microservices architecture supports a dynamic and forward-thinking development environment, enhancing the organization's ability to adapt to changing business demands and technology trends.

Chapter 9: Cloud Backup and Disaster Recovery

9.1 Backup Strategies in the Cloud: Ensuring Data Resilience and Business Continuity

Implementing effective backup strategies in the cloud is crucial for protecting data, ensuring business continuity, and mitigating the risks associated with data loss. By carefully considering key factors such as data classification, RPO/RTO requirements, encryption, redundancy, and compliance, organizations can develop comprehensive backup plans. Adhering to best practices such as automated backups, multiple storage locations, incremental backups, regular monitoring, and documented procedures ensures data integrity, minimizes downtime, and facilitates swift data recovery. With a well-executed backup strategy in the cloud, organizations can confidently navigate data protection challenges, safeguard their critical information assets, and maintain uninterrupted business operations in an ever-evolving digital landscape. The seamless integration of cloud-based backup strategies not only safeguards critical data but also establishes a strong foundation for future growth and success in an increasingly data-centric business world.

9.1.1. The Importance of Backup Strategies in the Cloud:

Backup strategies play a critical role in any organization's data management plan. In the cloud, where data is stored remotely, backup strategies become even more significant due to potential risks like security breaches, accidental deletion, natural disasters, or hardware failures. A well-designed backup strategy ensures data resilience, minimizes downtime, and facilitates quick data recovery, thereby safeguarding business continuity.

9.1.2. Key Considerations for Backup Planning:

When formulating a backup strategy in the cloud, several important factors should be considered:

- **Data Classification and Prioritization:** Classify and prioritize data based on its criticality and importance to the business. Identify the most critical data that requires frequent and immediate backups, ensuring that backup efforts are aligned with business priorities.

- **Recovery Point Objective (RPO) and Recovery Time Objective (RTO):** Define the acceptable timeframe for data loss (RPO) and the maximum tolerable downtime (RTO) for the business. These metrics help determine backup frequency and restoration timeframes, ensuring the backup strategy meets business requirements.

- **Data Encryption and Security:** Ensure that backup data is encrypted both during transit and at rest to protect it from unauthorized access. Implement robust access controls and authentication mechanisms to safeguard the backup infrastructure.

- **Compliance and Regulatory Requirements:** Consider any industry-specific regulations or compliance standards that govern data protection and retention. Align the backup strategy with these requirements to ensure adherence and avoid potential legal or regulatory issues.

- **Redundancy and Data Availability:** Evaluate the level of redundancy and data availability needed for the backup solution. Consider employing multiple storage locations or geographically distributed backups to ensure data resiliency and availability in the face of localized incidents or infrastructure failures.

- **Backup Retention Policies:** Establish backup retention policies based on legal requirements, business needs, and data sensitivity. Define the duration for which backups should be retained and establish mechanisms for purging outdated backups to optimize storage usage.

- **Testing and Validation:** Regularly test and validate backup and recovery processes to ensure their effectiveness. Conduct mock recovery exercises to verify the integrity of backup data and the reliability of the restoration process. This proactive approach helps identify and address any potential issues before they impact critical operations.

9.1.3. Best Practices for Backup Strategies in the Cloud:

To implement effective backup strategies in the cloud, organizations should adhere to the following best practices:

- **Automated and Regular Backups:** Implement automated backup processes to ensure consistency and eliminate the risk of human error. Schedule regular backups based on RPO requirements, considering factors such as data volatility and business operations.

- **Multiple Storage Locations:** Store backups in multiple geographically distributed storage locations to protect against data loss caused by regional disasters or infrastructure failures. Leverage the redundancy and durability features offered by cloud storage providers to enhance data resiliency.

- **Incremental and Differential Backups:** Consider using incremental or differential backup methods to reduce backup time and storage costs. These methods back up only the changes made since the last backup, minimizing data transfer and storage requirements while ensuring comprehensive protection.

- **Versioning and Snapshotting:** Leverage the versioning and snapshot capabilities provided by cloud storage services to maintain multiple copies of data at different points in time. This allows for easy restoration to specific versions or recovery points, offering added flexibility and protection against accidental data modification.

- **Offsite Backups:** Maintain offsite backups to safeguard against site-wide disasters or system failures. Cloud storage offers an ideal offsite backup location due to its durability and accessibility, providing an additional layer of protection for critical data.

- **Regular Monitoring and Auditing:** Continuously monitor the backup process and perform regular audits to ensure backups are running successfully and data integrity is maintained. Establish alerts and notifications for backup failures or anomalies to enable prompt remediation and prevent data loss.

- **Data Encryption and Secure Transfer:** Encrypt backup data both during transit and at rest to protect it from unauthorized access. Use secure protocols, such as SSL/TLS, for data transfer to prevent interception or tampering and ensure end-to-end security.

- **Documented Backup and Recovery Procedures:** Maintain clear and well-documented backup and recovery procedures. Include step-by-step instructions, contact information, and escalation paths for quick and efficient recovery in case of data loss or system failures. Regularly update and communicate these procedures to relevant stakeholders.

- **Disaster Recovery Planning:** Integrate backup strategies into a comprehensive disaster recovery plan. Define recovery priorities, establish communication channels, and regularly test and update recovery processes to ensure preparedness for unforeseen events. A robust disaster recovery plan ensures swift and efficient recovery from any disruptions.

9.2 Disaster Recovery Planning: Ensuring Business Resilience

9.2.1. The Importance of Disaster Recovery Planning:

This section emphasizes the significance of disaster recovery planning in safeguarding businesses against various disruptive events. It highlights the potential disasters, whether natural or technological, that can lead to business disruptions, data loss, financial losses, and reputational damage. A well-designed disaster recovery plan helps organizations recover critical systems, protect data, and minimize downtime. It also provides a systematic approach for responding to emergencies and mitigating the impact of disruptive events.

9.2.2. Key Considerations for Disaster Recovery Planning:

the key aspects organizations should consider when developing a disaster recovery plan:
- **Risk Assessment and Business Impact Analysis:** Organizations should conduct a thorough risk assessment to identify potential threats and vulnerabilities that may affect the business. Performing a business impact analysis (BIA) helps determine the criticality and dependencies of systems and data, aiding in prioritizing recovery efforts.

- **Recovery Time Objective (RTO) and Recovery Point Objective (RPO):** RTO defines the acceptable time frame for system recovery, while RPO establishes the maximum tolerable data loss. These metrics guide decision-making during the recovery process and help set recovery goals.

- **Data Backup and Replication:** Implementing a robust data backup strategy that includes regular backups, offsite storage, and data replication ensures data availability and integrity during recovery. Cloud-based backup solutions are recommended for scalability and redundancy.

- **Communication and Stakeholder Management:** Clear communication channels and protocols should be established to disseminate information during a disaster. Identifying key stakeholders, assigning responsibilities, and establishing a chain of command ensures effective communication and coordination.

- **Resource Requirements and Dependencies:** Organizations must identify critical resources and dependencies for recovery, including hardware, software, infrastructure, and personnel. Planning for resource allocation, procurement, and activation helps minimize downtime and expedite the recovery process.

- **Compliance and Legal Considerations:** Taking into account regulatory and compliance requirements relevant to the organization's industry ensures that the disaster recovery plan aligns with legal obligations, such as data privacy and confidentiality.

9.2.3. Essential Components of a Disaster Recovery Plan:
the essential components that a comprehensive disaster recovery plan should include:
- **Emergency Response Procedures:** Detailed step-by-step procedures for initiating the disaster recovery process, including activating the incident response team, communication protocols, and initial damage assessment.

- **Data Backup and Recovery Strategy:** Documentation of the data backup strategy, including backup frequency, storage location, encryption measures, and recovery processes, to ensure business continuity.

- **System and Infrastructure Recovery:** Defined processes and steps required to restore critical systems, applications, and infrastructure components, along with identifying necessary resources and configurations for timely recovery and minimal downtime.

- **Personnel and Vendor Management:** Outlining the roles and responsibilities of key personnel during the recovery process and establishing procedures for engaging external vendors or service providers if required.

- **Testing and Training:** Regular testing of the disaster recovery plan to ensure its effectiveness and conducting mock recovery exercises to validate recovery procedures. Providing training to personnel involved in executing the plan ensures their familiarity with their roles and responsibilities.

- Documentation and Maintenance: Detailed documentation of the entire disaster recovery plan, including contact information, configuration details, and recovery procedures, along with regular updates to reflect changes in the business environment or infrastructure.

9.2.4. Testing and Maintenance of the Disaster Recovery Plan:
the importance of regular testing and maintenance to ensure the disaster recovery plan's effectiveness:

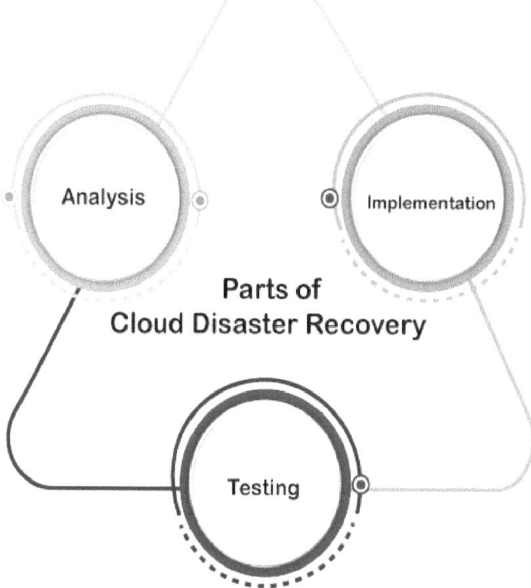

- Regular Testing: Conducting periodic tests, such as tabletop exercises and simulations, to evaluate the plan's effectiveness and identify areas for improvement. Testing recovery procedures, communication channels, and coordination among team members validates the plan's readiness.

- Scalability and Performance Testing: Assessing the plan's scalability by testing its ability to handle larger recovery scenarios or increased data volumes and conducting performance testing to optimize the recovery process for efficiency.

- Documentation Updates: Regularly reviewing and updating the disaster recovery plan documentation to reflect changes in infrastructure, applications, or business processes, ensuring that contact information, responsibilities, and procedures are up to date.

- Training and Awareness: Providing ongoing training to personnel involved in executing the plan and conducting awareness programs to ensure all employees are familiar with their roles and responsibilities during a disaster. Regularly communicating updates and changes to maintain awareness across the organization.

- Review and Audit: Periodic reviews and audits of the disaster recovery plan to assess its compliance with regulatory requirements and industry best practices. Engaging internal or external auditors validates the plan's effectiveness and identifies areas for improvement.

9.2.5. Best Practices for Disaster Recovery Planning:

Regularly reassess risks and update the plan accordingly to address emerging threats and vulnerabilities.
Maintain clear and up-to-date documentation, including contact information, procedures, and recovery steps.
Establish strong partnerships with vendors and service providers to ensure timely support and resources during a disaster.
Consider the use of cloud-based disaster recovery solutions for scalability, flexibility, and reduced infrastructure costs.
Establish a communication plan to promptly inform employees, customers, and stakeholders during a disaster and keep them updated on the recovery progress.
Foster a culture of preparedness and awareness by conducting regular training, awareness programs, and drills.
Conduct post-recovery evaluations and lessons learned sessions to continuously improve the plan's effectiveness and address any shortcomings.

9.3 High Availability and Fault Tolerance: Building Resilient Systems in the Cloud

9.3.1. Understanding High Availability and Fault Tolerance:

- **High Availability (HA):** This section defines high availability as the ability of a system or service to remain accessible and operational without disruptions for an extended period. It explains that HA aims to eliminate single points of failure and ensure uninterrupted service delivery, even in the face of hardware failures, network issues, or software glitches.

- **Fault Tolerance (FT):** This section defines fault tolerance as a system's ability to continue functioning properly despite the occurrence of faults or failures. It highlights that FT involves designing systems that can detect and respond to failures in real-time through redundancy and failover mechanisms, ensuring uninterrupted operation and data integrity.

9.3.2. Strategies for Achieving High Availability and Fault Tolerance in the Cloud:

various strategies to achieve high availability and fault tolerance in the cloud:

- **Redundancy and Load Balancing:** The article explains the importance of redundancy by deploying multiple instances of critical components across different servers, availability zones, or regions. It also highlights load balancing as a method to distribute incoming traffic across these redundant instances for optimal resource utilization and handling sudden spikes in demand.

- **Automated Monitoring and Self-Healing:** Implementing automated monitoring systems is described to continuously monitor the health and performance of components within the system. Intelligent monitoring tools capable of detecting anomalies, triggering alerts, and initiating self-healing actions, such as restarting failed instances or scaling resources, are recommended.

- **Data Replication and Backup:** This section stresses the need for data redundancy and integrity through data replication mechanisms like database replication or distributed file systems. Regularly backing up critical data to multiple geographically diverse locations is highlighted to protect against data loss and enable quick recovery.

- **Disaster Recovery Planning:** Developing a comprehensive disaster recovery plan (DRP) with backup strategies, data recovery plans, and system restoration methods is essential. Implementing backup systems and infrastructure in separate locations is recommended to ensure business continuity during disasters.

- **Elasticity and Auto Scaling:** The article suggests leveraging the cloud's elasticity and auto scaling capabilities to automatically adjust resource allocation based on demand. Implementing auto scaling policies that add or remove resources dynamically to handle varying workloads ensures optimal performance and availability.

- **Geographic Redundancy and Multi-Region Deployment:** Deploying critical components across multiple regions or availability zones is emphasized to ensure geographic redundancy. This distribution mitigates the impact of regional outages or disruptions, maintaining service availability.

- **Health Checks and Failover Mechanisms:** Implementing health checks and failover mechanisms to detect and respond to failures is crucial. Automated monitoring regularly checks the health of resources and redirects traffic to healthy instances in case of failures, minimizing service disruption.

9.3.3. Best Practices for Building Resilient Systems:

Best practices for building resilient systems in the cloud:

- **Architect for Failure:** Designing systems with the assumption that failures will occur is essential. Implementing redundancy, fault tolerance mechanisms, and component isolation minimizes the impact of failures on the overall system.

- **Use Managed Services:** Leveraging managed services offered by cloud providers, such as managed databases and load balancers, is recommended. These services often include built-in high availability and fault tolerance features, reducing the burden of managing these aspects at the application level.

- **Implement Automated Infrastructure as Code:** Using infrastructure as code (IaC) tools, such as AWS CloudFormation or Azure Resource Manager, is advised. This approach enables consistent and repeatable infrastructure deployment, making it easier to implement high availability and fault tolerance configurations.

- **Regularly Test and Simulate Failures:** Conducting regular testing and simulation exercises to validate system resilience is crucial. Testing failover mechanisms, disaster recovery procedures, and resource scaling ensures they function as expected and can handle failures effectively.

- **Monitor and Analyze Performance:** Implementing robust monitoring and logging solutions to gain real-time visibility into system performance is recommended. Analyzing performance metrics and logs helps identify potential bottlenecks, anticipate failures, and proactively optimize resources and configurations.

- **Stay Up to Date with Security Practices:** Following security best practices, including regular patching and updates, implementing robust access controls, and utilizing encryption, is crucial to protect data and prevent service disruptions.

- **Document and Share Knowledge:** Documenting system architectures, configurations, and recovery procedures is essential. Sharing this knowledge with the team ensures everyone is familiar with the system's high availability and fault tolerance mechanisms, facilitating effective troubleshooting and recovery during incidents.

Exercise
Multiple Choice Questions

1. What is the primary purpose of backup strategies in the cloud?

a. Reducing data storage costs

b. Ensuring data resilience and business continuity

c. Increasing data transfer speeds

d. Improving network security

2. What should be considered when defining a backup strategy's Recovery Point Objective (RPO)?

a. Maximum tolerable downtime for the business

b. Duration for which backups should be retained

c. The timeframe for data loss acceptable to the business

d. Level of data redundancy needed for the backup solution

3. Which backup method backs up only the changes made since the last backup?

a. Incremental backup

b. Full backup

c. Differential backup

d. Snapshot backup

4. How can organizations achieve geographic redundancy in the cloud?

a. By using multiple cloud service providers

b. By distributing critical components across different servers

c. By implementing load balancing for network traffic

d. By conducting regular disaster recovery drills

5. What role does automated monitoring play in building resilient systems in the cloud?

a. Providing security against cyber-attacks

b. Detecting and responding to system failures in real-time

c. Reducing the cost of cloud resources

d. Ensuring data encryption during transit

6. Which best practice involves regularly testing the disaster recovery plan to ensure its effectiveness?

a. Documenting backup and recovery procedures

b. Implementing data encryption during transit and at rest

c. Establishing a communication plan for stakeholders

d. Conducting mock recovery exercises and simulations

7. What does the term "Fault Tolerance" refer to in IT infrastructure design?

a. The ability of a system to handle a sudden spike in demand

b. The capability of a system to self-heal and recover from failures

c. The redundancy of multiple data centers in different geographic locations

d. The consistency of system performance over time

8. What is the purpose of using load balancing in achieving high availability in the cloud?

a. To distribute incoming traffic across multiple redundant instances

b. To automate the backup process and schedule backups

c. To encrypt data both during transit and at rest

d. To maintain data integrity during recovery operations

9. How can infrastructure as code (IaC) tools benefit the implementation of resilient systems in the cloud?

a. They provide real-time monitoring of cloud resources

b. They allow for automated backup scheduling

c. They enable consistent and repeatable infrastructure deployment

d. They automatically encrypt data stored in the cloud

Review Questions

1. What is the importance of backup strategies in the cloud?

2. What key factors should be considered for backup planning in the cloud?

3. How can organizations automate and schedule backups effectively in the cloud?

4. Why is using multiple storage locations for backups important in the cloud?

5. What are incremental and differential backups, and how do they benefit cloud-based backup strategies?

6. How can cloud-based disaster recovery solutions enhance fault tolerance?

7. How can organizations achieve high availability in the cloud?

8. What are the benefits of implementing automated monitoring and self-healing in the cloud?

9. How does data replication and backup contribute to fault tolerance in the cloud?

10. What role does disaster recovery planning play in achieving business resilience?

11. Why is documentation and regular testing essential for building resilient systems in the cloud?

Answer Secton

Multiple Choice Questions

1. b) Ensuring data resilience and business continuity

2. c) The timeframe for data loss acceptable to the business

3. a) Incremental backup

4. b) By distributing critical components across different servers

5. b) Detecting and responding to system failures in real-time

6. d) Conducting mock recovery exercises and simulations

7. b) The capability of a system to self-heal and recover from failures

8. a) To distribute incoming traffic across multiple redundant instances

9. c) They enable consistent and repeatable infrastructure deployment

Review Questions

1. Backup strategies are crucial in the cloud to protect against data loss caused by security breaches, accidental deletion, natural disasters, or hardware failures. They ensure data resilience, minimize downtime, and facilitate quick data recovery, safeguarding business continuity.

2. Data classification and prioritization, Recovery Point Objective (RPO) and Recovery Time Objective (RTO), data encryption and security, compliance and regulatory requirements, redundancy and data availability, backup retention policies, testing and validation.

3. Organizations can implement automated backup processes and schedule them based on RPO requirements, considering data volatility and business operations. This helps ensure consistency, eliminate human error, and align backup efforts with business needs.

4. Storing backups in multiple geographically distributed locations ensures protection against data loss caused by regional disasters or infrastructure failures. Leveraging redundancy and durability features of cloud storage enhances data resiliency.

5. Incremental and differential backups are backup methods that only back up changes made since the last backup. They reduce backup time and storage costs by minimizing data transfer and storage requirements while ensuring comprehensive protection.

6. Cloud-based disaster recovery solutions offer scalability, flexibility, and reduced infrastructure costs. They ensure the availability of redundant systems and data replication, enhancing fault tolerance by enabling rapid failover and recovery.

7. High availability in the cloud can be achieved through redundancy, load balancing, automated monitoring, self-healing, and geographic redundancy. These strategies eliminate single points of failure and ensure continuous access to services.

8. Automated monitoring continuously checks the health and performance of cloud resources, while self-healing mechanisms can automatically respond to failures by restarting instances or scaling resources. This ensures quick and efficient recovery, minimizing service disruptions.

9. Data replication ensures redundant copies of critical data in different locations, enabling data integrity and quick recovery. Regularly backing up data to multiple locations provides protection against data loss and enhances fault tolerance.

10. Disaster recovery planning provides a systematic approach to responding to emergencies, mitigating the impact of disruptive events, and ensuring business continuity. It includes backup strategies, data recovery plans, and system restoration methods.

11. Documentation ensures clear and up-to-date instructions for recovery procedures, while regular testing and simulation exercises validate system resilience and identify areas for improvement. This proactive approach helps organizations maintain robust and resilient infrastructures.

Chapter 10: Future Trends in Cloud Computing

10.1 Harnessing the Power of Edge Computing for IoT: Revolutionizing Data Processing and Connectivity

The transformative potential of edge computing in IoT By bringing computation and data processing closer to IoT devices, edge computing enables real-time analysis, reduced latency, enhanced security, and offline operation. The convergence of edge computing and IoT unlocks transformative applications across various industries, including industrial automation, smart cities, healthcare, retail, and autonomous vehicles. To successfully implement edge computing in IoT, organizations must carefully consider infrastructure requirements, data processing capabilities, security measures, integration with cloud services, and scalability. By harnessing the power of edge computing, organizations can fully realize the benefits of IoT, driving innovation and intelligent decision-making in our increasingly connected world.

10.1.1. Understanding Edge Computing and IoT:

Edge computing as a decentralized computing paradigm that processes data at the network edge instead of sending it to a centralized cloud or data center. It explains that IoT refers to the network of interconnected devices that collect, exchange, and analyze data, including sensors, wearables, smart appliances, and industrial equipment. These devices generate vast amounts of data that require processing and analysis.

10.1.2. Benefits of Edge Computing for IoT:

The key advantages of leveraging edge computing for IoT:

- **Reduced Latency:** Edge computing reduces data transmission time and enables real-time data processing. This reduced latency is crucial for time-sensitive applications, such as industrial automation, autonomous vehicles, and real-time monitoring, where instantaneous decision-making is vital.

- **Bandwidth Optimization:** By processing and filtering data at the edge, edge computing minimizes the amount of data that needs to be transmitted to the cloud. This optimization of bandwidth helps organizations save on network costs and improves overall system performance.

- **Enhanced Security and Privacy:** Edge computing allows sensitive data to be processed and analyzed locally, reducing exposure to potential security threats during data transmission. This distributed approach enhances data privacy and mitigates risks associated with data breaches.

- **Offline Operation:** Edge computing enables devices to operate autonomously even without a stable network connection. This capability is valuable in remote or disconnected environments where continuous connectivity may not be available.

- **Scalability and Flexibility:** Edge computing supports the scalability and flexibility required to accommodate the growing number of IoT devices. Edge nodes can be easily deployed and scaled based on the specific requirements of the IoT application, allowing for efficient resource utilization.

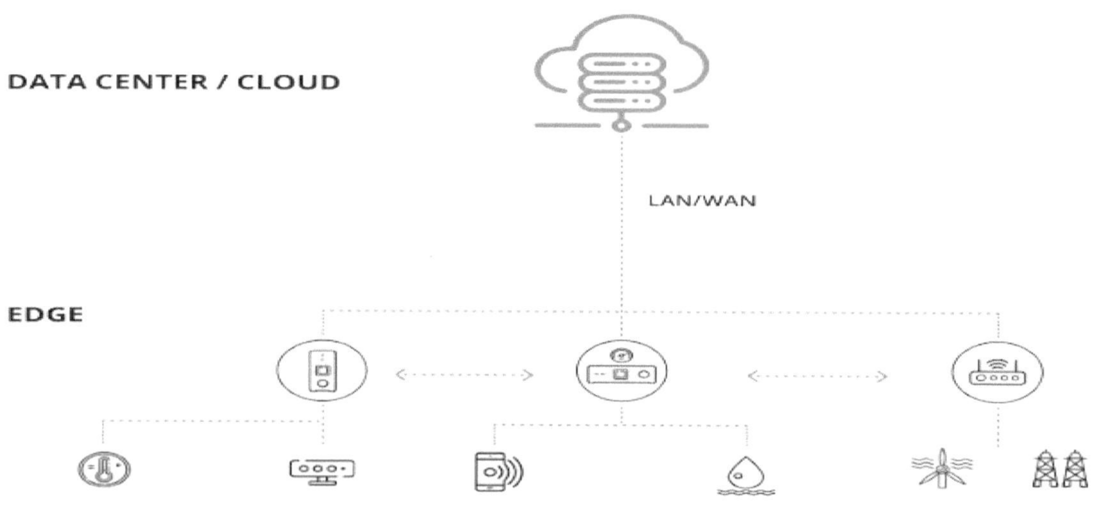

10.1.3. Use Cases and Applications of Edge Computing in IoT:
various use cases and applications where edge computing revolutionizes IoT:

- **Industrial IoT:** Edge computing facilitates real-time analytics, predictive maintenance, and process optimization in industrial settings. It enables efficient data processing and decision-making at the edge, enhancing operational efficiency, reducing downtime, and improving worker safety.

- **Smart Cities:** Edge computing enables intelligent management of urban infrastructure, such as smart grids, intelligent traffic systems, and environmental monitoring. Localized data processing and decision-making help optimize resource allocation, reduce congestion, and improve sustainability.

- **Healthcare:** Edge computing enables remote patient monitoring, real-time health data analysis, and personalized care delivery. It enhances healthcare services by providing timely insights, reducing response times, and supporting critical patient monitoring in remote or underserved areas.

- **Retail and Customer Experience:** Edge computing enables personalized marketing, real-time inventory management, and efficient supply chain operations. By processing customer data at the edge, retailers can deliver targeted promotions, optimize store layouts, and improve overall customer experience.

- **Autonomous Vehicles:** Edge computing plays a crucial role in enabling real-time decision-making and data processing for autonomous vehicles. It allows vehicles to process sensor data locally, reducing dependence on the cloud and enabling faster response times for critical driving tasks.

10.1.4. Key Considerations for Successful Implementation:
Important factors to consider when implementing edge computing in IoT:

- **Infrastructure and Network Considerations:** Strategic deployment of edge computing infrastructure, such as edge servers or gateways, close to IoT devices is essential. Organizations must evaluate network connectivity and latency requirements to optimize data transmission and processing.

- **Data Processing and Analytics:** Determining the appropriate data processing and analytics capabilities required at the edge is critical. Organizations must consider the volume and complexity of data generated by IoT devices and select suitable edge computing platforms and algorithms for efficient analysis.

- Security and Privacy: Implementing robust security measures to protect edge computing nodes and IoT devices from cyber threats is essential. Encryption of data during transmission and storage, access controls, and anomaly monitoring ensure data integrity and privacy.

- Integration with Cloud Services: Designing a hybrid architecture that seamlessly integrates edge computing with cloud services is important. Efficient data synchronization and bi-directional communication between edge nodes and the cloud leverage the scalability and advanced analytics capabilities of the cloud.

- Scalability and Management: Planning for scalability by considering the growth of IoT devices and the evolving requirements of edge computing infrastructure is crucial. Implementing centralized management and monitoring tools simplifies administration, orchestration, and deployment of edge computing resources.

10.2 Empowering the Future: Artificial Intelligence (AI) and Machine Learning (ML) in Today's World

AI and ML are transformative technologies that have reshaped industries with intelligent automation, predictive analytics, and data-driven decision-making. Responsible implementation is crucial, considering ethical factors like data privacy, bias, and transparency. With continued advancements and responsible use, AI and ML will drive positive change, unlocking new possibilities and unprecedented success in the digital era.

10.2.1. Understanding Artificial Intelligence and Machine Learning:

AI encompasses various technologies, such as natural language processing, computer vision, robotics, and expert systems. ML is introduced as a subset of AI, focusing on developing algorithms and statistical models enabling machines to learn from data and improve performance over time. ML algorithms analyze patterns to make predictions or decisions without explicit programming.

10.2.2. Significance of AI and ML:

the key importance of AI and ML in various ways:

- Automation and Efficiency: AI and ML automate repetitive and labor-intensive tasks, streamlining operations, improving efficiency, and optimizing resource allocation. Tasks like data entry, customer service, and data analysis can be automated, freeing up human capital for strategic activities.

- Predictive Analytics: ML algorithms analyze vast data to uncover patterns, trends, and correlations, enabling accurate predictions, anticipating customer behavior, optimizing processes, and identifying risks or opportunities.

- Personalized Experiences: AI-powered systems deliver personalized experiences by understanding user preferences, behavior, and historical data, enhancing customer satisfaction, engagement, and loyalty.

- Enhanced Decision-Making: ML algorithms analyze complex datasets, providing insights for data-driven decision-making. AI and ML enable informed decisions in real-time, considering numerous variables and factors.

- Intelligent Automation: AI and ML combine robotic process automation (RPA) with cognitive capabilities for intelligent automation, leading to increased productivity and reduced errors in complex tasks requiring cognitive abilities.

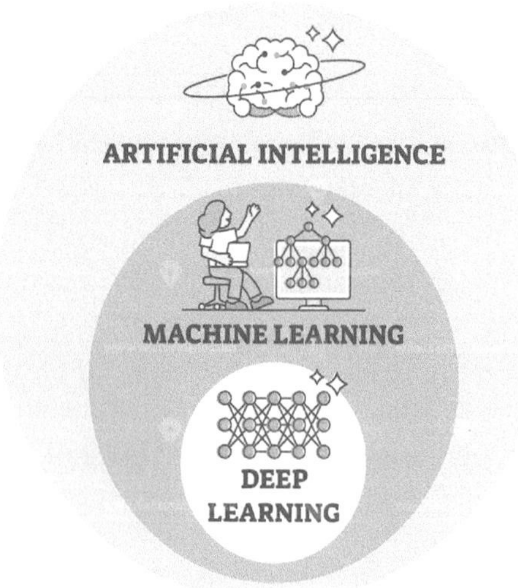

10.2.3. Practical Applications of AI and ML:
real-world applications of AI and ML:
- **Natural Language Processing (NLP):** NLP powers voice assistants, chatbots, and sentiment analysis, revolutionizing customer service, virtual assistants, and language translation.

- **Computer Vision:** Computer vision enables facial recognition, object detection, autonomous vehicles, and quality control in manufacturing, interpreting and understanding visual content.

- **Recommendation Systems:** ML-based recommendation systems offer personalized recommendations in e-commerce, streaming platforms, and content recommendation engines based on user behavior and preferences.

- **Fraud Detection:** ML algorithms detect patterns and anomalies, identifying fraudulent activities in real-time for banking, insurance, and e-commerce to prevent financial losses.

- **Healthcare and Medical Diagnosis:** AI and ML enable advanced medical diagnosis, image analysis, drug discovery, and personalized medicine, supporting early disease detection and treatment planning.

- **Autonomous Systems:** AI and ML power self-driving cars, drones, and robotics by using sensor data and making real-time decisions for autonomous navigation.

4. Ethical Considerations and Challenges:
Ethical considerations and challenges related to AI and ML:
- **Data Privacy and Security:** Responsible handling and protection of sensitive data are vital, ensuring compliance with data privacy regulations and robust security measures to safeguard against breaches.

- **Bias and Fairness:** Addressing bias in training data is essential to promote fairness in algorithmic decision-making, ensuring ethical and unbiased AI applications.

- **Transparency and Explainability:** The growing complexity of AI systems requires transparency and explainability, allowing users to understand how decisions are made.

- **Workforce Disruption and Upskilling:** AI and ML may automate certain job roles, necessitating investment in upskilling and reskilling programs to equip employees for an AI-driven future.

10.3 Quantum Computing and Cloud: Unleashing the Power of Quantum for Advanced Computing

The convergence of quantum computing and cloud presents unparalleled opportunities for advancing computational capabilities, problem-solving, and scientific discovery. Cloud-based quantum services make quantum resources accessible, scalable, and cost-effective, enabling organizations to explore quantum algorithms and applications without significant infrastructure investments. However,

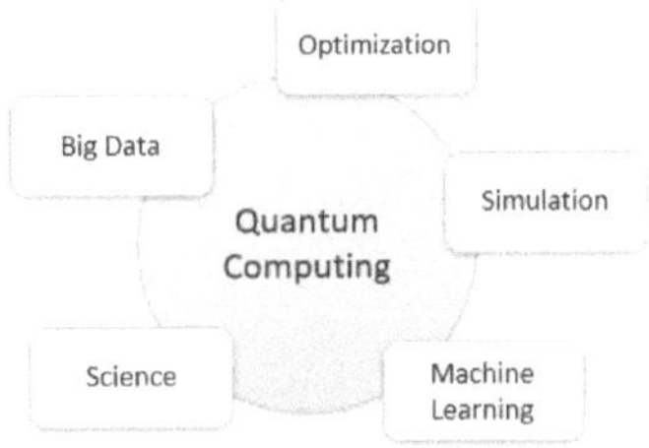

challenges related to error correction, security, quantum expertise, and standardization need to be addressed to fully unleash the potential of quantum computing in the cloud. Collaboration among researchers, cloud providers, and industry stakeholders will drive innovation, fuel breakthroughs, and shape the future of computing in the quantum era.

10.3.1. Understanding Quantum Computing:

The fundamental concepts of quantum computing:

- **Quantum Bits (Qubits):** Quantum computing utilizes qubits as the basic units of quantum information. Unlike classical bits that represent either 0 or 1, qubits can exist in a state of superposition, allowing them to represent multiple states simultaneously. This property enables quantum computers to perform complex calculations more efficiently.

- **Quantum Superposition and Entanglement:** Quantum superposition refers to the ability of qubits to exist in multiple states at once. Entanglement is a phenomenon where two or more qubits become linked, regardless of distance, resulting in correlated states. These properties form the basis for the unparalleled computational power of quantum computing.

10.3.2. Quantum Computing in the Cloud:

The integration of quantum computing with cloud platforms:

- **Cloud-based Quantum Services:** Cloud providers offer access to quantum computing resources through their platforms. Users can utilize quantum processors, run quantum algorithms, and analyze results through a cloud interface, eliminating the need for significant investments in quantum hardware.

- **Hybrid Quantum-Classical Computing:** Cloud-based quantum computing often adopts a hybrid approach, where classical computers collaborate with quantum processors. Classical computers handle pre- and post-processing tasks, while the quantum processor focuses on computationally intensive quantum operations. This hybrid model maximizes efficiency and scalability.

10.3.3. Significance and Potential Impact of Quantum Computing in the Cloud:

the importance of quantum computing in the cloud and its potential impact:

- **Advanced Computational Power:** Quantum computing can outperform classical computers in solving complex problems, such as optimization, cryptography, material science, drug discovery, and machine learning. Cloud-based quantum computing allows organizations to harness this power without the need for substantial upfront investments.

- Accessible Quantum Resources: Cloud-based quantum computing democratizes access to quantum resources, enabling businesses, researchers, and developers to explore and experiment with quantum algorithms and applications. This accessibility fosters innovation, accelerates discoveries, and promotes collaboration across diverse fields.

- Scalability and Flexibility: Quantum computing in the cloud provides scalability, allowing users to scale resources as needed without hardware limitations. Cloud platforms enable easy provisioning of additional qubits and computing power, ensuring that quantum resources can meet the demands of complex computations.

- Cost-Effectiveness: Cloud-based quantum computing offers a cost-effective approach to access quantum resources. Users can pay for the resources they consume, avoiding significant upfront costs associated with building and maintaining quantum hardware infrastructure.

10.3.4. Challenges and Considerations:

challenges related to quantum computing in the cloud:

- Quantum Error Correction: Quantum systems are susceptible to errors due to noise and decoherence. Effective quantum error correction techniques are crucial to ensuring the accuracy and reliability of quantum computations. Cloud providers and researchers need to develop robust error correction mechanisms to improve the stability of quantum systems.

- Security and Privacy: Quantum computing presents both threats and opportunities for cybersecurity. Quantum algorithms have the potential to break current encryption methods, necessitating the development of quantum-resistant cryptographic algorithms. Additionally, quantum systems require robust security measures to protect against unauthorized access and data breaches.

- Quantum Expertise: Quantum computing is a rapidly evolving field that requires specialized expertise. Bridging the gap between quantum experts and cloud users is essential to ensure the effective utilization of quantum resources in the cloud. Collaboration among researchers, cloud providers, and industry partners can facilitate knowledge sharing and skill development.

- Interoperability and Standardization: As quantum computing evolves, interoperability and standardization across different quantum platforms and cloud providers become crucial. Developing common standards and interfaces will promote compatibility, seamless integration, and interoperability among quantum systems in the cloud.

Exercise

Multiple Choice Questions

1. What is edge computing?

a. A centralized computing paradigm that processes data in a cloud or data center.

b. A decentralized computing paradigm that processes data at the network edge.

c. A technology that enables data transmission between IoT devices.

d. A method of data processing that relies on quantum computing.

2. Which of the following is NOT a benefit of leveraging edge computing for IoT?

a. Reduced latency

b. Enhanced security and privacy

c. Increased data transmission time

d. Offline operation capability

3. Which industry can benefit from edge computing by enabling real-time analytics, predictive maintenance, and process optimization?

a. Retail

b. Smart cities

c. Healthcare

d. Agriculture

4. What is one of the key challenges related to quantum computing in the cloud?

a. Increased data privacy and security risks

b. Lack of accessibility to quantum resources

c. Limited scalability and flexibility

d. Quantum error correction and stability

5. In quantum computing, what are basic units of quantum information called?

a. Bits

b. Bytes

c. Qubits

d. Quantum gates

6. Which technology enables facial recognition and object detection in various applications?

a. Natural Language Processing (NLP)

b. Computer Vision

c. Quantum Superposition

d. Quantum Entanglement

7. What makes quantum computing significantly more powerful than classical computing?

a. Ability to process data in the cloud

b. Use of classical bits for data representation

c. Quantum superposition and entanglement of qubits

d. Limited computational resources

8. How does edge computing reduce latency in data processing?

a. By transmitting data to a centralized cloud or data center.

b. By deploying edge nodes closer to IoT devices for real-time processing.

c. By utilizing quantum computing algorithms for faster data analysis.

d. By optimizing bandwidth to reduce data transmission time.

9. Which area of application can benefit from AI and ML in providing personalized experiences based on user behavior and preferences?

a. Industrial automation

b. Autonomous vehicles

c. E-commerce

d. Smart cities

10. What advantage does edge computing offer in scenarios where continuous connectivity may not be available?

a. Enhanced security and privacy

b. Reduced latency

c. Offline operation capability

d. Scalability and flexibility

Review Questions

1. What are qubits, and how are they different from classical bits in quantum computing?

2. How does cloud-based quantum computing democratize access to quantum resources?

3. In what ways does quantum computing in the cloud address the challenges of scalability and flexibility?

4. How can quantum error correction techniques address the challenges of noise and decoherence in quantum systems?

5. What potential applications can be revolutionized by the combination of quantum computing and cloud-based services?

6. How does quantum computing in the cloud impact the cost-effectiveness of accessing quantum resources?

7. What is the role of quantum computing in cybersecurity, and how does it pose both threats and opportunities?

8. How can collaboration between quantum experts and cloud users address the challenges of quantum expertise?

9. Why is standardization and interoperability essential for the future of quantum computing in the cloud?

Answer Secton

Multiple Choice Questions

1. b) A decentralized computing paradigm that processes data at the network edge.

2. c) Increased data transmission time

3. c) Healthcare

4. d) Quantum error correction and stability

5. c) Qubits

6. b) Computer Vision

7. c) Quantum superposition and entanglement of qubits

8. b) By deploying edge nodes closer to IoT devices for real-time processing.

9. c) E-commerce

10. c) Offline operation capability

Review Questions

1. Qubits are the basic units of quantum information in quantum computing. Unlike classical bits, which represent either 0 or 1, qubits can exist in a state of superposition, allowing them to represent multiple states simultaneously. This property enables quantum computers to perform complex calculations more efficiently and tackle problems that classical computers struggle to solve.

2. Cloud-based quantum computing offers scalable access to quantum resources through cloud platforms provided by vendors. Users can utilize quantum processors, run quantum algorithms, and analyze results without the need for significant investments in quantum hardware. This democratization enables businesses, researchers, and developers to explore and experiment with quantum computing, fostering innovation and collaboration across diverse fields.

3. Quantum computing in the cloud provides scalability and flexibility by allowing users to scale quantum resources as needed without hardware limitations. Cloud platforms enable easy provisioning of additional qubits and computing power, ensuring that quantum resources can meet the demands of complex computations. This scalability allows organizations to adapt and allocate resources according to their specific requirements, enhancing efficiency and performance.

4. Quantum error correction techniques are crucial for improving the stability of quantum systems by mitigating the impact of noise and decoherence. These techniques involve encoding quantum information redundantly across multiple qubits, allowing errors to be detected and corrected. By applying error correction codes, quantum systems can maintain the accuracy and reliability of quantum computations, making them more resilient to external disturbances.

5. The combination of quantum computing and cloud-based services can revolutionize various applications, such as optimization, cryptography, material science, drug discovery, and machine learning. Quantum computing's ability to solve complex problems exponentially faster than classical computers opens up new possibilities in these fields, leading to more efficient algorithms, enhanced simulations, and improved decision-making processes.

6. Cloud-based quantum computing offers a cost-effective approach to accessing quantum resources. Users can pay for the resources they consume, avoiding significant upfront costs associated with building and maintaining quantum hardware infrastructure. This cost-effectiveness democratizes access to quantum resources, making quantum computing more accessible to a wider range of users and organizations.

7. Quantum computing plays a crucial role in cybersecurity as it has the potential to both threaten existing cryptographic methods and offer opportunities for quantum-resistant cryptographic algorithms. Quantum algorithms can break current encryption methods, posing a threat to data security. However, the development of quantum-resistant cryptographic algorithms can address these vulnerabilities and enhance data protection in the future quantum era.

8. Collaboration between quantum experts and cloud users can bridge the gap in quantum expertise and facilitate effective utilization of quantum resources in the cloud. By working together, quantum experts can provide guidance, support, and knowledge sharing to help cloud users understand and utilize quantum capabilities effectively. This collaboration fosters skill development, accelerates research, and enables cloud users to leverage quantum computing for their specific applications.

9. Standardization and interoperability are vital for the future of quantum computing in the cloud as the field evolves and multiple quantum platforms emerge. Developing common standards and interfaces ensures compatibility and seamless integration among different quantum systems and cloud providers. This interoperability promotes collaboration, facilitates data exchange, and enhances the accessibility and usability of quantum resources in the cloud.

Chapter 11: Cloud Monitoring and Performance Optimization

11.1 Monitoring Tools and Techniques for Cloud: Maximizing Performance and Reliability

Monitoring tools and techniques are essential for managing and optimizing cloud-based services and applications. Comprehensive monitoring, real-time alerting, and cloud-native log analysis enable organizations to proactively detect performance issues, optimize resource allocation, and deliver a seamless user experience. Leveraging cloud provider monitoring services, historical trend analysis, and security-focused monitoring further enhances the effectiveness of cloud monitoring efforts. By adhering to best practices and continuously improving monitoring strategies, organizations can maximize the performance, availability, and reliability of their cloud-based solutions.

11.1.1. Importance of Monitoring in the Cloud:

The following aspects of cloud monitoring:

- **Performance Optimization:** Cloud monitoring allows organizations to track resource utilization, response times, and other performance metrics, identifying bottlenecks and optimizing resource allocation. It ensures that cloud services meet performance objectives and deliver an optimal user experience.

- **Proactive Issue Detection:** Real-time monitoring enables organizations to identify and address issues before they impact service availability or performance. Monitoring tools provide alerts and notifications, allowing for proactive troubleshooting and resolution.

- **Scalability and Resource Planning:** Cloud monitoring aids in resource planning by monitoring utilization trends and identifying capacity needs. Effective resource provisioning ensures optimal scalability to meet changing demands without overprovisioning or underutilization.

- **Cost Optimization:** By monitoring cloud resources, organizations can identify underutilized instances, inefficient resource allocation, or overprovisioning. Informed decisions about resource optimization and resizing maximize cost-efficiency.

11.1.2. Key Components of Cloud Monitoring Tools:

The essential components of cloud monitoring tools:

- **Resource Monitoring:** Cloud monitoring tools collect and analyze data on resource utilization, including CPU, memory, storage, network bandwidth, and disk I/O. This data provides insights into resource performance, bottlenecks, and optimization opportunities.

- **Application Performance Monitoring (APM):** APM focuses on monitoring application-specific metrics like response times, transaction rates, error rates, and user experience. APM tools help identify performance issues within applications running in the cloud and optimize application performance.

- **Infrastructure Monitoring:** This component tracks the health and performance of cloud infrastructure components, such as virtual machines, containers, databases, load balancers, and networking components. It provides visibility into infrastructure-level metrics and detects issues affecting overall system performance.

- **Log Monitoring and Analysis:** Log monitoring tools aggregate and analyze logs from various cloud resources and services. Log analysis aids in identifying errors, security threats, and operational issues, providing valuable insights for troubleshooting and compliance.

- **Dashboards and Visualizations:** Cloud monitoring tools offer dashboards and visualizations to present performance metrics and key indicators in a user-friendly manner. Visual representations facilitate effective monitoring, quick identification of trends, anomalies, and performance patterns.

11.1.3. Cloud Monitoring Techniques and Best Practices:

Best practices and techniques for effective cloud monitoring:

- **Comprehensive Monitoring:** Adopt a comprehensive monitoring approach that covers different layers of the cloud stack, ensuring visibility into all critical components and their interdependencies for effective performance management.

- **Real-time Monitoring and Alerting:** Implement real-time monitoring to capture performance metrics and receive alerts immediately when predefined thresholds are exceeded. Real-time alerts enable prompt action, minimizing the impact of performance issues and preventing service disruptions.

- **Autoscaling and Dynamic Resource Allocation:** Leverage cloud-native capabilities for autoscaling and dynamic resource allocation based on predefined thresholds or performance metrics. Autoscaling ensures that resources are provisioned or deprovisioned dynamically, optimizing performance and cost-efficiency.

- **Cloud-Optimized Log Analysis:** Utilize log monitoring and analysis tools designed specifically for cloud environments. These tools can aggregate logs from different cloud services, enable correlation across log data, and provide advanced analysis capabilities to identify performance issues and security threats.

- **Historical Trend Analysis:** Perform trend analysis by analyzing historical monitoring data to identify patterns, seasonality, and long-term performance trends. Historical trend analysis aids in capacity planning, predicting resource needs, and identifying potential performance issues.

- **Cloud Provider Monitoring Services:** Leverage native monitoring services provided by cloud providers, such as Amazon CloudWatch or Azure Monitor. These services offer deep integration with the cloud platform, providing detailed insights into cloud resources and services.

- **Security and Compliance Monitoring:** Implement monitoring tools that provide security-specific metrics and compliance checks. Monitor security events, access logs, and compliance frameworks to ensure the security and integrity of cloud resources and data.

11.1.4. Benefits of Effective Monitoring:

The advantages of an effective cloud monitoring strategy:

- **Improved System Availability:** Timely detection and resolution of issues minimize system downtime, improving overall availability. Proactive monitoring enables faster troubleshooting and reduced mean time to repair (MTTR).

- **Enhanced Performance and Scalability:** Monitoring tools provide insights into system performance, identifying bottlenecks and optimizing resource allocation. This optimization results in improved system responsiveness, reduced latency, and better user experiences.

- **Cost Optimization:** Effective monitoring helps optimize resource utilization, identifying underutilized resources and right-sizing infrastructure. This avoids unnecessary expenditures on overprovisioning and optimizes resource allocation, resulting in cost savings.

- **Compliance and Security:** Monitoring tools aid in meeting compliance requirements and enhancing security. By tracking security events, monitoring access controls, and detecting anomalies, organizations can strengthen security defenses, ensure regulatory compliance, and protect sensitive data.

11.2 Unveiling Cloud Performance: Metrics and Analysis for Optimal Cloud Operations

Performance metrics and analysis are crucial for optimizing cloud performance, ensuring efficient resource utilization, and delivering exceptional user experiences. By monitoring key performance metrics like response time, latency, throughput, error rates, and resource utilization, organizations can identify bottlenecks and optimize their cloud operations effectively. Employing analysis techniques such as trend analysis, comparative analysis, anomaly detection, and correlation analysis further enhances the ability to identify performance issues and optimize cloud resources. By following best practices, organizations can maximize the efficiency and reliability of their cloud-based services and applications, ultimately driving better business outcomes and user satisfaction.

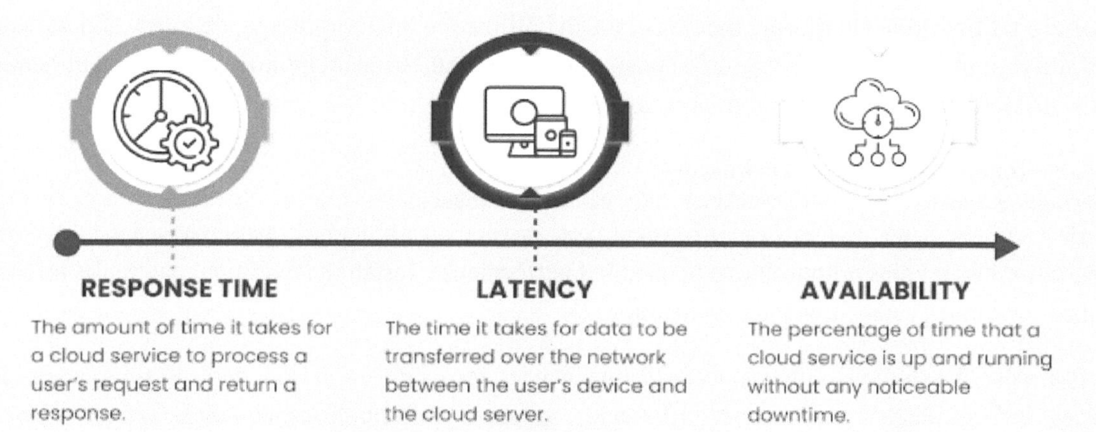

11.2.1. Importance of Performance Metrics in the Cloud:

The following aspects of performance metrics in the cloud:

- **Resource Utilization:** Performance metrics help monitor cloud resource utilization, including CPU, memory, storage, and network bandwidth. By gaining insights into resource usage patterns, organizations can identify bottlenecks and optimize resource allocation for optimal performance.

- **User Experience:** Performance metrics enable organizations to measure and enhance the user experience in cloud-based applications and services. Metrics such as response time, latency, and throughput provide insights into performance perceived by end-users, guiding areas for improvement.

- **Scalability and Capacity Planning:** Performance metrics aid in capacity planning by monitoring resource usage trends and forecasting future needs. They help ensure sufficient resources are available to handle increasing workloads and scale cloud infrastructure accordingly.

- **Cost Optimization:** Monitoring performance metrics related to resource utilization helps organizations identify underutilized or overprovisioned resources. Optimizing resource allocation based on these metrics can lead to cost savings by reducing unnecessary expenditures.

11.2.2. Key Performance Metrics in the Cloud:

This section elaborates on essential performance metrics in the cloud:

- **Response Time:** Measures the time taken for a request or operation to complete. It reflects the speed at which the cloud system responds to user requests and is critical for assessing user experience.

- **Latency:** Represents the time it takes for data to travel between the user and the cloud service. Monitoring latency helps identify network-related issues and optimize network configurations for faster data transmission.

- **Throughput:** Measures the rate at which the cloud system processes and delivers data. It indicates the system's capacity to handle concurrent requests and is vital for assessing scalability and performance.

- **Error Rates:** Tracks the frequency of errors or failures encountered during cloud operations. Monitoring error rates helps identify performance bottlenecks, software bugs, or configuration issues impacting system stability.

- **Resource Utilization:** Monitoring metrics like CPU utilization, memory usage, disk I/O, and network bandwidth provides insights into resource consumption and bottlenecks. Optimizing resource utilization ensures efficient operation and performance in the cloud.

11.2.3. Performance Analysis Techniques:

This section outlines various analysis techniques for cloud performance:

- **Trend Analysis:** Involves analyzing historical performance data to identify patterns, seasonality, and long-term trends. It helps organizations understand performance variations over time and make informed decisions for capacity planning and optimization.

- **Comparative Analysis:** Compares performance metrics across different time periods, regions, or cloud instances. It helps identify performance differences, optimize configurations, and make informed decisions based on historical data.

- **Anomaly Detection:** Utilizes machine learning algorithms and statistical analysis to identify abnormal behavior or deviations from normal performance patterns. Anomaly detection helps identify performance issues, security threats, or configuration errors.

- **Correlation Analysis:** Examines relationships between different performance metrics to identify dependencies and root causes of performance issues. Analyzing correlations helps prioritize optimizations and allocate resources effectively.

11.2.4. Best Practices for Performance Metrics and Analysis in the Cloud:

This section provides best practices for optimizing cloud performance:

- **Define Clear Performance Objectives:** Establish clear performance objectives based on business requirements and user expectations. These objectives serve as benchmarks for monitoring and analysis efforts.

- **Select Relevant Metrics:** Choose performance metrics aligned with specific cloud applications, services, and user requirements. Focus on metrics directly related to user experience, resource utilization, and critical processes.

- **Continuous Monitoring:** Implement continuous monitoring of performance metrics to capture real-time data. Continuous monitoring allows organizations to identify performance deviations promptly and address them before they impact users.

- **Combine Multiple Data Sources:** Aggregate and correlate performance metrics from different sources, such as cloud provider monitoring services, application logs, and infrastructure metrics. This provides a comprehensive view of cloud performance and helps identify root causes of issues.

- **Visualization and Reporting:** Utilize visualizations, dashboards, and reports to present performance metrics in a concise and understandable format. Visual representations facilitate quick identification of trends, anomalies, and optimization opportunities.

- **Regular Performance Reviews:** Conduct regular performance reviews to assess cloud performance, identify improvement opportunities, and adjust objectives or thresholds as needed. Regular reviews ensure continuous optimization and alignment with changing business needs.

- **Automation and Intelligent Alerts:** Leverage automation and intelligent alerting systems to proactively detect performance anomalies and trigger alerts based on predefined thresholds. Automation reduces manual effort and enables timely interventions for optimizations.

11.3 Troubleshooting and Optimization Strategies

11.3.1. Troubleshooting Strategies:

- **Monitoring and Alerting:** The article suggests implementing robust monitoring tools that capture performance metrics and provide real-time alerts when issues arise. By proactively monitoring, organizations can detect anomalies and deviations from expected performance, enabling prompt troubleshooting and resolution. Monitoring and alerting ensure that potential problems are identified before they impact end-users and help maintain optimal cloud performance.

- **Log Analysis:** Utilizing log analysis tools to aggregate and analyze logs from various cloud resources and services is crucial for troubleshooting. Analyzing logs helps identify errors, exceptions, and other valuable information for diagnosing and resolving issues effectively. Logs provide insights into the system's behavior, allowing administrators to track events and trace the sequence of actions leading to a problem.

- **Root Cause Analysis:** The article emphasizes conducting thorough root cause analysis to identify the underlying causes of performance issues. By analyzing system logs, metrics, and configuration settings, organizations can pinpoint the root cause and address it accurately. Root cause analysis is vital to prevent recurring issues and ensure long-term stability.

- **Collaborative Troubleshooting:** The article encourages fostering collaboration among different teams, including development, operations, and support, to collectively troubleshoot and resolve issues. Effective communication and knowledge sharing enhance problem-solving capabilities and accelerate issue resolution. Collaboration ensures that different perspectives are considered, leading to comprehensive solutions.

- **Performance Testing:** Regularly performing performance testing to proactively identify potential bottlenecks, scalability limitations, and resource constraints is essential. Techniques like load testing, stress testing, and performance profiling help validate system performance and identify areas for improvement. Performance testing aids in identifying potential issues before they occur in a production environment.

11.3.2. Optimization Strategies:

- **Right-sizing Resources:** this strategy advises continuously assessing resource utilization and optimizing cloud resources, such as CPU, memory, storage, and network allocation, based on actual usage patterns. This ensures cost-effective resource utilization that matches workload demands. Right-sizing resources prevents overprovisioning, which can lead to unnecessary expenses, and avoids underprovisioning, which may result in performance degradation.

- **Autoscaling:** Implementing autoscaling mechanisms to automatically adjust resource capacity based on demand is crucial for handling varying workloads. Autoscaling ensures that resources are provisioned or deprovisioned dynamically, maintaining optimal performance during peak times and reducing costs during low-demand periods.

- **Caching and Content Delivery Networks (CDNs):** Utilizing caching mechanisms and CDNs to reduce the load on backend services, improve response times, and enhance user experience is beneficial. Caching frequently accessed data and utilizing CDN edge locations reduce latency and network congestion, resulting in faster content delivery.

- **Database Optimization:** Optimizing database configurations, indexes, and query performance to improve database responsiveness and overall system performance is essential. Techniques like database sharding, indexing strategies, and query optimization can enhance database efficiency and reduce query execution times.

- **Content Optimization:** Compressing and optimizing content, such as images, CSS, and JavaScript files, to minimize network transfer times and improve page load speeds is recommended. Content optimization techniques like minification and compression reduce file sizes, resulting in faster loading times and better user experiences.

- **Network Optimization:** Optimizing network configurations, including routing, load balancing, and traffic management, is vital to improve network performance and reliability. Leveraging cloud-native networking services and global traffic management can optimize network traffic distribution, ensuring efficient data delivery.

- **Security Optimization:** Implementing security best practices to protect cloud resources and mitigate potential vulnerabilities is crucial. Regularly reviewing and updating security configurations, access controls, and encryption mechanisms ensures a secure cloud environment without compromising performance.

11.3.3. Best Practices for Troubleshooting and Optimization in the Cloud:

- **Continuous Monitoring:** Implementing continuous monitoring of performance metrics, resource utilization, and logs proactively identifies issues and performance bottlenecks. Regularly reviewing monitoring data and adjusting thresholds as needed ensures optimal performance is maintained.

- **Automation and Orchestration:** Leveraging automation and orchestration tools streamlines troubleshooting and optimization processes. Automating routine tasks like resource provisioning and configuration management improves operational efficiency and reduces human error.

- **Performance Baseline:** Establishing performance baselines and benchmarks to track performance trends and deviations allows organizations to quickly identify abnormal behavior and take appropriate actions. Performance baselines provide a reference point for comparing current performance metrics.

- **Cloud Provider Support:** Engaging with cloud provider support channels to seek assistance in troubleshooting and optimization efforts is recommended. Cloud vendors offer expertise and resources to address complex issues and optimize cloud configurations.

- **Documentation and Knowledge Sharing:** Maintaining comprehensive documentation of troubleshooting procedures, optimization strategies, and lessons learned fosters a culture of continuous improvement and expedites issue resolution. Knowledge sharing among team members ensures collective learning and knowledge dissemination.

Exercise

Multiple Choice Questions

1. Which of the following is a key advantage of leveraging edge computing for IoT?

a. Reduced network costs

b. Increased cloud storage

c. Decreased data processing speed

d. Enhanced reliance on centralized servers

2. What is the primary benefit of using cloud-based quantum services?

a. Cost savings on quantum hardware

b. Enhanced security measures

c. Faster quantum processing

d. Improved user interfaces

3. Which technique is used to analyze historical monitoring data to identify long-term performance trends?

a. Comparative analysis

b. Anomaly detection

c. Trend analysis

d. Correlation analysis

4. How does edge computing contribute to reduced latency in IoT applications?

a. Processing data at the central cloud

b. Utilizing slower network connections

c. Bringing computational power closer to IoT devices

d. Relying on edge nodes for data processing

5. What does APM stand for in the context of cloud monitoring tools?

a. Advanced Performance Metrics

b. Automated Process Management

c. Application Performance Monitoring

d. Adaptive Provisioning Mechanism

6. What is the purpose of implementing real-time monitoring and alerting in cloud environments?

a. To identify historical performance trends

b. To detect potential security threats

c. To automate cloud resource provisioning

d. To address issues before they impact users

7. Which technique uses machine learning algorithms to identify abnormal behavior in cloud performance data?

a. Trend analysis

b. Comparative analysis

c. Anomaly detection

d. Correlation analysis

8. How does autoscaling benefit cloud performance optimization?

a. Increases overall resource costs

b. Reduces network bandwidth

c. Enables dynamic resource allocation

d. Provides advanced visualization tools

9. Which component of cloud monitoring tools tracks the health and performance of cloud infrastructure components?

a. Resource monitoring

b. Log monitoring and analysis

c. Application Performance Monitoring (APM)

d. Infrastructure monitoring

10. What is the significance of comprehensive monitoring in cloud environments?

a. Focuses only on resource utilization metrics

b. Provides insights into cloud provider services

c. Covers different layers of the cloud stack

d. Improves cloud-native networking

11. What is the primary purpose of conducting root cause analysis in cloud troubleshooting?

a. To identify abnormal behavior in logs

b. To optimize resource utilization

c. To trace the sequence of actions leading to an issue

d. To establish clear performance objectives

12. How can content optimization improve cloud performance?

a. Reducing cloud service costs

b. Increasing network latency

c. Enhancing security measures

d. Minimizing data transfer times

Review Questions

1. Why is monitoring essential in the cloud environment?
2. What are some key performance metrics in the cloud?
3. How can anomaly detection be helpful in cloud performance analysis?
4. Why is collaborative troubleshooting important in cloud environments?
5. What is the significance of continuous monitoring in cloud performance optimization?
6. How does autoscaling benefit cloud environments?
7. What are some content optimization techniques to improve cloud performance?
8. Why is database optimization important in cloud environments?
9. How can security optimization be balanced with cloud performance?

10. What is the role of automation in troubleshooting and optimization?
11. How can performance baselines be helpful in cloud performance management?

Answer Secton
Multiple Choice Questions

1. a) Reduced network costs
2. a) Cost savings on quantum hardware
3. c) Trend analysis
4. c) Bringing computational power closer to IoT devices
5. c) Application Performance Monitoring
6. d) To address issues before they impact users
7. c) Anomaly detection
8. c) Enables dynamic resource allocation
9. d) Infrastructure monitoring
10. c) Covers different layers of the cloud stack
11. c) To trace the sequence of actions leading to an issue
12. d) Minimizing data transfer times

Review Questions

1. Monitoring is crucial in the cloud environment to track resource utilization, detect performance issues, ensure optimal user experience, and proactively address potential problems.

2. Key performance metrics in the cloud include response time, latency, throughput, error rates, and resource utilization metrics like CPU, memory, storage, and network bandwidth.

3. Anomaly detection uses machine learning algorithms and statistical analysis to identify abnormal behavior or deviations from normal performance patterns. It helps in identifying performance issues, security threats, or configuration errors.

4. Collaborative troubleshooting involves different teams working together, such as development, operations, and support, to collectively identify and resolve issues. Effective communication and knowledge sharing enhance problem-solving capabilities and accelerate issue resolution.

5. Continuous monitoring allows organizations to capture real-time data, promptly detect performance deviations, and take proactive actions to optimize cloud resources and maintain optimal performance.

6. Autoscaling automatically adjusts resource capacity based on demand, ensuring optimal performance during peak times and cost-efficiency during low-demand periods.

7. Content optimization techniques like minification and compression reduce file sizes, leading to faster loading times and better user experiences.

8. Database optimization improves database responsiveness and overall system performance by optimizing configurations, indexes, and query performance.

9. Security optimization involves implementing best practices to protect cloud resources while avoiding performance degradation. Regularly reviewing and updating security configurations and access controls ensures a secure environment without compromising performance.

10. Automation streamlines troubleshooting and optimization processes, improving operational efficiency and reducing human error in repetitive tasks.

11. Performance baselines provide a reference point for comparing current performance metrics, allowing organizations to quickly identify abnormal behavior and take appropriate actions for optimization.

Chapter 12: Cloud Governance and Management

12.1 Achieving Effective Cloud Governance: Frameworks for Success

Cloud governance frameworks are essential for organizations to establish effective policies, controls, and processes for managing cloud resources. By adopting a structured approach to cloud governance, organizations can mitigate risks, optimize costs, ensure compliance, and enhance operational efficiency. Popular frameworks such as CSA CCM, NIST CCSRA, ISO 27001, and CIS Controls provide valuable guidelines and best practices for implementing cloud governance. By leveraging these frameworks and tailoring them to their specific needs, organizations can achieve successful cloud adoption, secure their cloud environments, and maximize the value derived from cloud services.

12.1.1. Importance of Cloud Governance:

- **Risk Management:** Cloud governance helps identify and address risks related to cloud adoption, such as data breaches, compliance violations, and service disruptions. It establishes controls and policies to safeguard sensitive data, manage access, and enforce security measures.

- **Cost Optimization:** Governance frameworks enable organizations to optimize cloud costs by implementing policies and processes for resource allocation, usage tracking, and cost management. They provide visibility into cloud expenses and promote efficient resource utilization.

- **Compliance and Regulatory Requirements:** Cloud governance ensures adherence to industry-specific regulations and compliance standards. It establishes controls and processes to protect sensitive data, enforce privacy requirements, and facilitate audits and reporting.

- **Operational Efficiency:** Governance frameworks promote operational efficiency by establishing standardized processes, automation, and best practices for managing cloud resources. They enable organizations to streamline operations, enhance collaboration, and improve overall productivity.

12.1.2. Key Components of Cloud Governance Frameworks:

1. **Policies and Procedures:** Governance frameworks define policies and procedures for cloud resource provisioning, access management, data protection, and incident response. These policies guide decision-making and ensure consistent practices across the organization.

2. **Compliance and Security Controls:** Governance frameworks establish controls and mechanisms to ensure compliance with regulatory requirements and enforce security measures. They include identity and access management, encryption, network security, and vulnerability management.

3. **Risk Assessment and Management:** Governance frameworks incorporate risk assessment methodologies to identify and evaluate risks associated with cloud adoption. Risk management processes enable organizations to implement controls and mitigation strategies to address identified risks.

4. **Performance and Monitoring:** Governance frameworks establish performance metrics and monitoring processes to track and measure cloud resource utilization, service availability, and performance. Monitoring ensures compliance with service-level agreements (SLAs) and enables timely issue detection and resolution.

5. **Training and Awareness:** Governance frameworks include training and awareness programs to educate employees on cloud governance policies, security practices, and compliance requirements. Training ensures that individuals understand their responsibilities and adhere to established guidelines.

12.1.3. Popular Cloud Governance Frameworks:

- **Cloud Security Alliance (CSA) Cloud Control Matrix (CCM):** CCM provides a comprehensive set of security controls and best practices aligned with industry standards and regulations. It covers various domains, including data security, compliance, identity and access management, and incident response.

- **National Institute of Standards and Technology (NIST) Cloud Computing Security Reference Architecture (CCSRA):** CCSRA offers a framework for securing cloud computing environments. It provides a structured approach to identifying security requirements, assessing risks, and implementing appropriate security controls.

- **International Organization for Standardization (ISO) 27001:** ISO 27001 is a widely adopted information security standard that includes requirements for establishing, implementing, maintaining, and continually improving an information security management system (ISMS). It provides a systematic approach to managing security risks in cloud environments.

- **Center for Internet Security (CIS) Controls:** The CIS Controls framework offers a prioritized set of best practices for cybersecurity. It provides guidelines for implementing technical controls, security policies, and procedures to protect cloud resources from common cyber threats.

12.1.4. Benefits of Cloud Governance Frameworks:

- **Consistent Policies and Standards:** Governance frameworks establish consistent policies, standards, and procedures for cloud resource management across the organization. This promotes alignment, reduces inconsistencies, and ensures compliance with internal and external requirements.

- **Risk Mitigation:** Governance frameworks enable organizations to identify, assess, and mitigate risks associated with cloud adoption. By implementing appropriate controls and processes, organizations can proactively manage risks and prevent potential security breaches or compliance violations.

- **Enhanced Security and Compliance:** Governance frameworks ensure that cloud resources adhere to security and compliance requirements. They provide guidelines for implementing robust security controls, enforcing access management, and protecting sensitive data.

- **Cost Optimization:** Governance frameworks facilitate cost optimization by establishing policies and processes for resource provisioning, usage tracking, and cost management. Organizations can monitor and optimize cloud expenses, ensuring efficient resource utilization and reducing unnecessary costs.

- **Improved Operational Efficiency:** Governance frameworks promote standardized processes, automation, and best practices for managing cloud resources. This streamlines operations, enhances collaboration, and improves overall productivity and efficiency in the cloud environment

12.2 Resource Allocation and Management: Optimizing Cloud Resources for Efficiency

Efficient resource allocation and management are vital for maximizing the performance, scalability, and cost-effectiveness of cloud environments. By considering workload patterns, leveraging elasticity, right-sizing resources, and implementing effective monitoring and automation practices, organizations can optimize resource utilization and achieve significant cost savings. Load balancing, capacity planning, and regular optimization exercises further enhance resource efficiency. By adopting best practices and continuously evaluating resource allocation strategies, organizations can effectively manage their cloud resources, deliver optimal application performance, and achieve their business objectives in the cloud.

12.2.1. Importance of Resource Allocation and Management:

- **Cost Optimization:** Proper resource allocation and management directly impact cost optimization in cloud environments. By avoiding overprovisioning and underutilization of resources, organizations can align resource allocation with workload demands, leading to minimized unnecessary expenditures and overall cost-effectiveness.

- **Scalability and Performance:** Efficient resource allocation enables organizations to scale their cloud infrastructure based on demand. The ability to allocate resources dynamically and automatically allows organizations to ensure optimal performance during peak periods and accommodate fluctuating workloads without sacrificing efficiency.

- **Application Performance:** Resource allocation significantly influences application performance in the cloud. By allocating the right amount of resources, organizations can provide consistent and responsive user experiences, ensuring that applications perform optimally under varying workloads.

- **Governance and Compliance:** Resource allocation and management play a crucial role in ensuring compliance with governance policies, security standards, and regulatory requirements. Proper allocation and access controls help protect sensitive data and maintain compliance across the entire cloud environment.

12.2.2. Considerations for Efficient Resource Utilization:

- **Workload Analysis:** A thorough analysis of workload patterns, demand variations, and performance requirements is essential to understand resource needs accurately. By analyzing historical data and projecting future demands, organizations can allocate resources effectively and avoid wasteful practices.

- **Elasticity and Scalability:** Leveraging the elasticity and scalability features of the cloud is crucial for efficient resource allocation. Implementing auto-scaling mechanisms that automatically adjust resource capacity based on workload demands can optimize both performance and cost efficiency.

- **Right-sizing:** Right-sizing cloud resources involves matching the allocated resources with the actual workload requirements. By continuously monitoring resource utilization metrics and adjusting resource allocation accordingly, organizations can avoid overprovisioning or underutilization.

- **Resource Tagging and Labeling:** Implementing resource tagging and labeling strategies helps track and categorize cloud resources efficiently. This enables proper resource management, cost allocation, and easy identification of unused or underutilized resources.

- **Lifecycle Management:** Resource lifecycle management practices ensure efficient resource use throughout their lifespan. This includes decommissioning unused or outdated resources, optimizing storage utilization, and archiving data when appropriate.

12.2.3. Best Practices for Optimizing Cloud Resources:

- **Continuous Monitoring and Analysis:** Robust monitoring tools should be implemented to track resource utilization, performance metrics, and cost patterns continuously. Regularly analyzing this data helps identify resource bottlenecks, optimize allocation, and detect opportunities for cost savings.

- **Automation and Orchestration:** Leveraging automation and orchestration tools streamlines resource allocation and management processes. Automated provisioning, resource tagging, and policy-based allocation can optimize resource utilization and simplify management tasks.

- **Load Balancing:** Utilizing load balancing mechanisms ensures even distribution of workloads across available resources. Load balancers help achieve efficient resource utilization, improve application responsiveness, and enable scalability during traffic spikes.

- **Reserved Instances and Savings Plans:** Taking advantage of cloud providers' offerings, such as reserved instances or savings plans, can optimize costs for long-term resource requirements. These options provide discounted pricing and help organizations achieve significant cost savings.

- **Regular Capacity Planning:** Conducting regular capacity planning exercises allows organizations to assess resource needs, anticipate growth, and align resource allocation accordingly. Capacity planning ensures that organizations have the necessary resources in place to handle increasing workloads without unnecessary expenditures.

- **Cost Visibility and Optimization:** Implementing cost management tools and practices provides visibility into cloud expenses. Analyzing cost breakdowns, identifying cost drivers, and optimizing resource allocation based on cost-performance trade-offs can lead to more efficient resource usage.

- **Continuous Optimization:** Establishing a culture of continuous optimization involves regularly reviewing and fine-tuning resource allocation strategies. Organizations should evaluate the effectiveness of resource allocation decisions, explore new cloud services, and adopt emerging technologies to drive ongoing improvements.

12.3 Policy Enforcement and Compliance in the Cloud: Ensuring Governance and Security

Policy enforcement and compliance are vital components of cloud governance, enabling organizations to establish secure and compliant cloud environments. By developing comprehensive policies, leveraging automation, and enforcing access controls and configuration management, organizations can maintain robust policy enforcement. Regular monitoring, training, and collaboration with cloud providers contribute to effective policy enforcement and compliance. By following best practices, conducting regular policy reviews, and implementing continuous monitoring, organizations can ensure policy adherence, mitigate security risks, and demonstrate compliance with industry standards and regulatory requirements in the cloud. A strong policy enforcement and compliance framework will ultimately lead to a secure and well-governed cloud environment, safeguarding sensitive data and bolstering the organization's overall security posture.

12.3.1. Importance of Policy Enforcement and Compliance:

- **Security and Risk Mitigation:** Policy enforcement ensures that security controls, access management, and data protection measures are consistently applied across all cloud resources. By doing so, it helps mitigate security risks and protects sensitive information from unauthorized access or breaches.

- **Regulatory Compliance:** Compliance with industry-specific regulations, data protection laws, and privacy requirements is essential for organizations operating in the cloud. Policy enforcement ensures that cloud operations align with relevant regulations and compliance frameworks, avoiding potential legal and financial consequences.

- **Governance and Control:** Policy enforcement empowers organizations to maintain control over their cloud resources and applications. By establishing rules and guidelines for resource allocation, access management, data handling, and configuration management, it ensures consistent and secure practices.

- **Auditing and Accountability:** Policy enforcement facilitates auditing and accountability by providing a framework to track and monitor compliance with policies and regulations. This enables organizations to demonstrate adherence to internal controls and external requirements during audits and assessments.

12.3.2. Considerations for Effective Policy Enforcement and Compliance:

- **Policy Development:** Develop comprehensive policies that align with business objectives, security requirements, and regulatory frameworks. Well-defined policies should clearly outline expectations, guidelines, and standards for cloud resource usage, access controls, data handling, and incident response.

- **Automation and Orchestration:** Leverage automation and orchestration tools to enforce policies consistently across cloud resources. Automation helps ensure that policy enforcement is efficient, accurate, and scalable, reducing the risk of human errors or inconsistencies.

- **Access Controls and Identity Management:** Implement robust identity and access management (IAM) practices to enforce fine-grained access controls and user permissions. Assign appropriate roles and permissions to users, and regularly review and update access policies based on changing requirements.

- **Configuration Management:** Enforce configuration management policies to maintain consistency and security across cloud resources. Implement configuration management tools and processes to standardize configurations, prevent unauthorized changes, and detect configuration drift.

- **Monitoring and Auditing:** Deploy monitoring and auditing tools to track and log activities across cloud resources. Regularly review logs and audit trails to ensure policy compliance, detect policy violations, and investigate any suspicious activities or incidents promptly.

- **Training and Awareness:** Conduct regular training and awareness programs to educate employees on policies, security best practices, and compliance requirements. Promote a culture of security awareness and ensure that individuals understand their roles and responsibilities in maintaining policy compliance.

12.3.3. Best Practices for Policy Enforcement and Compliance:

- **Regular Policy Reviews:** Conduct periodic reviews of policies to ensure they remain up-to-date and aligned with evolving business and regulatory requirements. Involve stakeholders from different teams to gather feedback and make necessary adjustments.

- **Continuous Monitoring and Remediation:** Implement continuous monitoring of policy compliance using automated tools and processes. Monitor and track violations, and promptly address any non-compliance issues through remediation efforts and corrective actions.

- **Documentation and Documentation:** Maintain comprehensive documentation of policies, procedures, and controls. Document the rationale behind policy decisions, track changes, and maintain an audit trail to demonstrate compliance and facilitate future policy reviews.

- **Collaboration with Cloud Providers:** Leverage the security and compliance features provided by cloud service providers. Understand the shared responsibility model and collaborate with providers to ensure that policies and controls are effectively implemented in the cloud environment.

- **Regular Compliance Assessments:** Conduct regular compliance assessments and audits to validate policy enforcement and identify any gaps or non-compliance issues. Collaborate with internal or external auditors to assess the effectiveness of policy enforcement practices.

- **Incident Response and Reporting:** Develop an incident response plan that aligns with policy enforcement and compliance objectives. Establish procedures for reporting and addressing policy violations or security incidents, and ensure timely and appropriate response measures are implemented.

Exercise

Multiple Choice Questions

1. Cloud governance is essential for organizations seeking to achieve which of the following?

a. Reduced cloud costs

b. Increased data breaches

c. Compliance with security regulations

d. Dependency on centralized servers

2. Which factor does efficient resource allocation and management in the cloud directly impact?

a. Scalability and performance

b. Application development

c. Governance and control

d. Cost optimization

3. What is the primary purpose of leveraging automation and orchestration in cloud resource allocation?

a. Cost reduction

b. Efficient policy enforcement

c. Simplified management tasks

d. Increased scalability

4. What is the significance of compliance with industry-specific regulations in the cloud?

a. Increased resource costs

b. Protection from data breaches

c. Reduced application performance

d. Dependency on centralized servers

5. Which component of cloud governance establishes guidelines for resource allocation and data protection?

a. Continuous monitoring and analysis

b. Automation and orchestration

c. Policies and procedures

d. Resource tagging and labeling

6. What is the primary objective of implementing access controls and identity management in cloud environments?

a. Enforcing encryption mechanisms

b. Tracking resource utilization

c. Ensuring efficient resource allocation

d. Enforcing fine-grained access controls

7. How can organizations effectively optimize cloud costs through resource allocation?

a. Regularly reviewing performance metrics

b. Leveraging cloud provider offerings

c. Increasing overprovisioning

d. Implementing resource tagging

8. What role does automation play in policy enforcement?

a. Increases human errors

b. Simplifies compliance audits

c. Reduces the need for cloud services

d. Raises cloud costs

9. Why is continuous monitoring and analysis important in policy enforcement?

a. To maximize cloud scalability

b. To streamline resource allocation

c. To prevent human errors

d. To track policy compliance

10. How does proper configuration management contribute to policy enforcement?

a. Ensures compliance with regulations

b. Establishes standardized resource allocation

c. Mitigates security risks

d. Enables efficient cloud scaling

11. What is the primary objective of conducting regular compliance assessments?

a. Establishing automated policy enforcement

b. Identifying gaps in cloud governance

c. Reducing cloud costs

d. Increasing cloud scalability

12. What is the ultimate goal of effective policy enforcement and compliance in the cloud?

a. Reduced cloud resource allocation

b. Achieving regulatory compliance

c. Dependency on centralized servers

d. Ensuring efficient application development

Review Questions

1. What is the significance of cloud governance in organizations using cloud services?
2. How do cloud governance frameworks contribute to ensuring effective policy enforcement?
3. What are the key components of cloud governance frameworks, and how do they enhance cloud
4. security?
5. How does effective resource allocation in the cloud impact an organization's operational
6. efficiency?
7. What role does automation play in optimizing cloud resources?
8. How can organizations leverage cloud provider offerings to optimize costs?

1. What are the benefits of continuous monitoring and analysis in cloud resource optimization?
2. How does right-sizing of cloud resources contribute to cost optimization and performance
3. improvement?
4. What is the significance of collaboration with cloud providers in cloud governance?

Answer Section
Multiple Choice Questions

1. c) Compliance with security regulations
2. d) Cost optimization
3. c) Simplified management tasks
4. b) Protection from data breaches
5. c) Policies and procedures
6. d) Enforcing fine-grained access controls
7. b) Leveraging cloud provider offerings
8. b) Simplifies compliance audits
9. d) To track policy compliance
10. c) Mitigates security risks
11. b) Identifying gaps in cloud governance

12. b) Achieving regulatory compliance

Review Questions

1. Cloud governance plays a critical role in organizations using cloud services as it ensures secure, compliant, and efficient cloud operations. It involves creating policies, controls, and processes to manage cloud resources effectively, mitigating risks, and optimizing cloud usage. Through governance, organizations can safeguard sensitive data, enforce security measures, and adhere to regulatory requirements. It also promotes cost optimization by tracking and managing cloud expenses, optimizing resource allocation, and avoiding overprovisioning. Governance fosters operational efficiency by standardizing processes, promoting collaboration, and streamlining cloud resource management. Ultimately, it empowers organizations to achieve successful cloud adoption and maximize the value derived from cloud services.

2. Cloud governance frameworks establish comprehensive policies, procedures, and controls to guide policy enforcement effectively. These frameworks provide a structured approach to cloud resource management, ensuring consistency, security, and compliance across the organization. By defining clear policies for resource provisioning, access management, data protection, and incident response, organizations can enforce rules consistently. Additionally, governance frameworks often incorporate automation and orchestration tools to streamline policy enforcement. Automation ensures that policies are efficiently applied to cloud resources, reducing human errors and ensuring scalability. Overall, cloud governance frameworks play a crucial role in establishing a strong foundation for effective policy enforcement and maintaining a secure and well-governed cloud environment.

3. The key components of cloud governance frameworks include policies and procedures, compliance and security controls, risk assessment and management, performance monitoring, and training and awareness programs. Policies and procedures define guidelines for resource management, access controls, data protection, and incident response. Compliance and security controls ensure adherence to industry regulations and enforce security measures. Risk assessment identifies potential risks and implements mitigation strategies. Performance monitoring tracks resource utilization and service availability. Training and awareness programs educate employees on policies and security practices.

These components enhance cloud security by providing a systematic approach to managing cloud resources. Policies and controls protect sensitive data and enforce security measures. Compliance ensures adherence to regulations, and risk assessment mitigates security threats. Performance monitoring detects anomalies, and training promotes a culture of security awareness.

1. Effective resource allocation in the cloud significantly impacts an organization's operational efficiency. Proper allocation ensures that cloud resources align with workload demands, avoiding underprovisioning or overprovisioning. This optimization leads to better resource utilization and reduced costs, maximizing efficiency. Efficient resource allocation also enhances application performance by providing the necessary resources to meet user demands consistently. The ability to scale resources dynamically based on workload fluctuations ensures optimal performance during peak periods without compromising efficiency during low-demand periods. Overall, effective resource allocation streamlines operations, minimizes waste, and improves overall productivity and efficiency in the cloud environment.

2. Automation plays a crucial role in optimizing cloud resources by streamlining resource management tasks and ensuring efficiency and consistency. Automated provisioning allows organizations to scale resources based on demand, enabling them to optimize performance during peak times and reduce costs

during low-demand periods. It minimizes human errors and standardizes resource allocation, preventing overprovisioning or underutilization. Automation also facilitates policy enforcement by efficiently applying access controls and configuration management across cloud resources. By leveraging automation, organizations can achieve cost savings, operational efficiency, and improved scalability in their cloud environments, ultimately maximizing the value derived from cloud services.

3. Organizations can leverage cloud provider offerings to optimize costs by taking advantage of various cost-saving programs and services. For example, cloud providers offer discounted pricing options like reserved instances or savings plans, allowing organizations to commit to long-term usage at lower rates. By selecting the appropriate pricing model and optimizing resource allocation, organizations can achieve significant cost savings. Additionally, cloud providers often provide tools and services that enable cost tracking and optimization, helping organizations identify cost drivers and areas for improvement. By collaborating with cloud providers and utilizing their cost-saving offerings, organizations can effectively manage cloud expenses and optimize their cloud investments.

4. Continuous monitoring and analysis offer several benefits in cloud resource optimization. By tracking resource utilization, performance metrics, and cost patterns in real-time, organizations can identify resource bottlenecks and inefficiencies promptly. Regular analysis of monitoring data allows for quick detection of issues and the implementation of optimization measures before they escalate. It also provides insights into performance trends and patterns, enabling organizations to make informed decisions about resource allocation and capacity planning. Continuous monitoring ensures adherence to service-level agreements (SLAs) and enables timely issue detection and resolution. Overall, continuous monitoring and analysis play a crucial role in maintaining resource efficiency, cost optimization, and proactive management of cloud resources.

5. Right-sizing of cloud resources involves matching resource allocation with the actual workload requirements. By continuously monitoring resource utilization metrics and adjusting resource allocation accordingly, organizations can avoid overprovisioning or underutilization. Right-sizing contributes to cost optimization by ensuring that cloud resources are provisioned based on actual usage patterns, eliminating unnecessary expenses on unused resources. It improves performance by providing the necessary resources to meet workload demands accurately, resulting in optimized application responsiveness and user experiences. Right-sizing also enables efficient resource utilization, as organizations allocate resources precisely as needed, maximizing cost-effectiveness and performance in the cloud environment.

6. Collaboration with cloud providers is crucial in cloud governance as it allows organizations to leverage their expertise, services, and security features. Cloud providers offer native tools and services that align with governance requirements, such as identity and access management, encryption, and compliance controls. By understanding the shared responsibility model, organizations can ensure that their policies and controls align with those offered by the cloud provider. Collaborating with providers enables organizations to implement robust security measures and ensure compliance with industry standards and regulations. It also fosters ongoing communication and feedback, allowing organizations to adapt their governance strategies to changes in the cloud environment effectively.

Chapter 13: DevOps and Continuous Delivery in the Cloud

13.1 Introduction to DevOps: Bridging the Gap between Development and Operations

DevOps is a transformative approach that brings development and operations teams together to streamline software delivery, improve collaboration, and enhance business agility. By implementing DevOps principles such as collaboration, automation, continuous integration, and delivery, organizations can accelerate time-to-market, improve software quality, and drive innovation. By fostering a culture of collaboration, embracing automation, and adopting best practices, organizations can successfully implement DevOps and unlock the benefits of faster, more reliable software delivery. DevOps represents a fundamental shift in how software is developed and delivered, and organizations that embrace it stand to gain a competitive advantage in today's fast-paced digital landscape.

13.1.1. What is DevOps?

DevOps represents both a cultural and technical movement that seeks to unite development (Dev) and operations (Ops) teams. The primary objective is to foster a collaborative and communicative environment throughout the entire software development lifecycle. DevOps emphasizes breaking down traditional organizational silos, embracing automation, and cultivating a culture of continuous improvement, all with the aim of delivering software more rapidly and reliably.

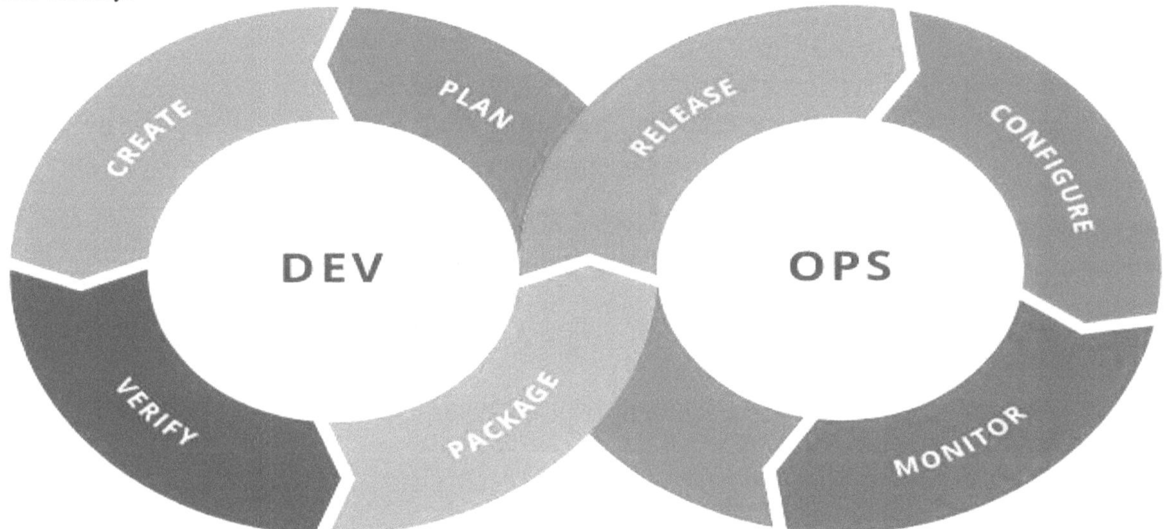

13.1.2. Key Principles of DevOps:

- **Collaboration and Communication:** DevOps places a strong emphasis on collaboration and open communication between development, operations, and other stakeholders involved in software delivery. It promotes cross-functional teams, shared responsibilities, and a culture of transparency.

- **Automation:** Automation lies at the core of DevOps practices. It involves automating repetitive tasks, such as building, testing, and deploying software, to reduce manual effort, minimize errors, and enhance overall efficiency.

- **Continuous Integration and Delivery:** DevOps encourages the practice of continuous integration (CI), which entails frequently integrating code changes into a shared repository, followed by automated testing to detect integration issues early. Continuous delivery (CD) focuses on automating the deployment process, enabling validated code to be delivered to production rapidly and reliably.

- **Infrastructure as Code:** Infrastructure as Code (IaC) treats infrastructure configurations as software code. This approach allows for version control, automation, and reproducibility of infrastructure, ensuring consistency across different environments.

- **Continuous Monitoring and Feedback:** DevOps emphasizes the importance of continuous monitoring of applications and infrastructure to gain insights into performance, availability, and user experience. Feedback loops help identify and address issues promptly, driving a culture of continuous improvement.

13.1.3. Benefits of DevOps:

- **Faster Time-to-Market:** DevOps enables rapid software delivery by automating processes, reducing manual errors, and facilitating faster feedback loops. This allows organizations to respond quickly to market demands and deliver new features and updates more frequently.

- **Improved Collaboration:** DevOps breaks down traditional barriers between teams, fostering collaboration and shared responsibility. This results in better communication, alignment, and knowledge sharing, leading to enhanced teamwork and overall efficiency.

- **Increased Agility and Flexibility:** DevOps enables organizations to adapt quickly to changing business requirements and market conditions. It facilitates rapid scaling, seamless deployments, and the ability to iterate and improve applications continuously.

- **Enhanced Software Quality:** DevOps practices, such as continuous integration, automated testing, and monitoring, significantly improve software quality. Issues are detected and addressed early in the development cycle, reducing defects and enhancing overall reliability.

- **Cost Optimization:** By automating processes and improving resource utilization, DevOps helps optimize costs. It minimizes manual effort, reduces the risk of errors, and ensures efficient use of infrastructure resources.

13.1.4. Best Practices for DevOps Implementation:

- **Cultural Transformation:** Successful DevOps implementation requires a cultural transformation. Organizations should encourage shared goals, transparency, and open communication between teams. Breaking down silos and fostering a mindset of continuous learning and improvement is essential.

- **Automation:** Identify and automate manual, repetitive tasks in the software development lifecycle. This includes building, testing, and deployment processes, as well as infrastructure provisioning and configuration management.

- **Continuous Integration and Delivery:** Implement CI/CD pipelines to automate code integration, testing, and deployment. Continuously deliver small, incremental changes to production, enabling rapid feedback and reducing the risk of larger failures.

- **Infrastructure as Code:** Treat infrastructure configurations as code, using tools and techniques to manage and provision infrastructure programmatically. This allows for version control, consistency, and reproducibility across environments.

- **Continuous Monitoring and Feedback:** Implement robust monitoring solutions to gain insights into application performance, infrastructure health, and user experience. Utilize feedback loops to capture user feedback, monitor metrics, and drive continuous improvement.

- **Security and Compliance:** Integrate security practices into the DevOps workflow from the beginning. Implement secure coding practices, automated security testing, and incorporate security reviews and compliance checks into the CI/CD pipeline.

13.2 CI/CD Pipelines in the Cloud: Streamlining Software Delivery and Deployment

CI/CD pipelines in the cloud have revolutionized software delivery and deployment, enabling organizations to achieve faster time-to-market, higher quality software, and enhanced collaboration. By implementing automated workflows, integrating testing at each stage, and leveraging cloud scalability, organizations can accelerate software development cycles and improve overall efficiency. Following best practices such as IaC adoption, parallel execution, environment isolation, and continuous improvement ensures the success of CI/CD pipelines in the cloud By embracing CI/CD practices

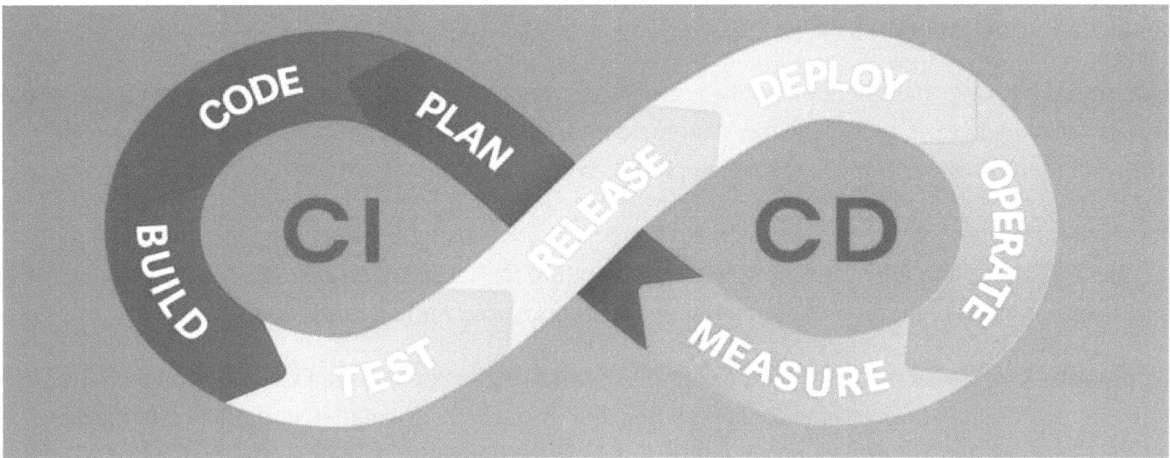

13.2.1. What are CI/CD Pipelines? z

CI/CD pipelines are automated workflows that facilitate the integration of code changes, the building of software artifacts, the execution of automated tests, and the seamless deployment of applications to production environments. These pipelines enable developers to continuously integrate code changes, validate them through automated tests, and deliver reliable software releases frequently.

13.2.2. Benefits of CI/CD Pipelines in the Cloud:

- **Faster Time-to-Market:** CI/CD pipelines empower rapid software delivery by reducing manual effort and minimizing errors. By automating processes and enabling quick feedback loops, organizations can deliver new features and updates to users faster, gaining a competitive edge.

- **Improved Collaboration and Efficiency:** CI/CD pipelines promote collaboration between development, operations, and other stakeholders. The automated nature of the pipelines streamlines workflows, reduces manual handoffs, and enhances overall efficiency and productivity.

- **Quality Assurance and Reliability:** Automated testing and quality assurance checks integrated into CI/CD pipelines ensure that code changes are thoroughly validated. This reduces the risk of introducing defects or regressions, resulting in more reliable software releases.

- **Scalability and Flexibility:** Cloud environments provide the scalability and flexibility required for CI/CD pipelines. Organizations can dynamically provision resources, scale infrastructure based on workload demands, and easily accommodate growing user bases.

- **Rollback and Recovery:** CI/CD pipelines simplify rollback and recovery processes in case of deployment issues or incidents. By following version control practices and maintaining artifact repositories, organizations can easily revert to a stable state and recover from failures.

13.2.3. Key Components of CI/CD Pipelines:

- **Source Control:** Utilize a version control system (e.g., Git) to manage code changes, track history, and enable collaboration among developers. A reliable source control system ensures proper versioning and facilitates code integration into the pipeline.

- **Automated Builds:** Implement build automation tools (e.g., Jenkins, CircleCI) to automate the compilation, packaging, and creation of software artifacts. Automated builds ensure consistency, reproducibility, and reduce manual effort.

- **Automated Testing:** Incorporate various testing types, such as unit tests, integration tests, and regression tests, into the CI/CD pipeline. Automated testing tools (e.g., JUnit, Selenium) ensure code quality and identify issues early in the development process.

- **Deployment Automation:** Automate the deployment process using infrastructure as code (IaC) tools (e.g., AWS CloudFormation, Terraform) and configuration management tools (e.g., Ansible, Chef). This enables consistent and reliable deployment of applications across multiple environments.

- **Continuous Monitoring:** Integrate monitoring solutions (e.g., Prometheus, Datadog) into the CI/CD pipeline to capture metrics and monitor application and infrastructure health. Continuous monitoring provides visibility into performance, availability, and user experience.

- **Release Management:** Implement release management practices to plan and coordinate software releases. Define release strategies, manage versioning, and control the rollout of new features or updates to production environments.

13.2.4. Best Practices for CI/CD Pipelines in the Cloud:

- **Infrastructure as Code (IaC):** Embrace IaC practices to define, provision, and manage infrastructure resources programmatically. This ensures consistency, reproducibility, and scalability in the cloud environment.

- **Automated Testing at Each Stage:** Include automated tests at each stage of the CI/CD pipeline to validate code changes thoroughly. This ensures that issues are detected early and reduces the risk of deploying faulty code to production.

- **Parallel Execution:** Optimize pipeline performance by parallelizing build and test processes. Distribute workloads across multiple compute resources to accelerate build times and provide faster feedback to developers.

- **Environment Isolation:** Isolate development, testing, and production environments to ensure the stability and reliability of each stage in the pipeline. Use separate infrastructure and configurations for each environment to avoid interference and maintain consistent behavior.

- **Continuous Feedback and Improvement:** Establish a culture of continuous feedback and improvement. Regularly review pipeline performance, collect feedback from stakeholders, and iterate on the pipeline to optimize processes and address pain points.

- **Security and Compliance:** Incorporate security measures into the CI/CD pipeline. Implement security testing, vulnerability scanning, and compliance checks to ensure that software releases meet security and regulatory requirements.

13.3 Infrastructure as Code (IaC): Streamlining Cloud Infrastructure Management

Infrastructure as Code (IaC) has revolutionized cloud infrastructure management, providing organizations with the ability to provision, manage, and scale infrastructure resources programmatically. By treating infrastructure as software, IaC enables consistency, scalability, and automation, resulting in improved efficiency, reduced errors, and better resource utilization. By adhering to key principles and best practices, organizations can successfully implement IaC, gain the benefits of infrastructure consistency, and achieve greater agility in managing their cloud environments.

13.3.1. What is Infrastructure as Code (IaC)?

Infrastructure as Code (IaC) is an approach that involves defining, managing, and provisioning infrastructure resources using code-based configurations and scripts. Instead of manually setting up and configuring infrastructure components, IaC allows organizations to automate the entire process, making infrastructure management more efficient and consistent.

13.3.2. Benefits of Infrastructure as Code:

- **Consistency and Reproducibility:** IaC ensures that infrastructure resources are provisioned consistently and reproducibly. Infrastructure configurations are defined in code, enabling easy replication of environments and reducing the risk of configuration drift or inconsistencies.

- **Scalability and Flexibility:** With IaC, organizations can dynamically scale infrastructure resources based on workload demands. This scalability enables efficient resource allocation and cost optimization, ensuring resources are provisioned as needed.

- **Version Control and Auditing:** IaC allows infrastructure configurations to be versioned, tracked, and audited. This provides visibility into changes, facilitates collaboration, and simplifies the process of rolling back or reviewing infrastructure changes.

- **Automation and Efficiency:** IaC automates the provisioning and management of infrastructure resources. This reduces manual effort, eliminates human errors, and improves overall efficiency in managing cloud infrastructure.

- **Disaster Recovery and Resilience:** IaC facilitates disaster recovery and resilience by enabling organizations to recreate infrastructure environments quickly and accurately. In the event of a failure or disaster, infrastructure can be redeployed using IaC scripts, minimizing downtime and data loss.

13.3.3. Key Principles of Infrastructure as Code:

- **Declarative Configuration:** IaC follows a declarative approach, where infrastructure configurations are specified as desired states rather than imperative commands. Infrastructure tools interpret these configurations and ensure the infrastructure matches the desired state.

- **Idempotency:** IaC scripts and configurations are designed to be idempotent, meaning they can be run multiple times without causing unintended side effects. This allows for repeatable and predictable infrastructure provisioning.

- **Modularity and Reusability:** IaC promotes modularity and reusability of infrastructure code. Infrastructure components can be defined as modules and reused across multiple projects or environments, reducing duplication and simplifying maintenance.

- **Continuous Integration and Delivery (CI/CD):** IaC integrates with CI/CD pipelines to automate infrastructure deployment and ensure consistent environments throughout the software delivery process. Infrastructure changes are versioned, tested, and deployed alongside application code changes.

- **Testing and Validation:** IaC configurations can be tested and validated to ensure they meet the desired requirements. Automated testing tools can be integrated into the CI/CD pipeline to validate infrastructure configurations and catch issues early in the process.

13.3.4. Best Practices for Implementing Infrastructure as Code:

- **Use Version Control:** Store infrastructure code in a version control system (e.g., Git) to track changes, facilitate collaboration, and enable rollback or review of infrastructure configurations.

- **Embrace Modularity:** Design infrastructure code in a modular and reusable manner. Define infrastructure components as modules and leverage them across projects or environments, promoting consistency and reducing duplication.

- **Leverage Cloud-Provider-Specific Tools:** Cloud providers offer tools and frameworks specific to IaC, such as AWS CloudFormation, Azure Resource Manager, or Google Cloud Deployment Manager. Leverage these tools to simplify infrastructure provisioning and management.

- **Test Infrastructure Code:** Incorporate testing into the CI/CD pipeline for infrastructure code. Utilize testing frameworks and tools to validate infrastructure configurations, catch errors, and ensure that desired states are achieved.

- **Establish Code Review Processes:** Implement code review processes for infrastructure code to ensure quality, adherence to best practices, and knowledge sharing among team members. Code reviews help identify potential issues or improvements early on.

- **Automate Configuration Management:** Utilize configuration management tools (e.g., Ansible, Chef, Puppet) to automate the configuration and management of infrastructure resources. These tools enable consistent application of configurations, ensuring infrastructure consistency.

13.4 DevOps Tools and Best Practices for Seamless Collaboration and Delivery

DevOps tools play a crucial role in enabling seamless collaboration, automation, and continuous delivery. By adopting the right set of tools and following best practices, organizations can streamline their software development lifecycle, improve efficiency, and achieve faster time-to-market. From source code management and continuous integration to deployment automation and monitoring, each tool serves a specific purpose in the DevOps toolchain. By selecting the appropriate tools, integrating them effectively, and following best practices, teams can embrace a DevOps culture, deliver high-quality software, and drive innovation in today's fast-paced development environments.

13.4.1. Source Code Management and Collaboration Tools:

- **Git:** Git is a widely adopted distributed version control system that enables teams to manage code repositories, track changes, and collaborate on code development efficiently. Git provides features such as branching, merging, and code review integrations, fostering collaboration and ensuring code integrity.

- GitHub, GitLab, Bitbucket: These platforms provide a web-based interface and additional collaboration features on top of Git. They offer features like issue tracking, pull requests, code reviews, and integration with CI/CD pipelines, enabling seamless collaboration and code sharing among team members.

13.4.2. Continuous Integration and Build Automation Tools:

- Jenkins: Jenkins is a popular open-source automation server that facilitates continuous integration and build automation. It enables developers to automate the process of building, testing, and deploying code changes. Jenkins integrates with various tools and supports a wide range of plugins, making it highly customizable.

- CircleCI, Travis CI: These cloud-based continuous integration platforms provide managed environments for running build and test jobs. They offer easy setup, scalability, and integration with popular version control systems, allowing teams to quickly set up and automate their CI pipelines.

13.4.3. Configuration Management and Infrastructure Provisioning:

- Ansible, Puppet, Chef: These configuration management tools automate the provisioning and management of infrastructure resources. They enable teams to define and apply configurations consistently across different environments, ensuring infrastructure integrity and repeatability.

- Terraform: Terraform is an infrastructure provisioning tool that enables teams to define and manage infrastructure resources using declarative code. It supports multiple cloud providers and allows infrastructure to be versioned and provisioned consistently, providing infrastructure as code capabilities.

13.4.4. Continuous Delivery and Deployment Tools:

- Kubernetes: Kubernetes is an open-source container orchestration platform that automates the deployment, scaling, and management of containerized applications. It provides features for service discovery, load balancing, and rolling deployments, making it an ideal tool for managing container-based applications in production.

- Docker: Docker is a containerization platform that simplifies the packaging and deployment of applications. It enables teams to encapsulate applications and their dependencies into containers, ensuring consistent deployment across different environments.

- Spinnaker: Spinnaker is a multi-cloud continuous delivery platform that provides a unified interface for deploying applications across multiple cloud providers. It offers features like canary deployments, automated rollbacks, and release management, facilitating reliable and controlled application deployments.

13.4.5. Monitoring and Observability Tools:

- Prometheus: Prometheus is an open-source monitoring and alerting toolkit that collects metrics from various systems and services. It enables teams to monitor application performance, infrastructure health, and generate alerts based on predefined thresholds or anomalies.

- ELK Stack (Elasticsearch, Logstash, Kibana): The ELK Stack is a set of open-source tools used for log management and analysis. Elasticsearch indexes and stores logs, Logstash processes and transforms log data, and Kibana provides a visualization and analytics interface for log exploration.

13.4.6. Best Practices for Effective DevOps Implementation:

- **Automation:** Automate repetitive tasks, such as build, test, and deployment processes, to reduce manual effort and ensure consistency.

- **Collaboration and Communication:** Foster open communication and collaboration between development, operations, and other stakeholders to align goals, share knowledge, and facilitate faster feedback loops.

- **Infrastructure as Code:** Treat infrastructure configurations as code and adopt IaC practices to ensure infrastructure consistency, repeatability, and version control.

- **Continuous Testing:** Integrate automated testing into the CI/CD pipeline to validate code changes and catch issues early in the development process.

- **Continuous Monitoring:** Implement continuous monitoring and observability practices to gain insights into application performance, infrastructure health, and user experience.

- **Security and Compliance:** Incorporate security practices into the DevOps workflow, including secure coding practices, vulnerability scanning, and compliance checks.

Exercise

Multiple Choice Questions

1. DevOps fosters collaboration and communication between which teams in the software delivery process?
a) Development and Marketing
b) Development and Operations
c) Marketing and Operations
d) Sales and Operations

2. Infrastructure as Code (IaC) treats infrastructure configurations as:
a) Physical hardware
b) Dynamic cloud resources
c) Software code
d) Unchangeable configurations

3. What is the primary objective of continuous integration (CI)?
a) Automatically deploying code to production
b) Identifying integration issues early
c) Managing cloud resources programmatically
d) Managing infrastructure as code

4. What key benefits do organizations gain by embracing DevOps and Continuous Delivery?
a) Slower time-to-market and reduced software quality
b) Faster time-to-market and increased software quality
c) Slower time-to-market and increased software quality
d) Faster time-to-market and reduced software quality

5. What is one of the key components of DevOps and Continuous Delivery in the Cloud that ensures reproducibility and easy rollback in case of issues?
a) Automated Build and Test
b) Configuration Management
c) Continuous Monitoring and Feedback
d) Version Control

6. Which practice involves automatically deploying validated code to production environments?
a) Continuous Integration (CI)
b) Continuous Monitoring and Feedback
c) Continuous Deployment (CD)
d) Continuous Delivery (CD)

7. Which DevOps best practice helps foster a culture of collaboration, trust, and shared responsibility among different teams?
a) Infrastructure Scalability and Resilience
b) Automation and Orchestration
c) Continuous Integration and Deployment Pipelines
d) Culture of Collaboration

8. What does Infrastructure as Code (IaC) allow organizations to do?
a) Automate cloud resource provisioning
b) Deploy software to production
c) Test applications continuously
d) Integrate security practices

9. Which practice in DevOps emphasizes the importance of continuously monitoring applications and infrastructure to gain insights into performance and availability?
a) Continuous Integration
b) Continuous Deployment
c) Continuous Monitoring and Feedback
d) Automation and Infrastructure as Code (IaC)

10. What does infrastructure scalability and elasticity align perfectly with?
a) Continuous Integration
b) DevOps and Continuous Delivery
c) Continuous Monitoring and Feedback

d) Automation and Orchestration

11. What type of tools are used to define, provision, and manage cloud resources programmatically in Infrastructure as Code (IaC)?

a) Monitoring tools
b) Configuration management tools
c) Collaboration tools
d) Version control tools

12. Which DevOps best practice involves implementing comprehensive monitoring solutions to capture performance metrics and user feedback?

a) Automation and Orchestration
b) Infrastructure Scalability and Resilience
c) Continuous Monitoring and Feedback
d) Continuous Integration and Deployment Pipelines

Review Questions

1. What are the key benefits of combining DevOps practices with the cloud environment for software development?

2. How does version control contribute to successful DevOps and continuous delivery in the cloud?

3. How does infrastructure automation contribute to the scalability and efficiency of DevOps in the cloud?

4. What are the key components of an efficient CI/CD pipeline for cloud-based DevOps?

5. How does a culture of collaboration contribute to the success of DevOps in the cloud environment?

6. How can organizations ensure security and compliance while implementing DevOps in the cloud?

7. How do cloud-native features contribute to the scalability and resilience of applications in a DevOps environment?

8. How does continuous monitoring and feedback contribute to continuous improvement in cloud-based DevOps?

9. How can DevOps practices in the cloud enable organizations to achieve faster time-to-market and innovation?

Answer Section
Multiple Choice Questions

1. b) Development and Operations

2. c) Software code

3. b) Identifying integration issues early

4. b) Faster time-to-market and increased software quality

5. d) Version Control

6. c) Continuous Deployment (CD)

7. d) Culture of Collaboration

8. a) Automate cloud resource provisioning

9. c) Continuous Monitoring and Feedback

10. b) DevOps and Continuous Delivery

11. b) Configuration management tools

12. c) Continuous Monitoring and Feedback

Review Questions

1. The combination of DevOps practices and the cloud environment brings numerous benefits to software development. Firstly, collaboration and communication are enhanced, as teams can work together on a shared platform, fostering efficient coordination. Automation becomes easier with cloud infrastructure, enabling streamlined processes and faster deployments. Scalability and elasticity of the cloud ensure optimal performance during varying workloads. Continuous Integration and Continuous Deployment (CI/CD) pipelines become seamless, reducing time-to-market. Additionally, cost-effectiveness is achieved through cloud resource management. Overall, the integration of DevOps with the cloud accelerates software delivery, improves software quality, and facilitates scalable and efficient development.

2. Version control plays a pivotal role in successful DevOps and continuous delivery in the cloud. It allows teams to manage and track changes to code, infrastructure definitions, and configuration files effectively. With version control, collaboration is seamless, enabling multiple developers to work on the same codebase simultaneously without conflicts. Rollbacks become effortless in case of issues, ensuring stability in the software development process. The ability to compare different versions helps in identifying improvements and issues. Furthermore, version control ensures transparency and traceability throughout the development lifecycle, promoting a well-organized and efficient cloud-based DevOps workflow.

3. Infrastructure automation is a cornerstone of DevOps in the cloud, playing a significant role in enhancing scalability and efficiency. With automation, provisioning, managing, and configuring cloud resources becomes effortless and consistent. Infrastructure as Code (IaC) tools facilitate the definition of infrastructure through code, enabling version control and testing. Automation reduces manual effort, minimizes human errors, and accelerates the deployment process. The dynamic nature of cloud environments aligns perfectly with automation, enabling rapid scaling up or down based on workload demands. Overall, infrastructure automation in the cloud streamlines DevOps practices, ensuring seamless collaboration, rapid deployments, and optimal resource utilization.

4. An efficient CI/CD pipeline for cloud-based DevOps comprises several key components. First, automated build and test processes ensure consistent software artifacts. Continuous Integration involves frequently merging code changes and running automated tests to identify integration issues early. The automated testing suite includes unit tests, integration tests, and regression tests, ensuring code quality and reliability. Additionally, infrastructure automation tools are employed to provision cloud resources programmatically. Configuration management ensures consistent deployments across cloud environments. Finally, continuous monitoring and feedback mechanisms provide insights into application

performance, user experience, and potential issues, allowing proactive resolutions. This cohesive CI/CD pipeline accelerates software delivery and ensures reliable and high-quality cloud-based deployments.

5. A culture of collaboration is fundamental to the success of DevOps in the cloud environment. By fostering a collaborative atmosphere, teams break down traditional silos and embrace a shared responsibility for software delivery. Collaboration promotes open communication, knowledge sharing, and cross-functional teams, leading to a holistic understanding of the entire development process. In a cloud-based DevOps setup, where teams may be distributed geographically, collaboration becomes even more critical. Teams work seamlessly on a shared platform, leveraging cloud features for real-time collaboration and resource sharing. Ultimately, a collaborative culture empowers organizations to achieve faster innovation, improved efficiency, and enhanced adaptability in the cloud-based DevOps journey.

6. Ensuring security and compliance during the implementation of DevOps in the cloud requires a proactive approach. From the outset, organizations must integrate security practices into the DevOps workflow. Secure coding practices should be adopted, minimizing vulnerabilities in the software. Vulnerability scanning tools help identify potential weaknesses early on. Security testing should be an integral part of the CI/CD pipeline, ensuring code integrity throughout deployment. Additionally, adherence to industry standards and regulations must be a priority, with compliance checks built into the deployment process. By prioritizing security and compliance in the cloud-based DevOps workflow, organizations can confidently deliver software that meets stringent security standards and compliance requirements.

7. Cloud-native features play a vital role in enhancing the scalability and resilience of applications in a DevOps environment. Features like autoscaling automatically adjust resource capacity based on demand, ensuring applications can handle varying workloads efficiently. Load balancing distributes traffic evenly across multiple instances, optimizing performance and minimizing downtime. Fault tolerance mechanisms ensure that applications can gracefully handle failures without widespread disruptions. By designing applications to be stateless and horizontally scalable, DevOps teams can take full advantage of cloud-native features, ensuring seamless growth and adaptability. Embracing cloud-native capabilities enhances application resilience and scalability, enabling rapid response to changing demands in a DevOps-driven cloud environment.

8. Continuous monitoring and feedback mechanisms are central to driving continuous improvement in cloud-based DevOps. Monitoring tools capture real-time performance metrics, logs, and user feedback, providing valuable insights into application behavior and user experience. By analyzing this data, DevOps teams can detect performance bottlenecks, identify potential issues early, and optimize resource utilization. Continuous monitoring enables proactive issue resolution, minimizing downtime and enhancing application reliability. Moreover, feedback loops between development, operations, and users facilitate a constant flow of information, driving iterative improvements in the software. As a result, cloud-based DevOps benefits from a culture of continuous learning, innovation, and refinement, ultimately leading to better software quality and user satisfaction.

9. DevOps practices in the cloud enable organizations to achieve faster time-to-market and innovation through various means. Firstly, streamlined collaboration and communication foster efficient teamwork and decision-making, expediting development cycles. Automation reduces manual effort, enabling faster and error-free deployments. Cloud scalability allows organizations to quickly adapt to changing demands,

launching products or features rapidly. Continuous Integration and Continuous Deployment (CI/CD) pipelines automate testing and deployment processes, shortening the software delivery lifecycle. Moreover, cloud-based DevOps empowers organizations to experiment and innovate with low-risk environments, encouraging continuous learning and improvement. By embracing cloud-based DevOps, organizations can accelerate innovation, enhance competitiveness, and deliver cutting-edge solutions to the market swiftly.

Chapter 14: Cloud Networking and Connectivity

14.1 Virtual Private Cloud (VPC): Secure and Scalable Cloud Network Infrastructure

Virtual Private Cloud (VPC) is a foundational component of cloud computing that offers organizations a secure and scalable network infrastructure within a public cloud environment. By leveraging VPC, organizations can design and manage their own isolated network environments, control access, and establish secure connectivity between resources. By following best practices such as proper planning, security measures, scalability considerations, and monitoring, organizations can create a robust VPC infrastructure that meets their specific requirements for performance, security, and compliance. A well-designed and effectively managed VPC enables organizations to fully leverage the benefits of the cloud while maintaining control, security, and flexibility in their network infrastructure.

14.1.1. Understanding Virtual Private Cloud (VPC):

Virtual Private Cloud (VPC) is a logically isolated and customizable virtual network environment within a public cloud provider's infrastructure. It enables organizations to provision and manage their own virtual network resources, including subnets, routing tables, IP address ranges, and security groups.

- **Isolation and Security:** VPC offers isolation from other tenants in the cloud, ensuring that resources and data are kept separate. It enables organizations to define network access control policies, establish secure communication, and implement network-level security measures.

- **Scalability and Flexibility:** VPC provides the flexibility to scale network resources based on demand. Organizations can easily add or remove subnets, adjust IP address ranges, and configure network routing to accommodate changing requirements and application workloads.

14.1.2. Key Components of Virtual Private Cloud (VPC):

- **Subnets:** Subnets are segmented portions of the VPC's IP address range. They allow organizations to logically divide their network and allocate resources to specific parts of their infrastructure. Subnets can be configured with different availability zones to ensure high availability and fault tolerance.

- **Routing:** VPC includes a routing table that determines how network traffic is directed within the VP Routing rules define how data flows between subnets, gateways, and external networks. Routing policies can be customized to optimize traffic flow and establish secure connections.

- **Security Groups:** Security groups act as virtual firewalls for resources within the VP They control inbound and outbound traffic based on specified rules. Security groups enable organizations to enforce granular access controls and restrict communication between resources.

- **Network Address Translation (NAT):** NAT allows resources within the VPC to communicate with external networks, such as the internet, by translating private IP addresses to public IP addresses. It enables outbound internet access for resources while maintaining their internal private IP addresses.

- Virtual Private Network (VPN) Connectivity: VPC supports VPN connections that enable secure and encrypted communication between the VPC and on-premises data centers. VPN connections establish a secure tunnel over the internet, allowing organizations to extend their network infrastructure to the cloud.

- Direct Connect: Direct Connect provides a dedicated and private network connection between on-premises data centers and the VP It offers higher bandwidth, lower latency, and enhanced security compared to internet-based VPN connections, facilitating seamless hybrid cloud integration.

14.1.3. Best Practices for Designing and Managing a VPC:

- Planning and Segmentation: Carefully plan the IP address ranges and subnet design to ensure efficient utilization of resources and avoid IP conflicts. Segment resources into appropriate subnets based on security requirements, availability needs, and application dependencies.

- Security and Access Controls: Implement strict security measures using security groups, network ACLs (Access Control Lists), and other mechanisms to control inbound and outbound traffi Follow the principle of least privilege and regularly review and update security policies to mitigate risks.

- Scalability and Elasticity: Design the VPC for scalability and flexibility by using multiple availability zones and properly distributing resources across them. Leverage auto-scaling capabilities to automatically adjust resource capacity based on demand.

- Monitoring and Logging: Implement monitoring and logging solutions to track network traffic, performance metrics, and security events within the VP Utilize cloud provider tools or third-party solutions to gain visibility into network activities and proactively detect anomalies or security incidents.

- Backup and Disaster Recovery: Establish backup and disaster recovery strategies for critical resources within the VP Regularly back up data, replicate resources across availability zones, and periodically test and validate disaster recovery procedures.

- Compliance and Governance: Adhere to industry-specific compliance requirements and best practices when designing and managing the VPC infrastructure. Implement controls to ensure data privacy, encryption, and compliance with regulations relevant to your organization's industry.

14.2 Network Security Groups and Firewalls: Safeguarding Cloud Networks

Network Security Groups (NSGs) and firewalls play critical roles in securing cloud networks by enforcing access controls, filtering traffic, and protecting resources from unauthorized access and cyber threats. NSGs provide granular control over inbound and outbound traffic within Virtual Private Clouds (VPCs), while firewalls serve as barriers between internal and external networks. By implementing NSGs and firewalls effectively and following best practices such as segmentation, regular rule review, logging, and centralized management, organizations can enhance the security posture of their cloud networks and protect their assets and data from potential security breaches. A well-designed and effectively managed network security framework is essential to safeguarding cloud environments and maintaining data integrity and confidentiality in today's digitally connected world.

14.2.1. Network Security Groups (NSGs):

Network Security Groups (NSGs) are virtual firewalls that allow organizations to filter and control inbound and outbound traffic to resources within a Virtual Private Cloud (VPC). NSGs operate at the network layer (Layer 3) and enforce security rules based on source and destination IP addresses, ports, and protocols.

- Traffic Filtering and Access Control: NSGs enable organizations to define rules to allow or deny specific types of traffic based on IP addresses, ports, and protocols. They provide granular control over inbound and outbound communication, ensuring only authorized traffic flows to and from resources.

- **Network Segmentation:** NSGs facilitate network segmentation by applying different security rules to different subnets or resource groups within the VP This helps enforce security policies and restrict communication between resources, reducing the attack surface and mitigating the impact of potential breaches.

- **Stateful Packet Inspection:** NSGs use stateful packet inspection to track the state of network connections and allow related incoming traffic. This ensures that only valid responses to outgoing requests are permitted, enhancing security by preventing unauthorized connections.

- **Logging and Monitoring:** NSGs provide logging and monitoring capabilities to track network traffic and security events. Organizations can analyze logs and monitoring data to detect anomalies, identify potential threats, and respond promptly to security incidents.

14.2.2. Firewalls:

- **Purpose and Function:** Firewalls are security devices or software solutions that monitor and control network traffic based on predefined security policies. They act as a barrier between internal networks (e.g., VPCs) and external networks (e.g., the internet) and inspect traffic to block malicious or unauthorized access attempts.

- **Types of Firewalls:** There are several types of firewalls, including:

- **Network Firewalls:** These operate at the network layer (Layer 3) and analyze IP addresses, ports, and protocols to filter traffic.

- **Application Firewalls:** These operate at the application layer (Layer 7) and can inspect and filter traffic based on application-specific rules.

- **Web Application Firewalls (WAF):** WAFs focus specifically on protecting web applications from common web-based attacks.

- **Security Policies and Rule Configuration:** Firewalls are configured with security policies that define allowed or blocked traffic based on specified criteria, such as IP addresses, ports, and protocols. Organizations can customize these policies to align with their security requirements.

- **Intrusion Detection and Prevention:** Some firewalls include intrusion detection and prevention capabilities. They can detect and block suspicious or malicious activities in real-time, providing an additional layer of protection against threats.

- **Centralized Management:** Firewalls often have centralized management consoles that allow administrators to configure, monitor, and update firewall rules across multiple devices or instances within the cloud network.

14.2.3. Best Practices for Implementing NSGs and Firewalls:

- **Segmentation and Least Privilege:** Apply the principle of least privilege by restricting network traffic between resources. Use NSGs and firewalls to enforce strict access controls and limit communication to only necessary connections.

- **Regular Rule Review and Updates:** Regularly review and update NSG and firewall rules to adapt to changing security requirements and address emerging threats. Remove unnecessary or obsolete rules to minimize the attack surface.

- **Defense in Depth:** Implement multiple layers of security controls, including NSGs, firewalls, and other security measures, to create a robust defense against threats. This multi-layered approach enhances security by adding redundancy and mitigating the impact of potential breaches.

- **Logging and Monitoring:** Enable logging and monitoring for NSGs and firewalls to capture network traffic, security events, and anomalies. Regularly analyze logs and monitoring data to detect and respond to security incidents promptly.

- **Automation and Centralized Management:** Leverage automation and centralized management tools to streamline the configuration and management of NSGs and firewalls. This simplifies rule updates, enhances consistency, and reduces the risk of misconfigurations.

- **Regular Security Audits:** Conduct regular security audits to assess the effectiveness of NSGs and firewalls in protecting the cloud network. Identify vulnerabilities, weaknesses, and potential improvements to ensure ongoing network security.

14.3 Hybrid Cloud Networking: Bridging On-Premises and Cloud Environments

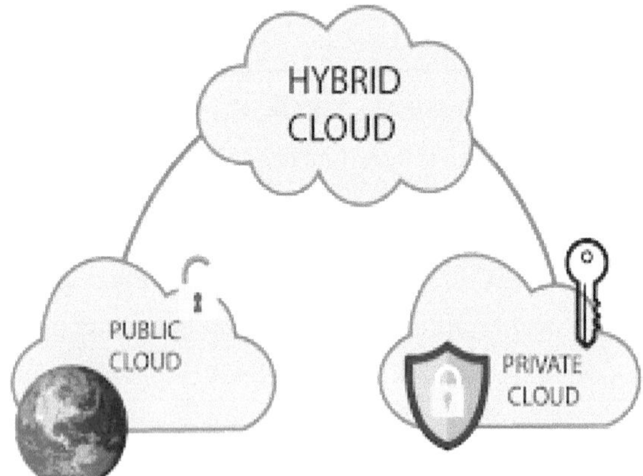

Hybrid cloud networking enables organizations to harness the advantages of both on-premises infrastructure and the cloud by establishing seamless connectivity and communication between the two environments. By implementing VPNs, direct connections, and other hybrid network connectivity solutions, organizations can securely extend their networks, access cloud resources, and leverage the scalability and flexibility of the clouBy following best practices such as thorough planning, robust security measures, network segmentation, and continuous monitoring, organizations can build a resilient and high-performing hybrid network infrastructure that supports their business requirements and enables seamless collaboration between on-premises and cloud environments. The successful implementation of hybrid cloud networking empowers organizations to optimize their IT infrastructure, achieve cost efficiencies, and drive innovation in today's dynamic and interconnected digital landscape.

14.3.1. Understanding Hybrid Cloud Networking:

Hybrid cloud networking refers to the integration of on-premises infrastructure with public cloud resources to create a unified and interconnected network environment. It enables organizations to extend their network infrastructure to the cloud while maintaining control over their on-premises data centers.

- **Connectivity and Communication:** Hybrid cloud networking facilitates secure connectivity and seamless communication between on-premises environments and cloud resources. It allows organizations to establish links, transfer data, and access applications and services across the hybrid network.

- **Flexibility and Scalability:** Hybrid cloud networking provides organizations with the flexibility to scale their infrastructure resources based on demand. It allows them to leverage the agility and scalability of the cloud while retaining the control and security of their on-premises environments.

14.3.2. Key Components of Hybrid Cloud Networking:

- **Virtual Private Network (VPN):** VPN technology establishes secure and encrypted communication tunnels over the internet, connecting on-premises networks with virtual private clouds. VPNs provide a cost-effective and flexible way to extend the on-premises network to the cloud securely.

- **Direct Connect:** Direct Connect enables organizations to establish dedicated and private network connections between their on-premises data centers and the cloud service provider's infrastructure. It offers higher bandwidth, lower latency, and enhanced security compared to internet-based VPN connections.

- **Hybrid Network Connectivity Solutions:** Cloud service providers offer specific solutions for hybrid cloud networking, such as AWS Transit Gateway, Azure Virtual WAN, or Google Cloud Interconnect. These solutions provide centralized management, simplified connectivity, and enhanced security for hybrid network architectures.

- **Network Address Translation (NAT):** NAT allows organizations to map private IP addresses used in their on-premises networks to public IP addresses in the cloud. This enables seamless communication between on-premises and cloud resources without exposing the internal IP addresses.

- **Load Balancers and Application Delivery Controllers (ADCs):** Load balancers and ADCs distribute network traffic across multiple servers or instances, ensuring efficient utilization of resources and high availability for applications deployed in both on-premises and cloud environments.

14.3.3. Best Practices for Hybrid Cloud Networking:

- **Planning and Architecture Design:** Thoroughly plan and design the hybrid cloud network architecture, considering factors such as security requirements, scalability, performance, and application dependencies. Identify the optimal connectivity solutions and network components that align with the organization's goals.

- **Security and Compliance:** Implement robust security measures to protect data and resources in transit between on-premises and cloud environments. Utilize encryption, access controls, and security policies to ensure data confidentiality and integrity.

- **Network Segmentation and Access Controls:** Segment the hybrid network into logical segments or virtual LANs (VLANs) to isolate traffic and enforce access controls. Utilize firewalls, network security groups, and other security mechanisms to restrict communication and protect sensitive resources.

- **Monitoring and Visibility:** Implement monitoring and logging solutions to gain visibility into the hybrid network. Monitor network traffic, performance metrics, and security events to identify potential issues, anomalies, or security breaches. Utilize centralized monitoring tools or cloud provider-specific monitoring services.

- **Network Performance Optimization:** Optimize network performance by leveraging content delivery networks (CDNs) for efficient content delivery, using caching mechanisms to reduce latency, and employing traffic routing techniques to minimize bottlenecks and ensure optimal performance.

- **Regular Testing and Disaster Recovery Planning:** Conduct regular testing and validation of the hybrid network infrastructure. Test failover and disaster recovery procedures to ensure business continuity in case of network disruptions or cloud service outages.

14.4 Content Delivery Networks (CDNs) for Cloud: Optimizing Content Delivery and Performance

CDNs for cloud environments play a vital role in optimizing content delivery, reducing latency, and improving user experience. By leveraging the distributed infrastructure of cloud providers, CDNs ensure efficient content delivery to global audiences. CDNs in the cloud offer benefits such as improved performance, global reach, scalability, and bandwidth optimization. By following best practices like effective caching strategies, continuous monitoring, and security considerations, organizations can harness the full potential of CDNs in the cloud to accelerate content delivery, enhance user experience, and ensure the seamless delivery of web applications, media files, and other digital content. Leveraging CDNs in the cloud empowers organizations to deliver content with maximum efficiency, delight users with a superior experience, and achieve business success in the digital era.

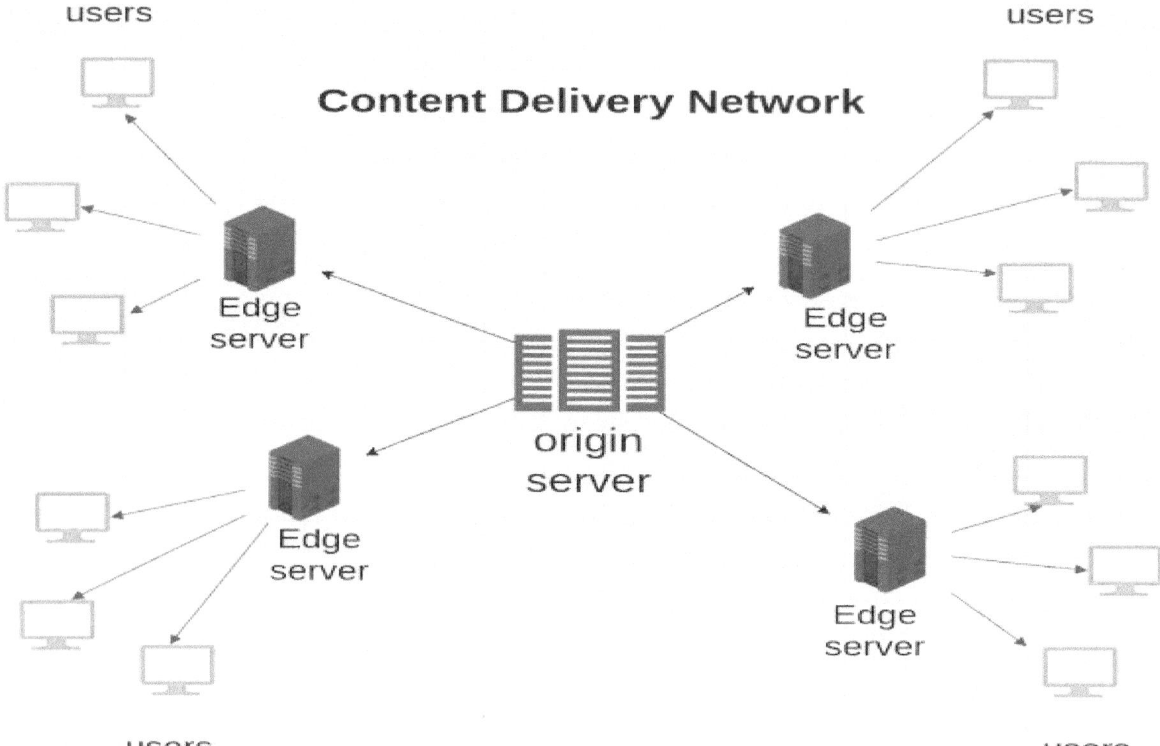

CDNs for cloud environments are specialized networks that store and deliver content from edge servers located in various data centers. These edge servers are part of a cloud provider's infrastructure, enabling efficient content delivery to end-users by reducing latency and improving performance.

- **Integration with Cloud Services:** CDNs in the cloud seamlessly integrate with cloud platforms and services, allowing organizations to leverage the scalability, flexibility, and global reach of the cloud. CDNs can be tightly integrated with cloud providers' offerings, such as storage, compute, and serverless services.

- **Dynamic Scaling:** CDNs in the cloud are designed to dynamically scale and adapt to changing demands. They can handle high traffic volumes, automatically provision additional edge servers, and distribute content efficiently to meet the needs of rapidly growing applications or sudden traffic spikes.

14.4.2. Benefits of CDNs for Cloud:

- **Improved Performance and Latency Reduction:** CDNs in the cloud minimize latency by caching content close to end-users. By delivering content from nearby edge servers, CDNs reduce the round-trip time, resulting in faster page load times, reduced buffering, and an enhanced user experience.

- **Global Content Reach:** CDNs for cloud enable organizations to deliver content worldwide through a network of edge servers located in various regions. This global reach ensures that content is delivered from the closest edge server to the end-user, irrespective of their geographic location.

- **Scalability and Elasticity:** CDNs in the cloud offer scalability and elasticity to handle varying traffic loads. They can dynamically scale up or down based on demand, ensuring that content delivery remains optimized and responsive, even during peak usage periods.

- **Bandwidth Optimization:** CDNs in the cloud reduce bandwidth consumption on the origin server by caching and delivering content from edge servers. This reduces the load on the cloud infrastructure and minimizes data transfer costs.

- **Content Security and DDoS Mitigation:** CDNs in the cloud often include built-in security features and DDoS protection mechanisms. They help protect applications and content from malicious attacks, ensuring the availability and integrity of services.

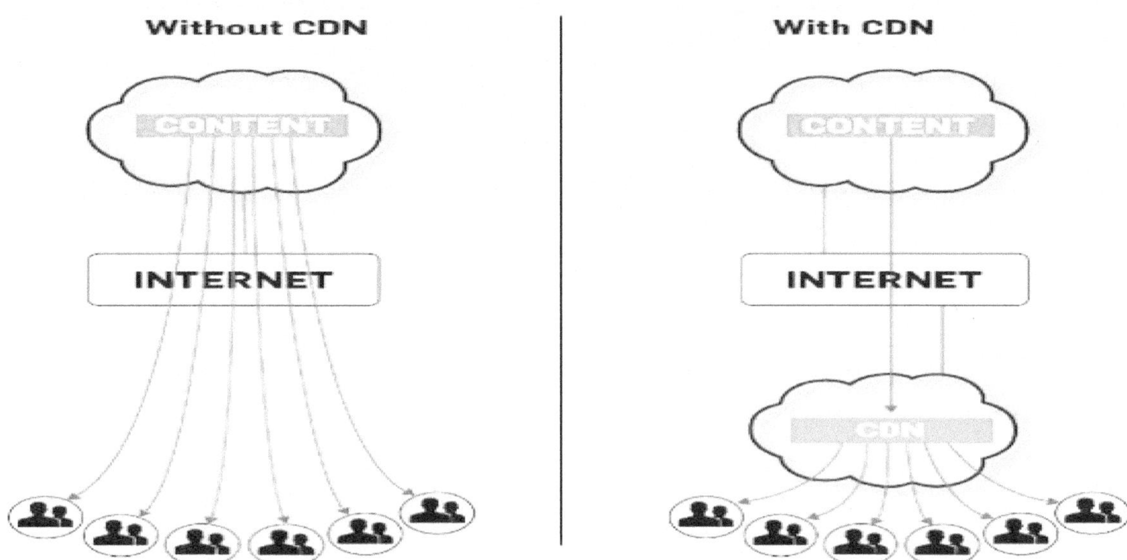

14.4.3. Key Components of CDNs for Cloud:

- **Edge Servers and Points of Presence (PoPs):** Edge servers deployed in data centers globally form the backbone of CDNs for cloud. These servers cache and deliver content to end-users based on their geographic location, ensuring optimized content delivery.

- **Origin Servers and Cloud Storage:** Origin servers in the cloud act as the source of content for CDNs. They store the original copies of content and serve as the origin point from which CDNs retrieve and cache content on edge servers. Cloud storage services often integrate seamlessly with CDNs to deliver and update content efficiently.

- **Caching and Purging Mechanisms:** CDNs for cloud employ caching mechanisms to store frequently accessed content on edge servers. Caching algorithms determine which content to cache and for how long. Purging mechanisms allow organizations to remove or update cached content in real-time.

- **Traffic Routing and Load Balancing:** CDNs for cloud utilize intelligent traffic routing and load balancing techniques to distribute requests across edge servers. This ensures optimal resource utilization, reduces server load, and improves overall content delivery performance.

- **Analytics and Reporting:** CDNs for cloud offer analytics and reporting capabilities that provide insights into content delivery performance, user engagement, and traffic patterns. These insights help optimize content delivery strategies, identify bottlenecks, and make informed decisions.

14.4.4. Best Practices for Leveraging CDNs in the Cloud:

- **Content Caching Strategy:** Implement an effective caching strategy to determine which content should be cached and for how long. Frequently accessed static content should have longer cache durations, while dynamic or personalized content may require shorter cache durations.

- **Content Versioning and Cache Invalidation:** Utilize content versioning techniques and cache invalidation mechanisms to ensure that updated or modified content is propagated to edge servers promptly. Implement cache invalidation APIs or tags to selectively purge or update specific content items.

- **Continuous Monitoring and Optimization:** Regularly monitor CDN performance metrics, such as cache hit rates, response times, and traffic patterns. Analyze these metrics to identify performance bottlenecks, optimize content delivery configurations, and make data-driven decisions for further optimization.

- **Security Considerations:** Implement appropriate security measures, such as SSL/TLS encryption, to ensure secure content delivery. Leverage CDNs that offer DDoS protection, web application firewalls, and other security features to mitigate potential attacks and ensure the integrity of content delivery.

- **Multi-CDN Strategy:** Consider implementing a multi-CDN approach by using multiple CDN providers or services. This diversifies content delivery options, enhances availability, and mitigates the risk of relying solely on a single CDN provider.

Exercise

Multiple Choice Questions

1. What is a Virtual Private Cloud (VPC)?

a. A publicly accessible cloud network environment.

b. A logically isolated and customizable virtual network environment within a public cloud.

c. A private on-premises network that is isolated from the internet.

d. A standalone physical server hosted in a data center.

2. Which of the following is a benefit of using VPC?

a. Shared resources with other tenants in the cloud.

b. Limited control over network configurations.

c. Inability to scale network resources based on demand.

d. Isolation and control over the virtual network environment.

3. What are the key components of Virtual Private Cloud (VPC)?

a. Subnets, firewall, and load balancer.

b. Security groups, NAT, and VPN connectivity.

c. Public IP addresses, application servers, and routers.

d. Encryption, CDN, and public cloud provider.

4. What is the purpose of a security group in VPC?

a. It provides encryption for data at rest.

b. It allows organizations to control inbound and outbound traffic based on rules.

c. It manages DNS resolution for resources within the VPC.

d. It optimizes network routing between subnets.

5. Which component of VPC allows resources within the VPC to communicate with external networks, such as the internet?

a. Routing table.

b. Security group.

c. Virtual Private Network (VPN) connectivity.

d. Network Address Translation (NAT).

6. What is the function of a Virtual Private Network (VPN) in VPC?

a. It allows resources to communicate within the same subnet.

b. It establishes secure and encrypted communication between VPC and on-premises data centers.

c. It provides load balancing for incoming traffic.

d. It manages access control for security groups.

7. How does Direct Connect differ from VPN connectivity in VPC?

a. Direct Connect provides a dedicated and private network connection between VPC and on-premises data centers.

b. VPN connectivity offers higher bandwidth and lower latency compared to Direct Connect.

c. Direct Connect establishes a secure tunnel over the internet.

d. VPN connectivity is only available in certain regions.

8. What is a best practice for designing and managing a VPC?

a. Implement security groups with no restrictions for inbound and outbound traffic.

b. Scale network resources independently of demand.

c. Use a single availability zone to ensure high availability.

d. Plan IP address ranges and subnet design efficiently to avoid IP conflicts.

9. Which of the following is NOT a best practice for securing a VPC?

a. Regularly reviewing and updating security policies.

b. Implementing network segmentation using subnets.

c. Enabling monitoring and logging to track network traffic and security events.

d. Allowing unrestricted access from any IP address to all resources.

10. What is the conclusion regarding Virtual Private Cloud (VPC)?

a. VPC is not a critical component of cloud computing.

b. VPC offers organizations a secure and scalable network infrastructure within a public cloud environment.

c. VPC provides no benefits in terms of network isolation and security.

d. VPC cannot be customized to meet specific requirements.

11. What is the role of Network Security Groups (NSGs) in cloud environments?

a. They act as physical firewalls for on-premises data centers.

b. They allow organizations to control inbound and outbound traffic to resources within a VPC.

c. They provide encryption for data at rest in the cloud.

d. They manage cloud storage services and data replication.

Review Questions

1. What are the key benefits of implementing a hybrid cloud networking strategy?
2. How do Network Security Groups (NSGs) contribute to cloud network security?
3. What is the primary purpose of Content Delivery Networks (CDNs) for cloud environments?
4. How do CDNs for cloud handle varying traffic loads?
5. What are the key components of a Virtual Private Cloud (VPC)?
6. How does planning and segmentation contribute to an effective Virtual Private Cloud (VPC) infrastructure?
7. How does Infrastructure as Code (IaC) contribute to the implementation and management of a secure and scalable Virtual Private Cloud (VPC) infrastructure?

8. How do CDNs in the cloud contribute to reducing bandwidth consumption and data transfer costs?

Answer Section

Multiple Choice Questions

1. b) A logically isolated and customizable virtual network environment within a public cloud.

2. d) Isolation and control over the virtual network environment.

3. b) Security groups, NAT, and VPN connectivity.

4. b) It allows organizations to control inbound and outbound traffic based on rules.

5. d) Network Address Translation (NAT).

6. b) It establishes secure and encrypted communication between VPC and on-premises data centers.

7. a) Direct Connect provides a dedicated and private network connection between VPC and on-premises data centers.

8. d) Plan IP address ranges and subnet design efficiently to avoid IP conflicts.

9. d) Allowing unrestricted access from any IP address to all resources.

10. b) VPC offers organizations a secure and scalable network infrastructure within a public cloud environment.

11. b) They allow organizations to control inbound and outbound traffic to resources within a VPC.

Review Questions

1. Implementing a hybrid cloud networking strategy offers several key benefits. Firstly, it allows organizations to leverage the best of both worlds by integrating on-premises infrastructure with public cloud resources. This provides greater flexibility and scalability, as organizations can dynamically scale their cloud resources based on demand. Additionally, hybrid cloud networking enables seamless communication between on-premises data centers and cloud environments, ensuring a cohesive network environment. It also allows organizations to meet specific compliance or data residency requirements by keeping sensitive data on-premises while utilizing the cloud for less sensitive workloads. Ultimately, a well-executed hybrid cloud networking strategy maximizes performance, enhances security, and optimizes resource utilization.

2. Network Security Groups (NSGs) play a crucial role in cloud network security by acting as virtual firewalls within a Virtual Private Cloud (VPC). NSGs enable organizations to define and enforce access control rules, allowing or denying specific types of network traffic based on source and destination IP addresses, ports, and protocols. By implementing NSGs, organizations can create a secure network environment, controlling inbound and outbound traffic to and from resources within the VPC. This granular control ensures that only authorized traffic is allowed, reducing the attack surface and mitigating potential security threats.

3. The primary purpose of Content Delivery Networks (CDNs) in cloud environments is to optimize content delivery performance and enhance user experience. CDNs leverage a distributed network of edge

servers strategically placed in data centers worldwide. These servers cache and deliver web content, applications, and media files closer to end-users, reducing latency and improving page load times. By delivering content from nearby edge servers, CDNs minimize the round-trip time, resulting in faster access to content, reduced buffering, and an overall smoother user experience, regardless of the end-user's geographic location.

4. CDNs for cloud are designed with dynamic scaling capabilities, allowing them to handle varying traffic loads effectively. When the demand for content increases, CDNs automatically provision additional edge servers to accommodate the increased traffic. These edge servers efficiently distribute content to end-users, ensuring that the content delivery performance remains optimized during peak usage periods. Conversely, during periods of low traffic, CDNs can scale down their resources, minimizing operational costs while still maintaining sufficient capacity to serve end-users. This dynamic scaling feature allows CDNs to adapt to changing traffic patterns, providing reliable and responsive content delivery.

5. A Virtual Private Cloud (VPC) comprises several key components that collectively create an isolated and customizable virtual network environment within a public cloud provider's infrastructure. These components include:

Subnets: Segmented portions of the VPC's IP address range that allow logical division of the network and allocation of resources to specific parts of the infrastructure.
Routing Table: Determines how network traffic is directed within the VPC, defining rules for data flow between subnets, gateways, and external networks.
Security Groups: Act as virtual firewalls for resources within the VPC, controlling inbound and outbound traffic based on specified rules.
Network Address Translation (NAT): Translates private IP addresses to public IP addresses, allowing resources within the VPC to communicate with external networks, such as the internet.
Virtual Private Network (VPN) Connectivity: Enables secure and encrypted communication between the VPC and on-premises data centers.
Direct Connect: Provides a dedicated and private network connection between on-premises data centers and the VPC, offering higher bandwidth, lower latency, and enhanced security.

1. Planning and segmentation are critical components of creating an effective Virtual Private Cloud (VPC) infrastructure. Proper planning involves carefully defining IP address ranges and subnet design to ensure efficient utilization of resources and avoid IP conflicts. By segmenting the VPC into appropriate subnets based on security requirements, availability needs, and application dependencies, organizations can enforce access controls and restrict communication between resources. This enhances security and minimizes the potential impact of security breaches. Well-executed planning and segmentation also lead to a more organized and manageable VPC infrastructure, making it easier to scale, optimize, and maintain the network environment.

2. Infrastructure as Code (IaC) plays a significant role in the implementation and management of a secure and scalable Virtual Private Cloud (VPC) infrastructure. IaC involves treating infrastructure configurations as code, allowing organizations to define, provision, and manage cloud resources programmatically. By leveraging IaC tools and frameworks, organizations can create version-controlled templates that represent the desired state of the VPC infrastructure. These templates can be automatically deployed and updated, ensuring consistency and minimizing human errors during infrastructure provisioning. IaC also facilitates rapid scalability by allowing resources to be provisioned or modified

automatically based on demand, streamlining VPC management and ensuring security best practices are consistently applied.

3. CDNs in the cloud reduce bandwidth consumption and data transfer costs through their caching mechanisms. When content is cached on edge servers distributed globally, it reduces the need for repeated content fetches from the origin server. As a result, less data is transferred between the origin server and the CDN, leading to reduced bandwidth usage. By delivering content from nearby edge servers to end-users, CDNs also minimize data travel over long distances, further optimizing data transfer costs. The efficient utilization of edge servers and reduced data transfers contribute to cost savings, making CDNs a cost-effective solution for content delivery in the cloud.

Chapter 15: Serverless Architecture and Functions-as-a-Service (FaaS)

15.1 Serverless Computing Overview: Embracing Scalability and Efficiency in the Cloud

Serverless computing has transformed the way applications are developed and deployed in the cloud, offering scalability, cost efficiency, and reduced operational overhead. By leveraging serverless technologies, developers can focus on writing code without the burden of managing infrastructure. With the ability to automatically scale, serverless functions handle varying workloads effectively, ensuring optimal performance and cost optimization. By following best practices such as granular function design, stateless architecture, security implementation, and performance optimization, organizations can fully harness the benefits of serverless computing and build scalable, cost-efficient, and agile applications in the cloud. Leveraging serverless computing empowers organizations to develop and deliver applications with maximum efficiency, optimize costs, and respond to changing demands in real-time, leading to enhanced user experiences and increased business success in the digital era.

15.1.1. Understanding Serverless Computing:

Serverless computing, also known as Function as a Service (FaaS), is a cloud computing model where developers write and deploy functions or application logic without having to provision or manage servers. The cloud provider dynamically allocates resources to execute the functions based on incoming requests or events.

- **Event-Driven Architecture:** Serverless computing follows an event-driven architecture, where functions are triggered by specific events, such as HTTP requests, database updates, file uploads, or time-based schedules. Functions are executed on-demand, scaling automatically to handle incoming workload spikes.

- **Stateless Functions:** Serverless functions are stateless, meaning they do not maintain persistent connections or store session data. Each function execution is isolated and self-contained, allowing for rapid scaling and parallel execution without resource contention.

15.1.2. Benefits of Serverless Computing:

- **Scalability and Elasticity:** Serverless computing enables automatic scaling of functions in response to workload fluctuations. Cloud providers handle the scaling and resource allocation, ensuring that applications can handle sudden spikes in traffic without manual intervention.

- **Cost Efficiency:** With serverless computing, you only pay for the actual execution time of functions. Cloud providers charge based on the number of invocations and the duration of function execution. Since there is no idle time or fixed infrastructure costs, serverless computing can be more cost-effective, especially for applications with sporadic or unpredictable workloads.

- **Reduced Operational Overhead:** Serverless computing eliminates the need for managing infrastructure, operating systems, and servers. Developers can focus on writing code and delivering business value rather than dealing with server provisioning, maintenance, and scalability challenges.

- **Rapid Development and Deployment:** Serverless architectures promote faster development cycles and deployment. Developers can quickly iterate and deploy smaller units of code without the need to manage the entire application infrastructure. This agility allows for more frequent updates and shorter time-to-market.

15.1.3. Key Components of Serverless Computing:

- **Functions:** Functions are the building blocks of serverless applications. They encapsulate specific units of code that perform specific tasks or operations. Functions are stateless and executed in response to events or triggers.

- **Event Sources:** Event sources, such as HTTP requests, database changes, message queues, or scheduled timers, trigger the execution of serverless functions. These events drive the serverless architecture and dictate when and how functions are invoked.

- **Cloud Provider Services:** Serverless computing relies on the services provided by cloud providers, such as AWS Lambda, Azure Functions, or Google Cloud Functions. These services handle function execution, scaling, event management, and other operational aspects.

15.1.4. Best Practices for Leveraging Serverless Computing:

- **Granular Function Design:** Decompose applications into smaller, granular functions that perform specific tasks. This allows for better scalability, reusability, and independent development and deployment of functions.

- **Stateless Design and Externalized State:** Ensure that serverless functions are stateless and do not maintain internal state or dependencies. Externalize state storage using databases, object storage, or caching services to achieve data persistence and scalability.

- **Security and Authentication:** Implement appropriate security measures, such as authentication, authorization, and encryption, to protect serverless functions and their associated resources. Use mechanisms provided by the cloud provider or third-party services to secure function endpoints and data transmission.

- **Performance Optimization:** Optimize function execution time by reducing unnecessary dependencies, optimizing code, and leveraging caching mechanisms. Design functions to be lightweight and use serverless-specific optimizations, such as cold-start mitigation techniques and connection pooling.

- **Monitoring and Logging:** Implement comprehensive monitoring and logging solutions to gain visibility into function performance, errors, and resource utilization. Leverage cloud provider-specific monitoring tools or third-party services to proactively detect issues and troubleshoot performance bottlenecks.

- **Automated Testing and Deployment:** Adopt automated testing and continuous integration/continuous deployment (CI/CD) practices to ensure the quality and rapid deployment of serverless functions. Use deployment pipelines and version control systems to manage and release function updates reliably.

15.2 AWS Lambda and Azure Functions for Cloud: A Comparison of Serverless Computing Platforms

AWS Lambda and Azure Functions are robust serverless computing platforms that offer scalability, cost efficiency, and simplified infrastructure management in the cloud. While both platforms provide similar benefits, they have specific strengths and integration capabilities within their respective cloud ecosystems. By considering factors such as language support, cloud service integration, development tools, management features, and cost considerations, you can make an informed decision when choosing between AWS Lambda and Azure Functions for your cloud-based applications.

Each platform has its unique strengths and capabilities, and the choice between AWS Lambda and Azure Functions depends on the specific requirements of your project, your team's expertise, and your cloud provider preferences. Both platforms offer reliable and scalable serverless computing solutions that can significantly streamline application development, reduce operational overhead, and enhance overall efficiency in the cloud environment.

15.2.1. AWS Lambda for Cloud:

AWS Lambda is a serverless computing service that allows developers to run code in response to events without the need to manage servers or infrastructure. Lambda is tightly integrated with other AWS services, making it a compelling choice for cloud-based applications.

- **Integration with AWS Services:** AWS Lambda seamlessly integrates with various AWS services, such as Amazon S3, Amazon DynamoDB, Amazon API Gateway, and more. This integration allows developers to build serverless applications that leverage the power of AWS infrastructure and services.

- **Cloud-native Development:** AWS Lambda promotes cloud-native development by providing native support for AWS services, event-driven architectures, and the ability to trigger functions in response to cloud events. It enables developers to build highly scalable and decoupled cloud applications.

- **Infrastructure Management:** With AWS Lambda, developers are relieved from infrastructure management tasks. AWS takes care of server provisioning, scaling, and high availability, allowing developers to focus solely on writing code and delivering business value.

- **Pricing Model:** AWS Lambda follows a pay-per-use pricing model, where you are billed based on the number of function invocations and the duration of each invocation. AWS Lambda provides a generous free tier for new users, making it cost-effective for applications with sporadic or low-volume workloads.

15.2.2. Azure Functions for Cloud:

Azure Functions is a serverless compute service offered by Microsoft Azure. It enables developers to build event-driven applications that automatically scale based on demand. Azure Functions is tightly integrated with other Azure services, making it a suitable choice for cloud-based development.

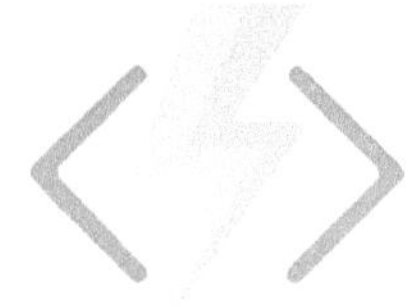

- **Integration with Azure Services:** Azure Functions seamlessly integrates with various Azure services, including Azure Blob Storage, Azure Cosmos DB, Azure Event Grid, and more. This integration enables developers to leverage the comprehensive ecosystem of Azure services in their serverless applications.

- **Event-driven Architecture:** Azure Functions is designed to follow an event-driven architecture, allowing developers to trigger functions in response to various cloud events, such as HTTP requests, timers, storage events, and message queue events. This architecture promotes scalability and loosely coupled application design.

- **Managed Infrastructure:** Azure Functions abstracts away the underlying infrastructure, providing managed execution environments for functions. Azure handles infrastructure management, including scaling, patching, and availability, enabling developers to focus on application logic.

- **Consumption-based Pricing:** Azure Functions adopts a consumption-based pricing model, where you are billed based on the actual consumption of resources during function execution. You only pay for the resources used, making it cost-effective for applications with variable or unpredictable workloads.

15.2.3. Considerations for Choosing a Platform:

- **Language Support:** Both AWS Lambda and Azure Functions support multiple programming languages, including popular choices like Node.js, Python, C#, and more. Consider the language support and ecosystem surrounding each platform to ensure compatibility with your development team's skills and project requirements.

- **Cloud Service Integration:** Evaluate the integration capabilities of each platform with other cloud services that are essential for your application. Both AWS Lambda and Azure Functions offer extensive integration with their respective cloud service ecosystems, enabling seamless utilization of additional cloud resources.

- **Development Tools and Ecosystem:** Assess the development tools, frameworks, and ecosystem surrounding each platform. Consider factors such as development environments, SDKs, deployment options, and community support to ensure a smooth development experience.

- **Management and Monitoring:** Compare the management consoles, monitoring capabilities, and debugging tools provided by AWS Lambda and Azure Functions. Evaluate the ease of monitoring, logging, and troubleshooting functions in each platform to ensure efficient management of your serverless applications.

- **Cost Considerations:** Understand the pricing models and associated costs of AWS Lambda and Azure Functions. Analyze your application's expected usage patterns, function execution durations, and scaling requirements to estimate the cost implications of each platform accurately.

15.3 Event-Driven Architecture with Serverless for Cloud: Building Scalable and Responsive Applications

Event-driven architecture combined with serverless computing offers a powerful approach for building scalable, responsive, and decoupled applications in the cloud. By leveraging the event-driven paradigm, developers can create applications that automatically scale and respond to events while benefiting from the cost efficiency and simplified infrastructure management provided by serverless computing. By following best practices such as identifying critical events, designing granular functions, using event brokers, implementing event-driven workflow orchestration, and monitoring event flow, organizations can harness the full potential of event-driven architecture with serverless in the cloud to build robust and scalable applications. The combination of event-driven architecture and serverless computing provides a winning strategy for developers aiming to create efficient and adaptable applications in the cloud.

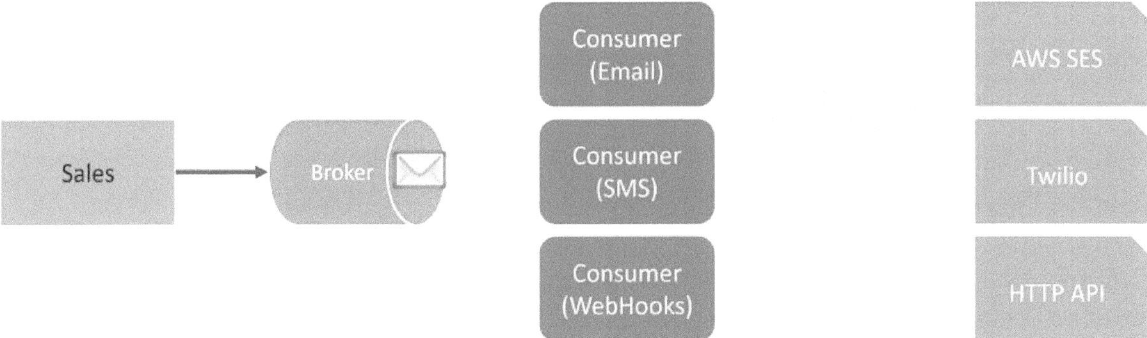

15.3.1. Understanding Event-Driven Architecture in the Cloud:

Event-driven architecture (EDA) in the cloud is an architectural approach where application components interact with each other through events. Events represent significant occurrences or changes in the system, such as user actions, system events, or data updates. In the cloud, EDA enables the creation of scalable and responsive applications that can handle dynamic workloads and efficiently respond to events.

- **Asynchronous Communication:** Event-driven architectures in the cloud rely on asynchronous communication between components. When an event occurs, it triggers a corresponding action or series of actions, which can be executed by serverless functions or other event-driven services. This asynchronous communication allows components to operate independently and decoupled from each other.

- **Scalability and Resilience:** By leveraging serverless computing in an event-driven architecture, applications can scale seamlessly and automatically based on incoming event load. Cloud providers manage the infrastructure and automatically allocate resources as needed, ensuring the application can handle varying workloads and maintain high availability.

15.3.2. Benefits of Event-Driven Architecture with Serverless in the Cloud:

- **Scalability:** Event-driven architecture combined with serverless computing enables applications to scale effortlessly based on event triggers. Cloud providers automatically allocate resources to handle event-driven workloads, ensuring that the application can scale up or down as needed without manual intervention.

- **Cost Efficiency:** Serverless computing follows a pay-per-use model, where you only pay for the actual execution time of functions triggered by events. This cost model eliminates the need to provision and manage resources continuously, resulting in cost savings for applications with sporadic or unpredictable event patterns.

- **Loose Coupling and Flexibility:** Event-driven architecture promotes loose coupling between application components, allowing them to operate independently and be easily modified or replaced without affecting other components. This flexibility enables agile development and enhances the application's ability to evolve and adapt to changing requirements.

- **Event-Driven Workflow:** With event-driven architecture, applications can easily define workflows that react to specific events. Events can trigger serverless functions, initiate data processing, trigger notifications, or invoke external services, enabling a dynamic and responsive application flow.

15.3.3. Key Components of Event-Driven Architecture with Serverless in the Cloud:

- **Events and Event Sources:** Events are the core building blocks of event-driven architectures. They can be generated by various sources such as user interactions, system events, external services, or data updates. Event sources can include HTTP requests, database triggers, message queues, or cloud service events.

- **Serverless Functions:** Serverless functions, such as those provided by AWS Lambda or Azure Functions, handle the execution of actions in response to events. These functions are event-triggered and perform specific tasks based on the event data. Serverless functions can be easily scaled, managed, and deployed on-demand.

- **Event Brokers or Message Brokers:** Event brokers or message brokers, such as AWS SNS (Simple Notification Service) or Azure Service Bus, facilitate the routing and distribution of events between different components. They ensure reliable event delivery and decouple event producers from event consumers.

- **Event Processing and Workflows:** Event-driven architectures often involve event processing and workflow management components. These components receive events, process them, and orchestrate the flow of actions or functions based on predefined rules or business logic. Tools like AWS Step Functions or Azure Logic Apps can be used for this purpose.

15.3.4. Best Practices for Event-Driven Architecture with Serverless in the Cloud:

- **Identify Events and Event Sources:** Determine the types of events that are critical to your application and identify the sources that generate those events. Consider user interactions, system events, external service integrations, or data updates as potential event sources.

- **Design Autonomous and Granular Functions:** Decompose application logic into small, autonomous serverless functions that perform specific tasks. This approach promotes loose coupling and allows for independent scaling and deployment of functions based on event triggers.

- **Use Event Brokers or Message Queues:** Utilize event brokers or message queues to decouple event producers from event consumers. This ensures reliable event delivery, provides fault tolerance, and allows for asynchronous processing.

- **Implement Event-Driven Workflow Orchestration:** Use workflow management tools or state machines, such as AWS Step Functions or Azure Logic Apps, to define and manage complex event-driven workflows. These tools provide visual representations of the workflow and enable reliable execution and error handling.

- **Monitor and Track Events:** Implement monitoring and logging mechanisms to track the flow of events and monitor the performance of serverless functions. Leverage cloud provider monitoring services, custom logging, or third-party tools to gain insights into event processing and application performance.

Exercise

Multiple Choice Questions

1. What is the main characteristic of Event-Driven Architecture (EDA) in the cloud?

a. Synchronous communication between components.

b. Asynchronous communication between components.

c. Centralized event handling.

d. Strict coupling between application components.

2. How does serverless computing enhance the scalability of applications in an event-driven architecture?

a. It allows direct communication between application components.

b. It automatically allocates resources to handle event-driven workloads.

c. It centralizes event processing for faster execution.

d. It eliminates the need for event brokers or message queues.

3. Which of the following is NOT a benefit of event-driven architecture combined with serverless computing in the cloud?

a. Scalability

b. Cost Efficiency

c. Tight Coupling between components

d. Flexibility

4. What is the role of event brokers or message queues in event-driven architecture?

a. They trigger serverless functions.

b. They handle the execution of actions in response to events.

c. They facilitate the routing and distribution of events between different components.

d. They provide monitoring and logging mechanisms for events.

5. What type of communication does event-driven architecture rely on between application components?

a. Synchronous communication

b. Asynchronous communication

c. Point-to-point communication

d. Broadcast communication

6. How do serverless functions in event-driven architectures handle the execution of tasks?

a. They continuously run in the background.

b. They are triggered by specific events and perform specific tasks based on event data.

c. They rely on a centralized event processing engine.

d. They communicate directly with other components for task execution.

7. Which cloud service feature allows event-driven architectures to handle varying workloads automatically?

a. Event Brokers

b. Message Queues

c. Infrastructure Provisioning

d. Automatic Resource Allocation

8. What is the pricing model of serverless computing for event-driven architectures?

a. Fixed monthly subscription

b. Pay-per-event

c. Pay-per-resource provisioned

d. Pay-per-use based on actual execution time

9. Which best practice ensures the independence and scalability of serverless functions in an event-driven architecture?

a. Avoiding the use of event brokers or message queues.

b. Designing autonomous and granular functions.

c. Increasing synchronous communication between functions.

d. Utilizing a centralized workflow management system.

10. What tool or service is commonly used to manage complex event-driven workflows in the cloud?

a. AWS Lambda

b. Azure Functions

c. AWS Step Functions

d. Azure Logic Apps

11. Which of the following is a critical consideration when designing an event-driven architecture with serverless computing in the cloud?

a. Maximizing synchronous communication between components.

b. Identifying critical events and event sources.

c. Avoiding the use of serverless functions.

d. Eliminating the need for monitoring and logging mechanisms.

Review Questions

1. What is serverless computing, and how does it differ from traditional cloud computing models?

2. What are the benefits of serverless computing in the cloud?

3. What is the significance of event-driven architecture in serverless computing?

4. What are the key components of serverless computing?

5. What best practices should be followed when leveraging serverless computing?

6. What are the distinguishing features of AWS Lambda for cloud applications?

7. How does Azure Functions compare to AWS Lambda as a serverless computing platform?

8. What considerations should be taken into account when choosing between AWS Lambda and Azure Functions?

9. What role does automated testing and continuous deployment play in serverless computing?

Answer Secton

Multiple Choice Questions

1. b) Asynchronous communication between components.
2. b) It automatically allocates resources to handle event-driven workloads.
3. c) Tight Coupling between components.
4. c) They facilitate the routing and distribution of events between different components.
5. b) Asynchronous communication.
6. b) They are triggered by specific events and perform specific tasks based on event data.
7. d) Automatic Resource Allocation.
8. d) Pay-per-use based on actual execution time.
9. b) Designing autonomous and granular functions.
10. b) AWS Step Functions.
11. b) Identifying critical events and event sources.

Review Questions

1. Serverless computing, also known as Function as a Service (FaaS), is a cloud computing model where developers write and deploy functions or application logic without having to manage servers. Unlike traditional cloud computing models, serverless computing abstracts away server management tasks, enabling developers to focus solely on code development, demand in response to specific events, such as HTTP requests or database updates. The cloud provider dynamically allocates resources to handle the incoming workload, scaling automatically based on demand, which optimizes cost efficiency and reduces operational overhead.

1. Serverless computing offers several benefits in the cloud environment. Firstly, it provides scalability and elasticity, allowing functions to automatically scale up or down in response to varying workloads. This ensures applications can handle traffic spikes efficiently. Secondly, serverless computing is cost-efficient as organizations are only charged based on the actual execution time of functions, avoiding idle time or fixed infrastructure costs. Additionally, serverless computing reduces operational overhead as developers are relieved from managing servers and infrastructure, enabling them to focus more on code development and business value. Moreover, it allows rapid development and deployment with smaller units of code, fostering agility and shorter time-to-market.

2. Event-driven architecture is a critical aspect of serverless computing. In this architecture, serverless functions are triggered by specific events, such as HTTP requests, database updates, or scheduled timers. When an event occurs, the corresponding function is executed on-demand, ensuring efficient resource utilization. Event-driven architecture enables automatic scaling based on workload demands, allowing applications to handle spikes in traffic seamlessly. As serverless functions are stateless and self-contained, they can be executed in parallel, optimizing performance and avoiding resource contention. The event-

driven approach in serverless computing enhances the agility and responsiveness of applications, making them suitable for various real-time use cases.

3. The key components of serverless computing are functions, event sources, and cloud provider services. Functions are the building blocks of serverless applications, containing specific units of code that perform tasks. Event sources, such as HTTP requests or database changes, trigger the execution of functions. Cloud provider services, such as AWS Lambda or Azure Functions, handle function execution, scaling, and event management. These services are crucial for serverless computing, providing the infrastructure and environment to run functions without server management. Together, these components create a seamless architecture for developing and deploying serverless applications in the cloud.

4. To maximize the benefits of serverless computing, organizations should follow several best practices. Firstly, adopt a granular function design by breaking applications into smaller, reusable functions to improve scalability and independent development. Secondly, ensure that serverless functions are stateless and externalize state storage to achieve data persistence and scalability. Implement appropriate security measures, such as authentication and encryption, to protect serverless functions and data transmission. Optimize function execution time by reducing dependencies and leveraging caching mechanisms. Implement comprehensive monitoring and logging solutions to proactively detect issues and troubleshoot performance bottlenecks. Finally, embrace automated testing and continuous deployment practices for rapid, reliable updates.

5. AWS Lambda offers several distinguishing features for cloud applications. It is tightly integrated with various AWS services, allowing developers to easily build serverless applications that leverage the full power of AWS infrastructure. With cloud-native development support, AWS Lambda enables developers to create applications that are highly scalable and decoupled, making them suitable for cloud environments. Furthermore, AWS Lambda's pay-as-you-go pricing model based on actual function execution time ensures cost efficiency for sporadic or unpredictable workloads. Additionally, AWS Lambda provides seamless infrastructure management, relieving developers from the burden of provisioning, scaling, and maintaining servers, allowing them to focus on business logic.

6. Azure Functions, like AWS Lambda, is a serverless computing platform that enables developers to run code without managing servers. It offers similar event-driven architecture, allowing functions to be triggered by events such as HTTP requests or timers. Azure Functions also provides seamless integration with various Azure services, making it easy to build cloud-native applications. In terms of pricing, both platforms follow a pay-as-you-go model based on actual function execution time. However, Azure Functions may have distinct features and service offerings compared to AWS Lambda. The choice between the two platforms depends on specific requirements, existing cloud ecosystem, and familiarity with the cloud provider.

7. When choosing between AWS Lambda and Azure Functions, several considerations come into play. Organizations should assess their existing cloud ecosystem and integration requirements with other cloud services. Both platforms have different pricing models and cost structures, so evaluating the cost implications based on expected workloads is essential. Considerations regarding developer expertise and familiarity with the cloud provider's environment should also be taken into account. Additionally, examining the performance, scalability, and feature offerings of both platforms in the context of the

specific application requirements will help make an informed decision. Conducting a thorough analysis of these factors will aid in choosing the right serverless computing platform.

8. Automated testing and continuous deployment are crucial for successful serverless computing. Automated testing ensures the quality and reliability of serverless functions, identifying and addressing issues early in the development process. Continuous deployment enables developers to release updates rapidly and frequently, supporting agile development cycles. Leveraging deployment pipelines and version control systems streamlines the process of managing and releasing function updates reliably. Automated testing and continuous deployment practices in serverless computing reduce the risk of deployment errors, improve application stability, and accelerate the delivery of new features and enhancements to users in real-time.

Chapter 16: Cloud Governance and Compliance

16.1 Cloud Security Frameworks: Strengthening Security in the Cloud

Cloud security frameworks play a crucial role in guiding organizations to secure their cloud environments effectively. By leveraging established frameworks such as the CSA Cloud Controls Matrix, CIS Controls, or the NIST Cybersecurity Framework, organizations can systematically assess risks, implement security controls, and ensure compliance with industry standards. These frameworks provide a structured approach to securing cloud-based systems, promoting risk management, best practices adoption, and continuous improvement. Implementing a cloud security framework is essential to establish a strong security foundation and protect sensitive data and critical assets in the cloud.

16.1.1. Understanding Cloud Security Frameworks:

Cloud security frameworks are structured approaches or guidelines that assist organizations in designing, implementing, and managing security controls and best practices for cloud environments. These frameworks provide a systematic methodology to assess risks, define security requirements, and implement appropriate security measures in the cloud.

- **Compliance and Standards:** Many cloud security frameworks align with established industry standards and compliance requirements, such as ISO 27001, NIST SP 800-53, or CSA's Cloud Controls Matrix (CCM). These frameworks help organizations demonstrate compliance with regulations and ensure adherence to industry-accepted security practices.

16.1.2. Popular Cloud Security Frameworks:

16.1.2.1 CSA Cloud Controls Matrix (CCM):

The Cloud Security Alliance (CSA) CCM is a widely adopted security framework that provides a catalog of security controls and best practices for cloud-based systems.

Key Components: CCM covers various domains, including governance, risk management, data protection, identity and access management, virtualization, and incident response. It offers a comprehensive set of control objectives and associated controls that organizations can adopt and customize for their cloud environments.

16.1.2.2 CIS (Center for Internet Security) Controls:

The CIS Controls are a set of 20 critical security controls developed by the Center for Internet Security. While not specific to the cloud, they provide a solid foundation for securing IT systems, including cloud environments.

Key Components: The CIS Controls cover areas such as inventory and control of hardware and software assets, secure configurations for hardware and software, continuous vulnerability management, controlled use of administrative privileges, and incident response capabilities. These controls can be applied to cloud infrastructure and applications to enhance security posture.

16.1.2.3 NIST Cybersecurity Framework:

The National Institute of Standards and Technology (NIST) Cybersecurity Framework is a widely recognized framework for managing and improving cybersecurity risk management processes across various industries.

Key Components: The NIST Cybersecurity Framework consists of five core functions - Identify, Protect, Detect, Respond, and Recover. It provides a flexible framework that organizations can tailor to their specific needs. The framework emphasizes risk assessment, continuous monitoring, incident response, and recovery planning, all of which are critical in securing cloud environments.

16.1.3. Significance of Cloud Security Frameworks:

- **Risk Assessment and Management:** Cloud security frameworks provide a structured approach to assess and manage risks associated with cloud adoption. They help identify potential vulnerabilities, prioritize security controls, and allocate resources effectively to mitigate risks.

- **Best Practices and Standards Compliance:** Cloud security frameworks align with established best practices and industry standards, enabling organizations to demonstrate compliance with regulatory requirements and industry-accepted security practices.

- Security Control Guidance: Cloud security frameworks offer comprehensive catalogs of security controls, enabling organizations to select and implement controls appropriate to their cloud environments. These frameworks provide guidance on implementing security measures and establishing a strong security posture.

- Continuous Improvement: Cloud security frameworks promote a culture of continuous improvement by emphasizing regular risk assessments, monitoring, and evaluation of security controls. They enable organizations to adapt and respond to evolving security threats and emerging technologies in the cloud.

16.2 Data Protection and Privacy in the Cloud: Safeguarding Sensitive Information

Data protection and privacy are paramount considerations when adopting cloud services. By implementing best practices such as data classification, strong access controls, encryption, compliance management, data backup, and incident response, organizations can effectively safeguard sensitive information in the cloud. It is essential to regularly review and update security measures, stay informed about evolving regulations, and collaborate closely with cloud service providers to ensure a robust security and privacy posture. By prioritizing data protection and privacy, organizations can maintain customer trust, comply with regulatory requirements, and safeguard sensitive information from unauthorized access or breaches in the cloud environment.

16.2.1 Understanding Data Protection and Privacy in the Cloud:

- Data Protection: Data protection encompasses a set of measures aimed at safeguarding data from unauthorized access, disclosure, alteration, or destruction. It involves implementing robust security controls, encryption mechanisms, access management policies, and data backup strategies to ensure both data integrity and confidentiality.

- Privacy: Privacy revolves around the protection of individuals' personal information and ensuring strict compliance with applicable privacy regulations. It entails obtaining informed consent for data collection, limiting data retention, and providing individuals with the ability to exercise control over their personal data.

16.2.2 Best Practices for Data Protection and Privacy in the Cloud:

16.2.2.1 Data Classification and Governance:

- Data Classification: Classify data based on its sensitivity and regulatory requirements. Apply appropriate security controls, access restrictions, and encryption protocols based on the data's classification to ensure that each level of data receives the appropriate level of protection.

- Data Governance: Establish comprehensive data governance policies and procedures to ensure proper data handling, retention, and disposal. Regularly review and update data governance practices to align with evolving regulations and industry standards.

16.2.2.2 Strong Access Controls and Authentication:

1. Role-Based Access Control (RBAC): Implement RBAC to assign access permissions based on user roles and responsibilities. Regularly review and update access privileges to ensure they align with the current business needs and minimize the risk of unauthorized access.

2. Multi-Factor Authentication (MFA): Enforce MFA for all user accounts to provide an additional layer of security and prevent unauthorized access. MFA requires users to provide multiple forms of identification, such as a password and a one-time code sent to their mobile device, to gain access to sensitive data.

16.2.2.3 Encryption and Data-at-Rest Protection:

- **Data Encryption:** Employ strong encryption mechanisms to protect sensitive data both in transit and at rest. Utilize robust encryption algorithms and ensure that encryption keys are securely managed and regularly rotated to maintain data confidentiality.

- **Secure Storage:** Choose cloud service providers that offer robust security measures and data encryption options. Regularly assess and validate the security controls implemented by the provider to ensure the integrity of data storage.

16.2.2.4 Data Residency and Compliance:

- **Data Residency:** Understand the location where data is stored and processed. Ensure compliance with data residency regulations and choose cloud providers that offer data centers within the desired jurisdictions to adhere to legal requirements.

- **Compliance Management:** Stay updated with applicable data protection and privacy regulations such as GDPR, CCPA, or industry-specific compliance requirements. Regularly assess and review compliance controls to maintain adherence and avoid potential legal issues.

16.2.2.5 Data Backup and Disaster Recovery:

- **Regular Backups:** Implement regular and automated data backup procedures to ensure data availability and resilience. Test the restoration process periodically to verify the integrity and effectiveness of backups and minimize data loss in case of system failures or cyber-attacks.

Disaster Recovery Planning: Develop a comprehensive disaster recovery plan to ensure data and system availability in case of unforeseen events. Regularly review and test the plan to address any gaps or emerging risks and expedite the recovery process.

16.2.2.6 Continuous Monitoring and Incident Response:

- **Security Monitoring:** Implement robust monitoring tools and processes to detect and respond to security incidents promptly. Monitor access logs, data transfers, and unusual activities to identify potential threats or breaches in real-time.

- **Incident Response:** Develop an incident response plan to outline the steps to be taken in the event of a security incident. Define roles, responsibilities, and communication channels to minimize the impact and mitigate risks quickly and efficiently.

16.3 Compliance Regulations and Audits for Cloud: Ensuring Regulatory Compliance in the Cloud

Compliance regulations and audits are indispensable in ensuring the security, privacy, and accountability of data stored and processed in the cloud. Organizations must have a comprehensive understanding of the regulatory landscape, implement appropriate security controls, and regularly assess their compliance posture. By adhering to key regulatory frameworks such as GDPR, HIPAA, PCI DSS, and FedRAMP, and following best practices such as conducting risk assessments, implementing strong access controls, encrypting data, and conducting regular audits, organizations can maintain compliance in the cloud environment. Compliance with regulatory requirements not only helps protect sensitive data but also builds trust with customers, partners, and regulatory authorities, positioning organizations for success in the cloud computing era.

16.3.1. Understanding Compliance Regulations and Audits in the Cloud:

- **Compliance Regulations:** Compliance regulations are legal frameworks that organizations must adhere to in order to protect sensitive data, ensure privacy, and meet industry-specific requirements. These regulations are designed to address concerns such as data protection, privacy, security, and accountability. Failure to comply with these regulations can lead to severe consequences, including fines and legal repercussions.

- **Audits:** Audits involve the thorough examination of an organization's systems, processes, and controls to ensure compliance with relevant regulations and industry standards. Audits provide an independent assessment of an organization's compliance posture and help identify areas for improvement. They play a critical role in ensuring that an organization's security measures and data handling practices align with regulatory requirements.

16.3.2. Key Regulatory Frameworks for Cloud Compliance:

- **General Data Protection Regulation (GDPR):** GDPR is a comprehensive regulation enacted by the European Union (EU) to protect the personal data and privacy of individuals within the EU. It imposes stringent data protection and privacy requirements on organizations, regardless of their physical location. Organizations handling personal data of EU residents must comply with GDPR.

- **Health Insurance Portability and Accountability Act (HIPAA):** HIPAA establishes regulations to safeguard the privacy and security of protected health information (PHI) in the healthcare industry. Covered entities and business associates that handle PHI must adhere to strict data protection standards and implement appropriate safeguards when using cloud services.

- **Payment Card Industry Data Security Standard (PCI DSS):** PCI DSS is a security standard designed to protect credit card data during storage, processing, and transmission. Organizations that handle credit card information must comply with PCI DSS requirements to ensure the security of cardholder data. Even though the cloud does not specifically fall under PCI DSS, organizations using cloud services need to ensure that the cloud provider meets PCI DSS compliance when processing or transmitting credit card data.

- Federal Risk and Authorization Management Program (FedRAMP): FedRAMP is a U.S. government program that provides a standardized approach to assessing and authorizing cloud services for use in federal agencies. It ensures that cloud service providers meet rigorous security and compliance requirements, making them suitable for government use.

16.3.3. Best Practices for Cloud Compliance:

- Understand Applicable Regulations: Identify the regulatory requirements that apply to your organization based on industry, geographic location, and the types of data being processed or stored in the cloud. Stay up-to-date with changes to relevant regulations to maintain compliance.

- Conduct Risk Assessments: Regularly assess the risks associated with cloud adoption and identify areas where compliance controls need to be strengthened. Implement security controls, data protection measures, and privacy safeguards accordingly to mitigate risks.

- Cloud Provider Due Diligence: When selecting a cloud service provider, conduct due diligence to evaluate their compliance posture and the specific services they offer to meet regulatory requirements. Ensure that the cloud provider has relevant certifications and accreditations.

- Data Classification and Encryption: Classify data based on its sensitivity and regulatory requirements. Implement encryption mechanisms to protect data at rest and in transit, adhering to industry-standard encryption algorithms.

- Access Controls and Monitoring: Implement strong access controls to ensure that only authorized personnel can access sensitive data in the cloud. Implement monitoring and auditing mechanisms to detect and respond to unauthorized access or suspicious activities promptly.

- Incident Response and Breach Notification: Develop an incident response plan to handle security incidents or data breaches effectively. Establish procedures for timely breach notification to relevant authorities and affected individuals, as required by regulations.

- Regular Audits and Assessments: Conduct internal and external audits or assessments to validate compliance with applicable regulations and industry standards. Regularly review and update security controls based on audit findings and recommendations to improve the overall compliance posture.

Exercise

Multiple Choice Questions

1. What is the primary purpose of cloud security frameworks?

a. To develop cloud-based applications

b. To manage and maintain cloud infrastructure

c. To provide a systematic approach to managing security risks and implementing security controls in the cloud

d. To ensure high availability of cloud services

2. Which cloud security framework provides a catalog of security controls and best practices for cloud-based systems and is developed by the Cloud Security Alliance (CSA)?

a. General Data Protection Regulation (GDPR)

b. Payment Card Industry Data Security Standard (PCI DSS)

c. Center for Internet Security (CIS) Controls

d. CSA Cloud Controls Matrix (CCM)

3. What is the purpose of the CIS (Center for Internet Security) Controls?

a. To secure credit card data during storage, processing, and transmission

b. To provide a standardized approach for assessing and authorizing cloud services for use in federal agencies

c. To establish regulations for safeguarding protected health information (PHI) in the healthcare industry

d. To provide a set of critical security controls for securing IT systems, including cloud environments

4. Which core functions are included in the NIST Cybersecurity Framework?

a. Identify, Protect, Detect, Respond, and Recover

b. Governance, Risk Management, Data Protection, and Incident Response

c. Encryption, Access Management, and Virtualization

d. Inventory Management, Incident Recovery, and Data Retention

5. What does GDPR stand for, and what does it aim to protect?

a. General Data Privacy Regulation; aims to protect credit card data during storage and transmission

b. General Data Protection Regulation; aims to protect personal data and privacy of individuals within the European Union

c. Government Data Protection Regulation; aims to protect government data from cyber-attacks

d. General Data Privacy Regulation; aims to protect health information in the healthcare industry

6. Why are audits essential in ensuring compliance in the cloud?

a. Audits help organizations avoid cloud adoption entirely

b. Audits provide a systematic approach to assessing risks in the cloud

c. Audits ensure that cloud providers adhere to industry standards

d. Audits provide an independent assessment of an organization's compliance posture and help identify areas for improvement

7. What are some best practices for maintaining cloud compliance?

a. Ignoring changes to relevant regulations to maintain compliance

b. Not conducting risk assessments in cloud environments

c. Implementing strong access controls and encryption

d. Avoiding cloud provider due diligence

8. What is the purpose of the FedRAMP program?

a. To protect credit card data during storage, processing, and transmission

b. To provide a standardized approach for assessing and authorizing cloud services for use in federal agencies

c. To safeguard the privacy and security of protected health information (PHI) in the healthcare industry

d. To ensure compliance with GDPR regulations in cloud environments

9. What does RBAC stand for, and what does it involve?

a. Role-Based Access Control; involves assigning access permissions based on user roles and responsibilities

b. Role-Based Access Compliance; involves monitoring cloud environments for security incidents

c. Role-Based Authentication Control; involves encrypting data at rest and in transit

d. Role-Based Authorization Compliance; involves conducting internal and external audits for cloud compliance

10. Why is data classification important for cloud compliance?

a. Data classification helps organizations avoid the use of cloud services

b. Data classification ensures that all data is encrypted

c. Data classification helps organizations apply appropriate security controls and access restrictions based on data sensitivity and regulatory requirements

d. Data classification is not relevant for cloud compliance

Review Questions

1. What is the purpose of cloud security frameworks, and how do they assist organizations in securing their cloud environments?

2. What are the key components of the General Data Protection Regulation (GDPR), and how does it impact organizations using cloud services?

3. How can organizations ensure regulatory compliance when using cloud services, particularly in industries like healthcare that must adhere to the Health Insurance Portability and Accountability Act (HIPAA)?

4. What are the primary considerations for organizations regarding data protection and privacy in the cloud, and how can they effectively safeguard sensitive information?

5. What role do compliance audits play in ensuring the security and privacy of data stored and processed in the cloud?

6. How can organizations effectively manage data governance in the cloud to meet regulatory requirements and ensure proper data handling?

7. How do cloud service providers contribute to ensuring regulatory compliance in cloud environments, and what factors should organizations consider when choosing a compliant cloud provider?

8. How can organizations foster a culture of continuous improvement to maintain regulatory compliance in the rapidly evolving landscape of cloud computing?

Answer Section

Multiple Choice Questions

1. c) To provide a systematic approach to managing security risks and implementing security controls in the cloud

2. d) CSA Cloud Controls Matrix (CCM)

3. d) To provide a set of critical security controls for securing IT systems, including cloud environments

4. a) Identify, Protect, Detect, Respond, and Recover

5. b) General Data Protection Regulation; aims to protect personal data and privacy of individuals within the European Union

6. d) Audits provide an independent assessment of an organization's compliance posture and help identify areas for improvement

7. c) Implementing strong access controls and encryption

8. b) To provide a standardized approach for assessing and authorizing cloud services for use in federal agencies

9. a) Role-Based Access Control; involves assigning access permissions based on user roles and responsibilities

10. c) Data classification helps organizations apply appropriate security controls and access restrictions based on data sensitivity and regulatory requirements

Review Questions

1. Cloud security frameworks serve as structured guidelines to design, implement, and manage security controls in cloud environments. They help organizations assess risks, define security requirements, and

apply appropriate measures to safeguard data and infrastructure. By providing a systematic methodology, these frameworks enable effective risk management, best practices adoption, and compliance with industry standards. Popular frameworks like CSA CCM, CIS Controls, and NIST Cybersecurity Framework offer comprehensive catalogs of controls and objectives that organizations can customize to their specific cloud setups, ensuring a robust security posture and enhanced protection against cyber threats.

2. GDPR is a comprehensive EU regulation focused on safeguarding the personal data and privacy of individuals. Its key components include data subject rights, informed consent, data protection officers, and mandatory data breach notification. GDPR applies to organizations worldwide if they handle personal data of EU residents. For cloud users, compliance involves adhering to GDPR principles when processing, storing, or transmitting personal data in the cloud. Organizations must ensure data protection measures, secure access controls, and privacy safeguards are in place to comply with GDPR requirements and avoid potential fines or legal consequences for mishandling personal data.

3. Ensuring regulatory compliance in the cloud, especially for healthcare organizations under HIPAA, requires a multi-faceted approach. Organizations must conduct thorough risk assessments, implement strong access controls, encrypt data, and enforce strict data governance. Cloud providers should be carefully selected based on their compliance with relevant regulations, including HIPAA Business Associate Agreements (BAAs). Regular audits and assessments are necessary to validate compliance. It is crucial to develop a comprehensive incident response plan and train staff on compliance procedures. By adopting industry best practices, healthcare organizations can effectively safeguard patient data and maintain HIPAA compliance in the cloud.

4. Organizations must consider data classification, access controls, encryption, and data residency requirements to protect sensitive information in the cloud. Data classification ensures that data is categorized based on its sensitivity, allowing appropriate security measures to be applied. Strong access controls, like Role-Based Access Control (RBAC) and Multi-Factor Authentication (MFA), limit access to authorized personnel. Encryption should be employed to protect data both at rest and in transit. Compliance with data residency regulations is essential for handling data in specific jurisdictions. By implementing these measures, organizations can effectively safeguard sensitive data, maintain data privacy, and prevent unauthorized access or breaches.

5. Compliance audits play a critical role in evaluating an organization's adherence to regulatory requirements and industry standards. They provide an independent assessment of an organization's security posture and data handling practices in the cloud. Audits help identify areas of non-compliance, security gaps, and potential vulnerabilities. By conducting regular internal and external audits, organizations can validate their compliance efforts, improve security controls, and address any issues or deficiencies promptly. Audits serve as a mechanism to demonstrate due diligence to regulators, customers, and partners, ensuring that data stored and processed in the cloud is adequately protected and privacy is maintained.

6. Effective data governance in the cloud requires a comprehensive strategy to handle data properly throughout its lifecycle. Organizations should define data ownership, data access controls, and data retention policies based on regulatory requirements and industry standards. Implementing data loss prevention (DLP) mechanisms helps prevent unauthorized data leakage. Regular data audits and access

reviews ensure that data handling practices align with data governance policies. Organizations must also provide training and awareness programs to educate employees on data handling best practices and privacy requirements. By establishing robust data governance practices, organizations can ensure data integrity, confidentiality, and compliance in the cloud.

7. Cloud service providers play a crucial role in ensuring regulatory compliance in cloud environments. They are responsible for maintaining a secure infrastructure, implementing appropriate security controls, and offering compliance certifications and audits. Organizations should choose cloud providers that align with relevant regulatory requirements and industry standards, such as GDPR or HIPAA compliance. Cloud providers should offer transparency regarding their security practices, data encryption, data residency options, and data breach notification procedures. Additionally, organizations must review and negotiate clear service-level agreements (SLAs) with cloud providers, outlining data protection responsibilities and contractual terms regarding compliance measures.

8. Organizations can foster a culture of continuous improvement for cloud compliance through ongoing risk assessments, regular audits, and security awareness training. Continuous monitoring of cloud environments ensures prompt detection and response to security incidents. Staying informed about changing regulations and industry standards helps organizations adapt their security measures to evolving requirements. Collaboration with cloud providers and participation in industry forums helps gain insights into best practices. By conducting regular internal reviews, organizations can identify areas for enhancement and apply lessons learned from incidents to bolster their cloud security and compliance posture. Emphasizing a proactive approach to compliance ensures that organizations are resilient in the face of emerging cloud security challenges.

Chapter 17: Cloud Native Development and Microservices

17.1 Introduction to Cloud Native: Building Scalable and Resilient Applications for the Cloud

Cloud native represents a paradigm shift in application development and deployment that harnesses the scalability, resilience, and flexibility of cloud computing. By embracing cloud native principles, organizations can build highly scalable, resilient, and cost-effective applications ideally suited for the cloud environment. The use of microservices, containers, container orchestration, infrastructure as code, service mesh, and observability tools enables the full realization of the potential of cloud native architecture. Embracing cloud native empowers organizations to rapidly innovate, deliver high-quality applications, and leverage the benefits of the cloud to stay competitive in today's fast-paced digital landscape.

17.1 1. Understanding Cloud Native:

Cloud native refers to an architectural approach and development methodology that optimizes the potential of cloud computing and its native services for designing, developing, and deploying applications. It revolves around building applications using cloud services, microservices, containers, and orchestrating them with modern DevOps practices.

Key Characteristics of Cloud Native:

- **Scalability and Elasticity:** Cloud native applications are meticulously designed to scale horizontally and vertically based on demand. They can dynamically adjust to fluctuating workloads and automatically allocate resources to ensure optimal performance.

- **Resilience and Fault Tolerance:** Cloud native applications are engineered to be highly resilient in the face of failures. They leverage redundancy, self-healing mechanisms, and fault-tolerant architectures to minimize downtime and ensure continuous availability.

- **Agility and Continuous Delivery:** Cloud native embraces agile development practices and emphasizes continuous integration, continuous delivery (CI/CD), and automated deployment pipelines. This approach enables rapid iteration, shorter release cycles, and faster time-to-market.

- **DevOps Collaboration:** Cloud native promotes a close collaboration between development and operations teams. It encourages the use of automation, infrastructure as code (IaC), and a culture of shared responsibility to streamline application deployment and management.

17.1 2. Benefits of Cloud Native:

- **Scalability and Flexibility:** Cloud native applications can scale effortlessly to accommodate changing workloads, allowing organizations to meet fluctuating demand without overprovisioning resources.

- **Resilience and High Availability:** Cloud native applications are designed to handle failures gracefully and recover swiftly, ensuring minimal downtime and improved reliability.

- **Cost Efficiency:** By leveraging cloud resources and scaling dynamically, cloud native applications optimize resource utilization, leading to cost savings compared to traditional infrastructure models.

- **Faster Time-to-Market:** The agile development practices and automation in cloud native enable faster development cycles, empowering organizations to release new features and updates rapidly.

- **Improved Developer Productivity:** Cloud native provides development teams with modern tools, technologies, and workflows that simplify application development, deployment, and management, leading to improved developer productivity.

17.1 3. Core Technologies and Principles of Cloud Native:

- **Microservices:** Cloud native applications are constructed using a microservices architecture, where applications are broken down into small, independently deployable services. This modular approach enables scalability, agility, and easier maintenance.

- **Containers and Container Orchestration:** Cloud native applications are often deployed in containers using technologies like Docker. Container orchestration platforms, such as Kubernetes, provide automated management and scaling of containers in a cloud environment.

- **Infrastructure as Code (IaC):** Infrastructure as Code is a fundamental principle of cloud native. It involves defining and managing infrastructure resources using code, allowing for consistent and repeatable deployments.

- **Service Mesh:** A service mesh, such as Istio or Linkerd, provides a dedicated infrastructure layer to manage communication between services in a cloud native application. It offers features like traffic routing, load balancing, and observability.

Observability and Monitoring: Cloud native applications leverage monitoring and observability tools to gain insights into application performance, troubleshoot issues, and ensure efficient resource utilization.

17.2 Building Microservices in the Cloud: Scalable and Decoupled Application Architectures

Building microservices in the cloud offers organizations the flexibility, scalability, and agility needed to develop modern, resilient, and highly scalable applications. By adhering to the key principles of microservices architecture and considering best practices such as service design, resilience, scalability, security, and observability, organizations can successfully leverage the benefits of microservices in the cloud. Embracing this architectural approach allows businesses to build modular and independent services that are well-suited for the dynamic and scalable nature of cloud computing, enabling them to deliver innovative and highly responsive applications in today's fast-paced digital landscape.

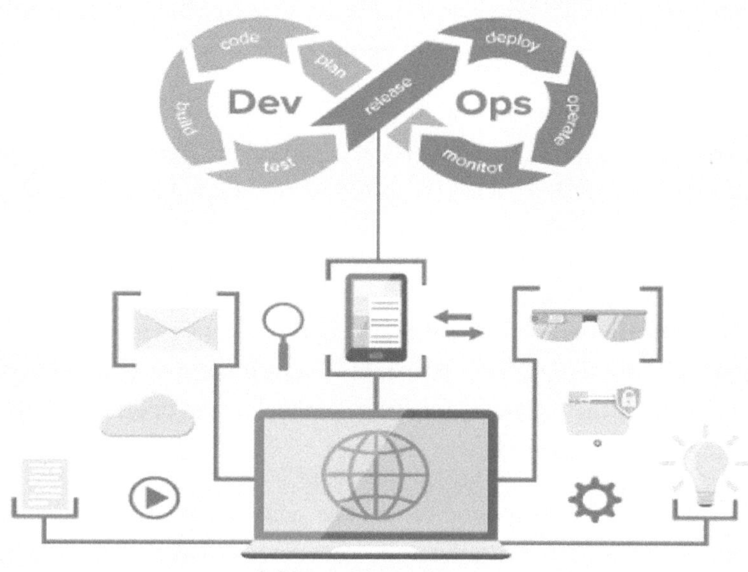

17.2.1. Understanding Microservices Architecture:

Microservices architecture is an architectural style that structures an application as a collection of loosely coupled services. Each service is self-contained, focused on a specific business capability, and can be independently developed, deployed, and scaled. This approach promotes agility, flexibility, and modularity in application development.

Key Principles of Microservices Architecture:

- **Service Independence:** Microservices are autonomous units that can be developed, deployed, and scaled independently of one another. This allows for parallel development and faster time-to-market.

- **Decentralized Data Management:** Each microservice has its own data store, enabling data management and modification within the service boundary, promoting loose coupling between services.

- **Communication via APIs:** Microservices interact with each other through well-defined APIs, facilitating loose coupling and service integration while abstracting the underlying implementation details.

- **Continuous Deployment and Scalability:** Microservices can be individually deployed and scaled based on demand, allowing for efficient resource utilization and dynamic scalability.

17.2.2. Benefits of Microservices Architecture in the Cloud:

- **Scalability:** Microservices architecture, combined with cloud computing, enables horizontal scaling of individual services, ensuring optimal performance under varying workloads and high user demands.

- **Agility and Faster Time-to-Market:** Independent development and deployment of microservices allow teams to work in parallel, facilitating faster iterations and enabling quicker delivery of new features and updates.

- **Resilience and Fault Isolation:** Microservices operate independently, isolating failures within a single service and ensuring that other services remain unaffected, leading to enhanced system resilience.

- **Flexibility in Technology Stacks:** Microservices allow organizations to use different technologies and programming languages for different services, enabling the best tool selection for specific business needs and preferences.

- **Simplified Maintenance and Evolvability:** Microservices promote modular development, making it easier to maintain, update, and enhance individual services without affecting the entire system, thereby simplifying long-term application management.

17.2.3. Building Microservices in the Cloud:

- **Service Design and Domain Boundaries:** Identify and define clear service boundaries based on business capabilities and domain-driven design principles to ensure proper separation of concerns. Strive for an optimal service granularity that balances functional cohesion and operational efficiency, avoiding services that are too large or too fine-grained.

- **Resilience and Fault Tolerance:** Implement mechanisms such as circuit breakers, retries, and timeouts to handle service failures and network issues gracefully. Leverage cloud-native infrastructure capabilities, such as auto-scaling, load balancing, and health checks, to ensure system resilience and maintain high availability.

- **Scalability and Performance:** Utilize cloud-based container orchestration platforms like Kubernetes to manage the deployment, scaling, and monitoring of microservices efficiently. Design services to scale horizontally, allowing for increased availability and efficient resource utilization during traffic spikes.

- **Security and Data Management:** Implement robust authentication, authorization, and encryption mechanisms to secure communication between microservices and protect sensitive data. Adopt cloud-native database services or consider distributed database solutions for efficient data management and scalability.

- **Observability and Monitoring:** Employ distributed tracing, logging, and monitoring tools to gain visibility into the behavior and performance of individual microservices and the entire system. Leverage cloud-native monitoring services to monitor service health, response times, and resource utilization, enabling timely detection and resolution of performance bottlenecks.

17.3 Service Mesh and Container Orchestration for Cloud: Enhancing Microservices Communication and Management

Service mesh and container orchestration technologies play pivotal roles in enhancing microservices communication and management within the cloud environment. Service mesh provides a dedicated infrastructure layer for service-to-service communication, offering robust features like traffic management, service discovery, and observability. Container orchestration platforms automate the deployment, scaling, and management of containers, ensuring efficient resource utilization and high availability. Together, these technologies enable organizations to build scalable, resilient, and manageable microservices architectures in the cloud. By leveraging the benefits of service mesh and container orchestration, businesses can enhance their microservices communication, improve scalability, ensure security, and simplify application deployment and management, ultimately delivering reliable and efficient cloud-native applications in today's dynamic digital landscape.

17.3.1. Understanding Service Mesh:

A service mesh is a dedicated infrastructure layer that provides a powerful communication framework between services in a microservices architecture. It efficiently handles service-to-service communication, managing essential functions such as traffic routing, load balancing, service discovery, and observability.

Key Components of Service Mesh:

- **Proxies (Sidecar):** A service mesh deploys a lightweight proxy, known as a sidecar, alongside each microservice instance. These proxies handle communication by intercepting and routing requests between services, enabling seamless service communication.

- **Service Registry:** The service mesh maintains a service registry that stores information about available services, their endpoints, and metadata, facilitating service discovery and dynamic routing based on real-time information.

- **Traffic Management:** Service mesh controls traffic flow between services, implementing advanced features like load balancing, circuit breaking, retries, and timeouts to ensure optimal performance and fault tolerance.

- **Observability:** Service mesh provides robust observability features, including monitoring and logging capabilities, allowing for metrics collection, distributed tracing, and error logging to gain valuable insights into service behavior and performance.

17.3.2. Understanding Container Orchestration:

Container orchestration involves the efficient management and scaling of containers that host microservices in a cloud environment. It automates container deployment, scaling, and load balancing to ensure optimal resource utilization, high availability, and seamless application management.

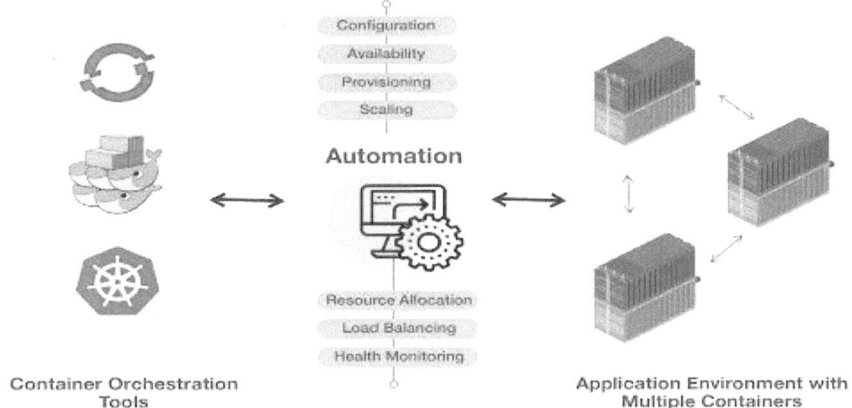

Key Components of Container Orchestration:

- **Container Runtime:** Container orchestration platforms, such as Kubernetes, manage container runtimes, including scheduling, provisioning, and lifecycle management of containers, streamlining container deployment and scaling.

- **Scaling and Load Balancing:** Container orchestration platforms dynamically scale containers based on workload demands, automatically adding or removing instances to handle varying traffic and ensure application resilience.

- **Service Discovery:** Container orchestration platforms provide mechanisms for service discovery, allowing services to locate and communicate with each other dynamically, regardless of changes in the infrastructure.

- **Self-Healing:** Container orchestration platforms continuously monitor container health and automatically restart or replace failed containers to maintain application availability and reliability.

- **Rolling Deployments and Updates:** Container orchestration enables seamless deployment and updates of containerized applications, ensuring zero-downtime releases and smooth rollbacks in case of issues, promoting uninterrupted service delivery.

17.3.3. Benefits of Service Mesh and Container Orchestration for Cloud:

- **Enhanced Communication:** Service mesh provides a dedicated infrastructure layer for managing service-to-service communication, enabling secure, reliable, and scalable interaction between microservices. It simplifies complex communication patterns and ensures proper load balancing and routing for efficient service interaction.

- **Scalability and Resilience:** Container orchestration platforms dynamically scale containers based on workload demands, ensuring applications can handle increased traffic and recover quickly from failures. This enhances application scalability and resilience.

- **Observability and Monitoring:** Service mesh and container orchestration platforms offer robust monitoring and observability capabilities, providing valuable insights into service performance, latency, and errors. This enhances troubleshooting, optimization, and the overall understanding of the system's behavior.

- **Security and Traffic Control:** Service mesh can implement robust security measures such as mutual TLS encryption and access control policies, ensuring secure communication between microservices. Container orchestration platforms offer traffic management capabilities, load balancing, and routing to optimize traffic flow, enhancing security and efficiency.

- **Simplified Deployment and Management:** Container orchestration platforms automate the deployment, scaling, and management of containerized microservices, reducing manual effort and simplifying application lifecycle management. This leads to streamlined development workflows and improved overall application management.

Exercise

Multiple Choice Questions

1. What is the primary goal of cloud native architecture?

a. Minimize cloud resource utilization

b. Achieve fully on-premises deployment

c. Create scalable, resilient, and highly available applications

d. Optimize traditional infrastructure models

2. Which of the following is NOT a key characteristic of cloud native applications?

a. Scalability and Elasticity

b. Resilience and Fault Tolerance

c. Agility and Continuous Delivery

d. Strict Monolithic Architecture

3. What benefit does cloud native architecture offer in terms of cost?

a. Increased cost due to overprovisioning resources

b. Reduced cost compared to traditional infrastructure models

c. Equal cost compared to traditional infrastructure models

d. No impact on cost

4. What development approach does cloud native embrace for faster time-to-market?

a. Waterfall development

b. Agile development practices

c. Heavy manual testing and verification

d. Traditional monolithic application development

5. What does cloud native promote to streamline application deployment and management?

a. Collaboration between development and sales teams

b. Use of traditional infrastructure models

c. Manual deployment practices

d. Automation, infrastructure as code (IaC), and shared responsibility culture

6. What is the key principle of microservices architecture that allows independent development and deployment of services?

a. Service Independence

b. Centralized Data Management

c. Tight Coupling

d. Manual Deployment

7. What is the benefit of independent development and deployment of microservices in the cloud?

a. Slower development cycles

b. Longer time-to-market

c. Faster iterations and quicker delivery of new features

d. Reduced scalability

8. What advantage does microservices architecture offer in terms of system resilience?

a. Increased susceptibility to failures

b. Isolation of failures within a single service

c. Inability to handle traffic spikes

d. Centralized data management

9. How does microservices architecture enable flexibility in technology stacks?

a. By enforcing the use of the same programming language for all services

b. By using a monolithic application structure

c. By allowing different technologies and programming languages for different services

d. By eliminating the need for independent deployment

10. What is the primary advantage of using container orchestration platforms like Kubernetes for microservices in the cloud?

a. Increased manual effort in managing containers

b. Reduced resource utilization

c. Seamless deployment, scaling, and load balancing of containers

d. Elimination of microservices architecture

11. What is the main purpose of a service mesh in a microservices architecture?

a. To serve as the user interface for microservices

b. To provide a dedicated infrastructure layer for service-to-service communication

c. To manage microservices database operations

d. To handle authentication and authorization for microservices

12. What components are part of a service mesh architecture?

a. Sidecars, circuit breakers, and databases

b. Proxies (sidecars), service registry, traffic management, and observability

c. Frontend user interface, load balancers, and message queues

d. API gateways, routers, and caching servers

13. What does container orchestration automate in a cloud environment?

a. Deployment of bare-metal servers

b. Management of virtual machines

c. Container deployment, scaling, and load balancing

d. Network firewall configurations

14. How does container orchestration contribute to system resilience?

a. By increasing the complexity of microservices communication

b. By using a monolithic application structure

c. By dynamically scaling containers based on workload demands

d. By centralizing data management for all services

15. Which technology enables service discovery and communication between microservices in a container orchestration platform?

a. Load balancers

b. API gateways

c. Service mesh

d. Message brokers

Review Questions

1. What are the key characteristics of cloud-native applications?

2. How do microservices architecture and cloud computing together enhance application scalability?

3. What are the benefits of using containers and container orchestration platforms like Kubernetes in cloud-native applications?

4. How does the use of Infrastructure as Code (IaC) benefit cloud-native application development?

5. How does service mesh facilitate efficient communication between microservices in a cloud-native architecture?

6. How does adopting cloud-native principles lead to faster time-to-market for applications?

7. How does microservices architecture promote better maintenance and evolvability of applications?

8. How do service mesh and container orchestration platforms enhance the security of cloud-native applications?

Answer Secton

Multiple Choice Questions

1. c) Create scalable, resilient, and highly available applications
2. d) Strict Monolithic Architecture
3. b) Reduced cost compared to traditional infrastructure models
4. b) Agile development practices
5. d) Automation, infrastructure as code (IaC), and shared responsibility culture
6. a) Service Independence
7. c) Faster iterations and quicker delivery of new features
8. b) Isolation of failures within a single service
9. c) By allowing different technologies and programming languages for different services
10. c) Seamless deployment, scaling, and load balancing of containers
11. b) To provide a dedicated infrastructure layer for service-to-service communication
12. b) Proxies (sidecars), service registry, traffic management, and observability
13. c) Container deployment, scaling, and load balancing
14. c) By dynamically scaling containers based on workload demands
15. c) Service mesh

Review Questions

1. Cloud-native applications exhibit key characteristics like scalability and elasticity, allowing them to dynamically adjust to fluctuating workloads by allocating resources for optimal performance. They are designed to be highly resilient, leveraging redundancy and self-healing mechanisms to minimize downtime and ensure continuous availability. Embracing agile development practices, they emphasize continuous integration, continuous delivery (CI/CD), and automated deployment pipelines, enabling faster time-to-market and rapid iteration. Furthermore, cloud-native applications promote DevOps collaboration, encouraging the use of automation, infrastructure as code (IaC), and a culture of shared responsibility to streamline application deployment and management.

2. Microservices architecture, when combined with cloud computing, enables horizontal scaling of individual services. Each microservice is self-contained and can be independently deployed and scaled based on demand. Cloud computing provides the infrastructure and resources required for dynamic scaling. As workload demands fluctuate, cloud-native applications can add or remove instances of microservices, ensuring optimal performance under varying workloads. This enhances application scalability, allowing it to handle increased traffic and user demands without overprovisioning resources.

3. Containers provide a lightweight and consistent environment for running cloud-native applications. They encapsulate application code, dependencies, and configuration, enabling portability and efficient

resource utilization. Container orchestration platforms, such as Kubernetes, automate the deployment, scaling, and management of containers in a cloud environment. Kubernetes ensures high availability, fault tolerance, and load balancing by dynamically managing container instances. It simplifies the management of complex microservices architectures, streamlines application deployment, and optimizes resource allocation, ultimately contributing to improved application resilience and scalability.

4. Infrastructure as Code (IaC) is a fundamental principle of cloud-native application development that involves defining and managing infrastructure resources using code. IaC enables consistent and repeatable deployments, reducing the likelihood of configuration errors and ensuring a reproducible environment. This practice improves the reliability of the infrastructure, simplifies the process of creating and managing resources, and facilitates version control and collaboration among development and operations teams. IaC also supports rapid application development and deployment, allowing organizations to adapt quickly to changing requirements and ensuring that the infrastructure aligns with the application needs.

5. A service mesh provides a dedicated infrastructure layer for managing service-to-service communication in a microservices architecture. It deploys lightweight proxies, known as sidecars, alongside each microservice instance. These proxies intercept and route requests between services, abstracting the underlying communication complexity from individual microservices. The service mesh also maintains a service registry that stores information about available services, facilitating service discovery and dynamic routing based on real-time information. With features like traffic management, load balancing, and observability, service mesh enhances communication efficiency, security, and reliability within a cloud-native application.

6. Cloud-native principles, such as agile development practices and continuous integration and delivery (CI/CD), contribute to faster time-to-market for applications. Agile development allows teams to work in parallel, speeding up the development process. CI/CD automates testing and deployment, reducing manual effort and enabling rapid iteration. Cloud-native infrastructure, with its scalability and elasticity, ensures that applications can handle varying workloads and user demands, allowing organizations to launch their products or updates without delays caused by provisioning and scaling traditional infrastructure. Altogether, cloud-native practices streamline the development and deployment pipeline, enabling organizations to release new features and updates rapidly.

7. Microservices architecture promotes better maintenance and evolvability by breaking down applications into small, independently deployable services. Each service focuses on a specific business capability and operates autonomously. This modular design makes it easier to update and enhance individual services without affecting the entire application. Microservices' loose coupling also reduces the impact of changes on other services, minimizing the risk of system-wide failures. As a result, organizations can perform upgrades, bug fixes, and feature additions more efficiently, without the need to take the entire application offline, leading to improved long-term application management.

8. Service mesh and container orchestration platforms play essential roles in enhancing the security of cloud-native applications. Service mesh enables secure communication between microservices by implementing robust security measures like mutual TLS encryption and access control policies. It ensures that data transmission within the microservices architecture remains confidential and authenticated. On the other hand, container orchestration platforms like Kubernetes provide advanced security features, such

as network policies and pod security policies, to restrict access between containers and secure the underlying infrastructure. By combining these technologies, organizations can establish a robust security posture for their cloud-native applications, protecting them from potential threats and vulnerabilities.

Chapter 18: Data Analytics and Machine Learning in the Cloud

18.1 Cloud-based Data Warehousing: Scalable and Analytics-Ready Data Storage

Cloud-based data warehousing empowers organizations with scalable, cost-effective, and analytics-ready data storage solutions. By leveraging cloud infrastructure, data integration capabilities, and advanced analytics tools, organizations can unlock the value of their data, gain valuable insights, and make data-driven decisions. To achieve success with cloud-based data warehousing, adherence to best practices in data modeling, integration, security, performance optimization, and backup and recovery is crucial. With cloud-based data warehousing, organizations can efficiently manage and analyze large volumes of data.

18.1.1. Understanding Cloud-based Data Warehousing:

Cloud-based data warehousing involves storing and managing large volumes of data in a centralized repository hosted and managed by cloud service providers. It harnesses cloud infrastructure and services to provide scalable, on-demand storage and processing capabilities for analytics and business intelligence.

Key Components of Cloud-based Data Warehousing:

- **Cloud Infrastructure:** Cloud-based data warehousing utilizes the infrastructure provided by cloud service providers, such as Amazon Web Services (AWS) or Google Cloud Platform (GCP), to store and process data. This cloud-based infrastructure eliminates the need for on-premises hardware investments.

- **Data Storage:** Data is stored in cloud-based storage systems, often using columnar or object storage formats optimized for efficient data retrieval and analysis. These storage systems enable quick access to vast amounts of data, essential for analytical workloads.

- **Data Integration:** Cloud-based data warehousing involves the integration of data from various sources, including on-premises systems, databases, and external data sources. This integration enables a unified view of the data, facilitating comprehensive analysis and reporting.

- **Data Processing and Analytics:** Cloud-based data warehousing platforms provide built-in data processing and analytics capabilities. These include data transformation tools, SQL query support, and integration with analytical tools, allowing organizations to perform complex queries, data transformations, and derive valuable insights from the stored data.

18.1.2. Benefits of Cloud-based Data Warehousing:

- **Scalability and Elasticity:** Cloud-based data warehousing allows organizations to scale storage and processing resources on-demand, accommodating varying workloads and ensuring optimal performance. This scalability enables organizations to handle data growth without costly and time-consuming infrastructure upgrades.

- **Cost-effectiveness:** Cloud-based data warehousing offers a pay-as-you-go model, where organizations pay for the storage and processing resources they consume. This eliminates the need for upfront infrastructure investments, enabling cost optimization and flexibility in managing data storage expenses.

- **Flexibility and Agility:** Cloud-based data warehousing empowers organizations to easily adapt and evolve their data models and analytics needs. With cloud resources readily available, organizations can rapidly develop, deploy, and iterate data models and analytical solutions, enabling agility in response to business needs.

- **Data Integration and Centralization:** Cloud-based data warehousing enables organizations to consolidate and integrate data from diverse sources into a single repository. This centralization provides a unified view of the data, simplifying analysis and reporting processes and enabling more informed decision-making.

- **Advanced Analytics Capabilities:** Cloud-based data warehousing platforms often provide built-in analytics tools, including data visualization, machine learning, and artificial intelligence capabilities. These advanced analytics capabilities empower organizations to derive deeper insights and make data-driven decisions.

18.1.3. Best Practices for Cloud-based Data Warehousing:

- **Data Modeling and Design:** Understand the data requirements and define a logical data model that aligns with the organization's analytics and reporting goals. Leverage schema design techniques suitable for columnar storage and optimized query performance, ensuring efficient data retrieval for analytical workloads. Implement data partitioning and indexing strategies to enhance query performance on large datasets, reducing response times for complex analytical queries.

- **Data Integration and ETL:** Establish robust data integration pipelines to extract, transform, and load data from various sources into the data warehouse. These pipelines ensure data consistency and maintain data integrity during the integration process. Implement data quality checks and validation processes to ensure the accuracy and consistency of the data stored in the data warehouse, enhancing data reliability and credibility.

- **Security and Compliance:** Implement appropriate access controls, encryption, and authentication mechanisms to protect sensitive data stored in the cloud-based data warehouse, safeguarding against unauthorized access and data breaches. Ensure compliance with relevant data privacy and security regulations, such as GDPR or HIPAA, when storing and processing sensitive data, avoiding potential legal and reputational risks.

- **Performance Optimization:** Monitor and tune the performance of queries and data processing jobs to ensure optimal execution and minimize latency, providing users with a responsive and efficient analytics experience. Utilize caching mechanisms, query optimization techniques, and indexing strategies to enhance query performance and reduce costs associated with data processing.

- **Backup and Disaster Recovery:** Implement regular backup and recovery mechanisms to protect data against accidental deletion, data corruption, or system failures, preserving data integrity and availability. Establish disaster recovery plans and replicate data across multiple geographic regions to ensure business continuity and minimize downtime in case of unforeseen disasters.

18.2 Data Lake Architectures for Cloud: Scalable and Flexible Data Storage and Analytics

Data lake architectures in the cloud provide organizations with scalable, flexible, and cost-effective solutions for storing and analyzing vast amounts of structured and unstructured data. By leveraging cloud storage, data processing frameworks, and analytics tools, organizations can gain valuable insights, drive data-driven decision-making, and unlock the potential of their data. Implementing best practices for data governance, data ingestion, data organization, security, and data processing is crucial for successful data lake architectures in the cloud. With data lake architectures, organizations can create a unified view of their data, break down data silos, and empower their teams to derive meaningful insights and drive innovation in today's data-intensive business landscape.

18.2.1. Understanding Data Lake Architectures:

Data lakes are centralized repositories that enable organizations to store and analyze large volumes of diverse data types, such as structured, semi-structured, and unstructured data. In the cloud, data lake architectures leverage cloud storage and computing capabilities to provide scalable and flexible solutions for data storage and analytics.

Key Components of Data Lake Architectures:

- Cloud Storage: Data lakes in the cloud utilize scalable and cost-effective cloud storage services, like Amazon S3 or Azure Blob Storage, to store data in its raw form without requiring a predefined schem This enables the storage of massive amounts of data without worrying about storage limitations.

- Data Ingestion: Data from various sources, including on-premises systems, databases, streaming platforms, and external sources, is ingested into the data lake. Ingestion can be performed in batch or real-time modes, allowing organizations to continuously update their data.

- Data Processing and Analytics: Cloud-based data lake architectures offer data processing and analytics capabilities through technologies like Apache Spark, Hadoop, or cloud-native analytics services. These tools enable data transformation, querying, machine learning, and advanced analytics, facilitating valuable insights and informed decision-making.

- Data Governance and Metadata Management: Effective data lake architectures incorporate data governance practices, including metadata management, data lineage, and access controls. These practices ensure data quality, security, and compliance throughout the data lake lifecycle.

18.2.2. Benefits of Data Lake Architectures for Cloud:

- Scalability and Flexibility: Data lake architectures in the cloud provide virtually unlimited scalability, enabling organizations to store and process data of any volume or variety. The cloud infrastructure automatically scales resources on-demand, accommodating growing data needs without additional manual configuration.

- Cost-effectiveness: Cloud-based data lakes follow a pay-as-you-go model, reducing upfront infrastructure costs. Organizations pay only for the storage and computing resources they use, allowing them to optimize costs and invest resources where needed.

- Data Exploration and Discovery: Data lakes store data in its raw form, preserving its original structure and enabling ad-hoc exploration and discovery. Analysts and data scientists can freely explore and analyze data without the need for predefined schemas, promoting data-driven innovation.

- **Advanced Analytics Capabilities:** Data lakes support a wide range of analytics tools, including data visualization, machine learning, and big data analytics frameworks. These tools can leverage the scale and processing power of the cloud to derive valuable insights from large and complex datasets.

- **Data Integration and Data Silo Breakdown:** Data lakes promote data integration by consolidating diverse data sources into a centralized repository. They enable organizations to break down data silos and create a unified view of the data for analytics and reporting purposes, improving data-driven decision-making.

18.2.3. Best Practices for Data Lake Architectures:

- **Data Governance and Metadata Management:** Establish robust data governance practices, including metadata management and data cataloging, to ensure data quality and facilitate data discovery. Implement access controls to ensure data security and compliance with data privacy regulations, protecting sensitive information.

- **Data Ingestion and Integration:** Define clear data ingestion strategies and establish robust data pipelines to ingest data from various sources efficiently. Leverage technologies like Apache Kafka or cloud-native streaming services for real-time data ingestion and processing, supporting continuous data updates.

- **Data Lake Structure and Organization:** Implement data lake structures that promote efficient data organization and querying, such as organizing data into folders, partitions, or logical data lakes based on business domains or data types. Utilize data lake governance frameworks to define policies and practices for data organization, including folder structures, naming conventions, and access controls.

- **Data Security and Access Controls:** Apply appropriate security measures, including encryption, access controls, and data anonymization, to protect sensitive data within the data lake. Implement role-based access controls (RBAC) and fine-grained permissions to control data access based on user roles and responsibilities.

- **Data Processing and Analytics:** Leverage cloud-native analytics services or distributed processing frameworks like Apache Spark to enable scalable and efficient data processing and analytics on the data lake. Implement data transformation and enrichment processes to prepare the data for analysis, ensuring data accuracy and reliability.

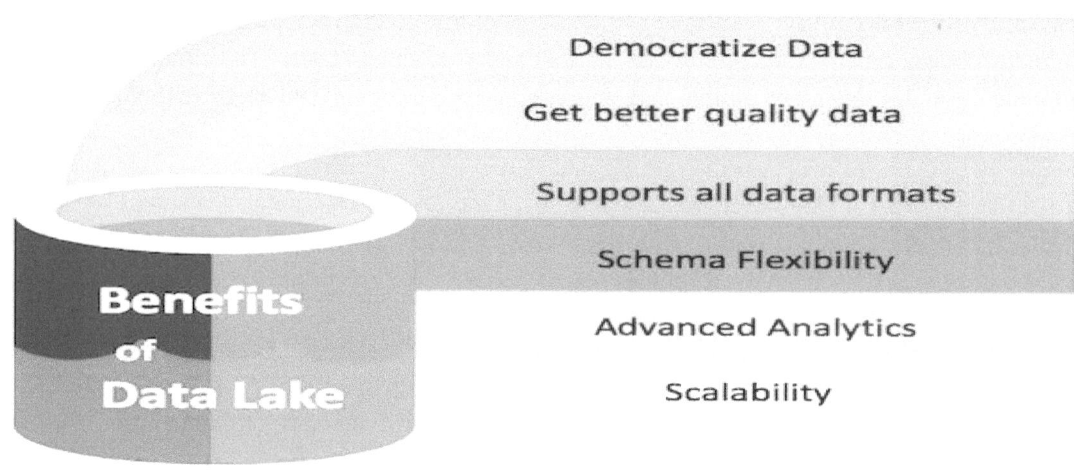

18.3 Machine Learning Services in the Cloud: Empowering Intelligent Applications

Machine learning services in the cloud offer organizations a powerful and accessible way to incorporate intelligent capabilities into their applications. By leveraging cloud-based infrastructure, pre-configured ML frameworks, and scalable computing resources, organizations can develop, train, deploy, and manage ML models more efficiently and cost-effectively. Following best practices for data preparation, model development, deployment, security, and collaboration will ensure successful utilization of machine learning services in the cloud. By embracing cloud-based ML services, organizations can unlock the potential of machine learning, drive innovation, and create intelligent applications that deliver value and insights in today's data-driven world.

18.3.1. Understanding Machine Learning Services in the Cloud:

Machine learning services in the cloud provide pre-built frameworks, tools, and infrastructure for training, deploying, and managing machine learning models. These services eliminate the need for organizations to build and maintain their own ML infrastructure, enabling faster development and deployment of intelligent applications.

Key Components of Machine Learning Services:

- **Model Training:** Cloud ML services offer scalable computing resources and distributed processing capabilities to train ML models using large datasets. They provide pre-configured ML frameworks and libraries for efficient model development.

- **Model Deployment:** Once trained, ML models can be deployed as web services or APIs, allowing applications to make predictions or perform complex tasks based on the model's capabilities.

- **Model Management and Monitoring:** ML services provide tools for monitoring model performance, managing model versions, and handling model updates and retraining as new data becomes available.

- **Data Processing and Feature Engineering:** ML services often include features for data preprocessing, feature engineering, and data transformation to prepare input data for training and inference.

18.3.2. Benefits of Machine Learning Services in the Cloud:

- **Scalability and Performance:** Cloud-based ML services offer on-demand scalability, allowing organizations to train and deploy ML models at any scale. They leverage distributed computing resources to handle large datasets and complex computations efficiently.

- **Cost-efficiency:** Cloud ML services follow a pay-as-you-go pricing model, allowing organizations to pay only for the resources consumed during training and inference. This eliminates the need for upfront hardware investments and ensures cost optimization.

- **Infrastructure and Tooling:** ML services in the cloud provide pre-configured ML frameworks, libraries, and development tools, reducing the complexity and time required to set up and manage ML infrastructure. This enables faster model development and deployment.

- **Accessibility and Collaboration:** Cloud-based ML services offer a user-friendly interface and APIs, making it easier for developers, data scientists, and domain experts to collaborate on ML projects. They enable seamless integration with other cloud services and provide access to extensive ML ecosystem resources.

- **Advanced Capabilities:** Cloud ML services often include advanced ML capabilities, such as automatic model tuning, hyperparameter optimization, and integration with deep learning frameworks. These capabilities streamline the development process and enhance model performance.

18.3.3 Best Practices for Leveraging Machine Learning Services in the Cloud:

- **Data Preparation and Exploration:** Ensure data quality and consistency by performing data cleaning, preprocessing, and feature engineering using cloud-based data processing tools. Leverage cloud-based data storage and analytics services to efficiently manage and explore large datasets for ML model training.

- **Model Development and Training:** Select the appropriate ML algorithms and frameworks that align with the problem domain and available data. Leverage cloud ML services' distributed training capabilities to scale model training and optimize performance. Monitor and track model training progress, evaluate model performance, and iterate on model development based on insights gained from monitoring.

- **Model Deployment and Management:** Follow best practices for deploying ML models as web services or APIs using cloud ML service capabilities. Implement versioning and monitoring of deployed models to ensure optimal performance and handle updates or retraining as required. Establish processes for monitoring model performance, gathering user feedback, and continuously improving the deployed models.

- **Security and Data Privacy:** Implement appropriate security measures, such as data encryption and access controls, to protect sensitive data used for training and inference. Comply with data privacy regulations and ensure that data used for ML training and inference follows ethical considerations.

- **Collaboration and Knowledge Sharing:** Foster collaboration between data scientists, developers, and domain experts to leverage their collective expertise for model development and deployment. Document and share knowledge regarding ML models, data processing pipelines, and deployment procedures to facilitate future iterations and model updates.

Exercise

Multiple Choice Questions

1. What is the key benefit of cloud-based data warehousing?

a. Cost-effectiveness

b. Advanced analytics capabilities

c. Scalability and elasticity

d. Data integration and centralization

2. Which component of cloud-based data warehousing enables organizations to perform complex queries and derive insights from stored data?

a. Cloud infrastructure

b. Data storage

c. Data integration

d. Data processing and analytics

3. What does cloud-based data warehousing utilize to store and manage large volumes of data?

a. On-premises hardware investments

b. Cloud service providers' infrastructure

c. External data sources

d. Cloud-native analytics services

4. What is a key benefit of data lake architectures for cloud?

a. Limited scalability

b. Increased infrastructure costs

c. Data silo creation

d. Virtually unlimited scalability

5. What are data lakes in the cloud designed to store?

a. Structured data only

b. Unstructured data only

c. Diverse data types, including structured, semi-structured, and unstructured data

d. None of the above

6. Which best practice ensures data quality and facilitates data discovery in data lake architectures?

a. Cloud-based data storage

b. Data integration and ETL

c. Data governance and metadata management

d. Data processing and analytics

7. What is a key component of machine learning services in the cloud that allows applications to make predictions based on trained models?

a. Data processing and feature engineering

b. Model training

c. Model management and monitoring

d. Model deployment

8. What is a benefit of machine learning services in the cloud for organizations?

a. Increased hardware investments

b. Reduced scalability

c. Pay-as-you-go pricing model

d. Limited model development capabilities

9. Which best practice for leveraging machine learning services in the cloud ensures data privacy and ethical considerations?

a. Data preparation and exploration

b. Collaboration and knowledge sharing

c. Security and data privacy

d. Model deployment and management

Review Questions

1. What is cloud-based data warehousing, and how does it provide scalable data storage and processing capabilities?

2. What are the key components of cloud-based data warehousing, and how do they contribute to its functionality?

3. What are the benefits of cloud-based data warehousing for organizations?

4. How can organizations ensure optimal performance and efficient data retrieval in cloud-based data warehousing?

5. How can organizations ensure data quality and security in cloud-based data warehousing?

6. What are data lake architectures, and how do they provide scalable and flexible data storage and analytics solutions?

7. What are the key benefits of data lake architectures for the cloud?

8. How can organizations ensure data quality and governance in data lake architectures for the cloud?

9. How can organizations leverage machine learning services in the cloud to empower intelligent applications?

Answer Section

Multiple Choice Questions

1. c) Scalability and elasticity

2. d) Data processing and analytics

3. b) Cloud service providers' infrastructure
4. d) Virtually unlimited scalability
5. c) Diverse data types, including structured, semi-structured, and unstructured data
6. c) Data governance and metadata management
7. d) Model deployment
8. c) Pay-as-you-go pricing model
9. c) Security and data privacy

Review Questions

1. Cloud-based data warehousing involves storing and managing large volumes of data in a centralized repository hosted and managed by cloud service providers. It harnesses cloud infrastructure and services, such as Amazon Web Services (AWS) or Google Cloud Platform (GCP), to offer on-demand and scalable storage and processing capabilities. This scalability allows organizations to handle varying workloads and data growth without the need for costly infrastructure upgrades. By leveraging the cloud's elastic resources, cloud-based data warehousing enables efficient data retrieval, data integration, and analytics for making data-driven decisions.

2. The key components of cloud-based data warehousing include cloud infrastructure, data storage, data integration, and data processing and analytics. Cloud infrastructure refers to the cloud service providers' infrastructure used for hosting and managing data. Data storage involves storing data in cloud-based storage systems, often optimized for quick data retrieval, while data integration facilitates unifying data from diverse sources. Lastly, data processing and analytics provide built-in tools for data transformation, SQL query support, and integration with analytical tools. These components together enable organizations to efficiently store, manage, and analyze large volumes of data for valuable insights.

3. Cloud-based data warehousing offers several benefits to organizations. These include scalability and elasticity, allowing organizations to scale storage and processing resources on-demand to accommodate varying workloads and data growth. The pay-as-you-go pricing model ensures cost-effectiveness, as organizations pay only for the resources they consume, eliminating the need for upfront infrastructure investments. Cloud-based data warehousing also promotes flexibility and agility, enabling organizations to adapt and evolve their data models and analytical needs rapidly. Moreover, it facilitates data integration and centralization, providing a unified view of data for improved analysis and reporting, and offers advanced analytics capabilities for deeper insights.

4. Organizations can ensure optimal performance and efficient data retrieval in cloud-based data warehousing by implementing best practices. These include understanding data requirements and designing a logical data model suitable for columnar storage and optimized query performance. Implementing data partitioning and indexing strategies also enhances query performance on large datasets, reducing response times for complex analytical queries. Additionally, utilizing caching mechanisms, query optimization techniques, and indexing strategies further enhances query performance and minimizes costs associated with data processing. Monitoring and tuning the performance of queries

and data processing jobs are essential for providing users with a responsive and efficient analytics experience.

5. Ensuring data quality and security in cloud-based data warehousing involves implementing best practices for data integration, security, and compliance. Establishing robust data integration pipelines ensures data consistency and maintains data integrity during the integration process. Implementing data quality checks and validation processes further enhances the accuracy and reliability of the data stored in the data warehouse. To ensure data security, organizations need to implement appropriate access controls, encryption, and authentication mechanisms to protect sensitive data stored in the cloud-based data warehouse, safeguarding against unauthorized access and data breaches. Additionally, compliance with relevant data privacy and security regulations, such as GDPR or HIPAA, is crucial to avoid potential legal and reputational risks.

6. Data lake architectures are centralized repositories that enable organizations to store and analyze large volumes of diverse data types, including structured, semi-structured, and unstructured data. In the cloud, data lake architectures leverage scalable and cost-effective cloud storage services, like Amazon S3 or Azure Blob Storage, to store data in its raw form without predefined schemas. This allows the storage of massive amounts of data without worrying about storage limitations. Data lakes support data ingestion from various sources in batch or real-time modes, enabling continuous data updates. Cloud-based data lake architectures also offer data processing and analytics capabilities through technologies like Apache Spark and Hadoop, facilitating valuable insights and informed decision-making.

7. Data lake architectures for the cloud offer several key benefits to organizations. One significant advantage is their virtually unlimited scalability, enabling organizations to store and process data of any volume or variety. The cloud infrastructure automatically scales resources on-demand, accommodating growing data needs without manual configuration. Another benefit is cost-effectiveness, as cloud-based data lakes follow a pay-as-you-go pricing model, reducing upfront infrastructure costs. Data exploration and discovery are promoted, as data lakes store data in its raw form, allowing ad-hoc exploration and analysis without predefined schemas. Furthermore, data integration and data silo breakdown are facilitated, as diverse data sources are consolidated into a centralized repository for improved data-driven decision-making.

8. To ensure data quality and governance in data lake architectures for the cloud, organizations can implement best practices. Establishing robust data governance practices, including metadata management and data cataloging, ensures data quality and facilitates data discovery. Implementing access controls helps ensure data security and compliance with data privacy regulations, protecting sensitive information. Defining clear data ingestion strategies and establishing robust data pipelines are essential for efficient data ingestion and integration from various sources. Leveraging technologies like Apache Kafka or cloud-native streaming services for real-time data ingestion and processing supports continuous data updates. Utilizing data lake governance frameworks also helps define policies and practices for data organization, including folder structures, naming conventions, and access controls.

9. Organizations can leverage machine learning services in the cloud to empower intelligent applications by using pre-built frameworks, tools, and infrastructure for training, deploying, and managing machine learning models. Cloud ML services offer scalable computing resources and distributed processing capabilities for training models using large datasets efficiently. Trained ML models can be deployed as

web services or APIs, enabling applications to make predictions or perform complex tasks based on the models' capabilities. By utilizing cloud-based ML services, organizations can avoid the complexity and time required to set up and manage ML infrastructure, allowing for faster model development and deployment. Access to a user-friendly interface and APIs promotes collaboration among developers, data scientists, and domain experts, driving innovation and creating intelligent applications that deliver

Chapter 19: Cloud-Native Database Services

19.1 Relational Databases in the Cloud: Scalable and Flexible Data Management

Relational databases in the cloud offer organizations scalable, flexible, and cost-effective solutions for data storage and management. By leveraging cloud infrastructure, organizations can benefit from the scalability, high availability, and security features provided by cloud-based relational databases. Implementing best practices for database design, security, scalability, backup, and performance optimization ensures successful implementation and efficient utilization of relational databases in the cloud. By adopting cloud-based relational databases, organizations can effectively manage their structured data, streamline application development, and leverage the advantages of cloud computing in today's data-driven world.

19.1.1. Understanding Relational Databases in the Cloud:

Relational databases in the cloud are cloud-hosted database management systems that enable organizations to store, manage, and retrieve structured data using a relational model. These databases adhere to the principles of traditional relational databases but leverage cloud infrastructure to offer scalability, availability, and ease of management.

Key Components of Relational Databases in the Cloud:

- **Cloud Infrastructure:** Relational databases in the cloud utilize the underlying infrastructure provided by cloud service providers, such as Amazon Web Services (AWS) or Microsoft Azure. This infrastructure encompasses compute resources, storage, and networking capabilities.

- **Database Engine:** The database engine serves as the core component responsible for data storage, retrieval, and query processing. It manages data consistency, transaction management, and enforces the relational model's integrity constraints.

- **Data Storage:** Cloud-based relational databases employ scalable and durable storage services offered by cloud providers, such as Amazon RDS or Azure SQL Database. These storage services ensure high availability, data redundancy, and automatic backups.

- **Management Tools:** Cloud-based relational databases offer management tools that simplify database administration tasks, including monitoring, performance optimization, backup and recovery, and security configuration.

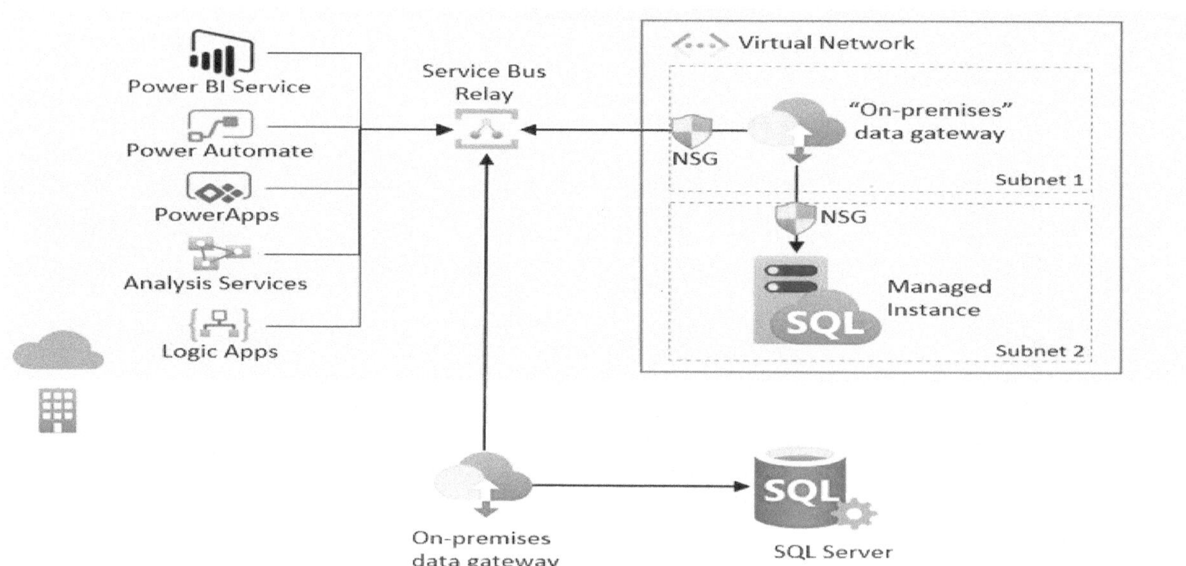

19.1.2. Benefits of Relational Databases in the Cloud:

- **Scalability and Elasticity:** Cloud-based relational databases provide scalability by allowing organizations to easily scale up or down their database resources based on demand. This ensures optimal performance during peak usage periods and cost savings during periods of lower demand.

- **High Availability and Durability:** Cloud-based relational databases offer built-in features for data replication, automatic backups, and disaster recovery. This ensures data durability, minimizes the risk of data loss, and provides high availability.

- **Cost-effectiveness:** Cloud-based relational databases follow a pay-as-you-go pricing model, eliminating the need for upfront hardware investments. Organizations only pay for the storage and compute resources they consume, resulting in cost optimization and reduced operational expenses.

- **Security and Compliance:** Cloud-based relational databases provide robust security features, including encryption at rest and in transit, access controls, and compliance with industry security standards. Cloud providers often have dedicated security teams and monitoring mechanisms to ensure data protection.

- **Ease of Management and Administration:** Cloud-based relational databases offer user-friendly management interfaces and automated administrative tasks. Database management tasks such as patching, upgrades, and backups are handled by the cloud provider, reducing the operational burden on organizations.

19.1.3. Best Practices for Relational Databases in the Cloud:

- **Database Design and Optimization:** Design the database schema carefully, considering normalization, data relationships, and performance requirements. Utilize indexing, query optimization, and caching techniques to enhance database performance. Regularly analyze database performance metrics and optimize queries to ensure efficient data retrieval.

- **Data Security and Compliance:** Implement strong access controls, user authentication, and data encryption to protect sensitive data stored in the database. Regularly monitor and audit database activity to identify and address security vulnerabilities or compliance violations. Comply with relevant data privacy regulations, such as GDPR or HIPAA, when storing and managing sensitive data.

- **Scalability and Performance:** Leverage auto-scaling capabilities provided by cloud-based relational database services to handle fluctuating workloads. Implement database sharding or partitioning techniques to distribute data across multiple nodes for improved performance and scalability.

- **Backup and Recovery:** Establish regular backup schedules and implement automated backup mechanisms to ensure data protection and minimize the risk of data loss. Test backup and recovery processes regularly to verify their reliability and effectiveness.

- **Monitoring and Performance Optimization:** Utilize monitoring tools and performance dashboards provided by the cloud provider to track database performance, resource utilization, and identify potential bottlenecks. Optimize database configurations, indexes, and queries based on performance metrics and tuning recommendations.

19.2 NoSQL Databases and Key-value Stores for Cloud: Scalable and Flexible Data Management

NoSQL databases and key-value stores in the cloud offer organizations scalable, flexible, and high-performance data storage solutions for managing diverse data types. By leveraging cloud infrastructure and distributed storage architectures, organizations can handle large volumes of data, achieve high availability, and ensure fault tolerance. Implementing best practices for data modeling, scalability, data consistency, security, and performance optimization is essential for successful implementation of NoSQL databases and key-value stores in the cloud. By adopting cloud-based NoSQL databases and key-value stores, organizations can efficiently manage unstructured and semi-structured data, build scalable applications, and leverage the advantages of cloud computing in today's data-intensive landscape.

19.2.1. Understanding NoSQL Databases and Key-value Stores:

NoSQL databases and key-value stores are non-relational data storage systems that provide flexible data models for storing and retrieving data. Unlike traditional relational databases, NoSQL databases and key-value stores do not enforce a fixed schema, enabling organizations to handle large volumes of unstructured or semi-structured data more efficiently.

Key Components of NoSQL Databases and Key-value Stores:

- **Data Model:** NoSQL databases offer various data models, such as key-value, document, columnar, or graph-based, each suited for specific use cases. Key-value stores focus on storing data as key-value pairs, allowing fast retrieval by key.

- **Scalable Architecture:** NoSQL databases and key-value stores are designed to scale horizontally, allowing organizations to distribute data across multiple nodes and handle high volumes of data and concurrent requests efficiently.

- **CAP Theorem:** NoSQL databases and key-value stores make design trade-offs based on the CAP (Consistency, Availability, Partition tolerance) theorem, prioritizing availability and partition tolerance over strong consistency.

- **Distributed Data Storage:** NoSQL databases and key-value stores utilize distributed storage architectures, such as Amazon DynamoDB or Apache Cassandra, to ensure fault tolerance, data replication, and high availability.

19.2.2. Benefits of NoSQL Databases and Key-value Stores in the Cloud:

- **Scalability and Performance:** NoSQL databases and key-value stores in the cloud offer horizontal scalability, allowing organizations to handle large volumes of data and high traffic loads efficiently. They distribute data across multiple nodes, enabling fast and parallel data retrieval.

- **Flexible Data Models:** NoSQL databases and key-value stores provide flexible data models, accommodating unstructured and semi-structured data. This flexibility allows organizations to store and process diverse data types, making them suitable for applications with evolving data requirements.

- **High Availability and Fault Tolerance:** Cloud-based NoSQL databases and key-value stores replicate data across multiple nodes, ensuring high availability even in the event of node failures. They provide built-in mechanisms for automatic data replication and failover.

- **Performance at Scale:** NoSQL databases and key-value stores are designed for high performance at scale. They can handle large datasets and support fast read and write operations, making them suitable for real-time applications and high-throughput scenarios.

- **Cost-effectiveness:** Cloud-based NoSQL databases and key-value stores follow a pay-as-you-go pricing model, allowing organizations to scale resources based on demand. This eliminates the need for upfront hardware investments and ensures cost optimization.

19.2.3. Best Practices for NoSQL Databases and Key-value Stores in the Cloud:

- **Data Modeling and Schema Design:** Understand the data access patterns and requirements to choose an appropriate data model, whether it's key-value, document, columnar, or graph-based. Optimize data schema design based on anticipated query patterns and performance requirements.

- **Scalability and Replication:** Leverage cloud-native NoSQL databases and key-value stores that provide automatic scaling and replication capabilities. Design data partitioning strategies to distribute data evenly across nodes and optimize performance.

- **Data Consistency and Conflict Resolution:** Understand the trade-offs between strong consistency and high availability when choosing a NoSQL database or key-value store. Implement conflict resolution mechanisms or employ eventual consistency approaches to handle data conflicts.

- **Security and Access Controls:** Implement appropriate access controls and authentication mechanisms to protect data stored in NoSQL databases and key-value stores. Utilize encryption mechanisms to secure data at rest and during transmission.

- **Monitoring and Performance Optimization:** Utilize monitoring and performance tuning tools provided by the cloud provider to monitor database performance and identify bottlenecks. Optimize queries, indexing strategies, and caching mechanisms to enhance read and write performance.

19.3 Managed Database Services for Cloud: Simplifying Data Management and Administration

Managed database services in the cloud simplify data management and administration, enabling organizations to focus on application development and data analysis. By leveraging the benefits of automated provisioning, high availability, scalability, and security features offered by managed database services, organizations can streamline their database operations and improve overall productivity. Implementing best practices for database selection, configuration, backup and recovery, performance optimization, security, and monitoring ensures successful implementation of managed database services in the cloud. By adopting managed database services, organizations can efficiently manage their data, achieve high performance, and leverage the advantages of cloud computing for their data-driven initiatives.

19.3.1. Understanding Managed Database Services in the Cloud:

Managed database services in the cloud refer to fully managed database offerings provided by cloud service providers. These services handle database administration tasks, such as provisioning, patching, backups, monitoring, and scaling, allowing organizations to focus on utilizing the database for their applications and data analytics needs.

Key Components of Managed Database Services:

- **Database Engine:** Managed database services offer a variety of database engines, including relational databases like MySQL, PostgreSQL, or SQL Server, and non-relational databases like MongoDB or Cassandr Each engine provides specific functionalities and caters to different use cases.

- **Automated Provisioning:** Cloud providers offer automated provisioning of databases, allowing organizations to quickly set up and deploy databases without the need for manual configuration or infrastructure management.

- **Monitoring and Alerts:** Managed database services provide built-in monitoring and alerting capabilities, enabling organizations to track database performance, resource utilization, and potential issues in real-time.

- **Scalability and Elasticity:** Managed database services offer automatic scaling capabilities, allowing databases to scale up or down based on demand. This ensures optimal performance during peak usage and cost efficiency during periods of lower demand.

19.3.2. Benefits of Managed Database Services in the Cloud:

- **Simplified Database Management:** Managed database services handle routine database administration tasks, such as software updates, backups, and scaling, freeing up resources and reducing the operational burden on organizations. This allows teams to focus on application development and data analysis.

- **High Availability and Reliability:** Managed database services provide built-in mechanisms for automatic backups, data replication, and failover, ensuring high availability and data durability. Cloud providers typically offer robust SLAs and guarantees for data availability.

- **Scalability and Performance:** Managed database services offer automatic scaling capabilities, allowing databases to handle increased workloads without manual intervention. This ensures consistent performance even during periods of high traffic or data growth.

- **Security and Compliance:** Managed database services implement robust security measures, including encryption, access controls, and compliance with industry standards and regulations. Cloud providers offer features and tools to protect data stored in managed databases.

- **Cost-effectiveness:** Managed database services follow a pay-as-you-go pricing model, allowing organizations to pay only for the resources they consume. This eliminates the need for upfront hardware investments and ensures cost optimization.

19.3.3. Best Practices for Managed Database Services in the Cloud:

- **Database Selection and Configuration:** Choose the appropriate database engine based on the specific requirements of the application, data model, and performance needs. Configure database settings, such as storage allocation, memory allocation, and connection pooling, to optimize performance and resource utilization.

- **Data Backup and Recovery:** Configure automated backup schedules and retention policies to ensure data durability and facilitate data recovery in case of accidental deletion or data corruption. Regularly test the backup and recovery processes to verify their reliability and effectiveness.

- **Performance Optimization:** Monitor database performance metrics, such as CPU utilization, query latency, and throughput, to identify potential bottlenecks. Optimize database indexes, query execution plans, and caching mechanisms to improve query performance and reduce latency.

- **Security and Access Controls:** Implement strong access controls, user authentication mechanisms, and encryption to protect data stored in managed databases. Regularly review and update access permissions to ensure that only authorized users have appropriate database access.

- **Monitoring and Alerting:** Utilize the monitoring and alerting capabilities provided by the managed database service to track database performance, resource utilization, and potential issues. Set up proactive alerts to notify administrators of critical events, such as high CPU usage, low disk space, or database failures.

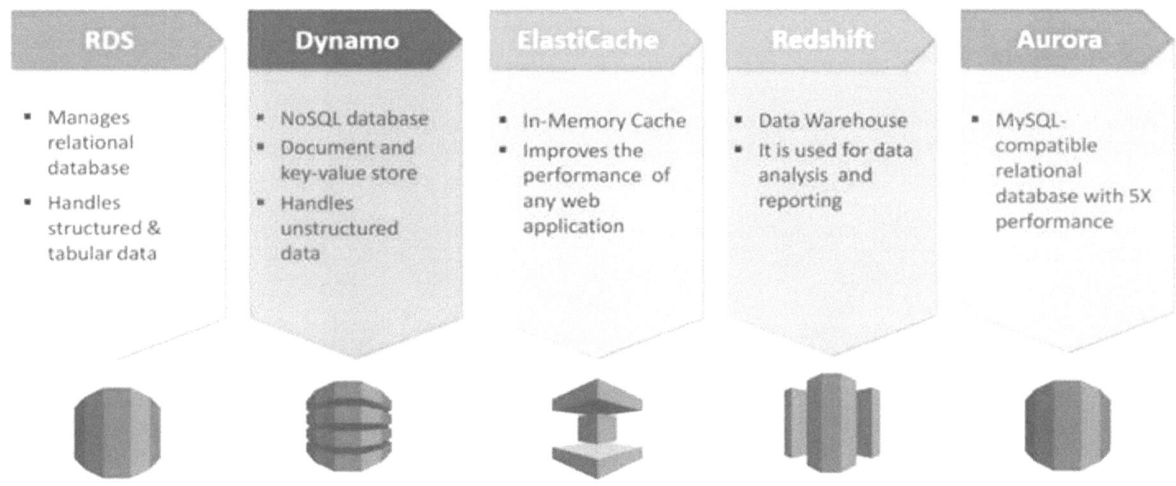

Exercise

Multiple Choice Questions

1. Which of the following is a key component of cloud-based relational databases?

a. Data modeling

b. Automatic scaling

c. Query optimization

d. CAP theorem

2. What is the primary advantage of using cloud-based NoSQL databases and key-value stores?

a. Strong consistency

b. Low cost

c. Horizontal scalability

d. Structured data support

3. Which database model is suitable for storing data in key-value pairs?

a. Relational model

b. Document model

c. Columnar model

d. Key-value model

4. What benefit do managed database services in the cloud provide?

a. Complete control over infrastructure management

b. Reduced application development effort

c. Manual scaling capabilities

d. Limited security features

5. Which best practice is essential for ensuring data durability in managed database services?

a. Frequent data backups

b. High consistency levels

c. Long data retention policies

d. Real-time data replication

6. Which component is responsible for enforcing the relational model's integrity constraints in cloud-based relational databases?

a. Data storage

b. CAP theorem

c. Database engine

d. Management tools

7. Which advantage do cloud-based NoSQL databases offer over traditional relational databases?

a. Fixed schema

b. Strong consistency

c. Automatic scaling

d. Vertical scalability

8. What is a characteristic feature of NoSQL databases and key-value stores in the cloud?

a. Relational data model

b. High cost of operation

c. Limited data volume support

d. Flexible schema

9. Which best practice ensures efficient data retrieval in managed database services?

a. Minimal data backups

b. Infrequent monitoring

c. Indexing strategies

d. No query optimization

Review Questions

1. What are the key components of cloud-based relational databases?

2. What benefits do organizations gain from adopting cloud-based NoSQL databases and key-value stores?

3. What makes NoSQL databases and key-value stores different from traditional relational databases?

4. How do managed database services in the cloud simplify data management for organizations?

5. What best practice ensures data durability in managed database services?

6. How do cloud-based NoSQL databases offer horizontal scalability?

7. What advantage do cloud-based NoSQL databases have over traditional relational databases in terms of data modeling?

8. How do managed database services in the cloud ensure high availability and reliability?

9. How can organizations optimize the performance of their managed database services?

Answer Section

Multiple Choice Questions

1. b) Automatic scaling

2. c) Horizontal scalability

3. d) Key-value model

4. b) Reduced application development effort

5. a) Frequent data backups

6. c) Database engine

7. c) Automatic scaling

8. d) Flexible schema

9. c) Indexing strategies

Review Questions

1. The key components of cloud-based relational databases include cloud infrastructure provided by the cloud service provider, the database engine responsible for data storage and query processing, data storage using scalable cloud storage services, and management tools for administration tasks.

2. Organizations benefit from horizontal scalability, allowing them to handle large volumes of data and high traffic efficiently. They also enjoy flexible data models, cost-effectiveness with pay-as-you-go pricing, and high availability through automatic backups and data replication.

3. Unlike traditional relational databases, NoSQL databases and key-value stores do not enforce a fixed schema, enabling them to store unstructured or semi-structured data efficiently. They prioritize availability and partition tolerance over strong consistency, as per the CAP theorem.

4. Managed database services handle database administration tasks, such as provisioning, backups, and scaling, allowing organizations to focus on their applications and data analysis. This reduces the operational burden and improves productivity.

5. Implementing frequent data backups and setting up automated backup schedules and retention policies ensure data durability and facilitate data recovery in case of data loss or corruption.

6. Cloud-based NoSQL databases employ distributed storage architectures, enabling them to distribute data across multiple nodes. This ensures efficient scaling to handle increased workloads without manual intervention.

7. Cloud-based NoSQL databases provide flexible data models, allowing them to accommodate unstructured and semi-structured data, making them suitable for applications with evolving data requirements.

8. Managed database services implement automatic backups, data replication, and failover mechanisms to ensure high availability and data durability. Cloud providers also offer robust SLAs and guarantees for data availability.

9. Organizations can optimize performance by monitoring database metrics, implementing performance tuning strategies, optimizing queries, indexes, and caching mechanisms, and regularly reviewing and updating access controls and permissions.

Chapter 20: Cloud Governance and Cost Optimization

20.1 Cloud Cost Allocation and Budgeting: Maximizing Cost Efficiency in the Cloud

Cloud cost allocation and budgeting are critical aspects of cloud cost management, enabling organizations to gain financial visibility, optimize resource utilization, and align cloud spending with business objectives. By implementing best practices for cloud cost allocation, organizations can attribute costs accurately, foster accountability, and make informed resource allocation decisions. Effective budgeting practices ensure cost control and facilitate proactive management of cloud spending. By leveraging cloud cost allocation and budgeting strategies, organizations can achieve cost efficiency, maximize their cloud investments, and optimize resource utilization in the dynamic cloud computing landscape.

20.1.1. Understanding Cloud Cost Allocation:

Cloud cost allocation involves attributing the costs of cloud resource usage to specific business units, departments, projects, or teams. This process provides visibility into resource consumption and helps identify areas of high expenditure.

Key Components of Cloud Cost Allocation:

- **Tagging and Labels:** Cloud providers offer tagging mechanisms to assign metadata to cloud resources. Tags can be used to categorize resources and track their associated costs, making it easier to understand expenses associated with different aspects of an organization.

- **Cost Allocation Reports:** Cloud providers offer cost allocation reports that enable organizations to view and analyze resource costs based on predefined tags or custom dimensions. These reports present a clear breakdown of expenses, aiding in financial decision-making.

- **Cost Allocation Tools:** Third-party tools and cloud management platforms provide advanced cost allocation capabilities, including automated tagging, cost attribution, and granular reporting. These tools streamline the process of allocating costs and optimizing resource utilization.

20.1.2. Benefits of Cloud Cost Allocation:

- **Financial Visibility:** Cloud cost allocation provides transparency into cloud spending by attributing costs to specific entities. This enables organizations to understand resource utilization patterns and make informed decisions regarding resource allocation and optimization. Financial transparency allows organizations to identify areas where cost-saving measures can be applied effectively.

- **Accountability and Governance:** Cost allocation fosters accountability by attributing costs to responsible entities, encouraging cost-conscious behavior, and facilitating governance and compliance requirements. When teams are aware of their usage and its associated costs, they are more likely to act responsibly and efficiently.

- **Resource Optimization:** By identifying areas of high expenditure, organizations can optimize resource utilization, identify cost-saving opportunities, and implement cost optimization strategies effectively. This leads to enhanced resource efficiency and reduced overall cloud expenses.

- **Data-Driven Decision Making:** Accurate cost allocation data empowers organizations to make data-driven decisions regarding resource allocation, capacity planning, and budgeting. Such decisions are based on concrete financial insights, which are essential for effective cloud cost management.

20.1.3. Best Practices for Cloud Cost Allocation and Budgeting:

- **Establish a Tagging Strategy:** Define a standardized tagging strategy that aligns with organizational goals and resource categorization requirements. Consistent tagging practices ensure that resources are appropriately categorized and easily trackable for cost attribution. Educate teams and stakeholders about the importance of consistent tagging practices to ensure their cooperation in the cost allocation process.

- **Align Cost Allocation with Organizational Structure:** Map cost allocation to reflect the organizational structure, business units, projects, or teams responsible for specific cloud resources. Aligning costs with organizational entities enhances accountability and enables better resource tracking. Regularly review and update cost allocation mappings to accommodate changes in the organizational structure or resource ownership, maintaining accuracy in cost attribution.

- **Automate Tagging and Cost Attribution:** Leverage automation tools and cloud management platforms to automatically apply tags and attributes to resources based on predefined rules or resource characteristics. Automation streamlines the cost allocation process and reduces the chances of human error. Utilize cloud provider APIs or third-party integrations to collect and consolidate cost allocation data efficiently, ensuring comprehensive and accurate reporting.

- **Implement Granular Cost Reporting:** Define meaningful cost allocation reports based on business requirements, utilizing tags or custom dimensions to capture relevant cost allocation criteria Granular cost reporting offers detailed insights into spending patterns, facilitating better decision-making. Leverage cost reporting tools to generate and analyze reports for better visibility and cost insights. These tools help identify trends and anomalies in cloud spending, aiding in cost optimization efforts.

- **Set and Monitor Budgets:** Establish cloud spending budgets aligned with business objectives and resource requirements. Budgets provide a framework for cost control and guide spending decisions in line with the organization's goals. Continuously monitor cloud spending against budgeted amounts and proactively manage cost overruns or budget deviations to maintain financial discipline.

- **Regularly Review and Optimize:** Conduct regular cost reviews and analysis to identify cost outliers, resource inefficiencies, and potential cost optimization opportunities. Periodic evaluations enable continuous improvement in cloud cost management. Implement cost optimization strategies, such as rightsizing instances, leveraging reserved instances, or utilizing spot instances, to optimize costs without sacrificing performance.

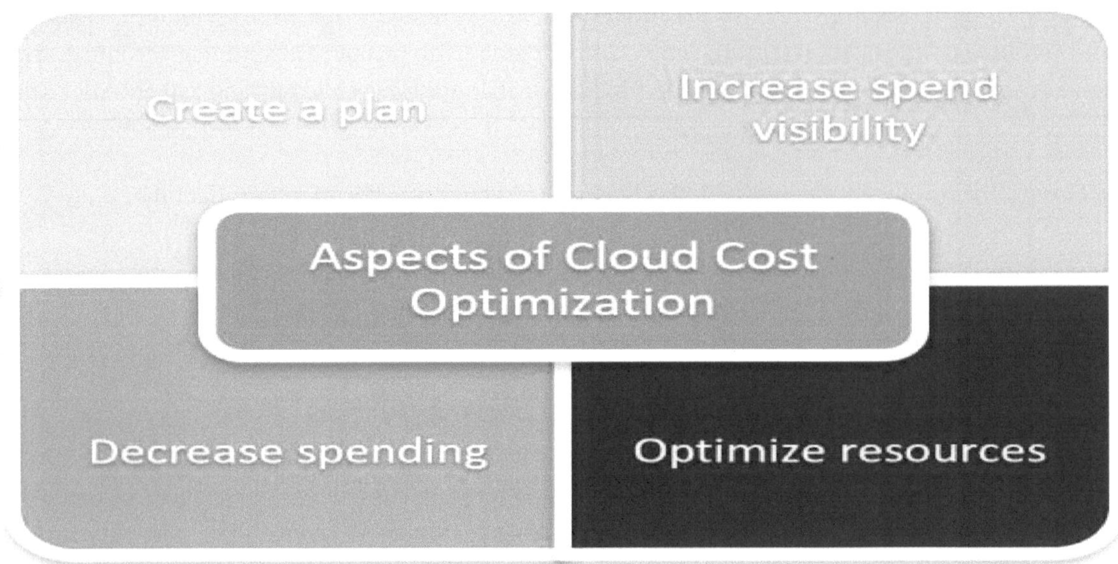

20.2 Right-sizing and Resource Optimization

Right-sizing and resource optimization are essential practices for achieving optimal performance and cost efficiency in the cloud. By analyzing workload patterns, monitoring resource utilization, and making informed optimization decisions, organizations can right-size their cloud resources to match workload requirements accurately. Implementing best practices for resource configuration, continuous monitoring, and optimization enables organizations to maximize efficiency, minimize costs, and improve overall performance in the cloud environment. By adopting right-sizing and resource optimization strategies, organizations can fully leverage the benefits of cloud computing while optimizing their resource utilization and cost-effectiveness.

20.2 1. Understanding Right-Sizing and Resource Optimization:

Right-sizing involves aligning cloud resources, such as compute instances or storage, to match the actual workload demands accurately. Resource optimization refers to analyzing and adjusting resource configurations and settings to achieve maximum efficiency and cost savings.

Key Components of Right-Sizing and Resource Optimization:

- **Performance Analysis:** To right-size resources effectively, organizations need to perform a thorough analysis of their workload patterns and usage metrics. This analysis includes monitoring performance data, such as CPU utilization, memory usage, and network traffic, to understand resource requirements and identify potential inefficiencies.

- **Resource Configuration:** Once performance analysis is complete, organizations can adjust resource specifications to optimize their cloud environment. This may involve selecting the appropriate instance types, storage capacity, or network configurations that best match the workload needs.

- **Performance Monitoring and Analytics:** To ensure ongoing efficiency and optimization, organizations must utilize monitoring tools and performance analytics. These tools continuously measure resource utilization, identify performance bottlenecks, and provide valuable insights to inform optimization decisions.

20.2 2. Benefits of Right-Sizing and Resource Optimization:

- **Cost Savings:** One of the primary benefits of right-sizing and resource optimization is the significant cost savings it brings. By accurately matching resources to workload demands and avoiding overprovisioning, organizations can minimize unnecessary expenses and optimize their cloud spending.

- **Improved Performance:** Optimized resource configurations ensure that applications and workloads have the appropriate resources to deliver optimal performance. This reduction in resource waste and improved allocation helps reduce latency and enhance user experience.

- **Scalability and Flexibility:** Right-sizing and resource optimization enable organizations to scale resources up or down dynamically based on workload requirements. This scalability and flexibility allow them to adapt to changing demands efficiently.

- **Environmental Impact:** By optimizing resource utilization and reducing overprovisioning, organizations can lower their energy consumption and carbon footprint. This contributes to sustainable and environmentally responsible practices.

20.2.3. Best Practices for Right-Sizing and Resource Optimization:

20.2.3.1 Performance Analysis and Workload Profiling:

- **Monitor Workload Patterns:** Regularly monitor workload patterns and resource utilization metrics to identify underutilized or overutilized resources. Understanding how resources are used at peak and average levels helps guide right-sizing decisions.

- **Continuous Monitoring:** Utilize cloud monitoring tools to track resource utilization and identify performance bottlenecks. Continuous monitoring ensures that resource optimization remains an ongoing process.

20.2.3.2Rightsizing Compute Instances:

- **Analyze Resource Utilization:** Analyze CPU, memory, and network utilization of compute instances to ensure optimal resource allocation. Matching the instance types and sizes to workload characteristics and performance requirements is essential.

- **Consider Scalability Needs:** Factor in the scalability needs of the workload when selecting compute instance types. Choose instances that can handle the potential growth in demand without incurring unnecessary costs.

20.2.3.3Storage Optimization:

- **Evaluate Data Storage Needs:** Evaluate the data storage needs, including data access frequency, data durability, and I/O requirements. This evaluation helps determine the most cost-effective storage solution while ensuring data availability and performance.

- **Utilize Storage Tiers:** Leverage storage tiers, such as hot, warm, and cold storage, to optimize costs based on data usage patterns. Frequently accessed data should be stored in higher-performance tiers, while less frequently accessed data can be stored in lower-cost tiers.

20.2.3.4Autoscaling and Elasticity:

- **Implement Autoscaling:** Implement autoscaling capabilities to dynamically adjust resources based on workload demands. Autoscaling ensures that the environment can handle fluctuating workloads without manual intervention.

- **Utilize Cloud Provider Features:** Utilize cloud provider features like Auto Scaling Groups or Elastic Load Balancers to automatically scale resources up or down based on predefined policies and triggers.

20.2.3.5Utilize Spot Instances and Reserved Instances:

- **Spot Instances:** Consider using spot instances, which offer spare capacity at lower prices, for non-critical workloads or time-flexible batch processing. Spot instances can provide significant cost savings when used strategically.

- **Reserved Instances:** Utilize reserved instances for workloads with consistent demand to achieve cost savings through discounted pricing. Reserved instances provide cost predictability for long-term workloads.

20.2.3.6Continuous Optimization and Cost Analysis:

- **Regular Cost Review:** Regularly review cost allocation reports and perform cost analysis to identify opportunities for further optimization. This continuous optimization approach ensures that the cloud environment remains cost-efficient over time.

- **Explore Cloud Provider Tools:** Cloud providers offer various cost optimization tools and services that provide insights into resource utilization and cost-saving opportunities. Leverage these tools to gain valuable data and recommendations for optimization.

20.3 Cost Reporting and Analysis for Cloud: Gaining Financial Insights and Optimizing Expenses

Cost reporting and analysis are integral components of effective cloud cost management. By adopting best practices for cost data collection, aggregation, visualization, and analysis, organizations can gain comprehensive financial visibility, optimize cloud spending, and make informed decisions regarding resource allocation and cost-saving measures. Continuous monitoring, analysis, and optimization of cloud costs enable organizations to maximize cost efficiency, prevent budget overruns, and optimize resource utilization in the dynamic cloud computing landscape. By implementing robust cost reporting and analysis practices, organizations can effectively manage their cloud expenses and unlock the full potential of cloud computing while maintaining financial control.

20.3.1. Understanding Cost Reporting and Analysis:

Cost reporting and analysis in the cloud involve the meticulous tracking, thorough analysis, and visual representation of cloud expenditure. The primary goal is to gain insights into resource consumption patterns, cost drivers, and opportunities for cost optimization. By doing so, organizations can achieve comprehensive financial visibility and make data-driven decisions for cost management.

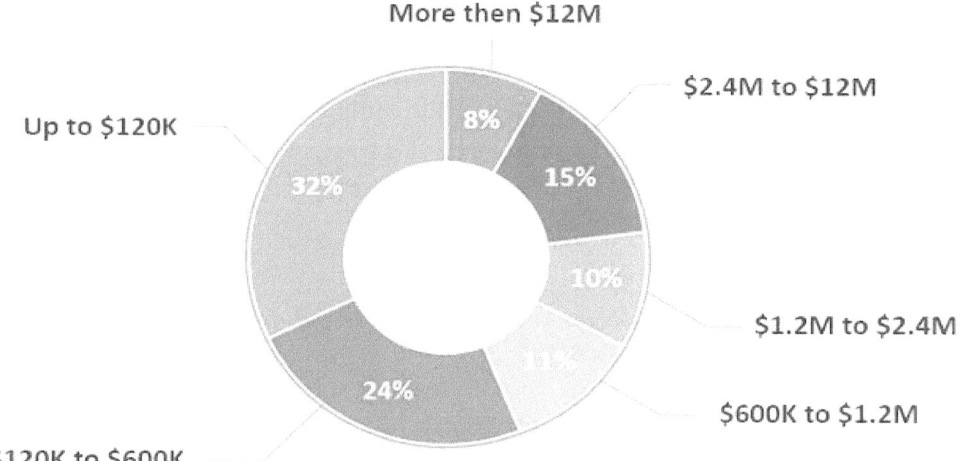

Key Components of Cost Reporting and Analysis:
- **Cost Data Collection:** The process of collecting detailed cost data from cloud service providers, including information on usage, pricing, and billing.

- **Data Aggregation and Consolidation:** Aggregating cost data from multiple sources or accounts to create a unified and coherent view of cloud spending.

- **Reporting and Visualization:** Presenting cost data through visually engaging dashboards, charts, and reports to provide clear visibility into spending patterns and trends.

- **Cost Analysis and Optimization:** Carefully analyzing cost data to identify cost drivers, uncover cost-saving opportunities, and devise strategies to optimize cloud spending.

20.3.2. Benefits of Cost Reporting and Analysis:
- **Financial Visibility:** Cost reporting and analysis offer a clear view of cloud spending patterns, helping organizations understand resource consumption, cost trends, and cost allocation across various departments, projects, or services.

- **Cost Optimization:** By analyzing cost data, organizations can identify underutilized resources, optimize resource allocation, and implement cost-saving strategies to minimize unnecessary expenses.

- **Budget Control:** Cost reporting and analysis enable effective budget management by tracking actual costs against budgeted amounts. This helps organizations control spending and take proactive measures to prevent cost overruns.

- **Data-Driven Decision Making:** Cost data insights facilitate informed decision-making regarding resource selection, capacity planning, pricing models, and cost optimization strategies. This leads to more efficient and cost-effective cloud resource management.

20.3.3. Best Practices for Cost Reporting and Analysis:
- **Define Cost Allocation and Tagging Strategy:** Establish a consistent tagging strategy to assign metadata to cloud resources, enabling effective cost allocation across departments, projects, or teams. Utilize predefined or custom tags to categorize resources and track costs accurately.

- **Implement Automated Cost Data Collection:** Leverage cloud provider APIs or third-party tools to automate the collection of detailed cost data, including usage, pricing, and billing information. Regularly reconcile cost data to ensure accuracy and completeness.

- **Centralize Cost Data and Aggregation:** Consolidate cost data from multiple cloud accounts, regions, or services into a centralized repository for unified reporting and analysis. Utilize cloud management platforms or third-party tools for seamless data aggregation.

- **Visualize and Present Cost Data:** Utilize visualization tools and dashboards to present cost data in a clear and easily understandable format. Generate reports and charts that provide insights into spending patterns, cost trends, and cost allocation across different dimensions.

- **Analyze Cost Drivers and Optimization Opportunities:** Perform cost analysis to identify cost drivers, such as overprovisioned resources, idle instances, or storage inefficiencies. Regularly review cost reports and conduct analysis to uncover optimization opportunities and implement cost-saving strategies.

- **Budget Tracking and Alerts:** Set and monitor cloud spending budgets, comparing actual costs against budgeted amounts. Implement alert mechanisms to notify stakeholders when spending approaches or exceeds predefined thresholds.

- **Regular Review and Continuous Optimization:** Conduct regular cost reviews and optimization assessments to identify potential cost-saving measures and validate the effectiveness of implemented strategies. Collaborate with stakeholders, including finance, operations, and technical teams, to align cost optimization efforts with business objectives.

Exercise

Multiple Choice Questions

1. What is the main purpose of cloud cost allocation?

a. To optimize cloud spending and resource utilization.

b. To achieve financial visibility and transparency.

c. To implement cost-saving strategies effectively.

d. To streamline the process of allocating costs.

2. What are the key components of cloud cost allocation?

a. Performance analysis, resource configuration, and performance monitoring.

b. Tagging and labels, cost allocation reports, and cost allocation tools.

c. Financial visibility, accountability, and data-driven decision making.

d. Resource optimization, cost data collection, and budget tracking.

3. How does cloud cost allocation foster accountability in organizations?

a. By implementing automated cost data collection.

b. By attributing costs to specific business units or teams.

c. By utilizing cloud provider APIs for data aggregation.

d. By setting and monitoring cloud spending budgets.

4. What is the benefit of continuous monitoring and analysis of cloud costs?

a. It enables effective budget management and cost control.

b. It allows organizations to maximize their cloud investments.

c. It provides insights into resource consumption patterns.

d. It helps organizations make data-driven decisions for cost management.

5. Which component of cloud cost allocation involves presenting cost data in a visually engaging format?

a. Performance analysis and workload profiling.

b. Implementing automated cost data collection.

c. Data aggregation and consolidation.

d. Reporting and visualization.

6. What is the primary goal of cost reporting and analysis in the cloud?

a. To streamline the process of allocating costs.

b. To achieve financial visibility and transparency.

c. To optimize cloud spending and resource utilization.

d. To foster accountability and governance.

7. Which best practice involves establishing a consistent tagging strategy for cloud resources?

a. Regularly reviewing and optimizing cloud costs.

b. Utilizing cloud provider APIs for data collection.

c. Defining meaningful cost allocation reports.

d. Establishing a tagging strategy for cost allocation.

8. How can organizations optimize cloud spending through cost reporting and analysis?

a. By implementing cost optimization strategies.

b. By utilizing cloud management platforms.

c. By setting and monitoring cloud spending budgets.

d. By analyzing cost data and uncovering opportunities for cost-saving.

9. What is the key component of cost reporting and analysis that involves aggregating cost data from multiple sources?

a. Visualizing and presenting cost data.

b. Implementing automated cost data collection.

c. Cost analysis and optimization.

d. Data aggregation and consolidation.

10. How does cloud cost allocation enable organizations to make data-driven decisions?

a. By implementing budget tracking and alerts.

b. By attributing costs to specific entities for accountability.

c. By providing insights into resource consumption patterns.

d. By establishing a standardized tagging strategy.

11. What is the benefit of continuously reviewing and optimizing cloud costs?

a. It enables effective budget management and cost control.

b. It provides financial visibility and transparency.

c. It fosters accountability and governance.

d. It allows organizations to maximize their cloud investments.

Review Questions

1. What is the purpose of cloud cost allocation, and how does it help organizations manage their cloud expenses effectively?

2. What are the key components of cloud cost allocation, and how do they contribute to accurate cost attribution?

3. How does cloud cost allocation foster accountability and cost-conscious behavior within organizations?

4. What are the benefits of implementing granular cost reporting in cloud cost management?

5. How can organizations align cloud cost allocation with their organizational structure for better resource tracking and accountability?

6. What role do automated tagging and cost attribution play in the cloud cost allocation process?

7. How can continuous review and optimization of cloud costs lead to long-term cost efficiency and better resource utilization?

8. How can cloud cost reporting and analysis contribute to effective budget management and cost control?

9. How does data-driven decision-making, facilitated by accurate cost allocation data, enhance cloud cost management?

Answer Section

Multiple Choice Questions

1. b) To achieve financial visibility and transparency.

2. b) Tagging and labels, cost allocation reports, and cost allocation tools.

3. b) By attributing costs to specific business units or teams.

4. c) It provides insights into resource consumption patterns.

5. d) Reporting and visualization.

6. b) To achieve financial visibility and transparency.

7. d) Establishing a tagging strategy for cost allocation.

8. d) By analyzing cost data and uncovering opportunities for cost-saving.

9. d) Data aggregation and consolidation.

10. c) By providing insights into resource consumption patterns.

11. a) It enables effective budget management and cost control.

Review Questions

1. The purpose of cloud cost allocation is to attribute the costs of cloud resource usage to specific entities, such as business units, projects, or teams. This process provides financial visibility and transparency, allowing organizations to understand resource consumption patterns and make data-driven decisions regarding resource allocation and optimization. Cloud cost allocation helps organizations manage their cloud expenses effectively by fostering accountability, enabling cost-saving measures, and facilitating compliance with budgetary constraints. By accurately attributing costs to responsible entities, organizations can optimize resource utilization, identify areas of high expenditure, and implement cost optimization strategies to minimize unnecessary expenses.

2. The key components of cloud cost allocation are tagging and labels, cost allocation reports, and cost allocation tools. Tags are used to categorize cloud resources and track their associated costs, providing a basis for accurate cost attribution. Cost allocation reports offer a clear breakdown of expenses based on predefined tags or custom dimensions, providing insights into resource spending patterns. Additionally, third-party cost allocation tools and cloud management platforms automate tagging, cost attribution, and granular reporting, streamlining the process of allocating costs and ensuring precise resource utilization data. Together, these components contribute to accurate cost attribution, enhancing financial visibility and informed decision-making.

3. Cloud cost allocation fosters accountability by attributing costs to specific business units, projects, or teams responsible for using cloud resources. When teams are aware of their usage and its associated costs, they are more likely to act responsibly and efficiently. This fosters cost-conscious behavior as team members become mindful of the financial impact of their cloud resource consumption. By holding individuals or departments accountable for their cloud spending, organizations can promote cost awareness, optimize resource utilization, and ensure that cloud expenses align with business objectives. Accountability, in turn, supports better governance and compliance with budgetary constraints.

4. Implementing granular cost reporting offers several benefits in cloud cost management. First, it provides detailed insights into spending patterns, enabling organizations to identify specific areas of high expenditure and potential cost-saving opportunities. Granular reports also facilitate better decision-making by presenting resource costs based on relevant business criteria, such as departments or projects. By analyzing granular cost data, organizations can optimize resource allocation, identify underutilized or inefficient resources, and implement targeted cost optimization strategies. Furthermore, granular cost reporting aids in compliance with budgetary constraints and supports data-driven decisions for resource allocation and capacity planning, leading to cost-efficient cloud operations.

5. To align cloud cost allocation with their organizational structure, organizations should map cost allocation to reflect the various business units, projects, or teams responsible for specific cloud resources. By doing so, costs can be attributed accurately to the entities using those resources, fostering

accountability and financial transparency. Regularly reviewing and updating cost allocation mappings to accommodate changes in the organizational structure or resource ownership ensures accuracy in cost attribution. Aligning cost allocation with the organizational structure also enables better resource tracking, allowing organizations to understand which entities drive specific cloud expenses, helping in optimizing resource utilization and budget management.

6. Automated tagging and cost attribution play a crucial role in the cloud cost allocation process. These mechanisms streamline and optimize the allocation of costs to cloud resources. Automated tagging applies metadata to resources based on predefined rules or resource characteristics, ensuring consistent and accurate categorization. This eliminates the need for manual tagging, reducing the chances of human error and ensuring all resources are appropriately labeled for cost attribution. Cost attribution, coupled with automated tagging, ties the tagged resources to the corresponding entities responsible for their usage. This automation improves the accuracy and efficiency of cost allocation, providing organizations with reliable financial insights for better resource management.

7. Continuous review and optimization of cloud costs are essential for achieving long-term cost efficiency and resource utilization. Regular cost reviews allow organizations to identify cost outliers, resource inefficiencies, and potential cost optimization opportunities. By continuously monitoring and analyzing cloud expenses, organizations can make data-driven decisions regarding cost-saving strategies, such as rightsizing instances or utilizing reserved instances. This ongoing optimization approach ensures that the cloud environment remains cost-efficient over time, aligning cloud spending with changing business needs. Moreover, continuous review and optimization foster a culture of cost awareness and accountability, driving better resource utilization and proactive management of cloud spending.

8. Cloud cost reporting and analysis contribute to effective budget management and cost control by providing insights into actual cloud spending against budgeted amounts. Through detailed cost data collection and consolidation, organizations can create comprehensive cost reports that present spending patterns, trends, and deviations from budgeted allocations. This enables stakeholders to monitor cloud spending in real-time and take proactive measures to prevent budget overruns. By analyzing cost drivers and uncovering optimization opportunities, organizations can implement cost-saving strategies to stay within budgetary constraints while optimizing resource utilization. Cloud cost reporting and analysis thus serve as powerful tools for financial visibility, facilitating informed decisions to maintain financial discipline.

9. Data-driven decision-making, facilitated by accurate cost allocation data, enhances cloud cost management by providing concrete financial insights. By analyzing detailed cost data, organizations can make informed decisions regarding resource allocation, capacity planning, and budgeting. This approach ensures that cloud resources are appropriately provisioned to meet workload demands without unnecessary overprovisioning. Data-driven decisions also support the implementation of cost-saving strategies, such as utilizing spot instances or leveraging reserved instances for predictable workloads. Furthermore, accurate cost allocation data enables organizations to assess the effectiveness of cost optimization efforts and continuously improve cloud cost management practices. By relying on data-driven insights, organizations can achieve cost efficiency and maximize the value of their cloud investments.

Chapter 21: Cloud Native Security

Securing cloud native architectures is essential to protect data and applications in modern cloud environments. By implementing best practices for secure containerization, microservices security, orchestration platform security, identity and access management, network security, and continuous security monitoring, organizations can mitigate risks and maintain a strong security posture. Regular security assessments and penetration testing further ensure ongoing protection against emerging threats. With a holistic approach to cloud native security, organizations can confidently leverage the benefits of cloud native architectures while safeguarding their critical assets.

21.1 Security Considerations in Cloud Native Environments

Securing cloud native environments is crucial to protect data and applications in the dynamic and scalable nature of modern cloud architectures. By implementing best practices such as securing containerization, network security, identity and access management, and secure orchestration platforms, organizations can mitigate security risks and safeguard their cloud native environments. Continuous security monitoring, vulnerability management, and regular security testing further ensure the ongoing protection of data and applications. With robust security measures in place, organizations can confidently embrace cloud native architectures while maintaining the highest levels of data and application security.

21.1.1. Understanding Cloud Native Environments:

Cloud native environments are characterized by the use of modern application development and deployment practices, such as containerization, microservices architectures, and orchestration platforms like Kubernetes. These environments allow organizations to build, deploy, and scale applications more efficiently, making them highly popular in cloud computing.

Key Components:

- **Containerization:** Containers provide lightweight, isolated runtime environments for applications, enhancing portability and scalability. They package the application code along with its dependencies, making it easier to move and run consistently across various environments.

- **Microservices Architecture:** In a microservices architecture, applications are broken down into smaller, loosely coupled services. Each service performs a specific function and communicates with other services through APIs. This architecture enables independent development, deployment, and scaling of services.

- **Orchestration Platforms:** Orchestration platforms like Kubernetes automate the deployment, scaling, and management of containerized applications. They simplify the management of container clusters, ensuring high availability and fault tolerance.

21.1.2. Security Risks in Cloud Native Environments:

- Container Vulnerabilities: Containers may introduce security risks if they are misconfigured or if images contain unpatched software or vulnerabilities. Attackers can exploit these weaknesses to gain unauthorized access to the container or execute malicious activities.

- Network Security: Microservices communicate over networks, and inadequate network security measures can lead to data breaches or unauthorized access. Securing communications between microservices is essential to protect sensitive data.

- Identity and Access Management: Cloud native environments often involve numerous services and components, making managing identities and access controls more complex. It's essential to implement proper authentication, authorization, and role-based access controls to prevent unauthorized access.

- Dynamic Nature of Orchestration: The dynamic nature of orchestration platforms introduces challenges in securing the control plane, securing inter-component communications, and ensuring secure configurations. Proper security measures are crucial to prevent unauthorized access or tampering.

21.1.3. Best Practices for Security in Cloud Native Environments:

21.1.3.1 Secure Containerization:

- Utilize Trusted Container Images: Use container images from reputable sources or official repositories. Regularly update and patch container images with the latest security fixes to reduce vulnerabilities.

- Container Runtime Security: Implement image scanning, runtime isolation, and container vulnerability management to identify and address security issues in containers.

21.1.3.2 Network Security:

- Secure Network Segmentation: Employ network security practices like secure network segmentation, encryption, and strict access controls to protect microservices communication and prevent lateral movement of attackers.

- Network Policies and Firewall Rules: Implement network policies and firewall rules to control traffic between microservices and external networks. This helps restrict access and prevent unauthorized communication.

21.1.3.3 Identity and Access Management:

- Robust Authentication Mechanisms: Implement robust authentication mechanisms, such as multi-factor authentication (MFA) and strong password policies, to ensure secure access to cloud native resources.

- Role-Based Access Controls (RBAC): Utilize RBAC and fine-grained access permissions to restrict access based on the principle of least privilege. This helps limit potential damage in case of a security breach.

21.1.3.4 Secure Orchestration Platforms:

- Secure Configurations: Implement secure configurations for orchestration platforms, including secure API endpoints, proper authentication mechanisms, and RBAC policies.

- Regular Updates and Patches: Regularly update and patch orchestration platform components to address security vulnerabilities and ensure the environment's overall security.

21.1.3.5 Security Monitoring and Logging:

- Comprehensive Logging and Monitoring: Implement logging and monitoring solutions to detect and respond to security incidents effectively. Monitor for abnormal activities, such as unauthorized access attempts or suspicious network traffi

21.1.3.6 Vulnerability Management:

- Establish a Vulnerability Management Program: Create a vulnerability management program to identify, assess, and remediate vulnerabilities in container images, orchestration platforms, and other cloud native components.

- Regular Software Updates: Regularly update and patch software components to address security vulnerabilities promptly. Staying up-to-date with security patches helps reduce the attack surface.

21.1.3.7 Continuous Security Testing:

- Regular Security Assessments: Conduct regular security assessments, penetration testing, and code reviews to identify and remediate security weaknesses in cloud native applications and infrastructure.

21.2 Container Security Best Practices

Container security is vital to protect applications and data in cloud environments. By following best practices such as securing container images, hardening container runtimes, implementing image verification, network segmentation, and access controls, organizations can enhance container security in the cloud. Regular monitoring, logging, and security assessments further strengthen the security posture of containerized environments. By incorporating container security measures throughout the development and deployment lifecycle, organizations can confidently leverage the benefits of containerization while ensuring the integrity and security of their applications in the cloud.

21.1.1. Understanding Container Security:

Containers provide lightweight and isolated runtime environments for applications, but their security depends on various factors, including proper configuration, secure container images, and robust runtime controls.

21.1.1.1 Key Considerations:

- Image Vulnerabilities: Container security can be compromised if insecure or outdated container images are used, which may contain software vulnerabilities or misconfigurations. Regularly updating and patching container images is crucial to address known vulnerabilities.

- Container Breakout: Containers run on the same host and share the host's kernel, which poses the risk of container breakout attacks. These attacks occur when an attacker gains unauthorized access to the host system or other containers. Ensuring proper isolation between containers is essential to mitigate this risk.

- Network Security: Implementing proper network segmentation and access controls is critical to prevent unauthorized access and protect sensitive data within containers. Properly configured network policies and firewall rules help control inbound and outbound traffic between containers and other network entities.

21.1.2. Container Security Best Practices:

21.1.2.1 Secure Container Images:

- Use Official and Trusted Images: Utilize container images from reputable sources or official repositories. This reduces the risk of using potentially compromised or unsecure images.

- **Regular Image Updates:** Regularly update and patch container images to address known vulnerabilities. Vulnerability scanning tools can help identify and remediate security issues in container images.

- **Image Scanning:** Implement image scanning tools that automatically check container images for known vulnerabilities before deployment. This ensures that only secure images are used in the environment.

21.1.2.2Harden Container Runtimes:
- **Security Profiles:** Utilize container runtimes with built-in security features, such as Docker's security profiles (e.g., seccomp, AppArmor or containerd's gVisor. These profiles limit the capabilities of containers and prevent privilege escalation.

- **Resource Constraints:** Employ resource constraints to limit container capabilities, such as CPU and memory usage. This helps reduce the potential impact of a compromised container.

21.1.2.3 Implement Image Verification:
- **Digital Signing:** Digitally sign container images to ensure their integrity and authenticity. Verifying image signatures before deployment helps prevent the use of tampered or unauthorized images.

21.1.2.4Secure Container Registry:
- **Access Controls:** Implement access controls and authentication mechanisms for container registries to prevent unauthorized image modifications or unauthorized access. Only authorized users should have the ability to push or pull images.

- **Registry Monitoring:** Regularly audit and monitor container registry activities to detect and respond to any suspicious or unauthorized activities, such as image tampering or unauthorized access attempts.

21.1.2.5Network Segmentation and Access Controls:
- **Isolation:** Employ network segmentation to isolate containers based on their functions or security requirements. Limit communication between containers to only necessary services and ports to minimize the attack surface.

- **Network Policies:** Implement network policies and firewall rules to control inbound and outbound traffic between containers and other network entities. This helps enforce network security and prevents unauthorized communications.

21.1.2.6Container Runtime Security:
- **Runtime Updates:** Regularly update and patch container runtimes to address any security vulnerabilities. Staying up-to-date ensures that security patches are applied promptly.

- **Network Encryption:** Implement container network encryption to protect data transmitted between containers, adding an extra layer of security to sensitive data.

21.1.2.7Monitoring and Logging:
- **Robust Monitoring:** Implement robust monitoring and logging solutions to track container activities, resource usage, and potential security events. This enables early detection and response to security incidents.

- **Intrusion Detection:** Utilize intrusion detection and prevention systems to identify and respond to any security threats or anomalies within the container environment.

21.1.2.8Container Lifecycle Management:
- **Secure Image Distribution:** Define clear container lifecycle management processes, including secure image distribution to prevent the use of unauthorized or tampered images.

- **Automation:** Automate container image updates and vulnerability scanning as part of the continuous integration and deployment (CI/CD) pipeline. This ensures that images are regularly checked and updated as new vulnerabilities are discovered.

21.1.2.9Regular Security Assessments and Penetration Testing:
- **Security Assessments:** Conduct periodic security assessments and penetration testing to identify vulnerabilities and assess the effectiveness of security controls. Remediate any identified security weaknesses promptly to maintain a robust security posture.

- **Continuous Improvement:** Ensure continuous improvement of container security by learning from security assessments and implementing necessary improvements based on the findings.

21.3 Vulnerability Management and Patching in the Cloud

21.3.1. Understanding Vulnerability Management:

Vulnerability management and patching are essential practices to maintain a secure cloud environment. By implementing best practices such as regular vulnerability scanning, prioritization, timely patch deployment, and collaboration with cloud service providers, organizations can mitigate security risks and protect their cloud infrastructure and applications. Continuous monitoring, reporting, and regular system updates further strengthen the security posture of the cloud environment. By incorporating vulnerability management and patching as integral parts of the overall security strategy, organizations can proactively address vulnerabilities, minimize the attack surface, and safeguard sensitive data in the cloud.

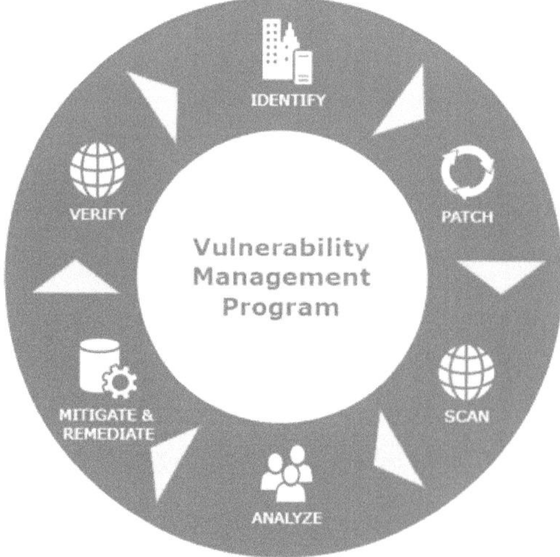

Key Considerations:
- **Vulnerability Scanning:** Regular vulnerability scanning is essential to discover weaknesses, misconfigurations, and potential security threats in the cloud environment. Vulnerability scanning tools conduct automated assessments to identify known vulnerabilities and provide valuable insights into areas that require attention.

- **Patch Management:** Patch management is a critical aspect of vulnerability management. It involves applying security patches promptly to address identified vulnerabilities. Security patches are updates released by software vendors to fix security flaws and vulnerabilities. By staying up-to-date with the latest patches, organizations can protect their systems from potential exploits.

- **Risk Prioritization:** Not all vulnerabilities have the same level of risk. It's crucial to prioritize vulnerabilities based on their severity, exploitability, and potential impact. This allows organizations to focus their efforts and resources on addressing high-priority vulnerabilities that pose the most significant threat to the cloud environment.

21.3.2. Vulnerability Management and Patching Best Practices:

- **Establish a Vulnerability Management Program:** Developing a comprehensive vulnerability management program is essential. This program should include clear policies, procedures, and defined roles and responsibilities for the teams involved in vulnerability management.

- **Regular Scanning Cadence:** Set up a regular scanning cadence to perform vulnerability assessments across all components of the cloud environment. This helps identify new vulnerabilities and monitor the overall security posture continuously.

21.3.3. Conduct Regular Vulnerability Scanning:

- **Automated Scanning Tools:** Employ automated vulnerability scanning tools to identify vulnerabilities efficiently. These tools can scan large and complex cloud infrastructures, making it easier to detect potential risks.

- **Continuous Scanning:** Implement continuous scanning to identify newly discovered vulnerabilities and emerging threats. Regular scans provide real-time insights into the cloud environment's security and allow for prompt actions.

21.3.4 Prioritize and Remediate Vulnerabilities:

- **Categorize Vulnerabilities:** Categorize vulnerabilities based on their severity, exploitability, and potential impact. This process helps in efficiently allocating resources to address the most critical risks first.

- **Focus on Critical Vulnerabilities:** Focus on remediation efforts for critical vulnerabilities that have the highest potential to be exploited and cause significant harm to the cloud environment.

- **Tracking and Documentation:** Establish a process to track and document all vulnerability remediation activities. This documentation ensures accountability, helps measure progress, and aids in compliance with security policies and regulations.

21.3.5 Implement Patch Management Processes:

- **Stay Informed:** Regularly review security advisories and patch releases from software vendors and cloud service providers. This ensures that your organization is aware of newly released patches to address vulnerabilities.

- **Patch Deployment:** Establish a patch management process that ensures timely deployment of patches across cloud infrastructure and applications. Testing patches in a non-production environment before deployment to production systems helps avoid potential disruptions.

21.3.6 Automated Patch Deployment:
- **Automation Tools:** Utilize automation tools and configuration management systems to streamline the patch deployment process. Automation reduces manual intervention and potential errors, making the patching process more efficient.

- **Scheduled Deployments:** Schedule regular patch deployments during maintenance windows or non-peak hours to minimize any adverse effects on services and users.

21.3.7 Monitor Patch Compliance:
- **Monitoring System:** Implement a monitoring system to track and evaluate patch compliance across the cloud infrastructure and applications. Regular assessment ensures that all critical patches have been successfully deployed.

- **Immediate Attention:** Identify any gaps or vulnerabilities that require immediate attention due to failed patch deployments or unresolved issues.

- **Regular System Updates:** Apart from patching, ensure that operating systems, software libraries, and dependencies are regularly updated. Keeping all components up-to-date ensures that known vulnerabilities are addressed promptly, and the cloud environment remains secure.

21.3.8 Vulnerability and Patch Reporting:
- **Reporting Mechanism:** Generate regular reports on vulnerability scan results, remediation efforts, and patch status. These reports provide visibility to stakeholders, such as management and security teams, helping them understand the current security posture and the effectiveness of vulnerability management efforts.

- **Collaboration:** Share vulnerability and patching reports with relevant teams to promote transparency, accountability, and collaboration in managing cloud security.

21.3.9 Collaboration with Cloud Service Providers:
- **Understand Provider Practices:** Stay informed about the vulnerability management practices and security features provided by cloud service providers. Familiarity with these practices allows you to align your vulnerability management efforts with the capabilities of the cloud service provider.

- **Leveraging Security Tools:** Take advantage of security tools, services, and guidance offered by the cloud service provider to enhance your vulnerability management efforts. Many cloud providers offer security services that can complement your in-house vulnerability management program.

Exercise

Multiple Choice Questions

1. What are the key components of cloud native environments?

a. Virtual machines, on-premises servers, and mainframes

b. Containerization, microservices architecture, and orchestration platforms

c. Cloud storage, load balancers, and firewalls

d. Network switches, routers, and gateways

2. Which of the following is a potential security risk in cloud native environments related to containers?

a. Network segmentation

b. Secure image distribution

c. Container vulnerabilities

d. Robust monitoring and logging

3. What is the purpose of implementing network segmentation and access controls in cloud native environments?

a. To secure container images

b. To prevent lateral movement of attackers

c. To automate container deployment

d. To enhance container runtime security

4. Which of the following practices helps ensure the integrity and authenticity of container images in the cloud?

a. Secure image distribution

b. Continuous scanning

c. Network encryption

d. Regular vulnerability scanning

5. Why is patch management crucial in vulnerability management for cloud environments?

a. To prioritize vulnerabilities based on their severity

b. To prevent unauthorized access to the cloud environment

c. To fix software vulnerabilities and address security flaws

d. To automate container deployment

6. What is the main purpose of categorizing vulnerabilities in vulnerability management?

a. To automate container deployment

b. To identify known vulnerabilities in cloud infrastructure

c. To streamline the patch deployment process

d. To efficiently allocate resources for remediation efforts

7. What is the significance of automation in vulnerability management and patch deployment?

a. To implement secure image distribution

b. To streamline the patch deployment process and reduce manual intervention

c. To prioritize vulnerabilities based on their severity

d. To prevent lateral movement of attackers

8. Why is regular monitoring and reporting essential in vulnerability management?

a. To identify known vulnerabilities in cloud infrastructure

b. To prevent unauthorized access to the cloud environment

c. To track and evaluate patch compliance

d. To enhance container runtime Security

9. How does collaboration with cloud service providers benefit vulnerability management efforts?

a. To prioritize vulnerabilities based on their severity

b. To automate container deployment

c. To understand the vulnerability management practices of cloud providers

d. To enhance container security by leveraging security tools and services offered by the cloud provider

Review Questions

1. What are the key components of cloud native environments, and how do they contribute to modern application development and deployment practices?

2. What are the security risks associated with containerization in cloud native environments, and how can organizations address them?

3. How can organizations ensure robust identity and access management (IAM) in cloud native environments?

4. How does regular vulnerability scanning contribute to effective vulnerability management in cloud environments?

5. What are the benefits of implementing network segmentation and access controls in cloud native environments?

6. How can organizations ensure secure image distribution in cloud native environments, and why is it crucial?

7. Why is collaboration with cloud service providers important for effective vulnerability management in the cloud?

8. What role does continuous monitoring play in vulnerability management for cloud environments?

Answer Section

Multiple Choice Questions

1. b) Containerization, microservices architecture, and orchestration platforms

2. c) Container vulnerabilities

3. b) To prevent lateral movement of attackers

4. a) Secure image distribution

5. c) To fix software vulnerabilities and address security flaws

6. d) To efficiently allocate resources for remediation efforts

7. b) To streamline the patch deployment process and reduce manual intervention

8. c) To track and evaluate patch compliance

9. d) To enhance container security by leveraging security tools and services offered by the cloud provider

Review Questions

1. The key components of cloud native environments are containerization, microservices architecture, and orchestration platforms like Kubernetes. Containerization allows applications to be packaged with their dependencies and run consistently across various environments, enhancing portability and scalability. Microservices architecture breaks down applications into smaller, loosely coupled services, enabling independent development and scaling. Orchestration platforms automate the deployment, scaling, and management of containerized applications, ensuring high availability and fault tolerance. Together, these components facilitate efficient application development, deployment, and management, making cloud native environments popular in modern cloud computing.

2. Containerization in cloud native environments introduces several security risks, including container vulnerabilities and the potential for container breakout attacks. Containers may contain unpatched software or misconfigurations, which attackers can exploit to gain unauthorized access or execute malicious activities. Additionally, containers running on the same host share the host's kernel, creating a risk of container breakout, where an attacker gains access to the host system or other containers. To address these risks, organizations should use trusted container images, regularly update and patch container images, and implement runtime isolation and vulnerability management. Proper network segmentation and access controls can also prevent lateral movement of attackers between containers.

3. Robust identity and access management (IAM) in cloud native environments can be achieved by implementing strong authentication mechanisms and role-based access controls (RBAC). Utilizing multi-factor authentication (MFA) and enforcing strong password policies enhances the security of user access. Role-based access controls help limit privileges to only what users need to perform their specific tasks,

reducing the risk of unauthorized access. Additionally, organizations should regularly review and audit IAM policies to ensure they align with the principle of least privilege. Proper IAM implementation ensures that only authorized users have access to cloud native resources, safeguarding the environment from potential threats.

4. Regular vulnerability scanning plays a crucial role in effective vulnerability management in cloud environments. Vulnerability scanning tools automatically assess cloud infrastructure, applications, and dependencies for known vulnerabilities. These scans provide valuable insights into potential security weaknesses and risks within the cloud environment. By conducting regular vulnerability scans, organizations can detect newly discovered vulnerabilities and emerging threats in real-time, allowing for prompt remediation efforts. Vulnerability scanning helps organizations prioritize security patches based on the severity of identified vulnerabilities, reducing the attack surface and maintaining a secure cloud infrastructure.

5. Implementing network segmentation and access controls in cloud native environments offers several benefits. Network segmentation helps isolate containers and microservices based on their functions or security requirements. This limits communication between containers and prevents unauthorized access, reducing the potential impact of a compromised container. Access controls ensure that only authorized users and services have the necessary permissions to interact with specific resources. Properly configured network policies and firewall rules restrict inbound and outbound traffic, preventing unauthorized communications and protecting sensitive data. Network segmentation and access controls enhance the overall security posture of cloud native environments, making them more resilient to potential cyber threats.

6. Secure image distribution in cloud native environments can be ensured by digitally signing container images. Digitally signing images helps verify their integrity and authenticity, ensuring that only authorized and tamper-free images are used in the environment. Before deploying container images, organizations should verify image signatures to prevent the use of unauthorized or maliciously modified images. Secure image distribution is crucial because using compromised or untrusted images can introduce security risks and vulnerabilities into the cloud environment. By ensuring the integrity of container images, organizations can maintain a strong security posture and reduce the likelihood of security breaches and unauthorized access.

7. Collaboration with cloud service providers is important for effective vulnerability management in the cloud because cloud providers often offer security tools, services, and guidance that complement an organization's vulnerability management efforts. Cloud service providers have expertise in securing their platforms and can provide valuable insights into the vulnerability management practices they employ. Understanding the security features and tools provided by the cloud provider allows organizations to align their vulnerability management strategies with the capabilities of the cloud environment. By leveraging the security offerings of the cloud provider, organizations can enhance their vulnerability management efforts and maintain a strong security posture in the cloud.

8. Continuous monitoring is a critical component of vulnerability management for cloud environments. It involves implementing robust monitoring and logging solutions to track cloud activities, resource usage, and security events in real-time. Continuous monitoring allows organizations to detect and respond to security incidents promptly, minimizing the potential impact of security breaches. By constantly

monitoring for abnormal activities, such as unauthorized access attempts or suspicious network traffic, organizations can quickly identify potential threats and take appropriate actions. Continuous monitoring also facilitates compliance with security policies and regulatory requirements, enabling organizations to maintain a vigilant and proactive approach to security in the cloud.

Chapter 22: Cloud Backup and Data Recovery Strategies

22.1 Backup and Restore Methods in the Cloud: Ensuring Data Resiliency and Business Continuity

Backup and restore methods in the cloud are critical for data resiliency, business continuity, and protection against data loss. By implementing suitable backup strategies, utilizing appropriate backup methods (full, incremental, differential, snapshots), and leveraging efficient restore approaches (point-in-time restore, DRaaS, cloud-to-cloud restore, hybrid restore), organizations can safeguard their data and systems in the cloud. Remember to define clear backup and recovery objectives, regularly test backups, ensure data security, and automate backup processes for efficiency. With robust cloud backup and restore practices, organizations can confidently embrace cloud computing while safeguarding their valuable data and ensuring uninterrupted business operations.

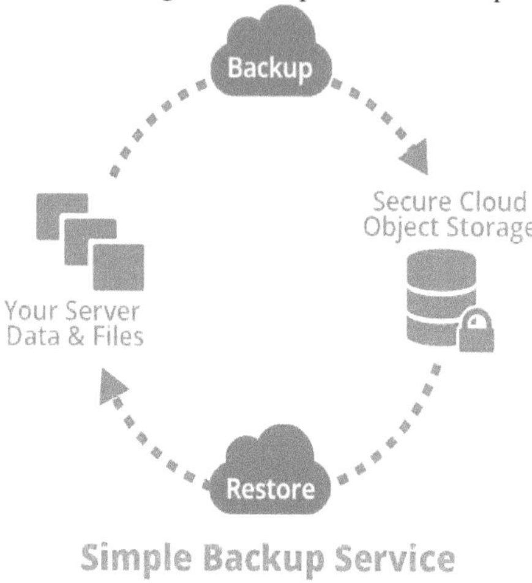

22.1.1. Importance of Cloud Backup and Restore: Cloud backup and restore methods are essential for mitigating risks associated with data loss and maintaining business continuity. Consider the following key reasons:

- **Data Protection:** Backing up data to the cloud safeguards against accidental deletions, hardware failures, natural disasters, and cyber threats. It provides an additional layer of protection to prevent permanent data loss.

- **Disaster Recovery:** Cloud-based backups enable rapid recovery in case of disasters. By leveraging the scalability and redundancy of cloud infrastructure, organizations can restore critical data and systems quickly, minimizing downtime and maintaining seamless operations.

- **Scalability and Flexibility:** Cloud-based backup solutions can scale seamlessly to accommodate growing data volumes. They offer flexible storage options and can adapt to changing business needs, ensuring data resiliency even as the organization expands.

22.1.2. Backup Methods in the Cloud:

When implementing backup strategies in the cloud, several methods can be utilized. Here are some common approaches:

- **Full Backups:** Full backups involve copying the entire dataset to the cloud. While they ensure complete data recovery, they can be time-consuming and resource-intensive, especially for large datasets. Full backups are typically performed periodically or as a baseline before incremental or differential backups.

- Incremental Backups: Incremental backups capture only the changes made since the last backup, significantly reducing backup time and storage requirements. During a restore, the full backup is combined with subsequent incremental backups to reconstruct the most recent state of the data. This method is efficient and saves storage space.

- Differential Backups: Differential backups capture the changes made since the last full backup. Unlike incremental backups, they do not rely on the previous backup chain during the restore process. However, differential backups require more storage space over time compared to incremental backups.

- Snapshot-Based Backups: Snapshots capture the state of the entire system or specific volumes at a specific point in time. They provide a quick and efficient way to create backups and enable near-instantaneous recovery. Snapshots are commonly used for data protection in cloud storage services, particularly in virtualized environments.

22.1.3. Restore Methods in the Cloud:

Effective restore methods are essential to quickly recover data and systems in the event of data loss or system failures. Consider the following approaches:

- Point-in-Time Restore: Many cloud storage services offer point-in-time restore capabilities, allowing you to restore data to a specific timestamp or version. This is particularly useful for recovering from accidental data modifications or data corruption.

- Disaster Recovery as a Service (DRaaS): DRaaS solutions enable organizations to replicate and recover entire systems or applications in the cloud. With DRaaS, businesses can quickly restore critical infrastructure and maintain business operations during outages or disasters.

- Cloud-to-Cloud Restore: In cases where data loss or service disruptions occur in one cloud provider, cloud-to-cloud restore enables recovery by replicating data and services to another cloud provider. This approach provides redundancy and ensures business continuity even if one cloud provider experiences downtime.

- Hybrid Restore: Hybrid restore methods involve recovering data and systems by combining on-premises backups with cloud backups. This approach provides flexibility and options for recovery in hybrid cloud environments, where data is distributed between on-premises infrastructure and cloud services.

22.1.4. Best Practices for Cloud Backup and Restore:

To ensure effective backup and restore operations in the cloud, follow these best practices:

- Define Backup and Recovery Objectives: Clearly define backup and recovery objectives, including recovery time objectives (RTOs) and recovery point objectives (RPOs). These metrics determine the acceptable downtime and data loss in case of a restore.

- Regular Testing and Validation: Regularly test backup and restore processes to verify the integrity and effectiveness of backups. Conduct periodic restoration drills to ensure that critical data and systems can be recovered successfully.

- Encryption and Data Security: Implement encryption mechanisms to protect backup data while in transit and at rest. Secure backup storage repositories with access controls and encryption to prevent unauthorized access to sensitive information.

- **Off-Site Storage and Redundancy:** Maintain off-site backups in geographically dispersed locations to protect against regional disasters. Utilize redundancy across multiple data centers or cloud regions to ensure data resiliency and enhance data availability.

- **Automated Backup and Monitoring:** Leverage automation tools to schedule and perform regular backups. Implement monitoring mechanisms to proactively identify backup failures and ensure the integrity of backup operations.

22.2 Disaster Recovery Planning and Testing for the Cloud: Ensuring Resilience and Business Continuity

Disaster recovery planning and testing are critical for ensuring resilience and business continuity in the cloud. By leveraging cloud-based replication, redundancy, and rapid recovery capabilities, organizations can effectively respond to disruptions and minimize downtime. Through careful disaster recovery planning, including business impact analysis, cloud provider selection, data replication strategies, and detailed runbooks, and regular testing of the recovery processes, organizations can confidently navigate unexpected events and protect their critical systems and data. Effective disaster recovery planning and testing in the cloud are essential elements of a comprehensive risk management strategy, allowing organizations to maintain operations and uphold customer trust even in the face of adversity

22.2.1. Understanding Disaster Recovery in the Cloud:

Disaster recovery refers to a set of strategies, processes, and technologies implemented to recover and restore critical systems and data in the event of a disaster. In the cloud, disaster recovery offers numerous benefits, including flexibility, scalability, and cost-efficiency. Consider the following key aspects:

- **Replication and Redundancy:** Cloud services allow organizations to replicate critical systems, applications, and data across multiple geographic regions or availability zones. This redundancy ensures that data and services remain accessible even if a specific region or zone experiences a disruption.

- **Rapid Recovery:** Cloud-based disaster recovery leverages the scalability and automation capabilities of cloud infrastructure. Organizations can quickly spin up replicated systems and restore data to minimize downtime and maintain business operations, leading to faster recovery times.

- **Cost Optimization:** Cloud-based disaster recovery eliminates the need for dedicated secondary data centers and hardware investments. Organizations can leverage cloud resources on-demand, reducing costs associated with infrastructure maintenance and allowing for a more cost-effective recovery strategy.

22.2.2. Disaster Recovery Planning for the Cloud:

Creating a comprehensive disaster recovery plan is crucial for effectively responding to and recovering from disruptions. Consider the following key steps and considerations:

- **Business Impact Analysis (BIA):** Conduct a BIA to identify critical systems, applications, and data that need to be prioritized for recovery. Determine recovery time objectives (RTOs) and recovery point objectives (RPOs) to establish recovery targets. The BIA helps organizations understand the impact of a potential disaster on business operations and guides the development of the recovery plan.

- **Cloud Provider Selection:** Choose a cloud provider that offers robust disaster recovery capabilities, including data replication, regional redundancy, and automated recovery processes. Consider factors such as provider reputation, service-level agreements (SLAs), and compatibility with your existing infrastructure. The right cloud provider can significantly enhance your disaster recovery capabilities.

- **Data Replication Strategies:** Determine the appropriate data replication strategy for your critical data. Options include synchronous replication for immediate failover, asynchronous replication for near-real-time replication, or periodic backup and restoration for less time-sensitive data. The choice of replication strategy depends on the criticality of the data and the desired recovery time.

- **Disaster Recovery Runbooks:** Develop detailed runbooks that document step-by-step procedures for recovering systems and applications in the event of a disaster. Include instructions for failover, data restoration, network reconfiguration, and post-recovery validation. Runbooks ensure that the recovery process is well-documented and can be executed efficiently during a crisis.

- **Backup and Recovery Testing:** Regularly test the backup and recovery processes to validate their effectiveness. Conduct scheduled drills and simulated disaster scenarios to identify potential gaps and refine the recovery procedures. Testing helps identify any weaknesses in the recovery plan and ensures that the organization is well-prepared to handle real-life disasters.

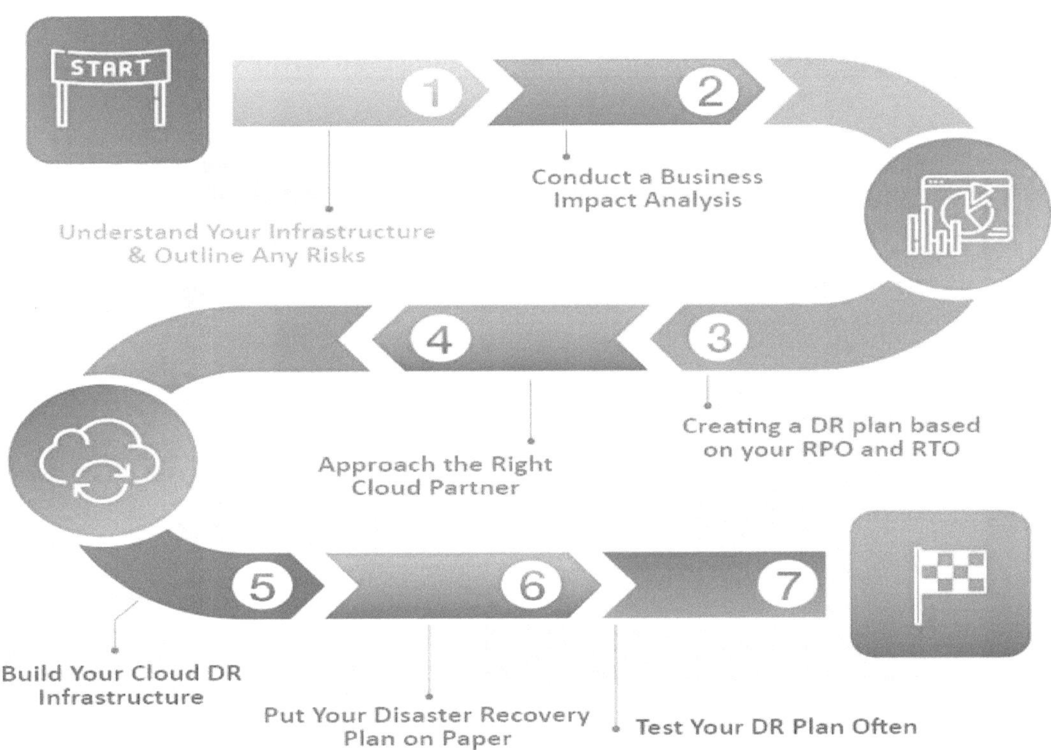

22.2.3. Disaster Recovery Testing in the Cloud:

Testing is a critical aspect of disaster recovery planning to ensure the readiness and effectiveness of the recovery processes. Consider the following best practices:

- **Testing Frequency:** Conduct regular disaster recovery tests to verify the functionality and efficiency of the recovery plan. The frequency of testing depends on the criticality of the systems and the rate of change in your infrastructure. Frequent testing ensures that the recovery plan remains relevant and effective over time.

- **Test Scope and Scenario Selection:** Define the scope of each test and select relevant disaster scenarios to simulate. Test various components, including data replication, failover, network connectivity, and application recovery, to ensure comprehensive validation. Testing different scenarios prepares the organization for a wide range of potential disasters.

- **Test Automation:** Leverage automation tools and scripts to streamline the testing process. Automated testing reduces human error, improves repeatability, and allows for more frequent testing without significant manual effort. Automation also makes it easier to conduct complex tests and scenarios.

- **Post-Test Analysis and Documentation:** After each test, analyze the results and document any issues or lessons learned. Use this feedback to refine the disaster recovery plan and update the runbooks accordingly. Documentation ensures that improvements are made based on past experiences and that the recovery plan evolves with the changing environment.

- **Compliance and Auditing:** Ensure that your disaster recovery testing aligns with industry regulations and compliance standards. Document the testing process, results, and any improvements made to meet auditing requirements. Compliance ensures that your disaster recovery plan meets industry best practices and regulatory requirements.

22.3 Data Replication and Redundancy in the Cloud: Ensuring Availability and Data Integrity

Data replication and redundancy are crucial for ensuring data availability, reliability, and integrity in the cloud. By implementing effective data replication strategies, leveraging regional redundancy, and following best practices such as automated replication, data integrity measures, and regular testing, organizations can minimize the risk of data loss and maintain uninterrupted access to critical information. Remember to align data replication strategies with business requirements and regularly assess and update your replication processes to adapt to changing needs and emerging technologies. Effective data replication and redundancy are essential elements of a comprehensive cloud infrastructure, providing organizations with the confidence to manage their data with utmost resilience and ensure uninterrupted business operations even in the face of adversity.

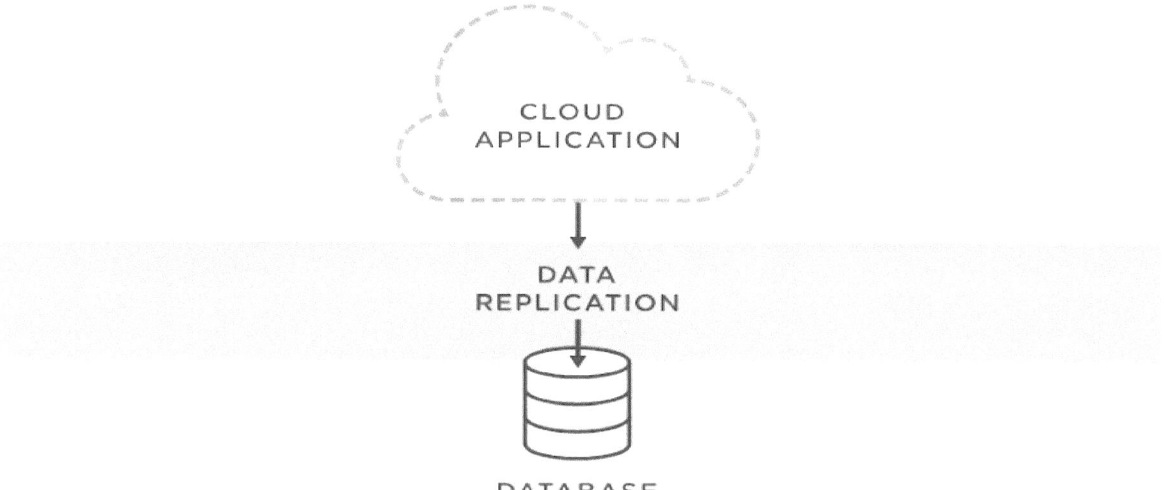

22.3.1. Understanding Data Replication in the Cloud:

Data replication involves creating multiple copies of data across different storage systems or locations. In the cloud, data replication is used to enhance availability, fault tolerance, and disaster recovery. Consider the following key aspects:

- **Replication Techniques:** Cloud providers offer various replication techniques, including synchronous and asynchronous replication. Synchronous replication ensures that data is written to multiple locations simultaneously, providing immediate consistency but potentially impacting performance due to the need for acknowledgment from multiple locations. Asynchronous replication involves replicating data with a slight delay, providing flexibility in terms of performance and geographic distance. Asynchronous replication is suitable for scenarios where minor data loss can be tolerated in exchange for improved performance.

- **Regional Replication:** Replicating data across different geographic regions or availability zones within a cloud provider's infrastructure ensures high availability. Regional replication protects against regional failures or natural disasters and allows for failover and quick recovery. This approach is particularly beneficial for critical applications and data that require continuous availability and minimal downtime.

- **Application-Level Replication:** Some cloud services offer application-level replication, where data is replicated at the application layer. This allows for consistency and availability guarantees specific to the application, ensuring seamless failover and recovery. Application-level replication is ideal for scenarios where certain applications have unique requirements for data consistency and availability.

22.3.2. Benefits of Data Replication and Redundancy in the Cloud:

Data replication and redundancy in the cloud provide numerous benefits that help ensure data availability, reliability, and integrity. Consider the following advantages:

- **High Availability:** By replicating data across multiple servers or regions, organizations can ensure continuous access to data, even in the event of hardware failures, network outages, or localized disruptions. High availability ensures that critical services remain accessible to users and customers at all times.

- **Fault Tolerance:** Replicating data across redundant systems reduces the risk of data loss and system downtime. If one server or location becomes unavailable, another replica can seamlessly take over, maintaining service continuity and minimizing the impact of failures.

- **Disaster Recovery:** Data replication enables efficient disaster recovery. By maintaining copies of data in geographically dispersed locations, organizations can quickly recover and restore data in the event of a disaster or data center failure. Disaster recovery becomes more streamlined and effective with multiple replicated copies available.

- **Performance Optimization:** Replicating data closer to users or applications reduces latency and improves performance. With data located in multiple regions, organizations can deliver content from the nearest replica, minimizing network latency and enhancing user experience.

22.3.3. Best Practices for Data Replication and Redundancy in the Cloud:

To ensure effective data replication and redundancy in the cloud, organizations should follow these best practices:

- **Data Replication Strategy:** Define a data replication strategy based on business requirements, including Recovery Point Objective (RPO) and Recovery Time Objective (RTO). Determine the frequency and granularity of replication based on the criticality of data and the acceptable data loss in case of a failure. Align replication strategies with the specific needs of each application or dataset.

- **Regional Redundancy:** Replicate data across different geographic regions or availability zones within the cloud provider's infrastructure. Ensure that data is stored in physically separated locations to protect against regional failures or disasters. Regional redundancy ensures that data remains accessible even if a whole region experiences an outage.

- **Automated Replication:** Leverage automation tools and cloud services to streamline data replication processes. Automated replication ensures consistency, reduces human error, and simplifies management. Automation also enables frequent and efficient updates to replicated dat

- **Data Integrity and Consistency:** Implement mechanisms to ensure data integrity and consistency across replicated copies. Employ checksums, encryption, and data validation techniques to maintain data integrity throughout the replication process. Data integrity measures prevent data corruption and maintain data accuracy across replicas.

- **Regular Monitoring and Testing:** Continuously monitor the status and health of replicated dat Regularly test the replication process and conduct data integrity checks to ensure that replicas are accurate and up to date. Periodic testing and monitoring help identify any issues or discrepancies in the replication process.

- **Disaster Recovery Planning:** Incorporate data replication and redundancy into your disaster recovery plan. Define recovery procedures and conduct regular drills to validate the effectiveness of your recovery strategy. Disaster recovery planning ensures that your organization is well-prepared to handle data-related crises.

Exercise

Multiple Choice Questions

1. Which of the following is NOT a key component of cost reporting and analysis in the cloud?

a. Cost data collection

b. Data aggregation and consolidation

c. Cloud provider selection

d. Reporting and visualization

2. What is the primary goal of cost reporting and analysis in the cloud?

a. To gain insights into resource consumption patterns and cost drivers

b. To automate cost data collection from cloud service providers

c. To create multiple copies of data across different storage systems

d. To minimize data loss and maintain uninterrupted access to critical information

3. How can organizations optimize cloud spending through cost reporting and analysis?

a. By implementing automated data replication

b. By leveraging regional redundancy

c. By identifying underutilized resources and implementing cost-saving strategies

d. By conducting disaster recovery drills

4. Which best practice helps organizations achieve effective cost data collection in the cloud?

a. Utilizing predefined or custom tags for resource categorization

b. Regularly reviewing and auditing IAM policies

c. Conducting regular vulnerability scanning

d. Utilizing visualization tools and dashboards

5. What is a key benefit of implementing network segmentation and access controls in cloud native environments?

a. High availability and fault tolerance

b. Data replication and redundancy

c. Enhanced financial visibility

d. Isolation of containers and prevention of unauthorized access

6. What is the purpose of conducting regular disaster recovery testing in the cloud?

a. To identify potential cost-saving opportunities

b. To streamline data replication processes

c. To validate the effectiveness of the recovery plan

d. To minimize network latency and improve performance

7. Which replication technique ensures immediate consistency but may impact performance due to acknowledgment requirements?

a. Synchronous replication

b. Asynchronous replication

c. Application-level replication

d. Redundant replication

8. What is one advantage of regional redundancy in data replication for the cloud?

a. Improved performance optimization

b. Simplified data integrity checks

c. Reduction of data corruption risks

d. Protection against regional failures or disasters

9. How can organizations ensure data integrity throughout the replication process in the cloud?

a. By regularly monitoring replicated data

b. By conducting disaster recovery drills

c. By implementing automated replication

d. By utilizing visualization tools for data analysis

Review Questions

1. What are the key components of cost reporting and analysis in the cloud?
2. How can organizations benefit from cost reporting and analysis in the cloud?
3. What are the best practices for data replication and redundancy in the cloud?
4. How does regional redundancy in data replication benefit organizations?
5. What are the key considerations for disaster recovery planning in the cloud?
6. How can organizations optimize cloud spending through cost reporting and analysis?
7. How does automated replication contribute to effective data replication in the cloud?
8. What are the benefits of data replication and redundancy in the cloud?

Answer Section

Multiple Choice Questions

1. c) Cloud provider selection
2. a) To gain insights into resource consumption patterns and cost drivers
3. c) By identifying underutilized resources and implementing cost-saving strategies
4. a) Utilizing predefined or custom tags for resource categorization
5. d) Isolation of containers and prevention of unauthorized access
6. c) To validate the effectiveness of the recovery plan
7. a) Synchronous replication
8. d) Protection against regional failures or disasters
9. a) By regularly monitoring replicated data

Review Questions

1. The key components of cost reporting and analysis in the cloud include cost data collection, data aggregation and consolidation, reporting and visualization, and cost analysis and optimization. Cost data

collection involves collecting detailed cost information from cloud service providers. Data aggregation and consolidation involve combining cost data from multiple sources to create a unified view. Reporting and visualization present cost data in a clear and understandable format through dashboards and reports. Cost analysis and optimization focus on identifying cost drivers and opportunities for cost-saving measures to optimize cloud spending.

2. Cost reporting and analysis in the cloud offer several benefits to organizations. It provides financial visibility, allowing them to understand resource consumption patterns and cost allocation across various departments or projects. By analyzing cost data, organizations can identify underutilized resources, optimize resource allocation, and implement cost-saving strategies to minimize unnecessary expenses. Cost reporting also enables effective budget control by tracking actual costs against budgeted amounts, helping organizations prevent cost overruns. Moreover, cost data insights facilitate data-driven decision-making, aiding in resource selection, capacity planning, pricing models, and cost optimization strategies.

3. Best practices for data replication and redundancy in the cloud include defining a data replication strategy based on business requirements and aligning it with Recovery Point Objectives (RPOs) and Recovery Time Objectives (RTOs). Organizations should replicate data across different geographic regions or availability zones to ensure high availability and fault tolerance. Implementing automated replication streamlines the process, while data integrity and consistency measures, such as checksums and data validation, ensure data accuracy across replicas. Regular monitoring, testing, and disaster recovery planning help maintain effective data replication and enhance overall data availability and reliability.

4. Regional redundancy in data replication offers significant benefits to organizations. By replicating data across different geographic regions or availability zones within a cloud provider's infrastructure, organizations ensure high availability of their critical data. In the event of a regional failure or natural disaster, data remains accessible from other replicated locations, preventing downtime and minimizing the impact of disruptions. Regional redundancy enhances disaster recovery capabilities, allowing organizations to quickly recover and restore data from an alternate location. This approach is particularly beneficial for critical applications and data that require continuous availability and uninterrupted access.

5. Disaster recovery planning in the cloud requires several key considerations. First, conducting a thorough Business Impact Analysis (BIA) helps identify critical systems, applications, and data that need priority for recovery. Defining Recovery Point Objectives (RPOs) and Recovery Time Objectives (RTOs) establishes recovery targets. Cloud provider selection is crucial; organizations should choose providers offering robust disaster recovery capabilities, regional redundancy, and automated recovery processes. Data replication strategies, such as synchronous or asynchronous replication, should align with the criticality of data and desired recovery time. Detailed runbooks, documenting recovery procedures, and regular disaster recovery testing are essential components of the plan.

6. Organizations can optimize cloud spending through cost reporting and analysis by identifying cost-saving opportunities and implementing efficient resource allocation strategies. Cost reporting provides financial visibility into cloud spending patterns, helping organizations understand resource consumption and identify areas for optimization. By analyzing cost data, organizations can identify underutilized resources, such as idle instances, and implement measures to optimize resource usage. Additionally, regular monitoring of actual costs against budgeted amounts helps control spending and prevent budget

overruns. With data-driven decision-making, organizations can select cost-effective cloud services and pricing models, further optimizing their cloud spending.

7. Automated replication streamlines data replication processes in the cloud, enhancing efficiency and accuracy. Automation tools and cloud services automatically handle the replication of data, reducing the need for manual intervention. This minimizes the risk of human error during the replication process. Automated replication also ensures consistency across replicas, as data is replicated at regular intervals or in real-time, depending on the chosen replication strategy. Frequent and efficient updates to replicated data are achieved with automation, contributing to timely disaster recovery and maintaining high data availability. Overall, automated replication simplifies management and strengthens data redundancy in the cloud.

8. Data replication and redundancy in the cloud offer several benefits that contribute to data availability and reliability. Replicating data across multiple servers or geographic regions ensures high availability, allowing organizations to access data even if certain servers or regions experience failures or outages. This fault tolerance reduces the risk of data loss and system downtime. In the event of a disaster, data redundancy enables quick recovery and restoration from alternate locations, minimizing the impact on business operations. Additionally, data replication and redundancy improve performance optimization by delivering content from the nearest replica, reducing latency and enhancing user experience.

Chapter 23: Cloud Governance and Compliance Frameworks

Cloud governance models and frameworks are essential tools for organizations to effectively manage their cloud environments. By implementing these models and frameworks, organizations can establish policies, controls, and processes that ensure compliance, security, cost optimization, and operational efficiency in the cloud. Addressing key components such as policy management, resource provisioning, access control, security, cost optimization, and continuous improvement, organizations can successfully navigate the complexities of cloud governance and maximize the benefits of their cloud investments. Proper cloud governance is crucial for organizations of all sizes and industries to ensure the reliability, security, and cost-effectiveness of their cloud-based operations.

23.1 Cloud Governance Models and Frameworks

23.2.1. Definition of Cloud Governance Models and Frameworks:

- **Cloud Governance Models:** Cloud governance models outline the high-level principles, objectives, and guidelines that govern an organization's cloud adoption and usage. These models provide a strategic overview of the governance approach, ensuring that cloud initiatives align with the organization's overall business goals and objectives.

- **Cloud Governance Frameworks:** On the other hand, cloud governance frameworks provide a more detailed and comprehensive set of practices, processes, and controls to operationalize and enforce cloud governance. These frameworks offer specific guidance on various aspects of cloud management, including resource provisioning, access control, compliance, security, cost management, and more. They help organizations implement governance practices consistently across their cloud environment.

23.2.2. Key Components of Cloud Governance Models and Frameworks:

- **Policy and Compliance Management:** A critical component of cloud governance is establishing policies and procedures to ensure compliance with regulatory requirements, industry standards, and internal guidelines. Regular assessments and controls are enforced to address any deviations from the established policies.

- **Resource Provisioning and Management:** Guidelines for resource provisioning are defined to ensure that cloud resources align with business requirements. This involves determining the appropriate type and size of resources, managing resource allocation, monitoring resource usage, and optimizing resource utilization to control costs and maintain operational efficiency.

- **Access Control and Identity Management:** Robust access controls and identity management practices are implemented to manage user identities, roles, and permissions within the cloud environment. Proper authentication and authorization mechanisms are enforced to ensure secure access to cloud resources and dat

- **Security and Risk Management:** Cloud governance frameworks include defining security policies, controls, and procedures to safeguard cloud resources from internal and external threats. Regular risk assessments are conducted, security measures are implemented, and incident response and recovery processes are established to address potential security breaches effectively.

- **Performance Monitoring and Optimization:** Monitoring tools and processes are implemented to track resource utilization, performance metrics, and service availability in the cloud. Performance optimization involves dynamically scaling applications, identifying performance bottlenecks, and making adjustments to improve efficiency and user experience.

- **Cost Management and Optimization:** To control cloud spending, cost management practices are established. These include monitoring cloud expenses, implementing cost allocation mechanisms to attribute costs accurately, budgeting, and implementing optimization strategies to achieve cost efficiency.

- **Change Management and Continuous Improvement:** Governance frameworks incorporate change management processes to manage and track changes to cloud resources, configurations, and applications. Continuous improvement practices ensure that cloud governance evolves with the changing needs of the organization, incorporates feedback, and aligns with emerging best practices.

23.2.3. Significance of Cloud Governance Models and Frameworks:

- **Risk Mitigation:** Cloud governance models and frameworks play a crucial role in mitigating risks by enforcing security measures, ensuring compliance with standards, and implementing access controls to protect cloud resources and sensitive data.

- **Cost Optimization:** Effective governance models and frameworks help organizations optimize cloud costs by implementing cost control mechanisms, monitoring resource usage, and optimizing infrastructure based on business needs. This prevents unnecessary overspending and ensures cost efficiency.

- **Compliance and Regulatory Alignment:** Governance models and frameworks provide guidelines and processes to ensure that cloud operations align with industry regulations, data protection laws, and internal policies. This helps the organization avoid legal and compliance issues.

- **Operational Efficiency:** By establishing consistent processes, automating tasks, and implementing best practices, cloud governance models and frameworks improve operational efficiency. This reduces the risk of errors and misconfigurations and enhances overall cloud management.

- **Scalability and Flexibility:** Cloud governance frameworks are designed to accommodate the dynamic nature of cloud environments. Organizations can scale their cloud resources and adapt to changing business needs while maintaining control and governance.

- **Collaboration and Alignment:** Governance models and frameworks facilitate collaboration among stakeholders, including IT teams, business units, compliance officers, and security personnel. This ensures alignment in cloud operations and decision-making processes, fostering better communication and cooperation.

23.2 Compliance Standards and Regulations

Compliance standards and regulations are instrumental in safeguarding data, maintaining privacy, and ensuring security in cloud computing environments. Adhering to these standards, such as GDPR, HIPAA, PCI DSS, ISO/IEC 27001, and the NIST Cybersecurity Framework, helps organizations meet legal requirements, protect sensitive information, and maintain customer trust. By implementing appropriate security measures and adhering to compliance standards, organizations can mitigate risks, demonstrate their commitment to data protection, and operate securely in the cloud. These compliance frameworks provide a robust foundation for organizations to build a secure and privacy-focused cloud infrastructure while meeting regulatory obligations.

Here is common compliance standards and regulations applicable to cloud environments and their significance in more detail:

23.2.1. General Data Protection Regulation (GDPR):

- Overview: GDPR is a comprehensive data protection regulation that applies to organizations handling personal data of individuals residing in the European Union (EU). It aims to protect individuals' privacy rights and harmonize data protection laws across EU member states.

- Key Provisions:- Lawful Basis for Data Processing: GDPR requires organizations to have a valid legal basis for collecting, processing, and storing personal data. Consent is one of the lawful bases for data processing.

- Data Subject Rights: GDPR grants individuals various rights, including the right to access, rectify, and erase their personal data, as well as the right to data portability.

- Data Breach Notification: Organizations must promptly notify relevant authorities and affected individuals in the event of a data breach that poses a risk to individuals' rights and freedoms.

- Data Protection Impact Assessments (DPIAs): DPIAs must be conducted for high-risk processing activities, helping organizations identify and mitigate privacy risks associated with their data processing activities.

23.2.2. Health Insurance Portability and Accountability Act (HIPAA):

- Overview: HIPAA is a U.S. federal law that applies to healthcare organizations and their service providers. Its primary goal is to protect the privacy and security of protected health information (PHI).

- Key Provisions:

- Administrative, Physical, and Technical Safeguards: HIPAA requires covered entities to implement appropriate administrative, physical, and technical safeguards to protect electronic PHI (ePHI).

- Privacy Rule: The Privacy Rule sets limits on the use and disclosure of PHI, requiring patient consent for certain uses and disclosures and providing individuals with rights over their health information.

- Breach Notification Rule: Covered entities must report breaches of unsecured PHI to affected individuals, the Department of Health and Human Services (HHS), and, in some cases, the medic.

23.2.3. Payment Card Industry Data Security Standard (PCI DSS):
- **Overview:** PCI DSS is a set of security standards designed to protect cardholder data and prevent credit card fraud. It applies to organizations that process, store, or transmit credit card information.

- Key Provisions:

- **Network and System Security:** PCI DSS mandates secure network and system configurations, regular vulnerability assessments, and secure transmission of cardholder data.

- **Access Controls:** Organizations must implement strong access controls, including unique user IDs, restricted access to cardholder data, and regular access reviews.

- **Encryption and Tokenization:** Cardholder data must be encrypted during transmission and when stored. Tokenization can be used to replace sensitive data with tokens to reduce the scope of PCI compliance.

23.2.4. ISO/IEC 27001:
- **Overview:** ISO/IEC 27001 is an internationally recognized information security management standard. It provides a framework for organizations to establish, implement, maintain, and continually improve an information security management system (ISMS).

- Key Provisions:

- **Risk Assessment and Treatment:** Organizations must conduct regular risk assessments, implement appropriate controls to mitigate identified risks, and maintain risk management processes.

- **Security Policy and Objectives:** An organization must establish an information security policy and define security objectives aligned with its business goals.

- **Continuous Monitoring and Improvement:** ISO/IEC 27001 promotes ongoing monitoring, measurement, analysis, and improvement of the ISMS to ensure its effectiveness and alignment with changing business needs.

23.2.5. NIST Cybersecurity Framework:
- **Overview:** The NIST Cybersecurity Framework provides a voluntary framework of standards, guidelines, and best practices for organizations to manage and mitigate cybersecurity risks.

- Key Components:

- **Identify:** Organizations must understand and document their cybersecurity risks, establish governance, and identify critical assets and systems.

- **Protect:** Implement safeguards to protect systems and data, including access controls, security awareness training, and secure configurations.

- **Detect:** Establish mechanisms for timely detection of cybersecurity events, such as security monitoring, intrusion detection, and incident response capabilities.

- **Respond:** Develop an incident response plan to effectively respond to and mitigate the impact of cybersecurity incidents.

- **Recover:** Establish plans and processes for system recovery and business continuity in the event of a cybersecurity incident

23.3 Risk Management in Cloud Environments

Risk management is crucial for organizations operating in cloud environments to ensure data security, business continuity, and compliance with regulatory requirements. By implementing effective risk management practices, organizations can identify and mitigate risks, protect sensitive data, and respond to security incidents effectively. It is important to develop risk management strategies tailored to the specific risks and challenges of the cloud environment, including vendor risks, data security, compliance, and operational continuity. By adopting risk management frameworks such as the NIST Cybersecurity Framework, COSO Enterprise Risk Management Framework, and ISO/IEC 31000, continuously monitoring risks, and promoting employee awareness and training, organizations can establish a robust risk management program that supports secure and resilient cloud operations.

23.3.1. Importance of Risk Management in Cloud Environments:

- **Data Security:** Cloud environments handle vast amounts of sensitive data, making it essential to identify and address potential security risks to protect against data breaches, unauthorized access, and data loss. Implementing security measures such as encryption, access controls, and data classification helps safeguard sensitive information.

- **Operational Continuity:** Effective risk management ensures that potential disruptions, such as system failures, service outages, or natural disasters, are mitigated to maintain business continuity and minimize downtime. Organizations can implement disaster recovery plans and backup strategies to ensure rapid recovery in case of disruptions.

- **Compliance and Legal Requirements:** Cloud environments often operate under various regulatory frameworks and legal obligations, such as GDPR, HIPAA, or PCI DSS. Risk management helps organizations identify and address compliance risks to avoid penalties and reputational damage.

- **Vendor and Third-Party Risks:** Cloud environments involve reliance on cloud service providers and third-party vendors. Risk management helps assess and manage risks associated with vendor relationships, including data privacy, service level agreements, and contractual obligations. Due diligence and regular vendor performance reviews are essential in this context.

23.3.2. Risk Management Practices for Cloud Environments:

- **Risk Identification:** To effectively manage risks, organizations must identify and document potential risks specific to the cloud environment. Examples include data breaches, unauthorized access, service provider failures, data loss, and compliance violations.

- **Risk Assessment:** Evaluate the impact and likelihood of identified risks to prioritize them based on their severity and potential impact on business operations, data security, and compliance. This allows organizations to focus resources on addressing high-priority risks first.

- **Risk Mitigation Strategies:** Develop risk mitigation strategies and controls to address identified risks. This may include implementing security measures, data encryption, access controls, disaster recovery plans, and incident response procedures.

- **Continuous Monitoring:** Regularly monitor and assess the effectiveness of implemented controls and mitigation strategies. Continuous monitoring helps detect security incidents, vulnerabilities, system performance issues, and compliance gaps, allowing for timely remediation.

- **Incident Response and Recovery:** Establish incident response plans and procedures to effectively respond to and recover from security incidents. Incident response involves detection, containment, investigation, and remediation of security breaches to minimize their impact.

- **Vendor Risk Management:** Assess the risks associated with cloud service providers and third-party vendors. Conduct due diligence, review contracts, and ensure they meet security and compliance requirements. Regularly reviewing and monitoring vendor performance and security practices is crucial.

- **Employee Awareness and Training:** Educate employees about security risks, best practices, and their roles and responsibilities in mitigating risks. Training should cover topics such as data protection, password hygiene, phishing awareness, and incident reporting.

- **Data Backup and Recovery:** Implement regular data backups and test data recovery procedures to ensure business continuity in the event of data loss or system failures. Consider off-site backups or utilize cloud-native backup services for added resilience.

- **Cloud Security Standards and Certifications:** Leverage industry-recognized cloud security standards and certifications such as SOC 2, ISO/IEC 27001, and CSA STAR to assess cloud service provider security practices and validate their compliance with security standards.

23.3.3. Risk Management Frameworks:

- NIST Cybersecurity Framework: The NIST framework provides a comprehensive approach to managing cybersecurity risks, including risk identification, protection, detection, response, and recovery. It is widely used and adopted by organizations to enhance their cybersecurity posture.

- COSO Enterprise Risk Management Framework: The COSO framework provides a broader perspective on risk management, encompassing both operational and strategic risks. It offers guidance for identifying, assessing, and managing risks across an organization, including those related to cloud environments.

- ISO/IEC 31000: ISO/IEC 31000 is an international standard that provides principles and guidelines for risk management. It offers a systematic and structured approach to identifying, analyzing, evaluating, treating, and monitoring risks, making it applicable to cloud risk management.

Exercise

Multiple Choice Questions

1. What is the primary purpose of cloud governance models?

a. To provide detailed practices and controls for cloud management.

b. To outline the strategic approach and high-level principles of cloud governance.

c. To enforce access controls and identity management in the cloud.

d. To implement disaster recovery plans for cloud environments.

2. Which of the following is a key component of cloud governance frameworks?

a. Cost management and optimization

b. Data replication and redundancy

c. Performance monitoring and optimization

d. Change management and continuous improvement

3. What is the purpose of policy and compliance management in cloud governance?

a. To enforce access controls and identity management.

b. To establish resource provisioning guidelines.

c. To ensure cloud initiatives align with business goals.

d. To address regulatory requirements and internal guidelines.

4. Which cloud governance component involves managing user identities, roles, and permissions?

a. Policy and compliance management

b. Resource provisioning and management

c. Access control and identity management

d. Security and risk management

5. Which compliance framework is designed to protect cardholder data and prevent credit card fraud?

a. ISO/IEC 27001

b. COSO Enterprise Risk Management Framework

c. General Data Protection Regulation (GDPR)

d. Payment Card Industry Data Security Standard (PCI DSS)

6. What is the main goal of the NIST Cybersecurity Framework?

a. To establish guidelines for managing cybersecurity risks.

b. To ensure compliance with industry regulations.

c. To address data protection laws in the EU.

d. To protect against unauthorized access in cloud environments.

7. Which risk management practice involves evaluating the impact and likelihood of identified risks?

a. Risk identification

b. Risk assessment

c. Risk mitigation strategies

d. Continuous monitoring

8. How do cloud governance models and frameworks contribute to cost optimization?

a. By defining access controls and identity management.

b. By establishing policies and procedures for compliance.

c. By providing guidance on resource provisioning and cost management.

d. By developing disaster recovery plans for cloud environments.

9. What is the primary purpose of risk management in cloud environments?

a. To ensure compliance with cloud governance frameworks.

b. To establish secure access controls for cloud resources.

c. To identify and mitigate potential security and operational risks.

d. To implement continuous monitoring for cloud environments.

Review Questions

1. What are the key components of cloud governance models and frameworks?

2. How do cloud governance models and frameworks contribute to risk mitigation?

3. What is the significance of compliance standards like GDPR and HIPAA in cloud environments?

4. How does continuous monitoring contribute to effective cloud risk management?

5. How can organizations optimize cloud costs through cloud governance frameworks?

6. What role does employee awareness and training play in cloud risk management?

7. How can cloud governance frameworks assist in disaster recovery planning?

8. Why is vendor risk management critical in cloud environments?

Answer Secton

Multiple Choice Questions

1. b) To outline the strategic approach and high-level principles of cloud governance.

2. a) Cost management and optimization

3. d) To address regulatory requirements and internal guidelines.

4. c) Access control and identity management

5. d) Payment Card Industry Data Security Standard (PCI DSS)

6. a) To establish guidelines for managing cybersecurity risks.

7. b) Risk assessment

8. c) By providing guidance on resource provisioning and cost management.

9. c) To identify and mitigate potential security and operational risks.

Review Questions

1. The key components of cloud governance models and frameworks include policy and compliance management, resource provisioning and management, access control and identity management, security and risk management, performance monitoring and optimization, cost management and optimization, change management and continuous improvement. These components collectively establish guidelines, procedures, and controls for effective cloud management and alignment with business goals.

2. Cloud governance models and frameworks aid in risk mitigation by enforcing security measures, defining access controls, and implementing policies to protect cloud resources and sensitive data. Regular risk assessments and compliance checks ensure adherence to regulatory requirements and industry standards, reducing the likelihood of data breaches and unauthorized access.

3. Compliance standards like GDPR and HIPAA are crucial for protecting data privacy and maintaining regulatory compliance in cloud environments. Organizations handling personal data or sensitive health information must adhere to these standards to ensure data security, transparency, and individual rights protection.

4. Continuous monitoring allows organizations to promptly detect security incidents, performance issues, and compliance gaps. It enables real-time assessment of cloud resources, allowing swift responses to potential risks and vulnerabilities, ensuring the ongoing security and reliability of cloud environments.

5. Cloud governance frameworks provide guidance on cost management practices, enabling organizations to monitor and control cloud expenses effectively. By optimizing resource usage, implementing cost allocation strategies, and aligning cloud spending with business needs, organizations can achieve cost efficiency and prevent unnecessary overspending.

6. Employee awareness and training are essential in cloud risk management as they educate staff about security best practices, data protection, and incident reporting. By promoting security awareness, organizations can reduce the risk of human errors and improve overall cloud security.

7. Cloud governance frameworks help organizations develop detailed disaster recovery plans by providing guidelines on resource provisioning, data replication, and continuous monitoring. By following these frameworks, organizations can ensure timely and effective recovery in case of disruptions or data breaches.

8. Vendor risk management is crucial in cloud environments because organizations often rely on cloud service providers and third-party vendors. Assessing and monitoring vendor security practices, contractual obligations, and data privacy measures ensures that third-party risks are minimized, safeguarding sensitive data and maintaining compliance.

9.

Chapter 24: Multi-Cloud and Hybrid Cloud Architectures

Multi-cloud deployments offer significant benefits, including avoiding vendor lock-in, leveraging service diversity, increasing resilience, optimizing costs, and accessing best-of-breed solutions. However, organizations must also address challenges such as complexity, interoperability, management overhead, skill requirements, data governance, and security. By carefully assessing the benefits and challenges, organizations can make informed decisions about adopting a multi-cloud strategy and develop robust management practices, security measures, and governance frameworks to ensure successful implementation and utilization of multi-cloud deployments. Proper planning, skilled personnel, and strong vendor relationships are key to making the most of the advantages multi-cloud environments can offer.

Multi-cloud deployment refers to the practice of utilizing multiple cloud computing platforms and services from different cloud providers to host and manage an organization's applications, data, and workloads. Instead of relying solely on a single cloud provider, businesses opt for a multi-cloud strategy to diversify their resources and avoid vendor lock-in.

24.1 Benefits and Challenges of Multi-Cloud Deployments

24.1.1. Benefits of Multi-Cloud Deployments:

- **Vendor Lock-In Avoidance:** One of the primary benefits of multi-cloud deployments is the ability to avoid vendor lock-in. By using multiple cloud service providers, organizations reduce their dependence on a single provider. This gives them the flexibility to choose services and negotiate contracts based on specific needs, rather than being tied to a single vendor's offerings.

- **Service and Feature Diversity:** Different cloud providers offer unique services, features, and pricing models. Multi-cloud deployments allow organizations to leverage the strengths of each provider and choose the most suitable services for different workloads or applications. This enables them to build a more versatile and tailored cloud infrastructure.

- **Increased Resilience and Redundancy:** Distributing workloads across multiple cloud providers enhances resilience and reduces the risk of downtime or service disruptions. If one provider experiences issues or outages, organizations can redirect traffic or switch to another provider seamlessly, ensuring continuous availability of their applications and services.

- **Improved Performance and Latency Optimization:** Multi-cloud deployments enable organizations to place workloads closer to end-users or leverage specific cloud regions for better performance and reduced latency. This is particularly beneficial for globally distributed applications or services, where minimizing latency is crucial for user experience.

- **Cost Optimization and Negotiation Power:** By leveraging multiple cloud providers, organizations can compare pricing, negotiate better deals, and take advantage of competitive pricing models. This helps optimize costs and potentially reduce overall cloud expenditure. Organizations can also negotiate better terms with providers based on their multi-cloud strategy.

- **Best-of-Breed Solutions:** Multi-cloud environments allow organizations to select the best-of-breed solutions from different providers. They can choose the most suitable services for their specific needs, maximizing the quality, functionality, and capabilities of their cloud infrastructure and services.

24.1.2. Challenges of Multi-Cloud Deployments:

- **Complexity and Management Overhead:** Managing multiple cloud providers introduces complexity in terms of configuration, monitoring, security, and resource management. Organizations must invest in additional tools, expertise, and processes to effectively manage a multi-cloud environment. This can increase operational overhead and require advanced cloud management skills.

- **Interoperability and Integration:** Integrating applications and services across different cloud platforms can be challenging due to differences in APIs, data formats, and authentication mechanisms. Organizations need to ensure seamless interoperability and data exchange between cloud providers to avoid siloed data and applications.

- **Skill and Resource Requirements:** Multi-cloud deployments often require specialized skills and resources to effectively manage and monitor different cloud platforms. Organizations must invest in training or hire personnel with expertise in multiple cloud environments to handle the diverse set of technologies.

- **Data Governance and Compliance:** Managing data governance and compliance across multiple cloud providers can be complex. Organizations must ensure that data protection, privacy, and regulatory requirements are met consistently across all cloud platforms. This involves developing clear data governance policies and monitoring adherence to compliance standards.

- **Vendor Management and Relationships:** Working with multiple cloud vendors involves managing multiple contracts, support channels, and service-level agreements (SLAs). Organizations must establish effective vendor management processes to ensure timely support and resolution of issues. Building strong relationships with providers is crucial for smooth operations.

- **Security and Risk Management:** Securing multi-cloud environments requires implementing consistent security controls and monitoring mechanisms across different platforms. Organizations need to address potential risks such as data breaches, misconfigurations, or vulnerabilities introduced by the use of multiple providers. Strong security measures and risk management practices are essential to protect sensitive data and ensure compliance.

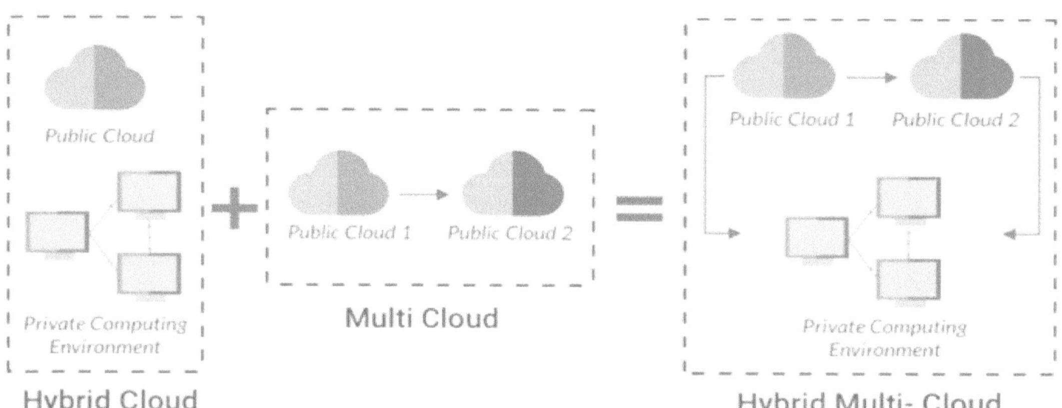

24.2 Hybrid Cloud Integration Strategies

Managing workloads across multiple cloud providers requires careful planning, consideration of workload characteristics, and effective management practices. By strategically placing workloads, optimizing resource utilization, managing data integration, ensuring security and compliance, and implementing robust governance and management processes, organizations can effectively leverage the benefits of multiple cloud providers while maintaining control, performance, and cost efficiency. Continuously monitoring and assessing the effectiveness of workload management strategies is essential, adapting as business needs evolve to ensure seamless operations and maximize the advantages of a multi-cloud approach.

24.2.1. Hybrid Cloud Integration Strategies:

- **Cloud Bursting:** Cloud bursting is a strategy where organizations utilize public cloud resources to handle workload spikes or high-demand periods. The on-premises infrastructure serves as the primary environment, and when additional capacity is needed, workloads are seamlessly migrated to the public cloud. This approach allows organizations to handle temporary resource demands without over-provisioning on-premises resources.

- **Data Integration:** Data integration involves synchronizing and replicating data between on-premises and cloud environments. This strategy ensures data consistency and availability across both environments, enabling applications to access and process data regardless of the location. Data integration is crucial for maintaining a unified view of data and supporting real-time analytics and decision-making.

- **Application Integration:** Application integration focuses on seamlessly integrating applications and services across hybrid cloud environments. This can involve utilizing APIs, messaging frameworks, and service-oriented architectures (SOA) to enable interoperability and data exchange between on-premises and cloud applications. Application integration allows for seamless collaboration and communication between systems hosted in different environments.

- **Dev/Test Environments:** Hybrid cloud integration can be used to create development and testing environments in the cloud while keeping production systems on-premises. This allows organizations to leverage the scalability and agility of the cloud for development and testing purposes while maintaining control over production systems. It accelerates application development and testing cycles and improves resource utilization.

- **Disaster Recovery (DR):** Hybrid cloud integration can be employed for disaster recovery purposes, where critical workloads are replicated and synchronized between on-premises and cloud environments. In the event of a disaster or outage, applications can be quickly switched to the cloud environment to ensure business continuity. Hybrid DR provides cost-effective and reliable disaster recovery capabilities.

24.2.2. Benefits of Hybrid Cloud Integration:

- **Scalability and Flexibility:** Hybrid cloud integration provides the ability to scale resources up or down based on demand. Organizations can leverage the cloud for burstable workloads while maintaining on-premises infrastructure for predictable or sensitive workloads. This scalability allows businesses to meet fluctuating demand efficiently.

- **Cost Optimization:** Hybrid cloud integration allows organizations to optimize costs by utilizing the most cost-effective resources for specific workloads. On-premises infrastructure can be utilized for stable workloads, while the cloud can be leveraged for temporary or variable workloads, resulting in cost savings. The pay-as-you-go model of the cloud minimizes capital expenditure.

- **Data Mobility and Accessibility:** Hybrid cloud integration enables seamless data movement and accessibility between on-premises and cloud environments. This promotes data sharing, collaboration, and real-time insights across the organization, supporting better decision-making and innovation.

- Enhanced Disaster Recovery: By replicating critical workloads and data to the cloud, organizations can improve their disaster recovery capabilities. In the event of a disaster, applications can be quickly restored in the cloud, ensuring business continuity and minimizing downtime. Hybrid DR provides geographic redundancy for added resilience.

- Flexibility in Application Deployment: Hybrid cloud integration provides flexibility in deploying applications. Organizations can choose to host certain applications on-premises for data sovereignty, compliance, or performance reasons, while leveraging the cloud for other applications to take advantage of its scalability and global reach. This allows businesses to optimize their application deployment based on specific requirements.

- Innovation and Agility: Hybrid cloud integration allows organizations to leverage the cloud's agility and innovation capabilities for development, testing, and experimentation, while maintaining control over production systems on-premises. This agility accelerates time-to-market for new products and services.

24.2.3. Considerations for Hybrid Cloud Integration:

- Security and Compliance: Organizations must ensure that data and applications are protected and compliant with security and privacy regulations across both on-premises and cloud environments. Security measures should be consistent and comprehensive, including data encryption, access controls, and security monitoring.

- Data Synchronization and Latency: Data synchronization between on-premises and cloud environments should be efficient and minimize latency to ensure real-time data availability and consistency. This requires choosing appropriate data replication and synchronization mechanisms.

- Connectivity and Network Infrastructure: Robust and reliable connectivity is essential for hybrid cloud integration. Organizations must assess their network infrastructure and bandwidth requirements to enable seamless data movement and application integration. Redundant and reliable connections are vital for data availability.

- Integration Middleware and Tools: Organizations should consider leveraging integration middleware and tools that facilitate seamless integration between on-premises and cloud environments. These tools provide connectivity, data transformation, and orchestration capabilities to simplify integration complexities and reduce manual effort.

- Monitoring and Management: Effective monitoring and management practices should be implemented to gain visibility and control over hybrid cloud environments. This includes monitoring performance, availability, and security across both on-premises and cloud resources. Centralized management tools can help streamline operations.

24.3 Managing Workloads Across Multiple Cloud Providers

Managing workloads across multiple cloud providers requires careful planning, consideration of workload characteristics, and effective management practices. By strategically placing workloads, optimizing resource utilization, managing data integration, ensuring security and compliance, and implementing robust governance and management processes, organizations can effectively leverage the benefits of multiple cloud providers while maintaining control, performance, and cost efficiency. Continuously monitoring and assessing the effectiveness of workload management strategies is essential, adapting as business needs evolve to ensure seamless operations and maximize the advantages of a multi-cloud approach.

24.3.1. Workload Placement and Resource Optimization:
- **Workload Analysis:** Before distributing workloads, it's crucial to assess their specific requirements, such as performance, security, compliance, and data sovereignty. This analysis helps determine which cloud provider is best suited for each workload based on their capabilities and features.

- **Cost Optimization:** Consider the cost implications of deploying workloads across different cloud providers. Evaluate pricing models, resource utilization patterns, and potential discounts to optimize costs and achieve a cost-effective workload distribution.

- **Performance Optimization:** Analyze workload performance requirements and consider the geographical locations and availability zones of cloud providers. This approach minimizes latency and ensures optimal performance for end-users.

- **Auto-scaling and Load Balancing:** Implement auto-scaling and load balancing mechanisms to dynamically distribute workloads across multiple cloud providers based on demand. This helps optimize resource utilization and maintains application performance during peak usage periods.

24.3.2. Data Management and Integration:
- **Data Governance and Compliance:** Establish data governance practices that ensure data privacy, security, and compliance across multiple cloud providers. Implement consistent data protection measures, encryption, access controls, and data lifecycle management strategies.

- **Data Replication and Synchronization:** Utilize data replication and synchronization techniques to ensure data consistency and availability across multiple cloud providers. This enables seamless data access and integration between workloads.

- **Data Transfer and Egress Costs:** Consider the costs associated with data transfer and egress between cloud providers. Optimize data transfer strategies, utilize data caching, and employ compression techniques to minimize data transfer costs.

- **Integration Middleware and Tools:** Employ integration middleware and tools that support interoperability and data integration between different cloud providers. These tools facilitate seamless data exchange, messaging, and orchestration across workloads.

24.3.3. Security and Compliance:
- **Consistent Security Controls:** Implement consistent security controls and practices across all cloud providers to maintain a unified security posture. This includes identity and access management, network security, encryption, and monitoring.

- **Security Monitoring and Incident Response:** Implement centralized security monitoring and incident response mechanisms to detect and respond to security incidents across multiple cloud providers. This ensures timely response and minimizes the impact of security breaches.

- **Compliance Management:** Ensure compliance with relevant regulations and industry standards across all cloud providers. Regularly review and update policies, conduct audits, and maintain documentation to demonstrate compliance.

24.3.4. Governance and Management:

- **Cloud Management Platform:** Consider using a cloud management platform that provides centralized management and control of workloads across multiple cloud providers. These platforms offer unified visibility, automation, and policy enforcement capabilities.

- **Service Level Agreements (SLAs):** Evaluate and negotiate SLAs with each cloud provider to ensure service availability, performance guarantees, and support levels. Monitor SLA compliance and address any issues promptly.

- **Cost and Resource Monitoring:** Implement robust cost and resource monitoring practices to track resource usage, analyze costs, and optimize resource allocation across multiple cloud providers. This helps identify cost-saving opportunities and ensure efficient resource utilization.

- **Vendor Management:** Establish effective vendor management processes to manage relationships with multiple cloud providers. This includes regular communication, contract management, performance reviews, and vendor governance.

Exercise

Multiple Choice Questions

1. Which of the following is a benefit of multi-cloud deployments?

a. Reduced complexity and management overhead

b. Limited vendor options and dependencies

c. Increased resilience and redundancy

d. Homogeneous service diversity

2. What does multi-cloud deployment refer to?

a. Using only one cloud provider for all services

b. Utilizing multiple cloud providers to manage applications and data

c. Leveraging hybrid cloud environments with on-premises and public clouds

d. Combining on-premises infrastructure with a single cloud provider

3. Which of the following is NOT a challenge of multi-cloud deployments?

a. Complexity in configuration and monitoring

b. Interoperability and integration between cloud providers

c. Skill and resource requirements for managing multiple providers

d. Reduced data governance and compliance requirements

4. What benefit do organizations gain from service and feature diversity in multi-cloud deployments?

a. Simplified management and monitoring

b. Homogeneous pricing models

c. Optimized costs through vendor lock-in

d. Leverage the strengths of each provider for specific needs

5. How does multi-cloud deployment help avoid vendor lock-in?

a. By selecting one cloud provider for all services

b. By utilizing a single cloud region for all resources

c. By distributing workloads across multiple cloud providers

d. By using private cloud infrastructure

6. Which of the following is a challenge related to multi-cloud deployments?

a. Reduced complexity and management overhead

b. Unified security controls across cloud providers

c. Reduced need for skilled personnel

d. Seamless data synchronization and exchange

7. What is a key consideration for successful multi-cloud deployments?

a. Limiting the number of cloud providers used

b. Reducing the need for data synchronization

c. Developing strong vendor relationships

d. Ignoring cost optimization strategies

8. Which benefit of multi-cloud deployments allows organizations to optimize costs based on specific needs?

a. Improved performance and latency optimization

b. Increased resilience and redundancy

c. Vendor lock-in avoidance

d. Cost optimization and negotiation power

9. What strategy enables organizations to utilize public cloud resources for workload spikes?

a. Cloud Bursting

b. Disaster Recovery

c. Application Integration

d. Data Replication

Review Questions

1. What are the benefits of multi-cloud deployments?

2. What challenges do organizations face in multi-cloud deployments?

3. How can organizations avoid vendor lock-in in multi-cloud deployments?

4. How does multi-cloud deployment enhance resilience and redundancy?

5. How can organizations optimize costs in multi-cloud deployments?

6. How can organizations ensure seamless data exchange in multi-cloud deployments?

7. How can organizations address security concerns in multi-cloud deployments?

8. What considerations should organizations make when choosing a multi-cloud deployment strategy?

Answer Section

Multiple Choice Questions

1. c) Increased resilience and redundancy

2. b) Utilizing multiple cloud providers to manage applications and data

3. d) Reduced data governance and compliance requirements

4. d) Leverage the strengths of each provider for specific needs

5. c) By distributing workloads across multiple cloud providers

6. b) Unified security controls across cloud providers

7. c) Developing strong vendor relationships

8. d) Cost optimization and negotiation power

9. a) Cloud Bursting

Review Questions

1. Multi-cloud deployments offer several advantages, including avoiding vendor lock-in, leveraging service diversity, increasing resilience, optimizing costs, and accessing best-of-breed solutions. By using multiple cloud providers, organizations can select the most suitable services and negotiate contracts based on specific needs, instead of being tied to a single vendor's offerings. Distributing workloads across

various cloud environments enhances resilience, ensuring continuous availability of applications and services even if one provider experiences issues. Moreover, leveraging the strengths of different cloud providers allows organizations to build a more versatile and tailored cloud infrastructure, leading to cost optimization and improved performance.

2. Multi-cloud deployments come with their share of challenges, including complexity, interoperability, management overhead, skill requirements, data governance, and security. Managing multiple cloud providers introduces complexity in terms of configuration, monitoring, and security. Ensuring seamless interoperability and data exchange between different cloud platforms can be challenging due to differences in APIs and data formats. Organizations must invest in additional tools, expertise, and processes to effectively manage a multi-cloud environment, increasing operational overhead. Additionally, multi-cloud deployments require specialized skills and resources to handle the diverse set of technologies involved, making it essential to invest in training or hire personnel with expertise in multiple cloud environments.

3. Organizations can avoid vendor lock-in in multi-cloud deployments by utilizing multiple cloud service providers simultaneously. By distributing workloads across different cloud environments, businesses reduce their dependence on a single provider and gain the flexibility to choose services and negotiate contracts based on specific needs. This approach allows them to select the most suitable cloud offerings for different workloads or applications, preventing them from being tied to a single vendor's offerings. By avoiding vendor lock-in, organizations can make informed decisions about their cloud strategies, optimize costs, and leverage the strengths of different cloud providers to achieve their business objectives.

4. Multi-cloud deployment enhances resilience and redundancy by distributing workloads across multiple cloud providers. If one cloud provider experiences issues or outages, organizations can seamlessly redirect traffic or switch to another provider. This ensures continuous availability of applications and services, reducing the risk of downtime and service disruptions. By diversifying their resources across various cloud environments, organizations are less susceptible to single points of failure. Multi-cloud deployments provide redundant options, enabling organizations to maintain operations and user access even in the face of unexpected failures or outages, thereby improving overall resilience and minimizing the impact of service disruptions.

5. Organizations can optimize costs in multi-cloud deployments by comparing pricing models, negotiating better deals, and leveraging competitive pricing from multiple cloud providers. By carefully assessing the cost implications of deploying workloads across different providers, organizations can select the most cost-effective resources for specific workloads. The pay-as-you-go model of the cloud allows organizations to scale resources up or down based on demand, minimizing unnecessary expenditures. Additionally, organizations can optimize costs by utilizing the most suitable cloud services from each provider for different workloads or applications, thereby achieving a balance between performance, features, and cost-efficiency.

6. To ensure seamless data exchange in multi-cloud deployments, organizations should focus on data synchronization and integration. Implementing data replication and synchronization techniques helps maintain data consistency and availability across different cloud environments. This enables applications to access and process data regardless of its location, promoting seamless data exchange. Additionally, organizations should consider employing integration middleware and tools that support interoperability

between different cloud platforms. These tools provide connectivity, data transformation, and orchestration capabilities, simplifying integration complexities and reducing manual effort in managing data exchange between workloads hosted on various cloud providers.

7. Organizations can address security concerns in multi-cloud deployments by implementing consistent security controls and practices across all cloud providers. This involves enforcing identity and access management, network security, data encryption, and security monitoring across different cloud environments. Centralized security monitoring and incident response mechanisms should be put in place to detect and respond to security incidents promptly. Compliance management practices should also be established to ensure that data protection, privacy, and regulatory requirements are met consistently across all cloud platforms. By taking a unified and comprehensive approach to security, organizations can protect sensitive data and maintain compliance in their multi-cloud deployments.

8. When choosing a multi-cloud deployment strategy, organizations should consider factors such as workload characteristics, cost optimization, security requirements, and management capabilities. Assessing the specific needs of each workload helps determine the most suitable cloud providers and features. Optimizing costs involves evaluating pricing models, resource utilization patterns, and potential discounts. Security considerations should focus on implementing consistent security controls and monitoring mechanisms across all cloud providers. Moreover, organizations should evaluate their management capabilities and invest in appropriate tools and skilled personnel to effectively manage and monitor a multi-cloud environment. Making informed decisions based on these considerations ensures a successful and well-managed multi-cloud deployment.

Chapter 25: Cloud-Native Application Development

25.1 Cloud-Native Application Design Principles

Cloud-native application design principles focus on leveraging cloud computing advantages to build scalable, resilient, and efficient applications. Adopting microservices, containers, automation, and DevOps practices enables organizations to deliver applications faster, improve scalability, and enhance resilience. By embracing cloud-native design principles, organizations can fully utilize cloud capabilities, achieve greater flexibility and agility, and drive innovation in their application development processes. Here's key principles:

25.1 1. Microservices Architecture:

Microservices architecture breaks down applications into small, independently deployable and manageable services. Each microservice focuses on a specific business capability and communicates with others through well-defined APIs. This approach allows for flexibility and agility as each component can be developed, deployed, and scaled independently, promoting faster development cycles and ease of maintenance.

25.1 2. Containers and Containerization:

Containers encapsulate applications and their dependencies in a consistent and lightweight runtime environment. Containerization enables portability, ensuring applications run consistently across different environments. It provides benefits such as efficient resource utilization, rapid deployment, and simplified management of application components.

25.1 3. DevOps and Automation:

DevOps practices foster collaboration between development and operations teams, promoting automation of various processes. Continuous Integration and Continuous Delivery (CI/CD) pipelines automate the build, test, and deployment processes, resulting in faster and more reliable application delivery. Infrastructure as Code (IaC) allows infrastructure configurations to be versioned, automated, and deployed alongside application code, making infrastructure changes more manageable.

25.1 4. Elasticity and Scalability:

Cloud-native applications are designed to scale horizontally by adding or removing instances dynamically based on demand. Horizontal scaling enables applications to handle variable workloads efficiently, ensuring optimal resource utilization. Autoscaling mechanisms automate the provisioning and deprovisioning of resources, allowing applications to scale seamlessly based on predefined rules or metrics.

25.1 5. Resilience and Fault Tolerance:

Cloud-native applications are built to handle failures gracefully and recover quickly from disruptions. Resilience is achieved through redundancy, load balancing, and fault isolation strategies. Techniques like circuit breakers, retries, and graceful degradation enable applications to maintain functionality even in the presence of failures.

25.1 6. Statelessness and Stateless Services:

Stateless services store session and state information outside the application, making them horizontally scalable. Requests can be handled by any available instance of the service, facilitating easy scaling and load balancing. Session and state information can be stored in external services, such as databases or caches, ensuring flexibility and resilience.

25.1 7. Cloud Services and Managed Services:

Cloud-native applications leverage cloud services and managed services provided by the cloud provider. Using managed services for databases, queues, caching, et, reduces operational overhead and allows developers to focus on application logi Cloud services offer scalability, resilience, and high availability out of the box, allowing applications to take full advantage of the underlying cloud infrastructure.

25.1 8. Monitoring and Observability:

Cloud-native applications incorporate robust monitoring and observability capabilities to gain insights into application performance and behavior. Monitoring tools, centralized logging, and metrics collection enable real-time visibility into application health and performance. Implementing distributed tracing and logging helps identify and diagnose issues across microservices and components.

25.1 9. Security and Compliance:

Security is a fundamental consideration in cloud-native application design. Strong identity and access management practices, encryption, and secure communication channels ensure data protection and compliance with regulatory requirements. Security measures should be applied at every layer, including infrastructure, application, and data, and regularly assessed and updated to maintain a secure environment.

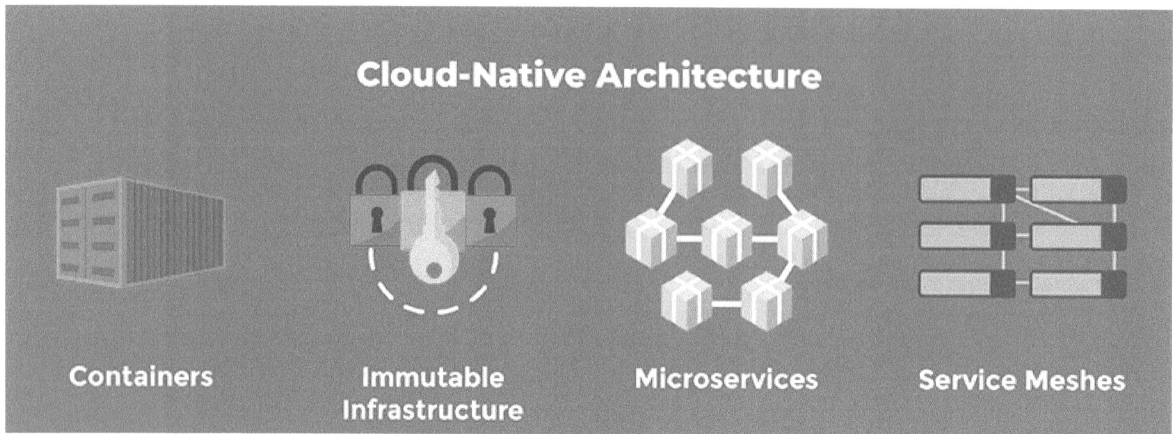

25.2Building Scalable and Resilient Applications

Building scalable and resilient applications in the cloud requires careful consideration of architecture, scalability, fault tolerance, and monitoring. By leveraging cloud-native services, adopting distributed architecture patterns, implementing automation and monitoring tools, and ensuring robust security measures, organizations can build applications that can handle varying workloads, recover quickly from failures, and provide a reliable user experience. Embracing cloud scalability and resilience practices empowers organizations to deliver high-performance applications while maximizing the benefits of cloud computing.

25.2.1. Microservices Architecture:

Adopting a microservices architecture involves breaking down applications into small, decoupled services. Each service can be independently developed, deployed, and scaled, leading to better resource utilization and improved scalability. Microservices promote fault isolation, ensuring that failures in one service don't impact the entire application. This architecture allows for greater flexibility and agility in application development and maintenance.

25.2.2. Horizontal Scaling:

Horizontal scaling is designing applications to scale by adding or removing instances dynamically based on demand. Cloud platforms offer auto-scaling mechanisms that automatically adjust resources based on predefined rules or metrics. Horizontal scaling enables applications to effectively handle increased workloads, ensuring optimal resource utilization while maintaining performance and responsiveness.

25.2.3. Load Balancing:

Load balancing techniques distribute incoming traffic evenly across multiple instances of an application. Load balancers play a crucial role in improving performance, scalability, and availability. By routing requests to healthy instances, load balancers prevent overloading specific instances and enable efficient resource usage. Load balancing ensures that applications can handle traffic spikes and distribute workloads evenly across resources.

25.2.4. Elasticity and Auto-scaling:

Leveraging cloud-native features like auto-scaling allows applications to automatically adjust the number of instances based on workload demands. Scaling policies can consider factors such as CPU utilization, network traffic, or queue length to dynamically scale resources up or down. Elasticity ensures that the application can handle varying workloads efficiently and optimizes costs by scaling resources only when needed.

25.2.5. Resilience and Fault Tolerance:

Designing applications with resilience in mind ensures they can withstand failures and recover quickly. Implementing fault-tolerant mechanisms, such as redundant instances, load balancing, and distributed caching, enhances the application's ability to handle disruptions and maintain availability. Utilizing cloud-native services like managed databases, object storage, and content delivery networks (CDNs) further improves resilience and data availability.

25.2.6. Distributed Architecture:

Leveraging distributed systems and data storage technologies improves scalability and resilience. Distributed databases, caches, and message queues facilitate large-scale data processing and communication between application components. Implementing data replication and synchronization techniques ensures data consistency across multiple regions or availability zones, contributing to better performance and reliability.

25.2.7. Monitoring and Alerting:

Comprehensive monitoring and alerting systems proactively identify performance issues, bottlenecks, or failures. Cloud monitoring services and application performance management tools collect metrics, monitor resource utilization, and track application health. Setting up alerts and notifications triggers actions based on predefined thresholds or abnormal behavior, enabling swift responses to potential issues.

25.2.8. Automated Deployment and Infrastructure as Code (IaC):

Automated deployment techniques and Infrastructure as Code (IaC) ensure consistent and repeatable application deployments. Configuration management and orchestration frameworks automate the provisioning and configuration of cloud resources. IaC provides version control, rapid provisioning, and easy replication of infrastructure components, reducing the risk of configuration errors and improving deployment speed.

25.2.9. Disaster Recovery and Backup:

Implementing robust disaster recovery strategies ensures business continuity in the event of infrastructure or application failures. Regularly backing up critical data and using cloud-based backup services facilitates easy data recovery in case of data loss. Regular testing of disaster recovery plans through drills ensures their effectiveness and identifies potential weaknesses in the recovery process.

25.2.10. Security and Compliance:

Strong security measures are essential to protect applications and data in the cloud. Following cloud security best practices, such as secure authentication and authorization mechanisms, data encryption, and regular security audits, helps safeguard sensitive information from unauthorized access and cyber threats. Ensuring compliance with relevant regulations and industry standards specific to the application and data handling maintains data integrity and builds trust with users and stakeholders.

25.3 Cloud-Native Tools and Frameworks

Cloud-native tools and frameworks play a crucial role in developing, deploying, and managing cloud-native applications. Whether it's container orchestration, service mesh, monitoring, automation, or infrastructure provisioning, these tools provide the necessary capabilities to leverage the full potential of the cloud. By adopting and utilizing these cloud-native tools and frameworks, organizations can enhance their application development processes, improve scalability, resilience, and observability, and maximize the benefits of cloud computing.

25.3.1. Kubernetes:

Kubernetes is an open-source container orchestration platform that automates the deployment, scaling, and management of containerized applications.It provides features like automatic scaling, load balancing, service discovery, and rolling updates, making it easier to deploy and manage applications in a distributed environment.Kubernetes allows organizations to abstract infrastructure details and focus on application development and scalability.

25.3.2. Docker:

Docker is a popular containerization platform that enables developers to package applications and their dependencies into portable containers. Containers provide a lightweight and consistent runtime environment, allowing applications to run reliably across different environments. Docker simplifies the process of building, distributing, and deploying applications, making it easier to adopt a microservices architecture and achieve scalability and portability.

25.3.3. Istio:

Istio is an open-source service mesh platform that provides a control plane for managing and securing microservices architectures. It offers features like traffic management, load balancing, observability, and security policies. Istio helps organizations manage the complexities of service-to-service communication, improve resilience, and enforce security across microservices.

25.3.4. Prometheus:

Prometheus is an open-source monitoring and alerting toolkit designed for cloud-native environments.
It provides a time-series database and a flexible query language for collecting, storing, and querying metrics from various sources. Prometheus enables organizations to monitor the performance, availability, and health of their cloud-native applications and infrastructure components.

25.3.5. Helm:

Helm is a package manager for Kubernetes that simplifies the deployment and management of applications on Kubernetes clusters. It allows organizations to define, install, and manage applications as reusable packages called "charts". Helm streamlines the deployment process and supports versioning, rollbacks, and configuration management, making it easier to manage complex application deployments.

25.3.6. Envoy:

Envoy is an open-source edge and service proxy that provides load balancing, service discovery, and observability functionalities. It can be used to enhance the performance, security, and resilience of cloud-native applications by managing traffic between services and providing features like rate limiting, circuit breaking, and observability.

25.3.7. OpenTelemetry:

OpenTelemetry is an open-source observability framework that helps organizations collect, correlate, and analyze telemetry data from distributed systems. It provides APIs, libraries, and instrumentation to capture metrics, traces, and logs from various components of cloud-native applications. OpenTelemetry facilitates better understanding and troubleshooting of application performance, enabling organizations to optimize and improve their cloud-native applications.

25.3.8. Jenkins:

Jenkins is an open-source automation server that supports continuous integration and continuous delivery (CI/CD) workflows. It enables organizations to automate the building, testing, and deployment of cloud-native applications, ensuring rapid and reliable delivery. Jenkins integrates with other cloud-native tools and frameworks, providing flexibility and extensibility in CI/CD pipelines.

25.3.9. Terraform:

Terraform is an infrastructure as code (IaC) tool that allows organizations to define and provision cloud resources using a declarative language. It supports multiple cloud providers and enables the creation, modification, and destruction of infrastructure resources in a reproducible and consistent manner. Terraform simplifies the management and provisioning of cloud infrastructure, making it easier to adopt cloud-native architectures.

25.3.10. AWS CloudFormation and Azure Resource Manager (ARM):

AWS CloudFormation and Azure Resource Manager (ARM) are infrastructure orchestration tools provided by AWS and Azure, respectively. These tools allow organizations to define and manage cloud resources using templates or scripts, enabling infrastructure provisioning and management as code. CloudFormation and ARM templates facilitate the automation and standardization of cloud infrastructure deployment, making it easier to adopt cloud-native practices.

Exercise

Multiple Choice Questions

1. What is the primary benefit of adopting a microservices architecture?

a. Faster application deployment

b. Simplified infrastructure provisioning

c. Enhanced security measures

d. Improved data governance

2. Which containerization platform enables applications to run consistently across different environments?

a. Kubernetes

b. Docker

c. Istio

d. Helm

3. Which cloud-native tool provides traffic management, load balancing, and security policies for microservices?

a. Prometheus

b. Jenkins

c. Helm

d. Istio

4. What is the primary purpose of a service mesh like Istio in a cloud-native environment?

a. Automate infrastructure provisioning

b. Simplify application deployment

c. Improve resilience and security of microservices

d. Provide monitoring and alerting capabilities

5. Which practice fosters collaboration between development and operations teams, leading to automation of processes like CI/CD?

a. Microservices architecture

b. Elasticity and scalability

c. DevOps and automation

d. Load balancing

6. What is the key advantage of horizontal scaling in cloud-native applications?

a. Simplified infrastructure management

b. Improved fault tolerance

c. Enhanced resource utilization

d. Reduced security risks

7. Which tool provides a time-series database and query language for monitoring cloud-native applications?

a. Kubernetes

b. Envoy

c. Prometheus

d. Terraform

8. What is the purpose of Infrastructure as Code (IaC) tools like Terraform?

a. Automate deployment of Kubernetes clusters

b. Enable containerization of applications

c. Simplify provisioning of cloud resources

d. Monitor application performance

9. What do AWS CloudFormation and Azure Resource Manager (ARM) enable organizations to do?

a. Define and manage cloud-native applications

b. Automate container orchestration

c. Provision and manage cloud infrastructure using templates

d. Implement service mesh for microservices

Review Questions

1. What are the key benefits of adopting cloud-native application design principles?
2. How does microservices architecture contribute to application development and maintenance?
3. What advantages do containers offer in cloud-native application design?
4. How does DevOps and automation facilitate cloud-native application development?
5. How does cloud-native application design ensure scalability and elasticity?
6. What strategies ensure the resilience and fault tolerance of cloud-native applications?
7. How do cloud-native applications ensure security and compliance?
8. What monitoring and observability practices are crucial for cloud-native applications?

Answer Section

Multiple Choice Questions

1. a) Faster application deployment

2. b) Docker
3. d) Istio
4. c) Improve resilience and security of microservices
5. c) DevOps and automation
6. c) Enhanced resource utilization
7. c) Prometheus
8. c) Simplify provisioning of cloud resources
9. c) Provision and manage cloud infrastructure using templates

REVIEW QUESTIONS

1. Cloud-native application design principles focus on leveraging cloud computing advantages to build scalable, resilient, and efficient applications. The benefits include faster application delivery, improved scalability, enhanced resilience, greater flexibility, and agility. By embracing microservices architecture, containers, automation, and DevOps practices, organizations can fully utilize cloud capabilities, optimize resource utilization, and drive innovation in their application development processes.

2. Microservices architecture breaks down applications into small, independently deployable and manageable services. Each microservice focuses on a specific business capability and communicates with others through well-defined APIs. This approach enables flexibility and agility as each component can be developed, deployed, and scaled independently. It promotes faster development cycles, ease of maintenance, and fault isolation, allowing organizations to innovate and adapt quickly to changing business needs.

3. Containers encapsulate applications and their dependencies in a consistent and lightweight runtime environment. They provide portability, ensuring applications run consistently across different environments. Containers offer benefits like efficient resource utilization, rapid deployment, and simplified management of application components. By utilizing containerization, organizations can achieve faster development and deployment cycles, seamless scaling, and improved resource efficiency.

4. DevOps practices foster collaboration between development and operations teams, promoting automation of various processes. Continuous Integration and Continuous Delivery (CI/CD) pipelines automate the build, test, and deployment processes, resulting in faster and more reliable application delivery. Infrastructure as Code (IaC) allows infrastructure configurations to be versioned, automated, and deployed alongside application code, making infrastructure changes more manageable. DevOps and automation enable rapid, reliable, and consistent application delivery in cloud-native environments.

5. Cloud-native applications are designed to scale horizontally by adding or removing instances dynamically based on demand. Horizontal scaling enables applications to handle variable workloads efficiently, ensuring optimal resource utilization. Autoscaling mechanisms automate the provisioning and deprovisioning of resources, allowing applications to scale seamlessly based on predefined rules or

metrics. This elasticity ensures that applications can handle varying workloads and optimize resource allocation, reducing operational costs.

6. Cloud-native applications are built to handle failures gracefully and recover quickly from disruptions. Resilience is achieved through redundancy, load balancing, and fault isolation strategies. Techniques like circuit breakers, retries, and graceful degradation enable applications to maintain functionality even in the presence of failures. Adopting these strategies enhances application reliability, availability, and user experience.

7. Security is a fundamental consideration in cloud-native application design. Strong identity and access management practices, encryption, and secure communication channels ensure data protection and compliance with regulatory requirements. Security measures should be applied at every layer, including infrastructure, application, and data, and regularly assessed and updated to maintain a secure environment.

8. Cloud-native applications incorporate robust monitoring and observability capabilities to gain insights into application performance and behavior. Monitoring tools, centralized logging, and metrics collection enable real-time visibility into application health and performance. Implementing distributed tracing and logging helps identify and diagnose issues across microservices and components. These practices allow organizations to proactively identify and address performance bottlenecks, ensuring optimal application performance and user satisfaction.

Chapter 26: Cloud Automation and Orchestration

26.1 Infrastructure Automation with Cloud APIs

Infrastructure automation with cloud APIs offers numerous advantages to organizations, empowering them to streamline and accelerate their cloud operations. Leveraging cloud APIs for provisioning, management, and scaling of cloud resources, organizations can achieve greater efficiency, cost optimization, consistency, and scalability. However, to ensure the reliability and resilience of automated processes, proper security, error handling, version management, and testing are essential. With careful planning and consideration of key factors, organizations can unlock the full potential of infrastructure automation with cloud APIs, enabling them to drive innovation and success in their cloud environments.

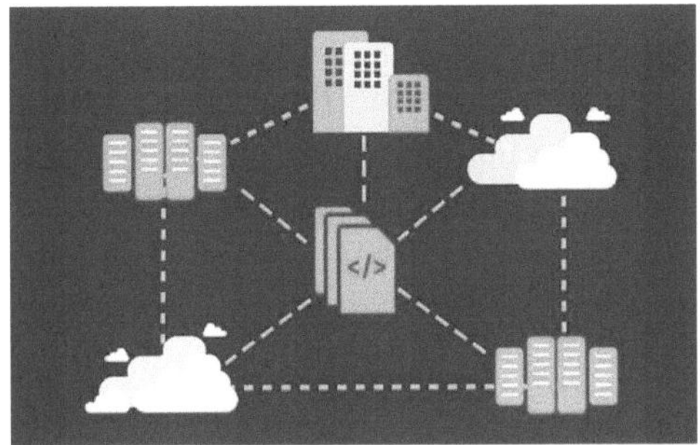

26.1.1. Benefits of Infrastructure Automation with Cloud APIs:

- **Speed and Efficiency:** Automation eliminates manual intervention, enabling rapid and consistent deployments. Developers can provision and configure cloud resources instantly through API calls, reducing the time-to-market for applications. This agility is crucial in today's fast-paced digital landscape.

- **Scalability:** Cloud APIs enable dynamic scaling of resources based on demand. Organizations can automatically scale up or down their infrastructure based on workload requirements, optimizing resource utilization and cost efficiency. This elasticity allows businesses to respond effectively to fluctuating workloads.

- **Cost Optimization:** Infrastructure automation allows organizations to programmatically manage cloud resources, ensuring that resources are provisioned and deprovisioned as needed. This prevents unnecessary costs associated with idle or underutilized resources, promoting cost optimization.

- **Consistency and Standardization:** Automation ensures that infrastructure configurations and deployments follow standardized processes. This reduces the risk of errors caused by manual interventions and ensures consistency across environments, promoting a stable and reliable infrastructure.

- **Version Control and Auditing:** Infrastructure automation through APIs enables version control of infrastructure configurations. This facilitates easy rollbacks in case of issues and provides an audit trail for compliance and security purposes, enhancing governance and accountability.

- **Disaster Recovery and High Availability:** With automation, organizations can automate disaster recovery procedures, enabling rapid recovery in case of failures or outages. Automation also facilitates the implementation of high availability configurations for critical services, minimizing downtime and ensuring business continuity.

26.1.2. Key Considerations for Infrastructure Automation with Cloud APIs:

- API Authentication and Security: Properly manage API authentication tokens and credentials to prevent unauthorized access. Utilize access control mechanisms to restrict API access and prevent exposure of sensitive resources.

- Error Handling and Fault Tolerance: Implement robust error handling mechanisms to handle failures and exceptions in API calls. Ensure that automated processes have built-in fault tolerance and can gracefully handle temporary API outages to maintain operational stability.

- Idempotency: Design automated processes to be idempotent, meaning that calling the same API multiple times produces the same result as calling it once. This ensures that repeated API calls do not cause unintended side effects and maintain consistent outcomes.

- Rate Limiting and Throttling: Be mindful of API rate limits imposed by cloud providers to prevent excessive API usage. Implement rate limiting and throttling mechanisms in automated scripts to avoid hitting API rate limits and ensure compliance with cloud provider policies.

- Monitoring and Reporting: Implement monitoring and logging to track API usage and identify potential issues. Monitor automated processes for errors, performance bottlenecks, and unexpected behavior, allowing proactive responses to potential incidents.

- Compliance and Governance: Ensure that automated processes adhere to compliance and governance policies. Implement proper access controls and permissions to ensure data security and privacy, mitigating the risk of data breaches and compliance violations.

- Version Management: Be aware that changes to API endpoints or behavior can affect automated processes. Implement version management strategies to ensure compatibility as APIs evolve, preventing disruptions due to changes in cloud provider APIs.

- Testing and Validation: Rigorously test automated scripts and processes in non-production environments before deploying them in production. Validate that automated configurations and deployments are functioning as expected to minimize the risk of unexpected behavior in live environments.

26.2 Orchestration Tools and Workflows

Orchestration tools and workflows have become integral components of cloud computing, empowering organizations to automate and streamline complex tasks and processes. By leveraging the benefits of automation, scalability, integration, and cost-effectiveness offered by orchestration tools, businesses can achieve greater operational efficiency and agility. Implementing best practices for creating workflows ensures that cloud operations are reliable, flexible, and compliant with industry standards. Ultimately, mastering orchestration tools allows businesses to harness the full potential of the cloud, driving innovation and success in the ever-evolving digital landscape.

26.2.1. Understanding Orchestration Tools:

Orchestration tools are powerful software solutions that facilitate the automation and management of complex tasks, processes, and workflows within cloud environments. These tools provide a centralized and standardized approach to coordinate and execute numerous interrelated tasks across multiple services and resources, simplifying cloud management for organizations.

26.2.2. Benefits of Orchestration Tools:

- Automation: One of the primary benefits of orchestration tools is automation. By automating repetitive and time-consuming tasks, cloud administrators can focus on more strategic initiatives. Automated workflows reduce human errors and enhance overall operational efficiency.

- **Scalability:** Orchestration tools enable organizations to effortlessly scale their cloud operations. As these tools can handle an increasing number of tasks and resources efficiently, scaling becomes seamless and hassle-free, ensuring the cloud environment can adapt to fluctuating workloads.

- **Integration:** Orchestration tools facilitate seamless integration and communication between different cloud services and components. They empower the creation of workflows that span across multiple cloud platforms, enabling hybrid and multi-cloud setups, and providing flexibility in choosing cloud providers.

- **Cost-Effectiveness:** By automating resource provisioning and deprovisioning, orchestration tools help optimize cloud resource usage. This minimizes unnecessary expenses, and the ability to scale resources automatically ensures that organizations pay only for what they need, optimizing cost efficiency.

- **Improved Governance and Compliance:** Orchestration tools play a significant role in enforcing standardized processes and policies. They ensure compliance with industry regulations and internal governance requirements, enhancing security and reducing the risk of non-compliance.

26.2.3. Common Orchestration Tools:

- **AWS CloudFormation:** AWS CloudFormation is a widely-used infrastructure as code (IaC) tool that allows users to define cloud resources using JSON or YAML templates. It automates the creation and management of AWS resources, providing a consistent and repeatable way to deploy and manage infrastructure.

- **Google Cloud Deployment Manager:** Google Cloud Deployment Manager allows users to define infrastructure as code using YAML or Jinja2 templates. It automates the creation and management of Google Cloud resources, making it easier to deploy complex applications.

- **Azure Resource Manager:** Microsoft Azure's Azure Resource Manager (ARM) enables users to define and deploy cloud resources using JSON templates. ARM provides a unified way to manage resources across Azure services, simplifying the deployment process.

- **Terraform:** Terraform is an open-source IaC tool that supports multiple cloud providers. It uses a declarative language to define infrastructure configurations, making it a flexible and powerful choice for orchestrating multi-cloud environments.

26.2.4. Creating Orchestration Workflows:

- **Task Sequencing:** Orchestration workflows define the sequence of tasks and dependencies among them. Users can specify which tasks should run concurrently or sequentially, ensuring proper execution and coordination.

- **Error Handling:** Workflows can incorporate error handling mechanisms to address potential issues that may arise during the execution of tasks. Error handling ensures that workflows can recover gracefully from failures, minimizing the impact on the overall process.

- **Input and Output Parameters:** Orchestration workflows can accept input parameters to customize execution based on specific requirements. Output parameters allow workflows to pass results or data between different tasks, enhancing flexibility and reusability.

- **Version Control:** Implementing version control for workflows helps manage changes, track revisions, and ensure consistency. Version control aids in maintaining documentation and simplifies collaboration among teams working on complex workflows.

26.2.5. Best Practices for Orchestration:

- **Start Small and Iterate:** It is advisable to begin with simple workflows and gradually expand as your understanding of the environment and requirements grows. Iteratively refine your workflows based on feedback and experience.

- **Test and Validate:** Regularly test and validate workflows in a non-production environment to ensure their accuracy and effectiveness. Identifying and addressing any issues before deploying them in the live environment helps avoid potential problems.

- **Use Parameterization:** Parameterize your workflows to make them reusable and customizable for different scenarios. This enhances the efficiency of your orchestration and allows for greater flexibility in handling various tasks.

- **Secure Credentials and Secrets:** Avoid hardcoding sensitive information in workflows. Instead, use secure methods to store and manage credentials and secrets, ensuring proper access controls and safeguarding sensitive data.

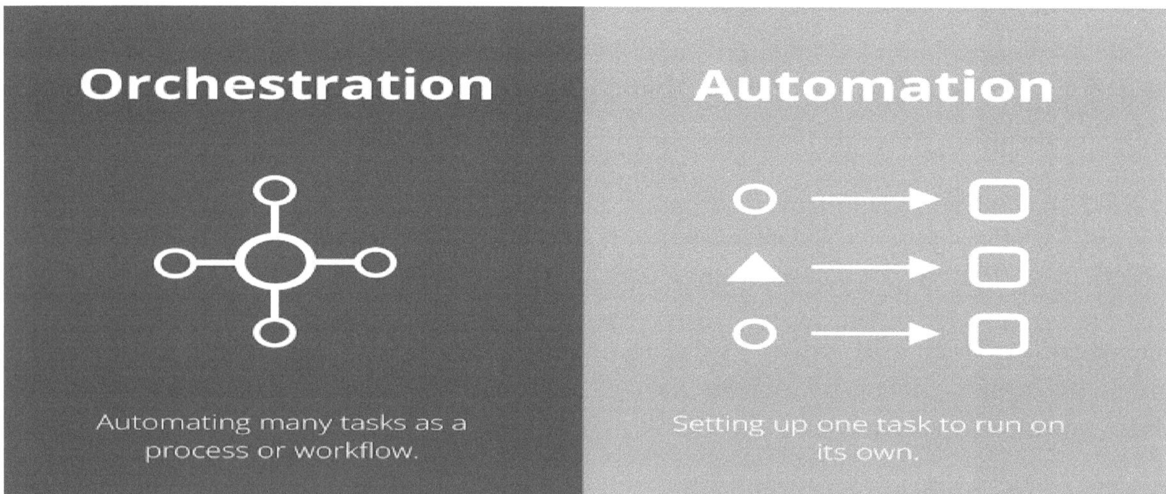

26.3 Infrastructure as Code (IaC) Best Practices

Infrastructure as Code (IaC) offers significant advantages in cloud computing, enabling organizations to automate and manage infrastructure through code. By adhering to best practices such as version control, modularity, parameterization, automated testing, CI/CD integration, security considerations, documentation, and treating infrastructure as data, businesses can harness the full potential of Ia Embracing IaC facilitates consistency, agility, and scalability in infrastructure management, leading to faster deployments, reduced human errors, and enhanced operational efficiency in the dynamic landscape of cloud computing. Adopting IaC is a transformative step towards a

26.3.1. Version Control and Collaboration:

Utilize version control systems, such as Git, to manage and track changes to your IaC code. Version control ensures that all changes are documented, enabling easy rollbacks and collaboration among team members. By adopting a collaborative approach, multiple team members can contribute to the IaC codebase, fostering a culture of continuous improvement and knowledge sharing. Proper version control also facilitates the creation of branches for new features or experiments without impacting the main codebase, enabling safe experimentation.

26.3.2. Modularity and Reusability:

Design IaC code in a modular and reusable manner. Break down infrastructure components into smaller, self-contained modules. This approach promotes consistency across deployments and allows for faster and more efficient provisioning. Reusable modules can be shared across different projects, reducing duplication of efforts and simplifying maintenance. Implementing modularity also helps manage the complexity of infrastructure configurations, making it easier to understand, maintain, and troubleshoot.

26.3.3. Immutable Infrastructure:

Adopt the principle of immutable infrastructure, wherein infrastructure components are treated as disposable and immutable. Instead of making direct changes to running instances, recreate the infrastructure from code whenever updates are required. This approach ensures that deployments are consistent, predictable, and reproducible, eliminating configuration drift. Immutable infrastructure also aids in faster recovery from failures as new instances can be quickly provisioned to replace failed ones.

26.3.4. Parameterization:

Parameterize your IaC code to make it flexible and customizable for different environments. Use variables to define configurations that can be adjusted based on specific requirements. Parameterization enables easy configuration changes without modifying the underlying code, streamlining the deployment process. Additionally, parameterization allows for the creation of environment-specific configurations, making it easier to manage dev, test, and production environments using the same IaC codebase.

26.3.5. Automated Testing:

Implement automated testing for your IaC code to validate its correctness and reliability. Use testing frameworks to check the syntax, logic, and behavior of the code. Automated testing helps identify errors early in the development process, reducing the risk of issues in production. Unit tests can verify individual components, while integration tests can assess the interaction between various infrastructure components. By ensuring the reliability of the IaC code through automated testing, organizations can deploy changes with greater confidence.

26.3.6. Continuous Integration and Continuous Deployment (CI/CD):

Incorporate IaC into your CI/CD pipeline to automate the deployment process. With CI/CD, changes to the IaC code are automatically tested, integrated, and deployed to production. This enables rapid and reliable delivery of infrastructure updates, promoting a culture of continuous delivery. CI/CD integration ensures that changes in the IaC code are thoroughly tested and validated before they reach the production environment, reducing the risk of errors and downtime.

26.3.7. Security and Compliance:

Ensure that security and compliance requirements are integrated into your IaC code. Use secure coding practices, encryption, and access controls to safeguard sensitive information. Regularly scan IaC code for security vulnerabilities, and enforce compliance policies to meet industry and organizational standards. Security considerations in IaC should include managing secrets and credentials securely, configuring appropriate network access controls, and applying security patches to infrastructure components.

26.3.8. Documentation:

Maintain comprehensive and up-to-date documentation for your IaC code. Document the purpose of each component, dependencies, and any specific deployment instructions. Well-documented code enhances transparency and makes it easier for team members to understand and contribute to the infrastructure codebase. Additionally, documentation serves as a knowledge base that future team members can refer to, ensuring consistency in infrastructure management.

26.3.9. Infrastructure as Data:

Adopt the concept of "infrastructure as data," where configurations are treated as data objects that can be stored, versioned, and analyzed. By treating infrastructure as data, it becomes easier to understand and manage the state of the environment. This approach can include using configuration management databases (CMDBs) or versioning systems to store infrastructure data, allowing for easy auditing, reporting, and change tracking.

26.3.10. Monitoring and Auditing:

Implement monitoring and auditing mechanisms for your IaC deployments. Monitor infrastructure changes, resource usage, and performance metrics. Regularly audit the infrastructure configurations to detect any deviations from the desired state. Monitoring helps ensure that the infrastructure remains in the intended state and that any unauthorized changes are quickly identified. Additionally, auditing allows organizations to assess the compliance of their infrastructure configurations with security and governance policies.

Exercise

Multiple Choice Questions

1. What is one of the primary benefits of infrastructure automation with cloud APIs?

a. Cost optimization

b. On-demand scaling

c. Modularity and reusability

d. Manual intervention

2. Why is version control essential in infrastructure as code (IaC) practices?

a. It ensures compliance with industry standards.

b. It allows for easy rollbacks and collaboration.

c. It automates disaster recovery procedures.

d. It provides automated testing capabilities.

3. What principle of infrastructure management treats infrastructure components as disposable and immutable?

a. Idempotency

b. Immutable infrastructure

c. Scalability

d. Version control

4. How can organizations achieve cost optimization in infrastructure automation with cloud APIs?

a. Implementing rate limiting and throttling mechanisms

b. Utilizing version control and modularity

c. Scaling resources dynamically based on demand

d. Programmatically managing cloud resources

5. Which best practice ensures that infrastructure configurations follow standardized processes?

a. Immutable infrastructure

b. Parameterization

c. Consistency and standardization

d. Automated testing

6. What is the primary purpose of automated testing in infrastructure as code (IaC)?

a. Achieving cost optimization

b. Improving governance and compliance

c. Validating correctness and reliability of code

d. Implementing version management strategies

7. Which tool facilitates the creation and management of Google Cloud resources using YAML or Jinja2 templates?

a. AWS CloudFormation

b. Google Cloud Deployment Manager

c. Azure Resource Manager

d. Terraform

8. What approach helps manage the complexity of infrastructure configurations in infrastructure as code (IaC)?

a. Parameterization

b. Immutable infrastructure

c. Modularity and reusability

d. Idempotency

9. How can organizations ensure the security of their infrastructure automation with cloud APIs?

a. Utilizing version control and collaboration

b. Treating infrastructure as data

c. Implementing robust error handling

d. Managing API authentication and credentials

Review Questions

1. What are the main benefits of infrastructure automation with cloud APIs?
2. How does immutable infrastructure differ from traditional infrastructure management?
3. What are the key considerations for implementing successful infrastructure as code (IaC) practices?
4. How does continuous integration and continuous deployment (CI/CD) integration enhance infrastructure as code (IaC) practices?
5. What role does version management play in infrastructure automation with cloud APIs?
6. Why is parameterization essential in infrastructure as code (IaC)?

7. How can organizations ensure the security of their infrastructure automation with cloud APIs?

8. What benefits does orchestration with cloud APIs offer to organizations?

Answer Section

Multiple Choice Questions

1. b) On-demand scaling

2. b) It allows for easy rollbacks and collaboration.

3. b) Immutable infrastructure

4. c) Scaling resources dynamically based on demand

5. c) Consistency and standardization

6. c) Validating correctness and reliability of code

7. b) Google Cloud Deployment Manager

8. c) Modularity and reusability

9. d) Managing API authentication and credentials

Review Questions

1. Infrastructure automation with cloud APIs offers several advantages, including increased speed and efficiency through the elimination of manual tasks and rapid provisioning. It enables scalability by allowing dynamic resource scaling based on demand, optimizing resource utilization and cost-effectiveness. Cost optimization is achieved by programmatically managing resources, ensuring that only necessary resources are provisioned, reducing unnecessary expenses. Automation also promotes consistency and standardization, reducing errors caused by manual interventions. Additionally, version management and auditing through API calls allow for better governance, accountability, and compliance.

2. Immutable infrastructure treats infrastructure components as disposable and immutable, meaning that instead of modifying running instances, new infrastructure is recreated from code whenever updates are required. This approach ensures consistency, predictability, and reproducibility of deployments, eliminating configuration drift and facilitating faster recovery from failures. In contrast, traditional infrastructure management involves modifying running instances directly, which can lead to configuration discrepancies and issues due to manual intervention.

3. Successful IaC implementation requires version control to manage changes, collaboration among team members, modularity for reusability, parameterization for flexibility, automated testing to validate code correctness, CI/CD integration for continuous delivery, security considerations to safeguard sensitive information, comprehensive documentation, and treating infrastructure as data to manage configurations effectively.

4. CI/CD integration automates the testing, integration, and deployment of IaC code changes. This ensures that code is continuously tested and validated before being deployed to production environments,

reducing the risk of errors and downtime. It enables a culture of continuous delivery, where changes can be delivered to production rapidly and reliably, increasing agility and operational efficiency.

5. Version management allows organizations to track and manage changes made to infrastructure configurations through cloud APIs. It enables easy rollbacks to previous versions in case of issues and provides an audit trail for compliance and security purposes. Version management ensures compatibility as APIs evolve, preventing disruptions due to changes in cloud provider APIs.

6. Parameterization allows IaC code to be customized and flexible for different environments. By using variables to define configurations, organizations can adjust settings based on specific requirements without modifying the underlying code. Parameterization facilitates the creation of environment-specific configurations and simplifies the management of development, testing, and production environments using the same IaC codebase.

7. To ensure security, organizations must manage API authentication tokens and credentials properly. Utilizing access control mechanisms helps restrict API access to prevent unauthorized access to sensitive resources. Securely managing secrets and credentials, configuring proper network access controls, and regular security scanning of IaC code for vulnerabilities are crucial security considerations.

8. Orchestration with cloud APIs empowers organizations to automate and manage complex tasks and workflows within cloud environments. It offers benefits such as automation, scalability, integration, cost-effectiveness, improved governance and compliance, and enhanced operational efficiency. Cloud orchestration simplifies cloud management, reduces human errors, and allows organizations to scale resources effortlessly based on fluctuating workloads, improving overall agility and responsiveness to changing business needs.

Chapter 27: Cloud Governance and Cost Optimization Strategies

27.1 Cloud Cost Governance and Budgeting

From an academic standpoint, cloud cost governance and budgeting are essential components of successful cloud adoption. Proper cost management practices optimize cloud spending, prevent budget overruns, and facilitate informed resource allocation decisions. By implementing best practices such as setting clear budgets, continuous monitoring, resource optimization, tagging, and governance policies, organizations can ensure cost efficiency and maximize the value of their cloud investments. Cloud cost governance fosters a financially responsible approach, enabling businesses to leverage the full potential of cloud computing while staying within their budgetary constraints.

27.1.1. The Significance of Cloud Cost Governance:

From an academic standpoint, cloud cost governance is a critical process that involves overseeing and optimizing cloud spending to ensure efficient resource utilization and cost control. It entails setting policies, procedures, and guidelines to manage cloud expenses effectively. With cloud cost governance, organizations can prevent unnecessary expenses, make informed decisions, and allocate resources judiciously, aligning with financial and strategic objectives.

27.1.2. Challenges in Cloud Cost Governance:

- **Lack of Visibility:** Academic research acknowledges that without proper monitoring and visibility into cloud usage, organizations may be unaware of resource inefficiencies and cost outliers, leading to higher expenses. Therefore, robust monitoring and reporting mechanisms are vital for effective cost governance.

- **Complexity of Pricing Models:** Cloud providers offer a wide array of pricing models, leading to complexities in predicting and managing costs. Academic research emphasizes the need for clear understanding and analysis of these models to optimize cost allocation.

- **Resource Mismanagement:** Inefficient resource provisioning and utilization can result in wasted cloud resources and unnecessary expenses. Research suggests implementing resource optimization techniques, such as auto-scaling and automated provisioning, to mitigate this challenge.

- **Lack of Accountability:** In a multi-team environment, a lack of clear ownership and accountability for cloud spending can lead to uncontrolled costs. Academic research advocates for the establishment of accountable roles and responsibilities to ensure cost transparency and control.

27.1.3. Best Practices for Cloud Cost Governance and Budgeting:

Academic research highlights several best practices for cloud cost governance and budgeting:

- **Set Clear Budget Limits:** Define and allocate cloud spending limits to different teams or projects. Regularly monitor spending against the budget and implement real-time alerts for approaching or exceeding budget thresholds.

- **Continuous Monitoring and Optimization:** Regularly monitor cloud usage, cost trends, and resource utilization. Use cloud management tools to identify opportunities for cost optimization, such as resizing instances or utilizing reserved instances.

- **Tagging and Resource Allocation:** Implement resource tagging to track and allocate costs to specific projects or teams. Properly tagged resources enable accurate cost attribution and help identify areas where optimization is needed.

- **Utilize Cost Management Tools:** Leverage cloud provider-native cost management tools or third-party cost optimization solutions to gain insights into cloud spending, identify cost-saving opportunities, and set up cost allocation reports.

- **Reserved Instances and Savings Plans:** Take advantage of cloud provider offerings like AWS Reserved Instances or Azure Savings Plans to commit to long-term usage and receive significant cost savings over pay-as-you-go pricing.

- **Rightsizing:** Analyze resource usage to identify underutilized or overprovisioned instances. Rightsize resources to match actual demand, thereby optimizing costs while maintaining performance.

- **Governance Policies:** Establish clear governance policies for cloud usage, covering resource provisioning, data retention, and access controls. Regularly review and enforce these policies to ensure compliance and cost efficiency.

- **Training and Awareness:** Educate cloud users and stakeholders about cloud cost management best practices and the impact of their actions on overall cloud spending. Encourage a culture of cost consciousness and accountability.

- **Regular Cost Review Meetings:** Conduct periodic cost review meetings with relevant stakeholders to discuss cost trends, budget adherence, and cost optimization strategies. Collaboratively identify areas for improvement and take necessary actions.

27.2 Cost Optimization Techniques and Best Practices

Cost optimization techniques and best practices are essential for organizations to effectively manage their cloud expenses. By employing right sizing, using reserved instances, leveraging spot instances, automating resource management, and utilizing cloud storage tiers, businesses can optimize costs while maintaining performance and scalability. Continuous monitoring, data analysis, and fostering a cost-conscious culture are equally vital in achieving sustainable cost optimization. With these practices in place, organizations can maximize the value of their cloud investments, drive business growth, and maintain a competitive edge in the ever-evolving cloud computing landscape.

27.2.1. Right Sizing:

Right sizing involves matching the size of cloud resources, such as virtual machines and storage, to the actual workload requirements. It requires careful analysis of resource utilization data to identify overprovisioned or underutilized resources. By rightsizing, organizations can avoid paying for unused capacity and ensure resources are optimally utilized. Continuous monitoring and analysis of resource utilization are critical for successful right sizing.

27.2.2. Use Reserved Instances or Savings Plans:

Cloud providers offer pricing options such as AWS Reserved Instances (RIs) or Azure Savings Plans, allowing organizations to commit to long-term usage in exchange for significant cost savings over pay-as-you-go pricing. By analyzing workload patterns and committing to reserved capacity for resources with predictable usage, organizations can maximize cost efficiency. Reserved Instances provide cost stability and are ideal for workloads with steady, consistent demand.

27.2.3. Spot Instances and Spot Fleets:

Spot Instances are unused cloud instances offered at significantly discounted prices compared to on-demand instances. Spot Fleets allow you to provision multiple Spot Instances to optimize availability and cost. Utilize Spot Instances for non-critical, fault-tolerant, and scalable workloads, taking advantage of cost savings when instances are available at reduced rates. It's important to note that Spot Instances are ephemeral and may be terminated when prices exceed your bid or when the underlying capacity becomes limited.

27.2.4. Automate Resource Management:

Implement automated resource management practices to optimize costs dynamically. Use automation tools to schedule the start and stop times of non-production resources, ensuring they are only active when needed. Automated scaling can also adjust resources based on workload demands, ensuring optimal performance and cost efficiency. By automating resource management, organizations can avoid paying for idle resources and achieve on-demand scalability.

27.2.5. Leverage Cloud Storage Tiers:

Cloud providers offer different storage tiers with varying performance and cost characteristics. Utilize the appropriate storage tier based on data access patterns and requirements. Frequently accessed data can reside in high-performance tiers, while infrequently accessed or archival data can be stored in lower-cost tiers. By choosing the right storage tier for each data type, organizations can optimize storage costs without compromising data accessibility.

27.2.6. Data Transfer and Egress Optimization:

Minimize data transfer costs between cloud services and regions. Utilize edge locations and content delivery networks (CDNs) for efficient content delivery and reduce egress charges by optimizing data transfer out of the cloud. Data transfer costs can accumulate significantly, especially for large-scale applications, making optimization in this area crucial for overall cost reduction.

27.2.7. Serverless and Managed Services:

Leverage serverless computing and managed services provided by cloud providers. These services automatically scale resources based on demand and charge only for actual usage, reducing the need for resource provisioning and management. Adopting serverless architectures and using managed services can significantly reduce operational costs and eliminate the need to manage underlying infrastructure.

27.2.8. Monitor and Analyze Cloud Costs:

Implement robust cost monitoring and reporting mechanisms. Use cost management tools to gain insights into cloud spending and identify cost trends and anomalies. Regularly analyze cost reports to detect opportunities for optimization and cost reduction. Cost monitoring helps organizations stay informed about their spending patterns and make data-driven decisions for cost optimization.

27.2.9. Tagging and Cost Allocation:

Implement consistent resource tagging to allocate costs accurately to departments, projects, or teams. Proper tagging enables granular visibility into cost distribution and helps identify areas for cost optimization. With accurate cost allocation, organizations can identify cost centers and track spending patterns to optimize resource usage effectively.

27.2.10. Educate and Foster Cost-Conscious Culture:

Educate all stakeholders, including developers and cloud users, about cost optimization best practices. Foster a culture of cost consciousness and accountability, where individuals understand the impact of their actions on cloud expenses and actively seek ways to optimize costs. Training and awareness programs empower teams to make cost-conscious decisions, leading to better cost governance across the organization.

27.3 Cloud Cost Analysis and Forecasting Tools: Maximizing Efficiency and Cost Control in the Cloud

Cloud cost analysis and forecasting tools play a pivotal role in achieving financial efficiency and cost control in cloud computing. By leveraging these tools, organizations can gain granular insights into their cloud expenses, identify optimization opportunities, and make informed decisions about resource allocation. Cloud cost analysis and forecasting are integral components of a robust cloud management strategy, enabling businesses to maximize the value of their cloud investments and maintain a competitive edge in the dynamic cloud landscape.

27.3.1. Understanding Cloud Cost Analysis Tools:

Cloud cost analysis tools are software solutions that help organizations track, monitor, and analyze their cloud expenses. These tools integrate with cloud service providers and gather detailed cost data, presenting it in a user-friendly interface. Cost analysis tools offer comprehensive insights into cloud spending across various services and resources, enabling stakeholders to make data-driven decisions.

27.3.2. Features and Functionalities of Cloud Cost Analysis Tools:

- **Cost Visualization Dashboards:** Cloud cost analysis tools provide real-time visualizations of cloud expenses through interactive dashboards. These dashboards present cost data in the form of charts, graphs, and heat maps, simplifying complex cost information for easy understanding.

- **Detailed Cost Breakdown:** Cost analysis tools offer a breakdown of cloud spending by services, resources, accounts, projects, and tags. This granularity helps stakeholders pinpoint areas of high spending, making it easier to identify cost optimization opportunities.

- **Historical Cost Data:** By leveraging historical cost data, analysis tools can generate trends and patterns, allowing businesses to identify seasonality or spikes in cloud spending. This historical perspective aids in predicting future expenses accurately.

- **Cost Allocation and Tagging:** Cloud cost analysis tools enable accurate cost allocation to different departments, projects, or teams. By applying tags to cloud resources, organizations gain granular insights into cost distribution and facilitate chargebacks.

- **Anomaly Detection:** Advanced analysis tools automatically detect unusual spending patterns or sudden cost spikes, alerting users to potential cost overruns or security breaches. Timely anomaly detection helps organizations take immediate action to rectify issues.

- **Cost Comparison Across Cloud Providers:** For businesses using multiple cloud providers or exploring a multi-cloud strategy, cost comparison features allow side-by-side analysis of cloud spending. This enables informed decisions about which provider offers the best pricing for specific needs.

- **Rightsizing Recommendations:** Cost analysis tools offer rightsizing recommendations by analyzing resource usage and performance metrics. This feature helps businesses optimize resource configurations to align with actual workload requirements, maximizing efficiency and reducing costs.

27.3.3. Significance of Cloud Cost Forecasting Tools:

Cloud cost forecasting tools utilize historical cost data and usage patterns to predict future expenses accurately. These tools help organizations plan budgets effectively, set realistic spending limits, and allocate resources judiciously.

27.3.4. Benefits of Cloud Cost Analysis and Forecasting Tools:

- **Proactive Cost Optimization:** Cloud cost analysis tools empower organizations to identify cost-saving opportunities and optimize spending before budget overruns occur.

- **Informed Decision-Making:** By providing clear insights into cloud spending, these tools enable stakeholders to make data-driven decisions about resource allocation and cloud usage.

- **Accurate Budget Planning:** Cloud cost forecasting tools aid in setting realistic budget limits based on historical data and anticipated workloads, ensuring financial efficiency.

- **Cloud Cost Control:** Armed with cost analysis and forecasting insights, businesses can maintain better control over their cloud expenses, preventing unexpected costs and ensuring cost predictability.

- **Resource Optimization:** By leveraging rightsizing recommendations and performance metrics, organizations can optimize resource utilization and reduce wasteful spending.

27.3.5. Integrating Cloud Cost Analysis and Forecasting into Cloud Strategy:

To fully capitalize on the benefits of cost analysis and forecasting tools, organizations should integrate these practices into their overall cloud management strategy. Regularly review cost reports, track cost trends, and analyze historical data to identify areas for improvement. Collaborate with stakeholders to optimize resource allocation and implement cost-saving measures effectively.

Exercise

Multiple Choice Questions

1. What is the primary goal of cloud cost governance?

a. Maximizing cloud spending without budget constraints.

b. Preventing unnecessary expenses and aligning with financial objectives.

c. Allocating unlimited cloud resources to different teams or projects.

d. Encouraging inefficient resource provisioning.

2. Which challenge is associated with cloud cost governance?

a. Lack of cloud service provider options.

b. Complexity of pricing models leading to cost predictability.

c. Limited visibility into cloud usage and cost outliers.

d. Accountability and clear ownership for cloud spending.

3. What best practice helps optimize cloud costs by matching resource size to actual workload requirements?

a. Tagging and resource allocation.

b. Cloud cost forecasting.

c. Right sizing.

d. Utilizing reserved instances.

4. Which cloud pricing option allows organizations to commit to long-term usage in exchange for significant cost savings?

a. Spot Instances

b. Savings Plans

c. Reserved Instances

d. On-demand Instances

5. What feature of cloud cost analysis tools allows side-by-side comparison of cloud spending across multiple providers?

a. Rightsizing recommendations.

b. Cost visualization dashboards.

c. Cost comparison across cloud providers.

d. Detailed cost breakdown.

6. Why is anomaly detection an essential feature of cloud cost analysis tools?

a. It helps automate resource management.

b. It provides rightsizing recommendations.

c. It aids in historical cost data analysis.

d. It alerts users to potential cost overruns or security breaches.

7. What benefit do cloud cost forecasting tools offer to organizations?

a. Proactive cost optimization.

b. Accurate budget planning.

c. Detailed cost breakdown.

d. Rightsizing recommendations.

8. What does cloud cost governance and budgeting seek to achieve?

a. Aligning with strategic objectives and avoiding cloud adoption.

b. Maximizing cloud spending without any cost control measures.

c. Optimizing cloud spending, preventing budget overruns, and informed resource allocation.

d. Ignoring cloud expenses and focusing solely on resource provisioning.

Review Questions

1. What are the key objectives of cloud cost governance and budgeting?

2. How can organizations overcome challenges in cloud cost governance, such as lack of visibility?

3. What is the significance of utilizing reserved instances or savings plans in cloud cost optimization?

4. How do cloud cost analysis tools facilitate informed decision-making in cloud resource allocation?

5. What is the role of tagging and resource allocation in cloud cost governance?

6. How does cloud cost forecasting aid in budget planning and cost control?

7. What are the benefits of integrating automated resource management into cloud cost optimization strategies?

8. How can fostering a cost-conscious culture benefit cloud cost governance efforts?

Answer Section

Multiple Choice Questions

1. b) Preventing unnecessary expenses and aligning with financial objectives.

2. c) Limited visibility into cloud usage and cost outliers.

3. c) Right sizing.

4. c) Reserved Instances

5. c) Cost comparison across cloud providers.

6. d) It alerts users to potential cost overruns or security breaches.

7. b) Accurate budget planning.

8. c) Optimizing cloud spending, preventing budget overruns, and informed resource allocation.

Review Questions

1. The main objectives of cloud cost governance and budgeting are to optimize cloud spending, prevent budget overruns, and ensure efficient resource utilization. By setting clear budgets, implementing monitoring and cost analysis, and adopting best practices like right sizing and using reserved instances, organizations can align their cloud expenses with strategic goals and financial constraints.

2. To address the challenge of limited visibility into cloud usage, organizations should invest in robust monitoring and reporting mechanisms. Implementing cloud cost analysis tools enables real-time tracking of cloud expenses and resource utilization, providing comprehensive insights into cost trends and anomalies. With improved visibility, businesses can identify inefficiencies and take proactive measures to optimize cloud spending.

3. Reserved instances or savings plans are crucial in cost optimization as they allow organizations to commit to long-term usage and receive significant cost savings over on-demand pricing. By analyzing workload patterns and committing to reserved capacity for predictable resources, businesses can achieve cost stability and reduce cloud expenses significantly, ensuring financial efficiency and budget control.

4. Cloud cost analysis tools provide detailed cost breakdowns, historical cost data, and visualizations through interactive dashboards. These features enable stakeholders to make data-driven decisions about resource allocation, ensuring that cloud spending is aligned with business needs and objectives. By having clear insights into cloud expenses, organizations can optimize resource usage and prioritize investments based on cost efficiency and value.

5. Tagging and resource allocation are essential in cloud cost governance as they enable accurate cost attribution to specific projects, teams, or departments. By implementing proper tagging practices, businesses gain granular visibility into cost distribution, facilitating chargebacks and cost accountability. This information helps identify areas for cost optimization and ensures that cloud expenses are transparently allocated to relevant stakeholders.

6. Cloud cost forecasting utilizes historical cost data and usage patterns to predict future expenses accurately. By leveraging forecasting tools, organizations can plan budgets effectively, set realistic spending limits, and allocate resources judiciously. This proactive approach to budget planning allows businesses to avoid unexpected costs and maintain better cost control, ensuring financial efficiency and predictability.

7. Automated resource management optimizes costs dynamically by scheduling start and stop times for non-production resources and adjusting resource allocation based on workload demands. By automating these processes, organizations can avoid paying for idle resources and achieve on-demand scalability, leading to significant cost savings and efficient resource utilization.

8. Encouraging a cost-conscious culture empowers individuals to understand the impact of their actions on cloud expenses and actively seek ways to optimize costs. By promoting awareness and accountability, organizations can create a collaborative environment where all stakeholders contribute to cost optimization efforts. This culture ensures that cloud cost governance becomes a collective responsibility, driving continuous improvement and cost efficiency across the organization.

Chapter 28: Serverless Computing and Event-Driven Architecture

Serverless computing is a powerful cloud computing model that abstracts infrastructure management and offers numerous benefits, including event-driven architecture, automatic scaling, pay-as-you-go pricing, and ease of use. By adopting serverless computing, organizations can build highly scalable, event-driven, and cost-effective applications with minimal operational overhead. The flexibility and agility provided by serverless computing make it a compelling choice for a wide range of use cases, including web and mobile applications, data processing, IoT applications, chatbots, scheduled tasks, and real-time data processing. As cloud providers continue to enhance their serverless offerings, this model is poised to become even more pervasive in the world of cloud computing.

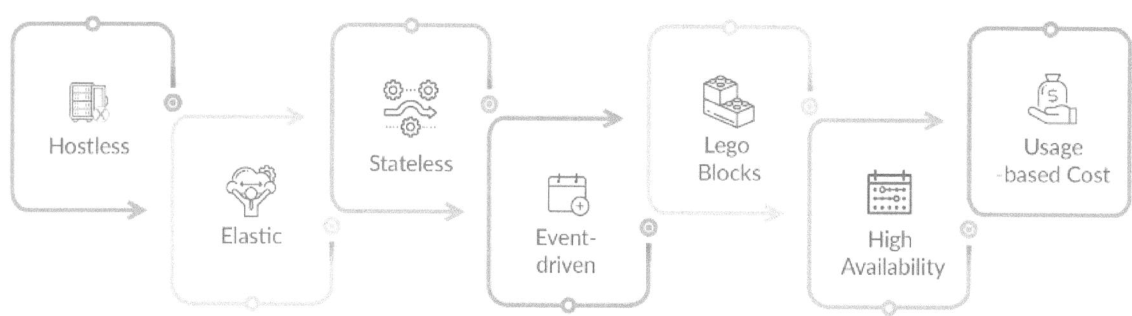

28.1 Serverless Computing Principles and Use Cases

28.1.1 Principles of Serverless Computing:

- **Event-driven Architecture:** One of the fundamental principles of serverless computing is its event-driven architecture. Serverless functions are triggered by specific events, such as HTTP requests, database changes, file uploads, or scheduled tasks. Each function is executed in response to a particular event, enabling event-driven and asynchronous application architectures. This event-based approach allows developers to build highly responsive, reactive, and decoupled systems.

- **Stateless Execution:** Serverless functions are stateless, which means they do not maintain any context or state between invocations. Each function execution is independent and isolated, making it easier to scale and distribute workloads without worrying about shared resources. Statelessness simplifies the management and scaling of serverless applications, as there is no need to manage session data or handle concurrent user requests on the same instance.

- **Automatic Scaling:** One of the key advantages of serverless computing is automatic scaling. Cloud providers manage the scaling of serverless functions automatically, based on the incoming request volume and workload demand. As the number of incoming events increases, the cloud platform dynamically provisions additional instances of the function to handle the load. Conversely, when the workload decreases, unused instances are automatically deprovisioned, ensuring efficient resource utilization and cost optimization.

- **Pay-as-you-go Pricing:** Serverless computing follows a pay-as-you-go pricing model. Organizations are billed only for the actual usage of functions, not for idle or unused resources. Users pay for the compute time and resources consumed during function execution. This makes serverless computing cost-effective for sporadic or low-traffic workloads, as organizations are only charged for the time the function is actively running.

- **No Server Management:** As the name suggests, serverless computing abstracts server management tasks from developers. Cloud providers handle tasks such as provisioning, monitoring, and scaling the underlying infrastructure. Developers can focus solely on writing code for the functions, without worrying about the operational aspects of managing servers. This abstraction allows developers to deliver business value more efficiently and accelerate the development lifecycle.

28.1.2 Use Cases of Serverless Computing:

- **Web and Mobile Applications:** Serverless computing is well-suited for handling backend services and APIs for web and mobile applications. Functions can be used to process HTTP requests, handle user authentication, and interact with databases and storage systems. The event-driven nature of serverless functions makes them highly responsive to incoming requests, providing a seamless experience for users.

- **Data Processing and Analytics:** Serverless functions are effective for data processing tasks, such as data transformation, filtering, and aggregation. They are particularly useful for real-time stream processing and ETL (Extract, Transform, Load) workflows. The ability to trigger functions based on events makes them ideal for processing data as it arrives.

- **Internet of Things (IoT) Applications:** Serverless computing is ideal for processing data generated by IoT devices. Functions can be triggered by device telemetry data, enabling real-time processing and analytics at scale. The automatic scaling capabilities ensure that the infrastructure can handle fluctuating loads from IoT devices.

- **Chatbots and Virtual Assistants:** Serverless functions are commonly used to power chatbots and virtual assistants. Functions can handle natural language processing, intent recognition, and integration with backend systems. The event-driven architecture enables chatbots to react in real-time to user input.

- **Scheduled Tasks and Cron Jobs:** Serverless computing is suitable for executing scheduled tasks and cron jobs. Functions can be triggered at specific intervals to perform tasks like data backups, report generation, and periodic data processing. This eliminates the need for dedicated server instances to handle such tasks.

- **File and Image Processing:** Serverless functions can be used to process and transform files and images uploaded to cloud storage. This includes tasks like resizing images, compressing files, and generating thumbnails. The on-demand execution of functions ensures efficient resource usage for sporadic file processing tasks.

- **Real-time Data Processing:** Serverless computing is well-suited for handling real-time data streams, such as event logs, social media feeds, and IoT data. Functions process incoming events as they occur, allowing for real-time analytics and decision-making. The automatic scaling ensures that the infrastructure can handle fluctuations in data stream volumes.

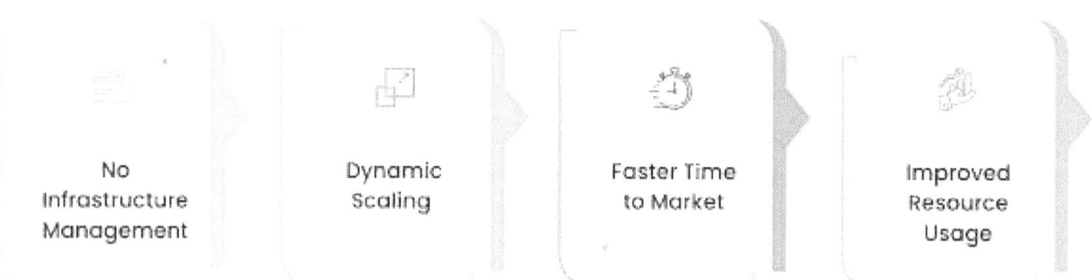

28.2 Event-Driven Architecture in Cloud Environments: Harnessing Real-Time Responsiveness and Scalability

Event-Driven Architecture in cloud environments offers a revolutionary way to design highly responsive, scalable, and flexible systems. By leveraging asynchronous communication through events, businesses can build data-intensive applications capable of meeting real-time demands. The decoupled nature of EDA allows for modular development, enhanced fault tolerance, and seamless scalability, making it an ideal choice for cloud-based applications. As organizations continue to embrace cloud computing, the adoption of Event-Driven Architecture is set to propel innovation and drive the transformation of modern applications in the dynamic landscape of cloud environments.

28.2.1. Understanding Event-Driven Architecture (EDA):

Event-Driven Architecture is an architectural style that emphasizes the production, consumption, and reaction to events. In this model, components of a system communicate asynchronously through events, which are notifications about significant changes or occurrences. Events can originate from various sources, such as user interactions, sensor data, or system activities, and are propagated to interested components without the need for direct interaction. EDA enables decoupling between different components, promoting modularity, scalability, and fault tolerance.

28.2.2. Key Components of Event-Driven Architecture:

- **Event Producers:** These are the sources that generate events. In cloud environments, event producers can be applications, microservices, IoT devices, or external services that emit events when specific conditions are met.

- **Event Brokers (Message Brokers):** Event brokers act as intermediaries that receive and store events. They ensure reliable delivery of events to their intended recipients and enable efficient event propagation across the system. Popular cloud-based event brokers include Apache Kafka, Amazon Kinesis, and Azure Event Hubs.

- **Event Consumers:** These are the components that react to events and perform specific actions based on the received event data. Event consumers can be microservices, functions (serverless), or data processing pipelines.

- **Event Processors:** Event processors are responsible for filtering, aggregating, or transforming events before they are consumed. They help in optimizing event handling and enable complex event processing.

28.2.3. Benefits of Event-Driven Architecture in Cloud Environments:

- Real-Time Responsiveness: EDA facilitates real-time responsiveness, as event-driven systems can react immediately to changes without waiting for synchronous requests or responses. This capability is crucial for applications that demand low latency, such as financial trading platforms, IoT systems, and real-time analytics.

- Scalability and Elasticity: Cloud environments offer the ideal infrastructure for EDA due to their inherent scalability and elasticity. As event loads increase, cloud-based event brokers and event consumers can dynamically scale to handle the surge in event processing, ensuring consistent performance.

- Flexibility and Agility: EDA promotes loose coupling between components, enabling easy integration and updates without disrupting the entire system. This agility allows businesses to iterate rapidly, add new functionalities, and adapt to changing requirements more efficiently.

- Reliability and Fault Tolerance: With event-driven systems, even if certain components fail temporarily, events can be stored in event brokers until the components are operational again. This fault-tolerant design ensures that events are not lost, enhancing system reliability.

- Event Traceability and Auditing: Events provide a natural audit trail of system activities, making it easier to trace the flow of data and understand how events trigger actions. This traceability aids in debugging, monitoring, and compliance requirements.

28.2.4. Implementing Event-Driven Architecture in Cloud Environments:

- Event Schema Design: Define clear event schemas with well-defined structures, ensuring consistency in event data. Adopting standards like Avro or Protocol Buffers can facilitate cross-platform compatibility.

- Message Broker Selection: Choose an appropriate cloud-based message broker that aligns with your performance, scalability, and data retention requirements.

- Event Validation and Error Handling: Implement mechanisms to validate incoming events and handle erroneous or duplicate events gracefully.

- Monitoring and Analytics: Integrate monitoring and analytics tools to track event flows, detect anomalies, and gain insights into event performance.

28.3 Building Serverless Applications with AWS Lambda and Azure Functions: Harnessing the Power of Function-as-a-Service

Serverless computing has revolutionized application development by providing a scalable and cost-effective way to build and deploy applications without managing infrastructure. AWS Lambda and Azure Functions are two leading Function-as-a-Service (FaaS) platforms that enable developers to focus solely on writing code without worrying about server provisioning or maintenance. In this article, we will explore the concept of serverless computing, the key features of AWS Lambda and Azure Functions, and how developers can leverage these platforms to build efficient and scalable serverless applications.

28.3.1. Understanding Serverless Computing:

Serverless computing is a cloud computing paradigm where developers can run code without managing the underlying servers. It abstracts away the infrastructure complexities, allowing developers to focus on writing application logic in the form of stateless functions. These functions are triggered by events and executed in response to those events, scaling automatically based on demand. The pay-as-you-go pricing model ensures cost-effectiveness, as developers only pay for the actual usage of resources during function execution.

28.3.2. Key Features of AWS Lambda and Azure Functions:

AWS Lambda:

- **Event-Driven Execution:** AWS Lambda functions can be triggered by a variety of events, including HTTP requests, changes in Amazon S3 buckets, updates in Amazon DynamoDB tables, or custom events via Amazon EventBridge. This event-driven architecture allows developers to build highly responsive applications.

- **Wide Language Support:** AWS Lambda supports multiple programming languages, including Node.js, Python, Java, C#, Go, and more. This flexibility allows developers to choose their preferred language for writing functions.

- **Seamless Integration:** Lambda integrates effortlessly with other AWS services, enabling developers to build complex applications by combining the functionalities of different services.

- **Automatic Scaling:** AWS Lambda automatically scales function instances to handle incoming requests, ensuring optimal performance and cost efficiency.

Azure Functions:

- **Event Triggers:** Azure Functions support various event triggers, such as HTTP requests, Blob storage changes, Azure Cosmos DB updates, and timers. This wide range of triggers enables developers to build event-driven applications.

- **Language Support:** Azure Functions support multiple programming languages, including C#, JavaScript, Python, Java, TypeScript, and more, giving developers the flexibility to use their preferred language.

- **Bindings:** Azure Functions offer bindings to connect functions with other Azure services, simplifying data input and output. Developers can easily interact with services like Azure Storage, Azure SignalR, and Azure Event Hubs.

- **Dynamic Scaling:** Azure Functions dynamically scales function instances based on incoming workload, ensuring efficient resource utilization and reduced costs.

3. Building Serverless Applications with AWS Lambda and Azure Functions:

- **Function Development:** Write stateless functions in your preferred programming language that perform specific tasks in response to events.

- **Event Trigger Configuration:** Configure event triggers to specify when and how your functions should be executed. Events can include HTTP requests, database updates, file uploads, timers, and more.

- **Integration with Other Services:** Leverage the extensive range of integrations provided by AWS Lambda and Azure Functions to connect your functions with various cloud services.

- **Logging and Monitoring:** Utilize built-in logging and monitoring features to track function performance, detect errors, and gain insights into application behavior.

- **Testing and Deployment:** Test your functions thoroughly in development environments before deploying them to production. Both platforms provide easy deployment options for serverless applications.

Exercise

Multiple Choice Questions

1. Which cloud computing model abstracts infrastructure management and allows developers to focus solely on writing code for individual functions?

a. Platform as a Service (PaaS)

b. Infrastructure as a Service (IaaS)

c. Function as a Service (FaaS)

d. Software as a Service (SaaS)

2. What is the fundamental principle of serverless computing that enables event-driven and asynchronous application architectures?

a. Stateless Execution

b. Automatic Scaling

c. Pay-as-you-go Pricing

d. Event-driven Architecture

3. Which of the following is a benefit of serverless computing's pay-as-you-go pricing model?

a. Predictable costs for idle resources

b. No billing for the actual usage of functions

c. Fixed monthly subscription fees

d. Unlimited resource allocation

4. Which cloud-based message broker acts as an intermediary, receiving and storing events in event-driven architecture?

a. Amazon EC2

b. Google Kubernetes Engine

c. Apache Kafka

d. Microsoft Azure Virtual Machines

5. What does "stateless execution" mean in the context of serverless computing?

a. Functions maintain context and state between invocations.

b. Functions execute in response to specific events.

c. Functions automatically scale based on workload demand.

d. Functions do not maintain context or state between invocations.

6. Which cloud provider offers Azure Functions as a Function-as-a-Service (FaaS) platform?

a. Amazon Web Services (AWS)

b. Google Cloud Platform (GCP)

c. Microsoft Azure

d. IBM Cloud

7. What makes event-driven architecture suitable for real-time responsiveness in applications?

a. Automatic Scaling

b. Stateless Execution

c. Event Producers

d. Asynchronous Communication through Events

8. Which benefit of Event-Driven Architecture (EDA) allows easy integration and updates without disrupting the entire system?

a. Real-Time Responsiveness

b. Reliability and Fault Tolerance

c. Scalability and Elasticity

d. Flexibility and Agility

9. Which cloud computing model revolutionizes application development by allowing developers to run code without managing the underlying servers?

a. Function as a Service (FaaS)

b. Infrastructure as a Service (IaaS)

c. Platform as a Service (PaaS)

d. Software as a Service (SaaS)

Review Questions

1. What is the key advantage of serverless computing over traditional cloud computing models?

2. How does event-driven architecture enable asynchronous and decoupled application design?

3. What are the benefits of using event-driven architecture in Internet of Things (IoT) applications?

4. How do cloud-based message brokers enhance the scalability and reliability of event-driven architecture?

5. What makes AWS Lambda and Azure Functions suitable for building efficient serverless applications?

6. How can organizations optimize costs in serverless computing?

7. What are the benefits of serverless computing for web and mobile applications?

8. How does event-driven architecture promote fault tolerance in cloud environments?

Answer Section
Multiple Choice Questions

1. c) Function as a Service (FaaS)

2. d) Event-driven Architecture

3. b) No billing for the actual usage of functions

4. c) Apache Kafka

5. d) Functions do not maintain context or state between invocations.

6. c) Microsoft Azure

7. d) Asynchronous Communication through Events

8. d) Flexibility and Agility

9. a) Function as a Service (FaaS)

Review Questions

1. The key advantage of serverless computing is its ability to abstract infrastructure management, allowing developers to solely focus on writing code for individual functions. With serverless, developers do not need to worry about provisioning, scaling, or managing servers, as cloud providers handle these tasks automatically. This abstraction enhances development productivity, reduces operational overhead, and enables a pay-as-you-go pricing model, where organizations are billed only for the actual usage of functions. The event-driven architecture of serverless computing further enhances its scalability and responsiveness, making it an ideal choice for various applications and use cases.

2. Event-driven architecture (EDA) enables asynchronous and decoupled application design by decoupling the components of a system and promoting communication through events. In EDA, components, also known as event consumers, react to events triggered by event producers, which can be external systems, user interactions, or internal processes. Since events are propagated without direct interaction, components can communicate asynchronously without waiting for responses, enhancing system responsiveness. This decoupling allows each component to function independently, making the

system more modular and flexible. As a result, developers can iterate, update, and scale different components without disrupting the entire application.

3. Event-driven architecture (EDA) offers several benefits for Internet of Things (IoT) applications. Since IoT devices generate vast amounts of data, EDA's event-based approach enables real-time processing and analytics at scale. IoT devices can trigger events based on sensor data, telemetry, or user interactions, allowing event consumers to process and react to this data in real time. The automatic scaling capabilities of EDA ensure that the system can handle fluctuating loads from IoT devices efficiently. Additionally, EDA's decoupled nature enables easy integration of new IoT devices and services without disrupting the entire IoT ecosystem, fostering flexibility and agility.

4. Cloud-based message brokers play a crucial role in enhancing the scalability and reliability of event-driven architecture (EDA). They act as intermediaries that receive and store events, ensuring reliable delivery to their intended recipients. By using message brokers, event consumers can process events at their own pace, decoupling the production of events from their consumption. This decoupling allows the system to handle spikes in event volume without overwhelming event consumers, enhancing scalability. Additionally, message brokers can persist events until they are successfully processed, ensuring event data is not lost even if consumers temporarily fail. This fault-tolerant design enhances the reliability of the overall system.

5. AWS Lambda and Azure Functions are suitable for building efficient serverless applications due to their function-as-a-service (FaaS) model. They allow developers to write code for individual functions, which are automatically triggered by specific events. This event-driven approach enables real-time responsiveness and event processing without the need for managing infrastructure. Both platforms offer seamless integration with other cloud services, making it easy to build complex applications using a combination of functionalities. The automatic scaling capabilities of AWS Lambda and Azure Functions ensure optimal resource allocation, reducing operational costs for organizations by charging only for the actual execution time of functions.

6. Organizations can optimize costs in serverless computing by leveraging its pay-as-you-go pricing model. Since serverless platforms charge based on actual function execution time, developers can optimize functions to run more efficiently and minimize the execution time. Right-sizing functions to match the workload's requirements can reduce idle time and resource waste, leading to cost savings. Utilizing reserved concurrency to limit the number of concurrent executions can help prevent unexpected spikes in costs. Additionally, organizations should implement best practices for resource management, such as intelligent scheduling, to ensure functions are only active when needed, further optimizing costs.

7. Serverless computing offers several benefits for web and mobile applications. Its event-driven architecture allows developers to handle backend services and APIs efficiently, processing HTTP requests and interacting with databases seamlessly. The automatic scaling capabilities ensure that applications can handle varying traffic loads without manual intervention. Pay-as-you-go pricing makes serverless cost-effective for web and mobile applications with sporadic or low-traffic workloads, as organizations are billed only for the actual function execution time. The decoupled nature of serverless functions also promotes modularity, making it easier to update and add new features to web and mobile applications without impacting the entire system.

8. Event-driven architecture (EDA) promotes fault tolerance in cloud environments by decoupling components and enabling asynchronous communication through events. When an event consumer temporarily fails, events are persisted in the message broker until the consumer is operational again. This ensures that event data is not lost and processing can resume seamlessly. Additionally, EDA's statelessness, where functions do not maintain context between invocations, simplifies scaling and distribution of workloads without worrying about shared resources. As a result, the system can recover from component failures and continue functioning without compromising the overall application's reliability and performance.

Chapter 29: Cloud Native Networking and Service Mesh

29.1 Service Mesh Concepts and Benefits

Service mesh has become an indispensable technology for managing the complex communication between microservices within distributed applications in cloud-native environments. By providing a dedicated infrastructure layer, service mesh enhances the reliability, observability, and security of service-to-service communication. With its traffic management, load balancing, observability, and security features, service mesh enables organizations to build and operate resilient and scalable cloud-native applications with confidence and efficiency. As cloud-native architectures continue to evolve, service mesh plays a critical role in maintaining the performance, security, and reliability of modern applications in the cloud.

1. What is a Service Mesh?

A service mesh is a specialized infrastructure layer in cloud computing that facilitates communication between microservices within a distributed application. It acts as a transparent intermediary between microservices, providing a dedicated set of lightweight proxies (sidecar proxies) deployed alongside each microservice. These proxies intercept and manage network traffic, enabling advanced features like load balancing, service discovery, encryption, traffic control, and more.

2. Key Concepts of Service Mesh:

- **Data Plane:** The data plane consists of the sidecar proxies deployed alongside each microservice. These proxies handle all incoming and outgoing network requests, intercepting and routing traffic based on the service mesh configuration. The data plane ensures that communication between microservices adheres to the established rules and policies.

- **Control Plane:** The control plane is responsible for managing and configuring the data plane proxies. It provides a centralized control interface where operators define communication policies, security measures, traffic routing rules, and other service mesh configurations. The control plane allows administrators to dynamically change the behavior of the service mesh without modifying the individual microservices.

- **Service Discovery:** Service mesh automates service discovery, allowing microservices to locate and communicate with each other without relying on hardcoded IP addresses or endpoints. This dynamic discovery enables easier scaling and adaptation to changes in the network topology. The service mesh ensures that each microservice can find and interact with other microservices seamlessly.

- **Load Balancing:** Service mesh includes intelligent load balancing algorithms that distribute incoming traffic evenly across multiple instances of a microservice. This ensures optimal resource utilization and high availability. Load balancing helps prevent overloading certain microservices and improves the overall responsiveness of the application.

- **Observability:** Service mesh provides extensive observability capabilities, including metrics, logs, and distributed tracing. These features help operators and developers monitor and troubleshoot the communication flow between microservices, identifying performance bottlenecks and errors. Observability is crucial for gaining insights into the health and performance of the entire distributed system.

- **Security and Encryption:** Service mesh offers built-in security features such as mutual TLS (mTLS) encryption to secure communication between microservices. mTLS ensures that all network traffic is encrypted and authenticated, preventing unauthorized access and eavesdropping. Security measures in the service mesh help protect sensitive data and prevent security breaches.

3. Benefits of Service Mesh in Cloud:
- **Simplified Communication:** Service mesh abstracts away the complexities of service-to-service communication, allowing developers to focus on building microservices without worrying about network concerns. It provides a consistent and standardized way of handling communication, making it easier to manage and understand the interactions between microservices.

- **Centralized Control:** The control plane provides a single point of control for managing service mesh configurations. This centralization promotes consistency and reduces operational overhead, making it easier to enforce policies and apply changes uniformly across the entire distributed application.

- **Scalability and Resilience:** Service mesh's traffic management features enable seamless scaling of microservices. The load balancing and dynamic routing capabilities ensure that traffic is intelligently distributed, avoiding service overload and maintaining the application's responsiveness and resilience.

- **Observability and Troubleshooting:** The observability features of service mesh provide valuable insights into the communication flow. Operators can monitor and analyze metrics, logs, and tracing data to identify performance issues, diagnose errors, and troubleshoot problems in real-time.

- **Enhanced Security:** Service mesh strengthens the security of cloud-native applications by providing encryption, authentication, and access control mechanisms for all inter-service communication. It helps ensure that only authorized services can communicate with each other, preventing potential security breaches and data leaks.

- **Cross-Platform Support:** Service mesh is platform-agnostic and can be deployed across various cloud providers and container orchestration platforms. This flexibility makes it suitable for multi-cloud and hybrid cloud environments, allowing organizations to maintain consistent communication patterns regardless of the underlying infrastructure.

29.1.4. Popular Service Mesh Implementations in Cloud:
- **Istio:** Istio is an open-source service mesh developed by Google, IBM, and Lyft. It is designed to work seamlessly with Kubernetes and provides robust traffic management, observability, and security features. Istio is widely adopted in the cloud-native community for its extensive capabilities and large ecosystem.

- **Linkerd:** Linkerd is a lightweight and fast service mesh specifically designed for cloud-native applications. It is built on top of the Rust programming language and offers strong performance and simplicity. Linkerd is known for its ease of use and minimal resource footprint.

- **Consul Connect:** Consul Connect is a feature of HashiCorp Consul, a service mesh and service discovery tool. Consul Connect provides secure service-to-service communication and service segmentation, making it a popular choice for organizations already using Consul for service discovery.

29.2 Implementing Service Mesh in Cloud Environments

Implementing service mesh in cloud environments requires careful consideration of the service mesh solution, proper infrastructure setup, and configuration of essential features like traffic routing, service discovery, security, and observability. By successfully deploying service mesh, you can enhance the reliability, scalability, and security of communication between microservices, enabling your cloud-native applications to operate efficiently and with greater confidence. As cloud-native architectures continue to evolve, service mesh plays a crucial role in managing the complexities of microservices communication and unleashing the full potential of cloud-native technologies in the cloud.

29.2.1. Choose a Service Mesh Solution:

When implementing service mesh in a cloud environment, the first step is to choose a suitable service mesh solution. Each service mesh implementation, such as Istio, Linkerd, and Consul Connect, comes with its own set of features, complexity, and compatibility with various cloud platforms. Consider factors like the specific requirements of your application, the level of integration with existing infrastructure, and the desired feature set when selecting a service mesh solution. Additionally, consider the maturity of the project, community support, and ease of use when making your choice.

29.2.2. Prepare the Infrastructure:

Before implementing service mesh, it is crucial to ensure that your cloud environment is properly set up. This typically involves having a container orchestration platform like Kubernetes in place, as most service mesh solutions are designed to work seamlessly with Kubernetes. Make sure that your microservices are containerized and deployed within the Kubernetes cluster.

29.2.3. Deploy the Data Plane Proxies:

The data plane proxies, often referred to as sidecar proxies, are fundamental components of the service mesh. These lightweight network proxies are deployed alongside each microservice in the Kubernetes cluster. They intercept and manage all incoming and outgoing network traffic for the associated microservice, providing the necessary communication functionalities offered by the service mesh.

29.2.4. Configure the Control Plane:

The control plane is responsible for managing and configuring the data plane proxies. It provides a centralized control interface where administrators define communication policies, security measures, traffic routing rules, and other service mesh configurations. The control plane allows operators to dynamically change the behavior of the service mesh without making changes to the individual microservices.

Depending on the selected service mesh solution, the control plane may be deployed as Kubernetes resources or managed through dedicated control plane management tools provided by the service mesh platform.

29.2.5. Define Traffic Routing Rules:

Once the control plane is set up, you can define traffic routing rules to control how traffic flows between microservices. This includes configuring load balancing algorithms, setting up retries, timeouts, and circuit breakers to enhance the resilience of your application. The service mesh can intelligently route traffic to different instances of a microservice, enabling better resource utilization and improving the overall performance and availability of the application.

29.2.6. Enable Service Discovery:

Service discovery is a critical feature of service mesh that enables microservices to locate and communicate with each other dynamically. The service mesh abstracts away the need for hardcoding IP addresses or endpoints, allowing microservices to adapt to changes in the network topology seamlessly. Ensure that service discovery is enabled and functioning correctly within your service mesh implementation to enable effective communication between microservices.

29.2.7. Implement Security Measures:

Enhance the security of your cloud-native application by enabling mutual TLS (mTLS) encryption and access control policies. mTLS ensures that all communication between microservices is encrypted and authenticated, preventing unauthorized access and eavesdropping. With mTLS, each microservice can verify the identity of its peers before establishing a secure connection, ensuring that only trusted services can communicate with each other. Additionally, the service mesh can enforce access control policies to restrict communication between microservices based on defined rules, providing an additional layer of security.

29.2.8. Set Up Observability:

Observability is essential for monitoring and troubleshooting the communication flow within your application. Service mesh implementations offer various observability features, including metrics, logs, and distributed tracing. These features help operators and developers gain insights into the performance and health of individual microservices and the overall application.

By configuring monitoring and logging capabilities, you can identify performance bottlenecks, diagnose errors, and promptly respond to issues in your cloud-native application.

29.2.9. Test and Monitor:

Thoroughly test your service mesh implementation to ensure that it functions as expected. Conduct testing scenarios to verify the correctness of traffic routing, load balancing, and security features. Test the resiliency of your application by simulating failures and traffic spikes to ensure that the service mesh can handle such situations gracefully.

Once the service mesh is deployed in production, continuously monitor its performance and behavior. Monitor metrics and logs to detect any anomalies or unexpected behavior, and use distributed tracing to follow the flow of requests through the microservices.

29.2.10. Scale and Optimize:

As your cloud-native application grows, monitor the performance of your service mesh and scale it accordingly to handle increased workloads. Scaling the service mesh involves adding more data plane proxies or upgrading the infrastructure to accommodate the growing number of microservices and communication traffic.

Continuously optimize your service mesh configuration and settings based on the observed performance and requirements of your application. Regularly review traffic patterns, resource utilization, and security policies to ensure the best possible performance and efficiency of your cloud-native architecture.

29.3 Traffic Management and Security with Service Mesh

Traffic management and security are fundamental aspects of service mesh in cloud-native environments. With intelligent traffic management capabilities, service mesh ensures optimal resource utilization, improved performance, and resilience. The robust security features, including mTLS encryption and access control, protect microservices from unauthorized access and ensure secure communication. Observability features like metrics, monitoring, distributed tracing, and logging provide valuable insights into the communication flow and assist in effective troubleshooting. By effectively managing traffic and enforcing strong security measures, service mesh enhances the overall reliability, scalability, and security of cloud-native applications in the cloud.

29.3.1. Traffic Management:

- **Load Balancing:** Service mesh employs intelligent load balancing algorithms to distribute incoming traffic evenly across multiple instances of a microservice. Load balancing ensures that each instance receives a fair share of requests, preventing overloading of any single instance and leading to optimal resource utilization. This feature improves the overall application performance and ensures high availability by evenly distributing the load.

- **Retries and Timeouts:** Transient failures can occur in distributed systems due to network issues or temporary unavailability of services. Service mesh allows for automatic retries of failed requests, reducing the impact of transient failures. Operators can configure the number of retries and set timeout thresholds for requests, preventing prolonged waits and freeing up resources in case of non-responsive services.

- **Circuit Breaking:** Circuit breaking is a crucial traffic management feature that prevents cascading failures. If a microservice experiences issues or becomes unresponsive, the service mesh stops sending requests to that service, isolating the failed component and minimizing the impact on downstream services. Circuit breaking enhances the resiliency of the application by limiting the scope of failures and allowing faster recovery.

- **Traffic Splitting:** Service mesh enables operators to split traffic, directing a portion of requests to specific versions of a microservice. This feature is useful during canary deployments or A/B testing when new versions of a service are gradually introduced to a subset of users. Traffic splitting allows operators to assess the new version's performance and stability before fully rolling it out.

- **Traffic Shifting:** With traffic shifting, operators can smoothly transition traffic from one version of a microservice to another. This enables seamless upgrades and rollbacks without service interruption. Traffic shifting is particularly useful during blue-green deployments, where the new version of a service is gradually introduced while the previous version is still running.

29.3.2. Security:

- **Mutual TLS (mTLS) Encryption:** Service mesh enforces mutual TLS (mTLS) encryption for all communication between microservices. mTLS ensures that all network traffic is encrypted and authenticated, providing end-to-end security. Each data plane proxy in the service mesh has its own identity, and all communication between proxies is encrypted with unique certificates. This robust encryption mechanism prevents unauthorized access to sensitive data and ensures the integrity of the communication flow.

- **Access Control and Authorization:** Service mesh supports access control and authorization policies, allowing operators to define which microservices can communicate with each other and what actions they are allowed to perform. This feature ensures that only authorized services can interact, reducing the risk of unauthorized access and potential security breaches.

- **Service Identity and Authentication:** Service mesh provides strong service identity through X.509 certificates, allowing each microservice to prove its identity when communicating with other services. This ensures that services can trust the identity of their counterparts and prevents man-in-the-middle attacks.

- **Secure Service-to-Service Communication:** By enforcing mTLS and implementing secure communication protocols, service mesh establishes a secure communication channel between microservices. This security measure protects sensitive data and ensures that communication between microservices remains confidential and tamper-proof.

- **Distributed Denial of Service (DDoS) Protection:** Service mesh can provide DDoS protection by enforcing rate limiting and traffic filtering policies. These measures help mitigate the impact of DDoS attacks by limiting the amount of incoming traffic and preventing service disruptions.

29.3.3. Observability:

- **Metrics and Monitoring:** Service mesh offers extensive metrics and monitoring capabilities, allowing operators to monitor the performance, latency, and error rates of microservices. These metrics provide valuable insights into the health of individual services and the overall application. Monitoring helps operators identify performance bottlenecks, diagnose issues, and optimize the application's performance.

- **Distributed Tracing:** Distributed tracing in service mesh allows operators to trace a request's journey as it flows through multiple microservices. This feature provides a detailed view of the communication flow and helps in diagnosing latency issues and understanding the interactions between services. Distributed tracing is crucial for troubleshooting complex issues in distributed systems.

- **Logging and Error Handling:** Service mesh can aggregate logs from all microservices, providing centralized error handling and logging. This centralized approach makes it easier to identify and respond to errors and issues affecting the application. By collecting and analyzing logs, operators gain better visibility into the application's behavior and can promptly address any anomalies or errors.

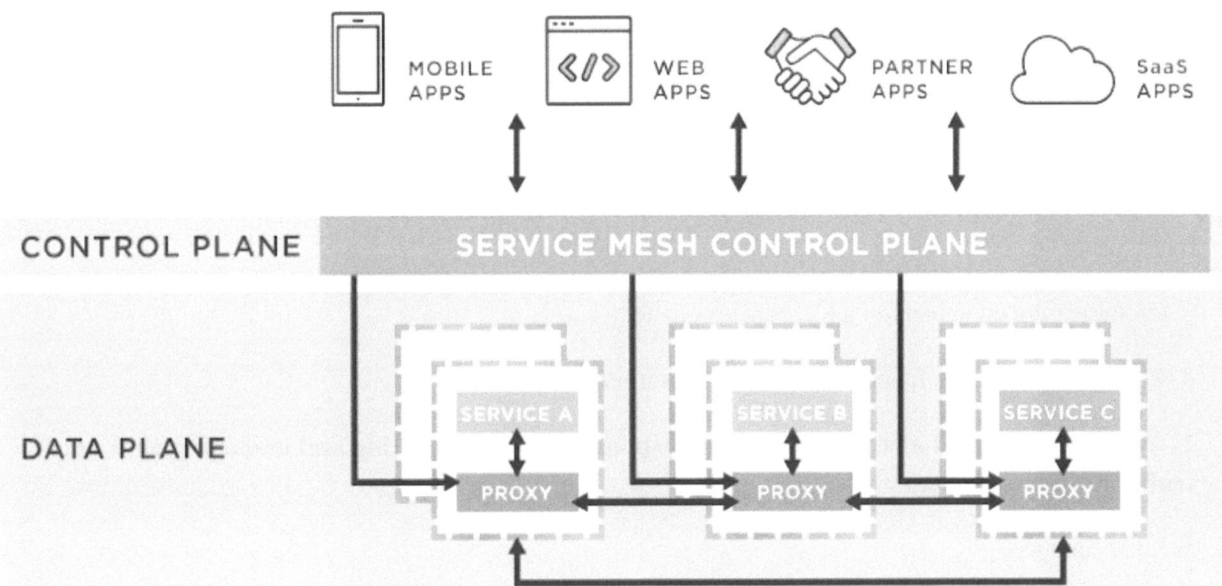

MOBILE APPS
WEB APPS
PARTNER APPS
SaaS APPS
CONTROL PLANE
SERVICE MESH CONTROL PLANE
DATA PLANE
SERVICE A
PROXY
SERVICE B
PROXY
SERVICE C
PROXY

Exercise

Multiple Choice Questions

1. What is the primary role of a service mesh in cloud-native environments?

a. Handling network infrastructure for microservices

b. Ensuring secure communication between microservices

c. Orchestrating containers in a Kubernetes cluster

d. Managing serverless functions in a cloud environment

2. Which component of a service mesh is responsible for intercepting and managing network traffic for microservices?

a. Load Balancer

b. Control Plane

c. Data Plane

d. Service Registry

3. What does service discovery enable within a service mesh?

a. Load balancing between microservices

b. Automatic scaling of microservices

c. Dynamic communication between microservices without hardcoded endpoints

d. Service isolation for improved security

4. What is the purpose of load balancing in a service mesh?

a. Encrypting communication between microservices

b. Ensuring even distribution of incoming traffic across microservice instances

c. Automatically retrying failed requests between microservices

d. Monitoring and analyzing metrics for microservices

5. Which security feature of service mesh encrypts all communication between microservices?

a. Access Control

b. Service Discovery

c. Mutual TLS (mTLS) Encryption

d. Load Balancing

6. What does the control plane of a service mesh allow administrators to do?

a. Handle network traffic for microservices

b. Configure load balancing for microservices

c. Dynamically change the behavior of the service mesh

d. Store data for microservices

7. How does service mesh enhance the reliability of cloud-native applications?

a. By automatically scaling microservices based on traffic demand

b. By providing centralized control and management of microservice communication

c. By securing communication between microservices with mTLS encryption

d. By providing extensive observability features for monitoring and troubleshooting

8. What is the benefit of distributed tracing in a service mesh?

a. Preventing DDoS attacks on microservices

b. Monitoring the performance and error rates of microservices

c. Diagnosing latency issues and understanding communication flow between microservices

d. Ensuring secure communication between microservices

9. Which service mesh implementation is known for its simplicity and minimal resource footprint?

a. Istio

b. Linkerd

c. Consul Connect

d. AWS Lambda

Review Questions

1. What are the main benefits of using a service mesh in cloud-native environments?

2. How does a service mesh ensure secure communication between microservices?

3. How does service discovery work in a service mesh?

4. What role does load balancing play in a service mesh?

5. How does the control plane of a service mesh enhance manageability?

6. How does service mesh assist in troubleshooting and monitoring cloud-native applications?

7. What is the significance of traffic management in a service mesh?

8. How does service mesh enable seamless scaling and adaptation in cloud-native environments?

Answer Section

Multiple Choice Questions

1. b) Ensuring secure communication between microservices
2. c) Data Plane
3. c) Dynamic communication between microservices without hardcoded endpoints
4. b) Ensuring even distribution of incoming traffic across microservice instances
5. c) Mutual TLS (mTLS) Encryption
6. c) Dynamically change the behavior of the service mesh
7. b) By providing centralized control and management of microservice communication
8. c) Diagnosing latency issues and understanding communication flow between microservices
9. b) Linkerd

Review Questions

1. The main benefits of using a service mesh in cloud-native environments include enhanced reliability, observability, and security of service-to-service communication. It simplifies communication between microservices, provides centralized control for managing configurations, and enables seamless scaling and adaptation to changes in the network topology. With traffic management features like load balancing and retries, service mesh ensures optimal resource utilization and high availability. The built-in security measures, such as mutual TLS encryption and access control, protect microservices from unauthorized access and potential security breaches. Observability features, like metrics and distributed tracing, assist in monitoring and troubleshooting the communication flow for better application performance.

2. A service mesh ensures secure communication between microservices through mutual TLS (mTLS) encryption and access control. mTLS ensures that all network traffic is encrypted and authenticated, providing end-to-end security. Each data plane proxy in the service mesh has its own identity, and all communication between proxies is encrypted with unique certificates. This robust encryption mechanism prevents unauthorized access to sensitive data and ensures the integrity of the communication flow. Additionally, access control policies in the service mesh allow administrators to define which microservices can communicate with each other and what actions they are allowed to perform, further enhancing the security of the communication.

3. Service discovery in a service mesh automates the process of locating and communicating with microservices without relying on hardcoded IP addresses or endpoints. The service mesh abstracts away the complexities of service discovery, making it dynamic and adaptable to changes in the network

topology. When a microservice needs to communicate with another microservice, it sends a request to the service mesh, which then uses its service registry to determine the location of the target microservice. The service mesh ensures that each microservice can find and interact with other microservices seamlessly, enabling easier scaling and adaptation to changes in the distributed application.

4. Load balancing in a service mesh ensures the even distribution of incoming traffic across multiple instances of a microservice. This feature improves resource utilization and prevents any single instance of a microservice from becoming overwhelmed with requests. The service mesh uses intelligent load balancing algorithms to distribute traffic based on factors like server health, capacity, and response time. By evenly distributing the load, load balancing ensures that all instances of a microservice share the request burden, leading to better performance, increased availability, and reduced chances of service overload.

5. The control plane of a service mesh provides a centralized control interface where operators define communication policies, security measures, traffic routing rules, and other service mesh configurations. This centralization promotes consistency and reduces operational overhead, making it easier to enforce policies and apply changes uniformly across the entire distributed application. Administrators can dynamically change the behavior of the service mesh without modifying the individual microservices, allowing for easier experimentation and adaptation to evolving application requirements. The control plane acts as the brain of the service mesh, providing a single point of control for managing and configuring the data plane proxies responsible for intercepting and managing network traffic.

6. Service mesh provides extensive observability capabilities, including metrics, logs, and distributed tracing, which assist in troubleshooting and monitoring cloud-native applications. Metrics and monitoring features allow operators to monitor the performance, latency, and error rates of microservices, providing valuable insights into the health of individual services and the overall application. Distributed tracing allows operators to trace a request's journey as it flows through multiple microservices, helping diagnose latency issues and understand the interactions between services. Logs aggregate information from all microservices, providing centralized error handling and logging for better visibility into the application's behavior and quick response to any anomalies or errors.

7. Traffic management in a service mesh plays a crucial role in optimizing the communication flow between microservices. It includes load balancing, retries, timeouts, circuit breaking, traffic splitting, and shifting. Load balancing ensures even distribution of incoming traffic across multiple instances of a microservice, preventing overloading and improving performance. Retries and timeouts automatically handle transient failures, reducing the impact of network issues. Circuit breaking isolates failed components, preventing cascading failures and enhancing the application's resilience. Traffic splitting allows for canary deployments and A/B testing, while traffic shifting enables smooth version upgrades and rollbacks without service interruption. All these features collectively ensure the reliability, scalability, and responsiveness of cloud-native applications.

8. Service mesh enables seamless scaling and adaptation in cloud-native environments by providing dynamic service discovery and traffic management features. With service discovery, microservices can locate and communicate with each other without relying on hardcoded endpoints, allowing for easy scaling as new instances are added. Traffic management features like load balancing and routing ensure that traffic is intelligently distributed, avoiding service overload and maintaining responsiveness as the

workload changes. Additionally, the central control plane allows administrators to dynamically change service mesh configurations, adapting the communication behavior of microservices in real-time. These capabilities enable cloud-native applications to efficiently scale and adapt to fluctuations in demand and network topology.

Chapter 30: Cloud Governance and Compliance Automation

30.1 Cloud Governance Automation Tools and Techniques

Cloud governance automation tools and techniques are indispensable for effectively managing cloud infrastructure at scale. By implementing infrastructure as code, configuration management, policy engines, continuous compliance monitoring, resource tagging automation, self-service portals, auto-scaling, security scanning, and audit logging automation, organizations can enhance governance efficiency, maintain compliance, and optimize cloud resource utilization. Automation reduces manual efforts, minimizes errors, and empowers organizations to manage their cloud environment with greater agility and confidence.

30.1.1. Infrastructure as Code (IaC):

Infrastructure as Code is a foundational automation technique for cloud governance. It involves managing cloud resources through code, using frameworks like AWS CloudFormation, Azure Resource Manager (ARM) templates, or Terraform. Organizations define their infrastructure as code, which allows them to version control and automate the deployment and management of cloud resources. IaC ensures consistency, reduces human errors, and enables quick and repeatable provisioning of cloud infrastructure.

30.1.2. Configuration Management:

Configuration management tools such as Chef, Puppet, and Ansible automate the configuration and management of cloud instances and applications. These tools enforce desired configurations, apply security policies, and perform updates across multiple instances at scale. Configuration management helps maintain a consistent and secure cloud environment by ensuring that configurations are aligned with organizational standards.

30.1.3. Cloud Governance Policy Engines:

Cloud governance policy engines enable organizations to define and enforce policies across their cloud resources. These engines evaluate cloud resources against predefined policies and provide automated remediation actions for non-compliant resources. Policy engines help organizations maintain compliance, security, and cost optimization by continuously monitoring and enforcing governance policies.

30.1.4. Continuous Compliance Monitoring:

Continuous compliance monitoring tools regularly assess cloud resources against industry standards and regulatory requirements. These tools provide real-time visibility into compliance status, identify deviations, and trigger alerts or remediation actions when violations occur. Continuous compliance monitoring ensures ongoing adherence to governance policies, reducing compliance risks.

30.1.5. Automated Resource Tagging:

Resource tagging automation tools automatically apply and enforce resource tags based on predefined rules. Tags help categorize and identify resources, making it easier to allocate costs, track usage, and apply security policies. By automating resource tagging, organizations can ensure consistent tagging practices and improve resource management.

30.1.6. Self-Service Portals:

Self-service portals provide a user-friendly interface for teams to request and provision cloud resources following predefined governance policies. Automation in self-service portals streamlines resource provisioning, ensuring that resources are deployed with the necessary approvals and compliance checks in place.

30.1.7. Auto-Scaling and Cost Optimization:

Cloud governance automation can leverage auto-scaling capabilities to dynamically adjust resources based on workload demands. This helps optimize resource utilization and reduce costs by scaling resources up or down automatically, ensuring efficient use of cloud resources.

30.1.8. Automated Security Scanning:

Automated security scanning tools continuously monitor cloud resources for security vulnerabilities, misconfigurations, and potential threats. These tools provide real-time security alerts and automatically remediate security issues, ensuring a secure and compliant cloud environment.

30.1.9. Audit Logging and Monitoring:

Automation of audit logging and monitoring enables organizations to track user activities, resource changes, and access permissions in their cloud environment. Automated logging simplifies compliance audits and helps detect and respond to security incidents promptly.

30.2 Compliance Monitoring and Enforcement

Compliance monitoring and enforcement are essential components of cloud governance. By implementing continuous compliance scanning, real-time alerts, audit logging, vulnerability management, and compliance dashboards, organizations can proactively monitor and maintain compliance in their cloud environments. Adhering to best practices such as defining policies, automated remediation, RBAC, regular audits, and employee training ensures that compliance remains a top priority across the organization. Leveraging cloud provider compliance services and engaging in third-party audits demonstrates the organization's commitment to compliance and security, instilling confidence in customers and stakeholders. Continuous compliance monitoring and enforcement foster a secure and compliant cloud environment, mitigating risks and ensuring the confidentiality, integrity, and availability of data and services.

30.2.1. Compliance Monitoring Components:

- **Continuous Compliance Scanning:** Automated tools continuously scan cloud resources to assess their compliance with relevant regulations and policies. These tools evaluate configurations, access controls, encryption, and other security measures to identify any deviations from compliance standards.

- **Real-Time Alerts and Notifications:** Setting up real-time alerts and notifications allows organizations to promptly address compliance violations. Automated alerts ensure that potential issues are quickly identified and remediated, reducing the risk of non-compliance and potential security breaches.

- **Audit Logging and Monitoring:** Enabling audit logging and monitoring tracks changes to cloud resources, user activities, and access permissions. Audit logs provide a detailed record of events, which is essential for compliance audits and investigations, ensuring transparency and accountability.

- **Vulnerability Management:** Automated vulnerability management tools scan cloud resources for security vulnerabilities and prioritize their remediation. Regular vulnerability scans help maintain a secure and compliant cloud environment by addressing potential security risks proactively.

- **Compliance Dashboards and Reporting:** Compliance dashboards and reporting tools provide a comprehensive view of the organization's compliance status and trends. These dashboards assist stakeholders in monitoring compliance efforts and identifying areas that require attention or improvement.

30.2.2. Best Practices for Compliance Enforcement:

- **Define and Document Policies:** Clearly defining and documenting compliance policies, including regulatory requirements and internal security standards, ensures that all relevant stakeholders are aware of and can adhere to these policies.

- **Implement Infrastructure as Code (IaC):** Leveraging Infrastructure as Code templates helps define and enforce compliance policies for cloud resources. IaC enables consistent provisioning and reduces the risk of misconfigurations that could lead to compliance issues.

- **Automated Remediation:** Implement automated remediation actions for common compliance violations. For example, automatically disabling public access to misconfigured S3 buckets helps maintain data security and compliance.

- **Role-Based Access Control (RBAC):** Enforcing RBAC ensures that access to cloud resources is restricted based on job roles and responsibilities. This approach limits access to authorized personnel, promoting data security and confidentiality.

- **Regular Compliance Audits:** Conducting regular compliance audits helps evaluate the effectiveness of compliance measures and identifies areas for improvement. Compliance audits enable organizations to stay proactive in maintaining compliance.

- **Training and Awareness:** Providing training and awareness programs for employees and stakeholders regarding compliance requirements and best practices fosters a culture of compliance and security within the organization.

- **Cloud Security Posture Management (CSPM):** Utilizing CSPM tools continuously monitors and assesses the security posture of cloud resources. These tools help identify security misconfigurations and enforce compliance policies.

- **Third-Party Auditing: Engaging third-party** auditing firms to conduct independent audits of the cloud environment ensures unbiased validation of compliance efforts, adding credibility to the organization's compliance posture.

30.2.3. Cloud Provider Compliance Services:

Leveraging compliance services provided by cloud providers, such as AWS Artifact and Azure Compliance Manager, offers access to compliance-related documentation, reports, and attestations that support internal and external audits.

30.3 Auditing and Reporting in Cloud Environments

Auditing and reporting are vital components of cloud governance, providing insights into compliance, security, and resource utilization. By centralizing and monitoring audit logs, organizations can promptly respond to security incidents and ensure compliance with regulatory requirements. Effective reporting practices, including defining requirements, regular reporting, executive summaries, and data visualization, enhance the clarity and usability of reports for various stakeholders. By implementing automation and leveraging cloud provider reporting services, organizations can streamline the auditing and reporting process, improving overall cloud governance and transparency.

30.3.1. Importance of Auditing and Reporting in the Cloud:

- **Compliance Verification:** Auditing verifies that cloud resources and operations comply with regulatory requirements, industry standards, and internal policies. It provides evidence of adherence to compliance measures during audits and ensures that the organization meets its obligations, avoiding potential legal and financial consequences.

- **Security and Risk Management:** Auditing helps identify security vulnerabilities, misconfigurations, and potential risks within the cloud environment. By regularly reviewing audit logs, organizations can detect and respond to security incidents promptly, safeguarding sensitive data and preventing breaches that could lead to data breaches and reputational damage.

- **Usage Tracking and Cost Optimization:** Cloud auditing tracks resource usage and expenditure, helping organizations optimize their cloud spending. It allows for accurate allocation of costs to specific projects or departments, identifies underutilized resources, and assists in making informed decisions for cost optimization and budget planning.

- **Incident Response and Forensics:** Auditing data supports incident response and forensic investigations. By tracing events and actions across cloud resources, organizations can reconstruct the timeline of security incidents and understand their impact, facilitating post-incident analysis and remediation.

- **Performance Monitoring:** Auditing provides insights into the performance of cloud services and applications. Analyzing audit data helps identify performance bottlenecks and aids in capacity planning for improved service delivery and customer experience.

30.3.2. Key Elements of Cloud Auditing:

- **Audit Logs:** Audit logs record events and activities performed within the cloud environment. These logs capture critical information, such as user actions, resource changes, and access attempts, facilitating post-incident analysis and compliance verification.

- **Log Aggregation and Centralization:** Centralized log aggregation gathers audit logs from multiple cloud services and regions into a centralized repository. This allows for consistent monitoring, analysis, and reporting, enabling a holistic view of the cloud environment.

- **Real-Time Monitoring:** Real-time monitoring of audit logs enables prompt detection of security incidents and potential compliance violations. Automated alerts and notifications ensure timely response to critical events, minimizing the impact of security breaches.

- **Data Retention and Archiving:** Establish data retention and archiving policies to ensure audit logs are preserved for the required duration, meeting compliance requirements and supporting investigations. Adequate data storage ensures historical data availability for future analysis.

30.3.3. Best Practices for Effective Reporting:

- **Define Reporting Requirements:** Define the key metrics, KPIs, and compliance objectives that need to be included in cloud reports. Tailor the reports to suit the needs of different stakeholders, such as IT teams, management, and auditors, to ensure they receive relevant and actionable information.

- **Regular and Scheduled Reporting:** Implement regular and scheduled reporting to maintain ongoing visibility into the cloud environment. Regular reports help in identifying trends and deviations over time, enabling proactive measures to address emerging issues.

- **Executive Summaries:** Provide executive summaries in reports to highlight critical insights, risks, and compliance status in a concise manner. These summaries help senior management make informed decisions and prioritize actions without delving into technical details.

- **Visualization and Dashboards:** Use data visualization techniques and dashboards to present audit data in an easy-to-understand format. Graphs, charts, and visual representations enhance the readability of reports, allowing stakeholders to quickly grasp key information.

- **Compliance Attestations:** Include compliance attestations and evidence in reports to support claims of adherence to specific compliance standards. This reinforces transparency and trust with customers, regulatory authorities, and other stakeholders.

- **Automation:** Automate the generation and distribution of reports to save time and ensure consistency. Automation reduces the risk of manual errors and ensures timely delivery of reports, enabling stakeholders to stay up-to-date with the latest information.

- **Secure Access to Reports:** Control access to audit reports and ensure they are available only to authorized personnel. Securely share reports with stakeholders and maintain data confidentiality to protect sensitive information.

30.3.4. Cloud Provider Reporting Services:

Leverage cloud provider reporting services such as AWS Config, AWS CloudTrail, Azure Monitor, and Google Cloud Audit Logs. These services offer built-in capabilities for collecting, analyzing, and visualizing audit logs, streamlining the auditing and reporting process. By utilizing these services, organizations can take advantage of cloud providers' expertise and tools to enhance their cloud governance efforts.

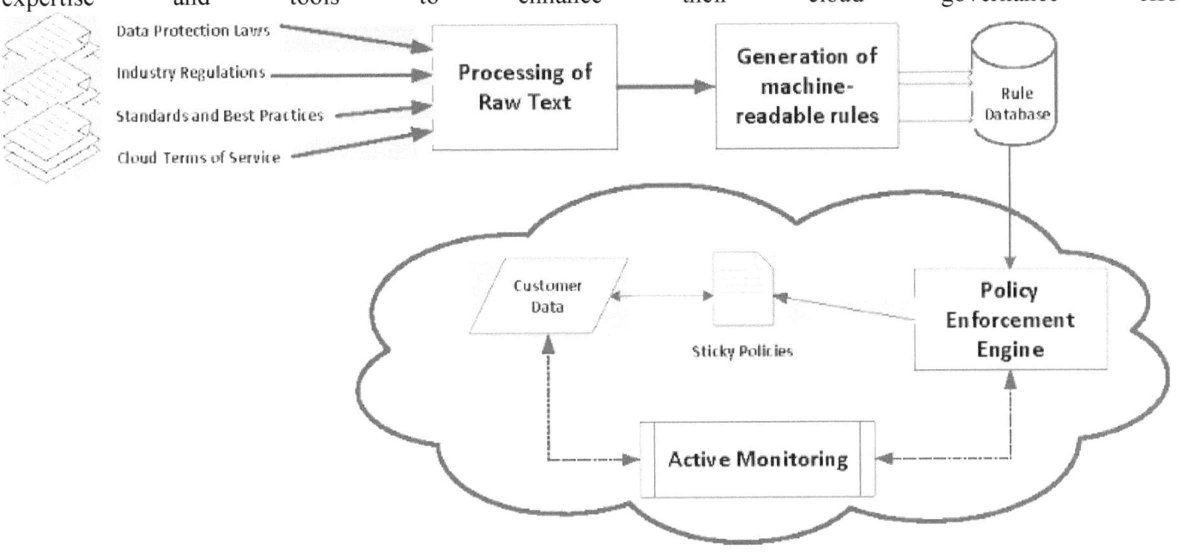

Exercise

Multiple Choice Questions

1. What is the primary benefit of using Infrastructure as Code (IaC) in cloud governance?

a. Improved cloud resource utilization

b. Faster deployment of cloud resources

c. Reduced manual efforts and human errors

d. Enhanced security of cloud infrastructure

2. Which tool enforces desired configurations and security policies across multiple cloud instances and applications?

a. AWS CloudFormation

b. Azure Resource Manager (ARM) templates

c. Chef

d. Terraform

3. What do Cloud Governance Policy Engines do?

a. Enforce security policies within cloud applications

b. Continuously monitor cloud resources for security vulnerabilities

c. Define and enforce policies across cloud resources

d. Manage the configuration of cloud instances

4. Which feature of cloud governance tools ensures resources are automatically scaled based on workload demands?

a. Continuous Compliance Monitoring

b. Self-Service Portals

c. Auto-Scaling

d. Infrastructure as Code (IaC)

5. What is the purpose of automated resource tagging in cloud governance?

a. Ensuring access control based on user roles

b. Enforcing encryption of cloud resources

c. Automatically applying resource tags based on predefined rules

d. Monitoring real-time compliance status

6. How do self-service portals streamline resource provisioning in cloud governance?

a. Enforce compliance policies during resource requests

b. Automate configuration management of cloud instances

c. Allow users to request and provision cloud resources with predefined policies

d. Implement continuous compliance monitoring for cloud resources

7. What does continuous compliance monitoring provide in cloud governance?

a. Real-time alerts for cloud resource utilization

b. Automated remediation actions for security issues

c. Audit logging and monitoring of cloud resources

d. Regular assessment of cloud resources against compliance standards

8. How do audit logs contribute to cloud governance?

a. Automate resource provisioning in cloud environments

b. Monitor cloud resource usage and cost optimization

c. Provide real-time security alerts and notifications

d. Track user activities and resource changes for compliance verification

9. What is the significance of data visualization in cloud governance reports?

a. Automate the generation of cloud governance reports

b. Present audit data in a concise format for executives

c. Provide evidence for compliance attestations

d. Continuously monitor cloud resources for security vulnerabilities

Review Questions

1. What are the key benefits of implementing infrastructure as code (IaC) in cloud environments?

2. How do configuration management tools such as Chef and Puppet contribute to cloud governance?

3. What role do cloud governance policy engines play in managing cloud resources?

4. How does continuous compliance monitoring contribute to cloud governance?

5. What are the advantages of automated resource tagging in cloud governance?

6. How do self-service portals enhance cloud governance?

7. How does auto-scaling contribute to cost optimization in cloud governance?

8. What role does automated security scanning play in cloud governance?

Answer Section

Multiple Choice Questions

1. c) Reduced manual efforts and human errors

2. c) Chef

3. c) Define and enforce policies across cloud resources

4. c) Auto-Scaling

5. c) Automatically applying resource tags based on predefined rules

6. c) Allow users to request and provision cloud resources with predefined policies

7. d) Regular assessment of cloud resources against compliance standards

8. d) Track user activities and resource changes for compliance verification

9. b) Present audit data in a concise format for executives

Review Questions

1. Infrastructure as code (IaC) allows organizations to manage their cloud resources through code, ensuring consistency and repeatability in the provisioning and management of cloud infrastructure. The primary benefits of IaC include reduced manual efforts and human errors, faster deployment of cloud resources, improved resource utilization, and better version control. By defining infrastructure configurations in code, teams can easily track changes, rollback to previous versions, and automate the entire provisioning process, leading to increased efficiency and agility in cloud operations.

2. Configuration management tools like Chef and Puppet automate the configuration and management of cloud instances and applications, ensuring they adhere to desired configurations and security policies. These tools enable organizations to maintain consistency across cloud resources by automatically enforcing configurations and applying updates at scale. By centralizing the management of configurations, organizations can efficiently monitor and control changes, reducing the risk of security vulnerabilities and ensuring compliance with internal standards and regulatory requirements.

3. Cloud governance policy engines allow organizations to define and enforce policies across their cloud resources. These engines continuously monitor cloud assets and services, evaluating them against predefined policies to identify compliance violations. In case of non-compliant resources, policy engines trigger automated remediation actions or notifications, ensuring that the cloud environment remains compliant with security, regulatory, and cost optimization requirements. By leveraging policy engines, organizations can maintain governance efficiency and minimize the potential risks associated with misconfigurations or unauthorized access.

4. Continuous compliance monitoring tools regularly assess cloud resources against industry standards and compliance requirements. These tools provide real-time visibility into compliance status, promptly identifying deviations or violations. By continuously monitoring cloud assets, organizations can proactively address compliance issues, minimize security risks, and maintain the desired security posture. Automated alerts and notifications ensure that relevant stakeholders are informed of compliance status and any necessary actions required to rectify non-compliant resources, promoting a secure and compliant cloud environment.

5. Automated resource tagging simplifies resource management and cost allocation in cloud environments. By applying tags automatically based on predefined rules, organizations can categorize resources, track usage, and allocate costs to specific projects or departments effectively. This automation ensures consistency in resource tagging practices, preventing human errors and reducing the risk of mislabeled or untagged resources. Additionally, resource tagging enables better control over access permissions and facilitates policy enforcement based on resource categories, contributing to improved governance and resource optimization.

6. Self-service portals streamline resource provisioning by providing a user-friendly interface for teams to request and deploy cloud resources following predefined governance policies. Through self-service portals, teams can access approved resources with the necessary security checks and compliance verifications in place. This automation reduces the burden on central IT teams and promotes agility in resource provisioning. Additionally, self-service portals enforce governance policies during resource requests, ensuring that cloud assets are provisioned according to organizational standards, leading to a more controlled and compliant cloud environment.

7. Auto-scaling automatically adjusts the number of cloud resources based on workload demands. By dynamically scaling resources up or down, organizations can optimize resource utilization and cost-effectiveness. During periods of high demand, auto-scaling provisions additional resources to handle the workload, ensuring optimal performance. Conversely, during periods of low demand, auto-scaling reduces resource instances, minimizing costs. This capability allows organizations to pay for resources only when needed, avoiding overprovisioning and unnecessary expenditures, thus contributing to efficient resource management and cost optimization.

8. Automated security scanning continuously monitors cloud resources for security vulnerabilities, misconfigurations, and potential threats. By providing real-time security alerts and notifications, automated security scanning tools enable organizations to promptly respond to security incidents, minimizing the impact of potential breaches. Additionally, these tools often offer automated remediation actions, allowing quick and efficient resolution of security issues. By integrating automated security scanning into cloud governance practices, organizations can maintain a strong security posture, ensuring the confidentiality, integrity, and availability of data and services in the cloud.

Chapter 31: Cloud Native Storage Solutions

31.1: Object Storage in the Cloud - A Deep Dive

Object Storage in the cloud has revolutionized the way businesses handle data storage and management. Its scalable, reliable, and cost-effective nature, combined with the flat namespace and metadata-driven approach, offers simplicity, flexibility, and data durability. From media content distribution to data backup and IoT data storage, Object Storage caters to a wide range of cloud-based use cases, making it a foundational element in the modern cloud computing landscape. Its impact is felt across various industries, driving innovation and efficiency in managing ever-expanding volumes of data in the cloud era.

31.1.1. Understanding Object Storage

In contrast to traditional file or block storage, Object Storage takes a unique approach to organize and store data. Instead of organizing data into a hierarchical file system with directories and folders, Object Storage treats each piece of data as an individual entity called an "object." An object consists of three essential components:

- **Data:** The actual content, whether it's a document, image, video, audio file, or any other type of unstructured data.

- **Metadata:** Descriptive information about the object, which can include attributes such as creation date, author, size, and custom-defined metadata relevant to the specific use case.

- **Unique Identifier:** Each object is associated with a Universally Unique Identifier (UUID) or a similar identifier. This unique identifier ensures that the object is addressable and easily retrievable, regardless of its physical location within the Object Storage infrastructure.

- The use of unique identifiers allows Object Storage to adopt a flat namespace. In a flat namespace, all objects are stored in a single, large pool, and they are not organized into complex directory structures. This simplicity makes Object Storage highly scalable and efficient for handling massive volumes of unstructured data.

31.1.2. Core Principles of Object Storage

- **Scalability:** One of the primary advantages of Object Storage is its exceptional scalability. Organizations can store an almost limitless amount of data without facing traditional fixed capacity limits. Object Storage achieves scalability by distributing data across multiple storage nodes or data centers. As data storage needs grow, new nodes can be added seamlessly, allowing for the dynamic expansion of the storage infrastructure.

- **Durability and Redundancy:** Object Storage ensures data durability and availability through data replication. Objects are redundantly stored across multiple storage nodes or geographically dispersed data centers. This redundancy reduces the risk of data loss due to hardware failures or catastrophic events. Even if one storage node fails, the data remains accessible and intact from other replicas.

- **Data Accessibility:** The unique identifier associated with each object enables easy and efficient data access from anywhere within the cloud infrastructure. This is particularly beneficial for distributed applications and services that require data access across different geographic regions. Developers and applications can directly reference objects by their unique identifiers without navigating complex directory structures.

- **Simplicity and Flexibility:** Object Storage's flat namespace and metadata-driven approach simplify data management. Unlike traditional storage methods that may require adherence to specific file system structures, Object Storage accommodates various data types seamlessly. This flexibility makes it well-suited for storing diverse data, ranging from simple documents to large multimedia files.

31.1.3. Benefits of Object Storage in the Cloud

- **Cost-Effectiveness:** Object Storage follows a pay-as-you-go model, where users only pay for the storage they consume. This cost-effective approach eliminates the need for upfront investments in hardware, making Object Storage a compelling option for businesses of all sizes. It allows organizations to scale their storage infrastructure according to actual usage, reducing unnecessary expenses.

- **Data Resilience and Reliability:** The data redundancy and distribution mechanisms of Object Storage ensure high levels of data resilience and reliability. With multiple replicas of each object, data remains available even if individual storage nodes or data centers experience failures. This robustness enhances data protection and reduces the risk of data loss.

- **Scalability on Demand:** Object Storage's inherent scalability allows organizations to adapt to changing data storage requirements without disrupting operations. Scaling up or down can be achieved easily and seamlessly, providing the agility needed to meet evolving business demands.

- **Global Accessibility:** Object Storage's distribution across multiple data centers in various regions enables low-latency data access for users around the world. This global accessibility is particularly crucial for applications with a geographically diverse user base, ensuring a consistent user experience regardless of the user's location.

31.1.4. Use Cases of Object Storage in the Cloud

- **Media and Content Distribution:** Object Storage is an ideal solution for hosting and distributing media content, including images, videos, and audio files. Its scalability and global accessibility facilitate efficient content delivery to end-users, ensuring a smooth user experience.

- **Data Backup and Archiving:** Businesses can utilize Object Storage for secure and cost-efficient data backup and long-term archiving. The redundancy and durability features of Object Storage make it a reliable choice for data retention, ensuring data remains safe and accessible for extended periods.

- **IoT Data Storage:** The Internet of Things (IoT) generates vast amounts of data from connected devices. Object Storage efficiently handles the storage and processing of this data, supporting real-time analysis and decision-making for IoT applications.

- **Web Applications and Content Management:** Object Storage is well-suited for web applications, especially those that require the storage and delivery of dynamic content and user-generated dat Its ability to handle various data types and accommodate fluctuating demands makes it an excellent fit for modern web applications.

31.2: Block Storage Options and Use Cases - A Deep Dive

Block storage options in the cloud provide businesses with high-performance, scalable, and reliable storage solutions for a wide range of applications and workloads. Whether hosting databases, running critical enterprise applications, managing virtualized environments, or conducting data-intensive analytics, block storage forms the underlying foundation for efficient and effective data management in the cloud. By choosing the appropriate block storage type and implementing it with best practices, organizations can optimize their cloud infrastructure and elevate their overall computing performance, ensuring a seamless and reliable experience for their applications and users.

31.2.1. Understanding Block Storage

Block storage operates by managing data in fixed-sized chunks known as "blocks." Each block is treated as an individual unit, and the storage system assigns a unique address to it. Unlike Object Storage, which organizes data as objects with associated metadata and unique identifiers, block storage lacks hierarchical structures or specific identifiers for individual blocks.

Block storage is typically accessed through storage protocols like iSCSI (Internet Small Computer System Interface) or Fibre Channel. This raw storage capacity can be directly formatted and used by an operating system or application, making it a flexible and versatile solution for various data storage needs.

31.2.2. Block Storage Options in the Cloud

- **Amazon Elastic Block Store (EBS):** Amazon Web Services (AWS) offers Elastic Block Store (EBS), a scalable block storage service specifically designed for use with Amazon EC2 instances. EBS volumes provide persistent and high-performance storage for applications running on EC2 instances. AWS offers several types of EBS volumes, each optimized for specific use cases:

- **General Purpose SSD (GP2):** Offers balanced performance for a wide range of workloads.

- **Provisioned IOPS SSD (IO1):** Provides high-performance storage for I/O-intensive database workloads.

- **Cold HDD (SC1):** Delivers cost-effective storage for less frequently accessed dat

- **Google Persistent Disk (PD):** Google Cloud Platform (GCP) offers Persistent Disk (PD) as its block storage solution for Google Compute Engine instances. PD volumes provide consistent performance and durability. GCP offers two types of PD:

- **Standard Persistent Disk:** Suitable for general-purpose workloads.

- **SSD Persistent Disk:** Offers high-performance storage for I/O-intensive applications.

- **Microsoft Azure Managed Disks:** Microsoft Azure provides Azure Managed Disks, which are persistent and scalable disks designed for use with Azure virtual machines. Azure Managed Disks come in three types:

  - **Standard HDD:** Offers cost-effective storage for non-critical workloads.
  - **Standard SSD:** Provides a balance of performance and cost for general-purpose applications.
  - **Premium SSD:** Delivers high-performance storage for mission-critical workloads.

31.2.3. Use Cases of Block Storage

- **Database Hosting:** Block storage is particularly well-suited for hosting databases that require high-performance and low-latency access to data. Databases, being central to many applications, demand reliable and fast storage to handle transactional and analytical workloads effectively.

- **Enterprise Applications:** Business-critical applications, such as ERP (Enterprise Resource Planning) systems and CRM (Customer Relationship Management) software, often require persistent and high-performance storage. Block storage provides the performance and data durability necessary to support these mission-critical applications and ensure smooth operations.

- **Virtual Machine Storage:** In virtualized environments, block storage serves as the underlying storage for virtual machine instances. Virtual machines rely on block storage for boot volumes and application data, enabling seamless migration and management of virtualized workloads. Block storage's low-latency access ensures optimal performance for virtualized environments.

- **Big Data and Analytics:** Data-intensive workloads, such as big data analytics and machine learning, require fast and efficient data processing. Block storage offers the necessary capacity and performance to handle vast amounts of data and support complex computational tasks, making it a vital component for these demanding workloads.

31.3 File Storage and Network-Attached Storage (NAS) in the Cloud: Empowering Seamless Data Management and Collaboration - A Deep Dive

File storage and Network-Attached Storage (NAS) are integral components of cloud computing, revolutionizing the way data is managed, shared, and accessed. Their centralized nature, ease of collaboration, scalability, data redundancy, and global accessibility make them essential tools for businesses seeking efficient data management solutions. Whether for document collaboration, media management, VDI, or personal file sharing, file storage and NAS in the cloud empower organizations and individuals alike to embrace a more streamlined and productive data-driven future. By leveraging these powerful storage technologies, businesses can harness the full potential of cloud computing to enhance collaboration, productivity, and data scalability in an ever-evolving digital landscape.

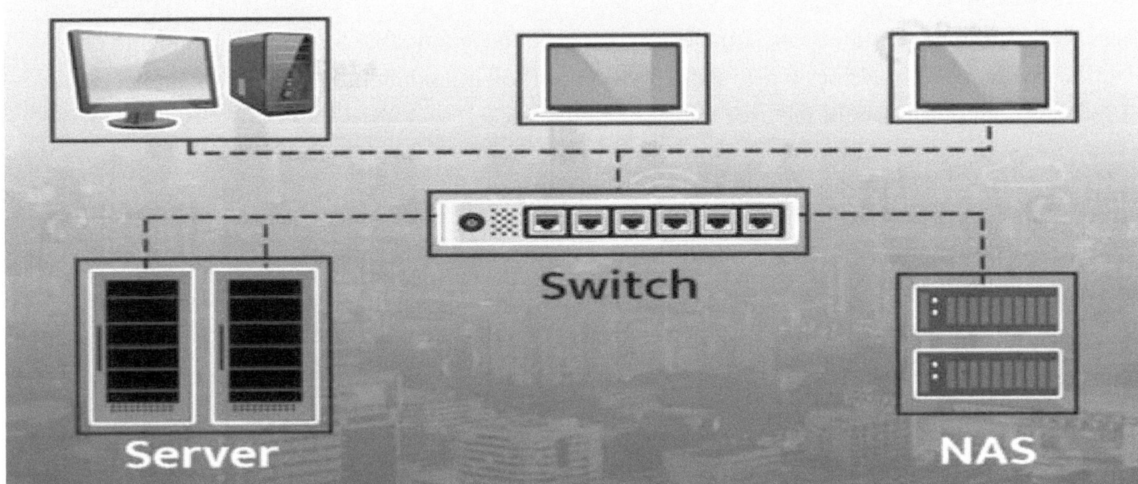

31.3.1. File Storage in the Cloud

File storage represents a straightforward and widely adopted method for storing and organizing data in the cloud. Unlike block storage, which manages data in fixed-sized blocks, file storage organizes data in a hierarchical structure of files and folders. Each file contains data, while folders provide a logical way to group and categorize related files. This hierarchical arrangement simplifies data organization, allowing users to navigate and locate specific files easily.

31.3.2. Network-Attached Storage (NAS) in the Cloud

Network-Attached Storage (NAS) takes file storage to the next level by providing a dedicated storage appliance that is directly connected to a network. In the context of cloud computing, NAS is a file-level storage solution accessed over a network, typically through standard file sharing protocols like NFS (Network File System) or SMB/CIFS (Server Message Block / Common Internet File System).

One of the key advantages of NAS is its ability to facilitate simultaneous access to files by multiple users and applications. It acts as a shared repository accessible over the network, making it an excellent solution for collaborative environments and scenarios where seamless data sharing and access are critical.

31.3.3. Features and Benefits of File Storage and NAS in the Cloud

- **Centralized Data Repository:** Both file storage and NAS offer a centralized repository for data, consolidating all relevant information in one location. This centralized approach simplifies data management, ensuring data consistency and reducing the chances of data fragmentation across different environments or systems.

- **Easy Data Sharing and Collaboration:** File storage and NAS excel in facilitating seamless data sharing and collaboration among users and teams. Cloud-based file storage systems often come with built-in sharing and access control features, making it simple to grant appropriate permissions and share files securely. This enhances productivity and teamwork across distributed teams and remote workers.

- **Scalability and Flexibility:** Cloud-based file storage and NAS solutions are highly scalable, allowing organizations to expand their storage capacity as their data requirements grow. Cloud providers handle the underlying infrastructure, eliminating the need for businesses to invest in and manage hardware upgrades. This scalability ensures that data storage can easily adapt to changing business needs.

- **Data Redundancy and Reliability:** Many cloud providers offer data redundancy and disaster recovery capabilities for file storage and NAS services. By replicating data across multiple data centers or geographical regions, they guarantee data integrity and availability, even in the event of hardware failures or natural disasters. This level of redundancy enhances data reliability and ensures business continuity.

- **Global Accessibility:** Cloud-based file storage and NAS enable users to access their data from anywhere with an internet connection. This feature is particularly valuable for distributed teams or organizations with multiple offices worldwide, fostering efficient collaboration and real-time access to critical information, regardless of the user's physical location.

31.3.4. Use Cases of File Storage and NAS in the Cloud

- **Document Management and Collaboration:** File storage and NAS are ideal for document management and collaboration scenarios, facilitating seamless sharing of documents, spreadsheets, and presentations among team members, regardless of their physical locations. Teams can collaborate in real-time and track version histories, improving productivity and document control.

- **Media and Content Management:** Cloud-based file storage and NAS are commonly used in media and content management industries, where large files, such as images, videos, and audio files, need to be stored, organized, and shared with stakeholders, customers, or the public. This enables efficient content distribution and management for media companies, marketing teams, and creative professionals.

- **Virtual Desktop Infrastructure (VDI):** In Virtual Desktop Infrastructure (VDI) environments, NAS plays a crucial role in providing shared storage for virtual desktops. With a central storage repository, VDI deployments can ensure consistent user experiences across multiple virtual machines while efficiently managing user data and profiles.

- **Home Directory and Personal File Sharing:** Cloud-based NAS is valuable for individual users who wish to maintain a centralized repository for personal files. Personal cloud storage solutions leverage NAS capabilities to provide a secure and private storage space accessible across users' various devices, ensuring data synchronization and easy file access.

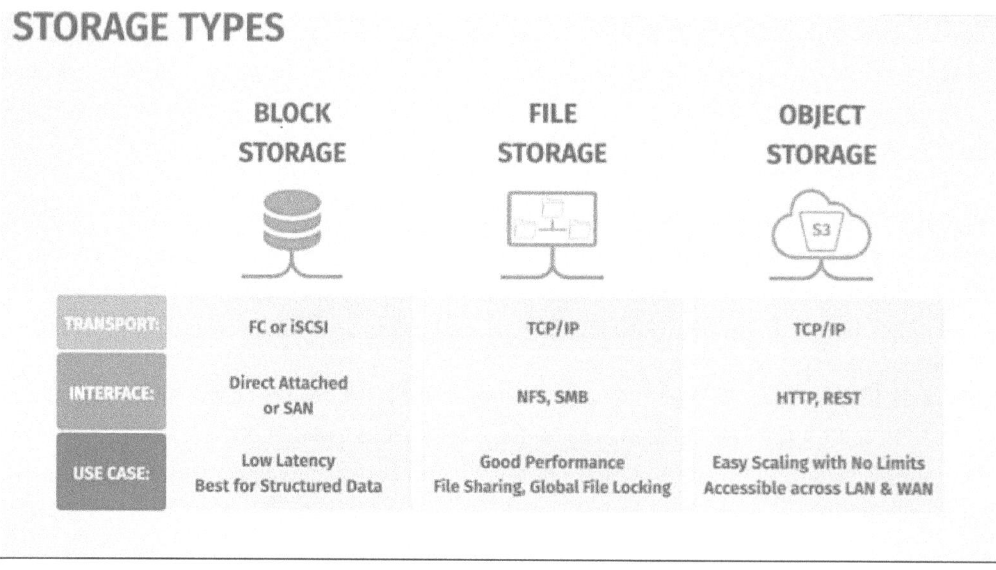

Exercise

Multiple Choice Questions

1. What makes Object Storage different from traditional file or block storage?
a) Object Storage organizes data into hierarchical file systems, while file and block storage treat each piece of data as an individual object.
b) Object Storage uses unique identifiers for each data object, while file and block storage use standard file paths or block addresses.
c) Object Storage stores data in fixed-sized blocks, while file and block storage store data as individual objects with metadata.
d) Object Storage allows data to be accessed directly through the storage protocols iSCSI or Fibre Channel, while file and block storage require additional middleware.
2. What are the core principles of Object Storage?
a) Low latency access and hierarchical data organization
b) Scalability, data redundancy, and file system hierarchy
c) Simplicity, high-performance storage, and metadata-driven approach
d) Scalability, durability, and flat namespace with unique identifiers
3. What is one of the primary advantages of Object Storage?
a) Reduced data redundancy for better cost optimization
b) High-latency access for faster data retrieval
c) Limited scalability due to fixed capacity limits
d) Ability to store almost limitless amounts of data
4. What storage option in the cloud is best suited for hosting databases with high-performance and low-latency access requirements?
a) File Storage
b) Network-Attached Storage (NAS)
c) Amazon Elastic Block Store (EBS)
d) Object Storage
5. Which cloud provider offers "Standard SSD" as a type of block storage?
a) Microsoft Azure
b) Google Cloud Platform (GCP)
c) Amazon Web Services (AWS)
d) IBM Cloud
6. In the context of cloud computing, what is the primary benefit of Network-Attached Storage (NAS)?
a) Efficiently managing data in fixed-sized blocks
b) Supporting dynamic expansion of storage infrastructure
c) Enabling direct access to data through iSCSI or Fibre Channel
d) Facilitating simultaneous access to files by multiple users
7. Which of the following is NOT a feature or benefit of file storage and NAS in the cloud?
a) Scalability and Flexibility
b) Data Resilience and Reliability
c) Global Accessibility
d) Hierarchical Data Organization
8. What cloud storage type is particularly well-suited for media content distribution and efficient content delivery to end-users?
a) Block Storage
b) File Storage
c) Network-Attached Storage (NAS)
d) Object Storage
9. In a cloud-based file storage system, how does data redundancy enhance reliability and data availability?
a) Data is distributed across multiple storage nodes, reducing latency.
b) Data is stored in fixed-sized blocks, ensuring efficient data retrieval.
c) Multiple replicas of each file are created, ensuring accessibility if one storage node fails.
d) Data is organized hierarchically in a single large pool, enabling scalability.

Review Questions

1. What are the key components of an object in Object Storage, and how does the use of unique identifiers contribute to its flat namespace?

2. Explain how Object Storage achieves data durability and redundancy, and how it ensures data availability in the event of hardware failures or catastrophic events.

3. What are the benefits of Object Storage in terms of cost-effectiveness, data resilience, and global accessibility?

4. Compare and contrast the use cases of Object Storage and Block Storage in the cloud, citing examples of scenarios where each storage type excels.

5. What are the core principles of Block Storage, and how does it differ from Object Storage in terms of data organization and access methods?

6. Describe the advantages of using Network-Attached Storage (NAS) in the cloud for document collaboration and media content management.

7. Explain how File Storage and NAS in the cloud enhance data scalability and accessibility for distributed teams and organizations with multiple offices worldwide.

8. Compare the advantages of Object Storage, Block Storage, and File Storage in terms of data organization, scalability, and suitability for specific cloud-based use cases.

Answer Section

Multiple Choice Questions

1. b) Object Storage uses unique identifiers for each data object, while file and block storage use standard file paths or block addresses.

2. d) Scalability, durability, and flat namespace with unique identifiers

3. d) Ability to store almost limitless amounts of data

4. c) Amazon Elastic Block Store (EBS)

5. a) Microsoft Azure

6. d) Facilitating simultaneous access to files by multiple users

7. d) Hierarchical Data Organization

8. d) Object Storage

9. c) Multiple replicas of each file are created, ensuring accessibility if one storage node fails.

Review Questions

1. An object in Object Storage consists of three components: data (the actual content), metadata (descriptive information), and a unique identifier. The use of unique identifiers allows each object to be addressable and easily retrievable, regardless of its physical location within the storage infrastructure. As a result, objects are stored in a single, large pool without complex directory structures, creating a flat namespace. This simplicity and addressability enable efficient scalability and easy data access, making Object Storage highly suitable for handling massive volumes of unstructured data.

2. Object Storage ensures data durability and redundancy by replicating objects across multiple storage nodes or geographically dispersed data centers. Each object has multiple replicas, which are updated synchronously or asynchronously. In case of hardware failures or catastrophic events, the data remains accessible from the surviving replicas, mitigating the risk of data loss. The distributed nature of Object Storage ensures that data is redundantly stored, providing data resilience and availability even in the face of individual storage node failures.

3. Object Storage follows a pay-as-you-go model, allowing users to pay only for the storage they consume. This cost-effectiveness eliminates the need for upfront investments in hardware and allows organizations to scale their storage infrastructure based on actual usage, reducing unnecessary expenses. Moreover, Object Storage's data redundancy mechanisms ensure high levels of data resilience and reliability. Objects are redundantly stored across multiple nodes or data centers, safeguarding data from hardware failures or disasters. Additionally, the unique identifier-based access enables global accessibility, allowing users to access their data from anywhere with an internet connection.

4. Object Storage is ideal for scenarios where unstructured data needs to be stored and accessed efficiently, such as media content distribution, data backup, and IoT data storage. It excels in handling large multimedia files and supports global accessibility for content delivery. On the other hand, Block Storage is best suited for hosting databases and enterprise applications that demand high-performance and low-latency access to data. Examples include hosting critical ERP systems, CRM software, and virtual

machine storage in virtualized environments. Both storage types offer unique advantages based on the specific needs of applications and workloads.

5. Block Storage manages data in fixed-sized chunks called "blocks" and assigns a unique address to each block. Unlike Object Storage, which treats each data piece as an individual object with unique identifiers, Block Storage lacks hierarchical structures or specific identifiers for individual blocks. Block Storage is accessed through storage protocols like iSCSI or Fibre Channel, allowing raw storage capacity to be directly formatted and used by an operating system or application. While Object Storage offers a flat namespace and metadata-driven approach, Block Storage operates at a lower level and does not provide inherent metadata.

6. Network-Attached Storage (NAS) facilitates simultaneous access to files by multiple users and applications, making it an excellent choice for document collaboration. It offers a shared repository accessible over the network, allowing teams to collaborate in real-time, track version histories, and improve document control. NAS also excels in media content management, where large files, such as images, videos, and audio, need to be organized and shared with stakeholders. Its centralized and scalable nature ensures efficient content distribution, making it valuable for media companies, marketing teams, and creative professionals.

7. File Storage and NAS in the cloud provide centralized data repositories, simplifying data management and reducing fragmentation across different systems. With scalable cloud-based solutions, organizations can easily expand their storage capacity to meet changing data requirements without investing in hardware upgrades. This scalability ensures that data remains accessible from anywhere with an internet connection, making it suitable for distributed teams and organizations with multiple global offices. Users can collaborate in real-time, share files securely, and access critical information regardless of their physical location, enhancing productivity and teamwork.

8. Object Storage offers a unique approach to data organization with its flat namespace and metadata-driven system, making it highly scalable for handling massive volumes of unstructured data. It excels in scenarios like media content distribution, data backup, and IoT data storage. Block Storage, with its fixed-sized blocks and direct access protocols, is ideal for hosting databases, critical applications, and virtual machine storage. It ensures low-latency access and high-performance storage. File Storage provides hierarchical data organization, simplifying data management and sharing. It's well-suited for document collaboration, media management, VDI, and personal file sharing. Each storage type caters to specific cloud-based use cases, offering unique advantages based on data requirements and application needs.

Chapter 32: Cloud Governance and Security Compliance

32.1: Security Governance in Cloud Environments - A Deep Dive

Security governance is a crucial aspect of cloud computing, ensuring the protection of valuable assets and sensitive data from a wide range of cyber threats. By adhering to sound security principles, addressing challenges proactively, and adopting best practices, organizations can build a secure cloud environment that fosters innovation, enhances customer trust, and propels business growth in the digital age. A robust security governance framework is fundamental to maximizing the benefits of cloud computing while minimizing security risks, enabling organizations to confidently embrace the full potential of the cloud.

32.1.1. Understanding Security Governance in Cloud Computing

Security governance is the foundation of a comprehensive security strategy in any organization. It refers to the framework of policies, processes, and controls that govern an organization's approach to security. In the context of cloud computing, security governance is paramount due to the critical importance of protecting sensitive data, applications, and infrastructure in a dynamic and distributed environment.

32.1.2. Principles of Security Governance in the Cloud

- **Risk Assessment and Management:** Effective security governance starts with a thorough risk assessment. Organizations must identify potential threats and vulnerabilities specific to their cloud environment. Risk management strategies, including risk mitigation plans and incident response protocols, should be in place to handle security incidents effectively.

- **Compliance and Regulatory Adherence:** Security governance ensures that the cloud environment complies with relevant data protection regulations, industry standards, and the organization's internal security policies. Compliance involves addressing data privacy, confidentiality, integrity, and other regulatory requirements.

- **Identity and Access Management (IAM):** IAM is a fundamental component of security governance in the cloud. It involves managing user identities, authentication mechanisms, access controls, and privileged access management. Proper IAM implementation ensures that only authorized users can access resources and data, reducing the risk of unauthorized access.

- **Data Encryption and Protection:** Data encryption plays a critical role in security governance. Encrypting data at rest and in transit protects sensitive information from unauthorized access or data breaches. Robust encryption mechanisms safeguard data confidentiality and integrity.

- **Continuous Monitoring and Auditing:** Regular monitoring, logging, and auditing of cloud resources are vital for detecting anomalies and potential security breaches. Continuous monitoring enables rapid incident response and helps organizations stay ahead of evolving threats, enhancing overall security posture.

32.1.3. Challenges in Security Governance for Cloud Environments

- **Shared Responsibility Model:** Cloud service providers follow a shared responsibility model, which means they are responsible for securing the underlying cloud infrastructure, while customers are responsible for securing their data, applications, and configurations. Understanding and effectively managing this shared responsibility model is crucial to avoid security gaps and misconfigurations.

- **Cloud Service Complexity:** Cloud environments often comprise multiple services and configurations, leading to increased complexity in managing security across diverse cloud services. Ensuring consistency in security controls across the environment can be challenging.

- **Data Sovereignty and Jurisdiction:** Data residing in cloud data centers located in different countries may be subject to varying data protection laws, leading to data sovereignty and jurisdiction challenges. Organizations must navigate these complexities to ensure compliance with relevant regulations.

32.1.4. Best Practices for Security Governance in the Cloud

- **Establish a Clear Security Policy:** Develop a comprehensive security policy that outlines roles, responsibilities, and best practices for all stakeholders involved in the cloud environment. Clearly define security controls and procedures to ensure adherence to security standards.

- **Continuous Education and Training:** Educate employees and users about security best practices and potential threats through regular training and awareness programs. An informed and vigilant workforce is an essential line of defense against cyber threats.

- **Implement Multi-Factor Authentication (MFA):** Enforce MFA to add an extra layer of security to user accounts. MFA significantly reduces the risk of unauthorized access, even if login credentials are compromised.

- **Regular Security Audits:** Conduct periodic security audits and penetration testing to identify vulnerabilities and address security gaps. Regular audits help organizations stay ahead of emerging threats and maintain a proactive security approach.

- **Use Security Automation:** Embrace security automation tools and technologies to implement security controls consistently and efficiently across the cloud environment. Automation helps reduce human errors and ensures uniform application of security measures.

32.2: Regulatory Compliance in the Cloud - A Comprehensive Exploration

Regulatory compliance in the cloud is a fundamental aspect for organizations handling sensitive data. Adhering to relevant regulations ensures data privacy, security, and integrity, building trust with customers and stakeholders. By understanding applicable regulations, choosing compliant cloud providers, and implementing strong security practices, organizations can confidently navigate the complex landscape of cloud compliance. Embracing best practices and obtaining relevant certifications and frameworks empowers organizations to harness the benefits of cloud computing while safeguarding sensitive information, thereby propelling them towards a secure and successful cloud journey.

32.2.1. The Importance of Regulatory Compliance in the Cloud

Regulatory compliance is a critical aspect of cloud computing, as it involves adhering to specific laws, regulations, and industry standards applicable to cloud service providers and their clients. Compliance is essential to protect sensitive data, maintain data privacy, and ensure data security, which fosters trust between organizations and their customers.

32.2.2. Challenges in Achieving Cloud Regulatory Compliance

- **Data Sovereignty and Jurisdiction:** Cloud data centers may be located in different countries, exposing organizations to diverse data protection and privacy laws. Ensuring compliance with varying regulations across multiple jurisdictions can be complex, especially when data crosses borders.

- **Shared Responsibility Model:** The shared responsibility model followed by cloud service providers means that both the provider and the customer have specific security responsibilities. Understanding and effectively meeting individual responsibilities within this model can pose challenges, especially if there is any misunderstanding about each party's obligations.

- **Auditing and Validation:** Compliance often requires periodic auditing and validation to ensure adherence to regulatory requirements. Maintaining a comprehensive trail of evidence and documentation for audits can be resource-intensive and time-consuming.

- **Data Protection and Encryption:** Different regulations may impose various data protection and encryption requirements. Organizations must implement robust encryption mechanisms and ensure that data is adequately protected throughout its lifecycle.

32.2.3. Best Practices for Ensuring Cloud Regulatory Compliance

- **Understand Applicable Regulations:** Identify and thoroughly understand the regulations relevant to your industry and the countries where data is processed and stored. Stay updated with changes in regulations to maintain ongoing compliance.

- **Select Compliant Cloud Providers:** Choose cloud service providers that have established compliance with relevant industry standards and certifications. Look for providers that offer transparency and detailed documentation on their security practices.

- **Data Classification and Segmentation:** Classify data based on sensitivity and regulatory requirements. Segregate data to ensure that it is adequately protected and accessible only to authorized personnel.

- **Implement Strong Access Controls:** Enforce robust identity and access management (IAM) practices. Utilize multi-factor authentication (MFA) and role-based access control (RBAC) to limit access to sensitive dat

- **Data Encryption and Key Management:** Implement end-to-end data encryption to protect data at rest and in transit. Employ proper key management practices to safeguard encryption keys and ensure their availability when needed.

- **Conduct Regular Audits and Assessments:** Perform regular internal and external audits to assess compliance status. Use third-party assessments to validate compliance and identify areas for improvement.

32.2.4. Cloud Compliance Certifications and Frameworks

- **ISO/IEC 27001:** An internationally recognized information security management system standard that covers a broad range of security controls.

- **SOC 2:** A report on the controls relevant to the security, availability, processing integrity, confidentiality, and privacy of cloud services. SOC 2 reports are commonly requested by customers and partners to evaluate a service provider's security controls.

- **HIPAA:** U.S. regulations that govern the privacy and security of protected health information (PHI). Organizations handling healthcare data must comply with HIPAA requirements to ensure the confidentiality and integrity of patient information.

- **GDPR:** The General Data Protection Regulation, a regulation in EU law on data protection and privacy for individuals within the European Union. GDPR imposes strict requirements on organizations that process personal data of EU residents.

32.3: Security Auditing and Incident Response - A Comprehensive Exploration

Security auditing and incident response are integral components of a robust cloud security strategy. Regular security audits help organizations identify and address vulnerabilities, while incident response ensures a swift and effective response to security breaches. By following best practices for security auditing and incident response, organizations can proactively safeguard their cloud environments and data, mitigating risks and enhancing overall security posture. By continuously evaluating and improving security measures, organizations can stay resilient in the face of evolving cyber threats and foster a secure cloud computing environment.

32.3.1. Security Auditing in the Cloud

Security auditing is a crucial process that involves assessing an organization's cloud infrastructure, applications, and processes to identify vulnerabilities, compliance gaps, and potential risks. The primary goal of security auditing is to ensure that the implemented security measures align with industry standards and regulatory requirements, thereby safeguarding sensitive data and maintaining a secure cloud environment.

32.3.2. Best Practices for Security Auditing in the Cloud

- **Regular Audits:** Conduct periodic security audits to assess the effectiveness of security controls and identify areas for improvement. Comprehensive audits should encompass all aspects of the cloud environment, including data access controls, identity management, encryption, and network security.

- **Third-Party Assessments:** Engage third-party security experts to conduct independent audits. Third-party assessments provide an unbiased perspective and can offer valuable insights into security vulnerabilities that may have been overlooked.

- **Compliance Checks:** Ensure that security audits include checks for compliance with relevant data protection regulations and industry standards. Evaluating data privacy, confidentiality, and integrity should be an integral part of security auditing.

- **Vulnerability Scanning and Penetration Testing:** Utilize automated vulnerability scanning and penetration testing tools to identify potential weaknesses and security gaps in the cloud infrastructure and applications. Regularly perform these tests to stay ahead of emerging threats.

- **Audit Trail and Documentation:** Maintain a comprehensive audit trail and documentation of security controls, configurations, and changes made to the cloud environment. This documentation is essential for future audits and incident investigations.

32.3.3. Incident Response in the Cloud

Incident response is a systematic approach to detecting, analyzing, and mitigating security incidents in the cloud environment. Effective incident response minimizes the impact of security breaches and helps organizations recover swiftly from such events.

32.3.4. Best Practices for Incident Response in the Cloud

- **Incident Response Plan:** Develop a detailed incident response plan that outlines the roles, responsibilities, and procedures for detecting, reporting, and responding to security incidents. Regularly update and communicate this plan to all relevant stakeholders.

- **Automated Incident Detection:** Implement automated monitoring and alerting mechanisms to quickly detect suspicious activities and potential security breaches. This can involve the use of security information and event management (SIEM) tools.

- **Escalation Procedures:** Establish clear escalation procedures to ensure that security incidents are promptly escalated to the appropriate personnel, including management and security teams. Rapid communication is essential for timely incident resolution.

- **Containment and Mitigation:** Once an incident is detected, take immediate action to contain the threat and mitigate its impact on the cloud environment. This may involve isolating affected systems or disabling compromised accounts.

- **Forensics and Investigation:** Conduct thorough forensic investigations to understand the scope and nature of the security incident. Preserve evidence and collect data to support incident analysis and, if needed, legal proceedings.

- **Communication and Reporting:** Communicate transparently with relevant stakeholders about the incident, its impact, and the steps being taken to address it. Timely and clear reporting is essential for maintaining trust and credibility.

Exercise

Multiple Choice Questions

1. What is the primary objective of security governance in cloud computing?

a. To ensure maximum data storage capacity in the cloud.

b. To protect valuable assets and sensitive data from cyber threats.

c. To achieve the lowest possible cost for cloud services.

d. To implement the latest cloud technologies.

2. Which principle of security governance involves identifying potential threats and vulnerabilities specific to the cloud environment?

a. Data Encryption and Protection

b. Compliance and Regulatory Adherence

c. Risk Assessment and Management

d. Continuous Monitoring and Auditing

3. What is the shared responsibility model in cloud computing?

a. Cloud providers are solely responsible for all security aspects.

b. Customers are solely responsible for all security aspects.

c. Cloud providers are responsible for the underlying infrastructure, and customers are responsible for securing their data and applications.

d. Customers are responsible for the underlying infrastructure, and cloud providers are responsible for securing their data and applications.

4. Which best practice for cloud regulatory compliance involves enforcing an extra layer of security to user accounts?

a. Implement Multi-Factor Authentication (MFA)

b. Continuous Education and Training

c. Data Classification and Segmentation

d. Regular Security Audits

5. What is the primary goal of security auditing in the cloud?

a. To minimize cloud service complexity.

b. To achieve compliance with all data protection regulations.

c. To assess the effectiveness of security controls and identify vulnerabilities and risks.

d. To ensure data sovereignty and jurisdiction compliance.

6. Which best practice for incident response in the cloud involves isolating affected systems or disabling compromised accounts?

a. Automated Incident Detection

b. Escalation Procedures

c. Containment and Mitigation

d. Forensics and Investigation

7. How can organizations ensure consistent security controls across a diverse cloud service environment?

a. By conducting regular security audits and penetration testing.

b. By choosing cloud providers with a strong reputation for security.

c. By implementing automated monitoring and alerting mechanisms.

d. By clearly defining roles, responsibilities, and best practices in a security policy.

8. Why are third-party security assessments valuable in security auditing?

a. They provide an unbiased perspective and offer valuable insights into security vulnerabilities.

b. They are mandatory for regulatory compliance.

c. They are cheaper than conducting internal security audits.

d. They guarantee complete protection against cyber threats.

9. What is the primary objective of continuous monitoring and auditing in the cloud?

a. To maintain data sovereignty and jurisdiction compliance.

b. To ensure maximum data storage capacity in the cloud.

c. To reduce human errors and ensure uniform application of security measures.

d. To detect anomalies and potential security breaches for rapid incident response.

Review Questions

1. What is the significance of security governance in cloud computing, and how does it contribute to an organization's overall security posture?

2. What are the core principles of security governance in the cloud, and how do they contribute to an organization's security strategy?

3. What are the challenges organizations may face in achieving cloud regulatory compliance, and how can these challenges be overcome?

4. How can organizations ensure consistent security controls across diverse cloud services and environments?

5. Explain the significance of incident response in the cloud and its role in minimizing the impact of security breaches.

6. What are the best practices for conducting security audits in the cloud, and how do they contribute to a secure cloud environment?

7. Why is continuous monitoring and auditing critical in the cloud environment, and how does it enhance overall security?

8. Explain the significance of data encryption and protection in cloud security and its role in safeguarding sensitive information.

Answer Section

Multiple Choice Questions

1. b) To protect valuable assets and sensitive data from cyber threats.

2. c) Risk Assessment and Management

3. c) Cloud providers are responsible for the underlying infrastructure, and customers are responsible for securing their data and applications.

4. a) Implement Multi-Factor Authentication (MFA)

5. c) To assess the effectiveness of security controls and identify vulnerabilities and risks.

6. c) Containment and Mitigation

7. d) By clearly defining roles, responsibilities, and best practices in a security policy.

8. a) They provide an unbiased perspective and offer valuable insights into security vulnerabilities.

9. d) To detect anomalies and potential security breaches for rapid incident response.

Review Questions

1. Security governance in cloud computing is crucial as it establishes the framework of policies, processes, and controls that guide an organization's approach to security. By adopting a robust security governance strategy, organizations can protect valuable assets and sensitive data from cyber threats, comply with relevant regulations, and build customer trust. It ensures that security measures align with best practices and industry standards, allowing businesses to confidently embrace the cloud while minimizing security risks. Overall, security governance plays a pivotal role in enhancing an organization's security posture and fostering a secure cloud environment.

2. The core principles of security governance in the cloud encompass risk assessment and management, compliance and regulatory adherence, identity and access management (IAM), data encryption and protection, and continuous monitoring and auditing. Risk assessment enables organizations to identify potential threats and vulnerabilities, helping them proactively address security gaps. Compliance ensures adherence to data protection regulations and industry standards, mitigating legal and reputational risks. IAM controls user access to resources, reducing the risk of unauthorized data breaches. Data encryption safeguards sensitive information from unauthorized access. Continuous monitoring and auditing enable the detection of security incidents for swift response and improvement.

3. Challenges in achieving cloud regulatory compliance include data sovereignty and jurisdiction issues, shared responsibility model complexities, and the resource-intensive nature of compliance checks. Overcoming these challenges involves understanding and navigating data protection laws in various countries, clarifying responsibilities with cloud providers to ensure comprehensive security coverage, and using automated tools for compliance checks. Additionally, maintaining thorough documentation and adopting efficient compliance management practices can streamline the compliance process.

4. To ensure consistent security controls across diverse cloud services and environments, organizations should establish a clear security policy that outlines roles, responsibilities, and best practices for all stakeholders. Implementing multi-factor authentication (MFA) and role-based access control (RBAC)

helps limit access to sensitive data. Regular security audits and penetration testing identify weaknesses and ensure uniform application of security measures. Utilizing security automation tools and technologies enforces security controls consistently and efficiently. By adopting these best practices, organizations can maintain a strong security posture and safeguard their cloud environments effectively.

5. Incident response in the cloud involves a systematic approach to detecting, analyzing, and mitigating security incidents. It plays a critical role in minimizing the impact of security breaches by promptly detecting and containing threats. An effective incident response plan, coupled with automated incident detection mechanisms, ensures rapid response to security incidents. Containment and mitigation actions help prevent further damage, while forensic investigations aid in understanding the incident's scope and nature. Transparent communication with stakeholders maintains trust, and regular incident response plan updates enhance an organization's ability to recover swiftly from security breaches.

6. Best practices for conducting security audits in the cloud include regular audits, third-party assessments, compliance checks, vulnerability scanning, and maintaining documentation. Regular audits assess the effectiveness of security controls, identify vulnerabilities, and improve security posture. Third-party assessments provide unbiased insights into security vulnerabilities and enhance overall security confidence. Compliance checks ensure adherence to data protection regulations and industry standards. Vulnerability scanning and penetration testing help identify weaknesses for proactive mitigation. Documentation of security controls and changes facilitates future audits and supports incident investigations. By following these best practices, organizations can establish a secure cloud environment.

7. Continuous monitoring and auditing are critical in the cloud environment because they enable organizations to detect anomalies and potential security breaches in real-time. Rapid incident detection allows for swift responses to security threats, minimizing their impact. Proactive monitoring helps identify vulnerabilities before they are exploited by cyber attackers. Regular auditing ensures ongoing compliance with security standards and regulatory requirements. By continuously evaluating security measures and responding promptly to incidents, organizations enhance their overall security posture and maintain a proactive approach to cybersecurity in the cloud.

8. Data encryption and protection are crucial components of cloud security as they safeguard sensitive information from unauthorized access. By encrypting data at rest and in transit, organizations ensure that even if an attacker gains access to the data, it remains incomprehensible without the appropriate decryption keys. Encryption protects data confidentiality, preventing unauthorized disclosure. Additionally, encryption enhances data integrity, as any tampering with encrypted data becomes evident upon decryption. By employing robust encryption mechanisms, organizations ensure that sensitive data remains secure throughout its lifecycle, bolstering the overall security and privacy of their cloud environment.

9.

Chapter 33: Cloud Disaster Recovery as A Service (Draas)

33.1: Introduction to Cloud Disaster Recovery as a Service (DRaaS)

Cloud Disaster Recovery as a Service (DRaaS) is a powerful and innovative solution that empowers organizations to enhance their disaster recovery capabilities while reducing costs and complexity. By leveraging the scalability, flexibility, and geographic redundancy of cloud computing, Cloud DRaaS ensures that critical systems and data are protected and readily recoverable in the face of unexpected events. As more organizations embrace the cloud for disaster recovery, Cloud DRaaS continues to redefine and optimize the way businesses achieve and maintain business continuity in an ever-changing technological landscape. By adopting Cloud DRaaS, organizations can strengthen their disaster recovery strategies, improve their resilience, and confidently navigate any disruptions that may arise in the dynamic business landscape.

33.1.1.Cloud Disaster Recovery as a Service (DRaaS)

Cloud DRaaS is a cloud-based solution that provides organizations with offsite backup and disaster recovery capabilities for their critical systems and data. It involves continuously replicating data from the organization's primary data center to a remote cloud environment, ensuring that the cloud-based data remains up-to-date and mirrors the production environment. In the event of a disaster or data loss at the primary site, organizations can initiate a failover to the cloud environment, making the cloud-based applications and data active and ensuring business continuity. Once the primary site is restored, a failback process synchronizes the data back to the original location.

33.1.2. How Does Cloud DRaaS Work?

- **Data Replication:** Cloud DRaaS relies on continuous data replication from the primary data center to a remote cloud environment. This ensures that the cloud-based data remains current and consistent with the production environment, minimizing data loss in the event of a disaster.

- **Recovery Point Objective (RPO) and Recovery Time Objective (RTO):** Organizations define their Recovery Point Objective (RPO) and Recovery Time Objective (RTO) as part of their disaster recovery strategy. RPO represents the acceptable data loss window, while RTO represents the maximum tolerable downtime. Cloud DRaaS solutions are designed to meet specific RPO and RTO requirements to align with the organization's recovery goals.

- **Failover and Failback:** During a disaster, the organization initiates a failover to the cloud environment. The cloud-based applications and data become active, ensuring uninterrupted business operations. Once the primary site is restored, a failback process is executed to synchronize the data back to the original location, resuming normal operations.

33.1.3. Benefits of Cloud DRaaS

- **Cost-Effectiveness:** Cloud DRaaS eliminates the need for costly upfront investments in dedicated disaster recovery infrastructure. Organizations pay only for the resources they consume during failover and testing, resulting in cost savings.

- Scalability and Flexibility: Cloud DRaaS offers scalability to accommodate changing data requirements. Organizations can easily adjust the storage and compute resources based on their disaster recovery needs, ensuring optimal performance.

- Automated and Reliable Failover: Cloud DRaaS solutions automate the failover process, reducing the risk of human errors during recovery procedures. Automated failover ensures swift and reliable recovery, minimizing downtime.

- Geographic Redundancy: Cloud DRaaS leverages the cloud provider's global data centers, allowing organizations to have geographic redundancy for their disaster recovery infrastructure. This mitigates the impact of regional disasters, ensuring business continuity.

- Testing and Compliance: Cloud DRaaS solutions enable organizations to perform regular disaster recovery testing without affecting the production environment. This helps validate the effectiveness of the disaster recovery strategy and ensures compliance with industry regulations.

33.1.4. Use Cases for Cloud DRaaS

- Mission-Critical Applications: Cloud DRaaS protects mission-critical applications, ensuring continuous availability and minimal data loss in the event of a disaster. This is crucial for organizations that heavily rely on critical systems for their operations.

- Data Protection and Compliance: Cloud DRaaS provides a secure and compliant backup and disaster recovery solution, ensuring that sensitive data is protected and regulatory requirements are met. This is especially relevant for organizations dealing with sensitive data or subject to industry-specific regulations.

- Risk Mitigation: Cloud DRaaS helps organizations mitigate the risk of data loss, downtime, and financial losses associated with disaster events. This enhances overall business resilience and minimizes the impact of unforeseen disruptions.

33.2: Implementing a Cloud-Based Disaster Recovery Strategy

Implementing a cloud-based disaster recovery strategy is a proactive approach that protects critical data, applications, and systems from unexpected events. By carefully assessing business requirements, choosing the right cloud provider, implementing data replication and backup, conducting regular testing, and ensuring security and compliance, organizations can confidently embrace cloud-based disaster recovery as an efficient and reliable means to achieve business continuity and protect their valuable assets. A comprehensive approach to cloud-based disaster recovery enables organizations to enhance their resilience, minimize downtime, and maintain business continuity even in the face of unforeseen disruptions.

33.2.1. Assessing Business Requirements

- Identify Critical Systems and Data: Begin by identifying the systems, applications, and data that are essential for business operations. This assessment will help prioritize what needs to be protected through the disaster recovery strategy. Critical systems and data should be the focus of the cloud-based disaster recovery plan.

- Define Recovery Objectives: Set Recovery Point Objectives (RPO) and Recovery Time Objectives (RTO) based on the organization's business needs. RPO defines the acceptable data loss window, while RTO indicates the maximum tolerable downtime. Aligning RPO and RTO with business requirements is crucial for tailoring the disaster recovery strategy to the organization's unique needs.

33.2.2. Choosing the Right Cloud Disaster Recovery Provider

- Cloud Provider Selection: Evaluate various cloud service providers based on their disaster recovery capabilities, data center locations, security measures, and compliance with relevant regulations. The chosen provider should offer the necessary features and support to meet the organization's disaster recovery objectives.

- Service Level Agreements (SLAs): Review SLAs carefully to ensure they align with the organization's RTO and RPO requirements. The SLA should guarantee the availability and reliability of the cloud-based disaster recovery environment to meet the organization's recovery goals.

33.2.3. Data Replication and Backup

- Data Replication: Implement continuous or periodic data replication from the primary data center to the cloud environment. This ensures that data in the cloud remains up-to-date and mirrors the production environment, minimizing data loss in the event of a disaster.

- Backup Strategy: Implement regular backups of critical data and applications in the cloud. Backups provide an additional layer of data protection and allow for easy restoration if needed. The backup strategy should be aligned with the RPO to ensure that data can be restored to an acceptable state in case of a disaster.

33.2.4. Testing and Validation

- Disaster Recovery Testing: Regularly conduct disaster recovery testing to validate the effectiveness of the cloud-based recovery strategy. Testing should simulate various disaster scenarios and recovery procedures to identify and address any potential issues proactively.

- Failover Testing: Test the failover process to the cloud environment to ensure that the transition is smooth and that systems and applications function as expected in the cloud. Failover testing provides insights into the performance of the cloud-based disaster recovery environment.

33.2.5. Security and Compliance

- Data Encryption: Ensure that data is encrypted both during transit and at rest in the cloud environment. Encryption enhances data security and helps protect against unauthorized access during data replication and storage.

- Access Controls: Implement strong identity and access management (IAM) controls to restrict access to the cloud-based disaster recovery environment to authorized personnel only. IAM policies should be regularly reviewed and updated to maintain security.

- Compliance Requirements: Ensure that the cloud-based disaster recovery strategy aligns with relevant industry regulations and data protection requirements. Compliance should be maintained throughout the disaster recovery lifecycle.

33.2.6. Monitoring and Maintenance

- Continuous Monitoring: Implement automated monitoring and alerting mechanisms to detect potential issues or anomalies in the cloud environment. Continuous monitoring ensures prompt detection and response to any deviations from normal operations.

- **Performance Optimization:** Regularly assess and optimize the performance of the cloud-based disaster recovery environment to ensure efficient operation during failover. Performance optimization contributes to seamless disaster recovery operations.

33.2.7. Documentation and Communication

- **Document the Disaster Recovery Plan:** Create a comprehensive disaster recovery plan that outlines all the steps, procedures, and roles involved in implementing and executing the cloud-based disaster recovery strategy. The documentation should be regularly updated to reflect changes in the organization's infrastructure and requirements.

- **Communication Plan:** Develop a communication plan to ensure that all relevant stakeholders are informed about the disaster recovery strategy, their roles, and the contact information for key personnel during an incident. Clear communication ensures effective collaboration during disaster recovery operations.

33.3: Testing and Failover in DRaaS Environments

Testing and failover are indispensable aspects of a successful Disaster Recovery as a Service (DRaaS) environment. Regular testing ensures that the disaster recovery plan is effective, data integrity is maintained, and recovery objectives are met. Failover tests validate the execution of recovery processes and build confidence in the disaster recovery capabilities. By implementing best practices for testing and failover, organizations can bolster their disaster recovery readiness, ensuring business continuity, and protecting critical data and applications in the face of unforeseen events

33.3.1. Importance of Testing in DRaaS Environments

- **Validation of DR Plan:** Testing is crucial to validate the effectiveness of the Disaster Recovery as a Service (DRaaS) plan. By conducting tests, organizations can identify any gaps, weaknesses, or potential issues that might hinder the successful execution of the disaster recovery process.

- **Ensuring Data Integrity:** Testing ensures that data replication and synchronization between the primary environment and the DRaaS environment are functioning as expecte This validation is essential to maintain data integrity during the recovery phase.

- **Validation of RPO and RTO:** Testing enables organizations to verify that the defined Recovery Point Objective (RPO) and Recovery Time Objective (RTO) are achievable and in alignment with the business needs. RPO defines the maximum tolerable data loss, while RTO sets the maximum allowable downtime.

33.3.2. Best Practices for Testing in DRaaS Environments

- **Regular Testing Schedule:** Organizations should establish a regular testing schedule to conduct both planned and surprise disaster recovery tests. Regular testing ensures that the DRaaS environment is up-to-date and allows teams to practice recovery procedures consistently.

- **Testing Scope and Objectives:** Clearly defining the scope and objectives of each testing scenario is essential. Organizations can consider testing individual applications, systems, or the entire infrastructure to ensure a comprehensive evaluation of the disaster recovery capabilities.

- **Test Plan and Documentation:** Developing a detailed test plan is critical. It should outline the steps, procedures, and expected outcomes for each testing scenario. Proper documentation of the test results and any identified issues allows for further analysis and remediation.

- **User Acceptance Testing (UAT):** Involving end-users and stakeholders in user acceptance testing is beneficial to ensure that the recovered systems meet business requirements and user expectations.

3. Importance of Failover Testing

- **Validation of Recovery Processes:** Failover testing simulates a real disaster scenario and is crucial for validating the effectiveness of the recovery processes. It assesses the ability to transition to the DRaaS environment seamlessly.

- **Performance Assessment:** Failover tests assess the performance of the DRaaS environment during an actual recovery. They help identify any performance bottlenecks or issues that may arise during the failover process.

- **Personnel Familiarity:** Conducting failover tests allows the disaster recovery team to become familiar with the failover process, which increases their confidence and readiness in handling real disaster events.

33.3.4. Best Practices for Failover Testing

- **Scheduled and Controlled Tests:** Planning failover tests carefully is essential to ensure minimal disruption to the production environment. Organizations should schedule tests during periods of low user activity to reduce potential impact.

- **Partial Failover Tests:** Initially, organizations can consider conducting partial failover tests for critical applications to assess the process and identify potential issues. Gradually expanding testing to include the entire infrastructure provides more comprehensive insights.

- **Backout Plan:** Always having a backout plan is crucial in case the failover test encounters unexpected issues. The backout plan should allow for a smooth transition back to the production environment.

33.3.5. Learning and Continuous Improvement

- **Review and Analysis:** After each testing and failover event, conducting a thorough review and analysis of the results is essential. It helps identify areas of improvement and address any shortcomings in the disaster recovery strategy.

- **Lessons Learned:** Documenting lessons learned from each test and incorporating them into the disaster recovery plan and future testing scenarios is important for continuous improvement. Learning from past experiences enhances the effectiveness of the DRaaS environment.

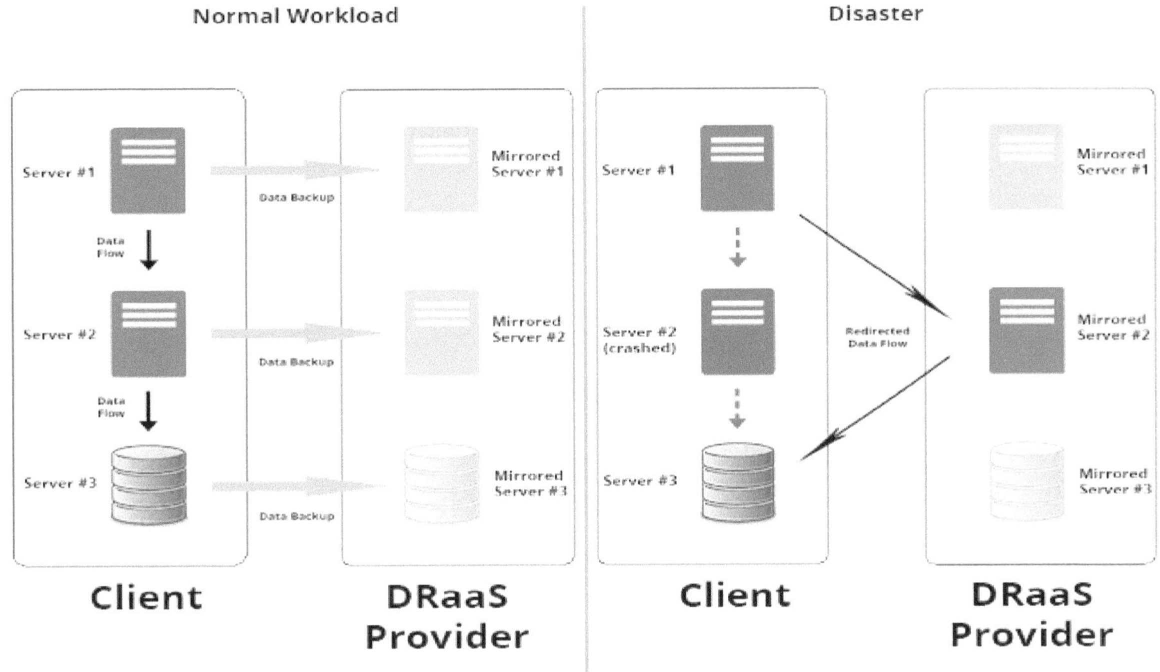

Exercise

Multiple Choice Questions

1. What is the primary purpose of Cloud Disaster Recovery as a Service (DRaaS)?

a. To provide cost-effective cloud storage for organizations

b. To enhance disaster recovery capabilities while reducing costs and complexity

c. To offer unlimited scalability and flexibility for cloud-based applications

d. To replace traditional on-premises data centers

2. How does Cloud DRaaS ensure data availability during a disaster?

a. By creating physical backups at an offsite location

b. By replicating data from the primary data center to a remote cloud environment

c. By relying on traditional tape backups stored in a secure facility

d. By using virtual machines for failover and recovery

3. What does Recovery Point Objective (RPO) represent in a disaster recovery strategy?

a. The maximum allowable downtime during a disaster

b. The acceptable data loss window after a disaster

c. The minimum number of servers required for failover

d. The recovery time needed to restore data from backups

4. Which benefit does Cloud DRaaS offer in terms of cost-effectiveness?

a. Elimination of disaster recovery testing costs

b. Reduction of manual intervention during failover

c. Elimination of upfront investments in dedicated disaster recovery infrastructure

d. Reduction of cloud storage costs during normal operations

5. What is a use case for Cloud DRaaS?

a. Data processing and analytics

b. Secure file sharing and collaboration

c. Protecting mission-critical applications

d. Customer relationship management (CRM) implementation

6. What should organizations consider when choosing a Cloud DRaaS provider?

a. The number of data centers the provider has globally

b. The provider's support for virtualization technologies

c. The provider's response to recent security breaches

d. The alignment of Service Level Agreements (SLAs) with RPO and RTO requirements

7. Why is user acceptance testing (UAT) important in disaster recovery testing?

a. To evaluate the performance of the cloud-based disaster recovery environment

b. To involve end-users and stakeholders in testing the recovery processes

c. To ensure compliance with industry regulations during testing

d. To simulate various disaster scenarios for thorough testing

8. What is the main purpose of conducting failover testing in a DRaaS environment?

a. To identify potential issues and shortcomings in the disaster recovery strategy

b. To assess the performance of the cloud-based disaster recovery environment

c. To simulate real disaster scenarios and test recovery processes

d. To evaluate the effectiveness of data encryption during failover

9. How does continuous monitoring contribute to a successful DRaaS environment?

a. It reduces the need for disaster recovery testing.

b. It detects potential issues or anomalies in the cloud environment promptly.

c. It eliminates the need for failover testing.

d. It ensures compliance with industry regulations during recovery operations.

Review Questions

1. What is Cloud Disaster Recovery as a Service (DRaaS), and how does it differ from traditional disaster recovery solutions?

2. What role does data replication play in Cloud DRaaS, and why is it critical for disaster recovery?

3. What are Recovery Point Objective (RPO) and Recovery Time Objective (RTO) in the context of Cloud DRaaS, and why are they important?

4. How does Cloud DRaaS contribute to cost-effectiveness for organizations, compared to traditional disaster recovery methods?

5. How does Cloud DRaaS provide geographic redundancy, and what benefits does it offer for disaster recovery?

6. How does Cloud DRaaS support disaster recovery testing, and what benefits does it offer for organizations?

7. What factors should organizations consider when choosing the right Cloud DRaaS provider for their disaster recovery needs?

8. How does automation play a vital role in Cloud DRaaS, and what benefits does it offer for disaster recovery operations?

9. How can organizations ensure continuous improvement and effectiveness in their Cloud DRaaS environment?

Answer Section

Multiple Choice Questions

1. b) To enhance disaster recovery capabilities while reducing costs and complexity.

2. b) By replicating data from the primary data center to a remote cloud environment.

3. b) The acceptable data loss window after a disaster.

4. c) Elimination of upfront investments in dedicated disaster recovery infrastructure.

5. c) Protecting mission-critical applications.

6. d) The alignment of Service Level Agreements (SLAs) with RPO and RTO requirements.

7. b) To involve end-users and stakeholders in testing the recovery processes.

8. c) To simulate real disaster scenarios and test recovery processes.

9. b) It detects potential issues or anomalies in the cloud environment promptly.

Review Questions

1. Cloud DRaaS is a cloud-based solution that provides offsite backup and disaster recovery capabilities for critical systems and data. It continuously replicates data from the primary data center to a remote cloud environment, ensuring up-to-date data. Unlike traditional solutions that require dedicated infrastructure, Cloud DRaaS leverages the cloud's scalability and geographic redundancy. In the event of a disaster, organizations can initiate failover to the cloud environment, ensuring business continuity. Once the primary site is restored, a failback process synchronizes the data back. Cloud DRaaS offers cost-effectiveness, flexibility, and automated failover, revolutionizing disaster recovery.

2. Data replication is a fundamental aspect of Cloud DRaaS. It involves continuously copying data from the primary data center to a remote cloud environment. This process ensures that the cloud-based data remains current and mirrors the production environment, minimizing data loss in case of a disaster. Data replication provides a reliable, up-to-date backup of critical systems and data, enabling organizations to quickly restore operations with minimal data loss. By maintaining real-time data synchronization, Cloud DRaaS ensures that the cloud environment is ready for failover, enhancing disaster recovery capabilities and business continuity.

3. RPO represents the acceptable data loss window, indicating how much data an organization is willing to lose during a disaster. RTO, on the other hand, denotes the maximum tolerable downtime for recovery. Both RPO and RTO are crucial elements of a disaster recovery strategy. Organizations must define these objectives based on their business needs and criticality of systems and data. Cloud DRaaS solutions are designed to meet specific RPO and RTO requirements, aligning with an organization's recovery goals. Meeting these objectives ensures that data loss and downtime are minimized, maintaining business continuity.

4. Cloud DRaaS offers significant cost-effectiveness compared to traditional disaster recovery solutions. With traditional methods, organizations need to invest in dedicated disaster recovery infrastructure, which involves substantial upfront costs. In contrast, Cloud DRaaS eliminates the need for such investments, as it leverages the cloud provider's infrastructure. Organizations only pay for the resources they consume during failover and testing, resulting in a pay-as-you-go model. Additionally, Cloud DRaaS reduces maintenance and operational expenses, as the cloud provider handles hardware updates, scalability, and maintenance. This cost-efficient approach allows organizations to optimize their disaster recovery budget effectively.

5. Cloud DRaaS leverages the cloud provider's global data centers, offering geographic redundancy for disaster recovery infrastructure. This means that data and applications are replicated and stored in multiple data centers located in different geographic regions. Geographic redundancy ensures that even if one region experiences a disaster, data and operations can failover to a different region seamlessly. This mitigates the impact of regional disasters, enabling continuous business operations. By diversifying data

storage across multiple regions, Cloud DRaaS enhances resilience and reduces the risk of data loss, providing organizations with robust disaster recovery capabilities.

6. Cloud DRaaS solutions enable organizations to perform regular disaster recovery testing without affecting the production environment. Testing is crucial to validate the effectiveness of the disaster recovery strategy, identify any weaknesses, and ensure compliance with industry regulations. With Cloud DRaaS, testing can be conducted in the cloud environment, simulating various disaster scenarios to evaluate recovery procedures and assess the performance of the DRaaS setup. Testing provides insights into the recovery process's reliability and helps organizations refine their disaster recovery plans, ensuring they are well-prepared for actual disaster events.

7. When selecting a Cloud DRaaS provider, organizations should consider several factors. Firstly, evaluate the provider's disaster recovery capabilities, including data replication frequency and recovery speed, to meet specific RPO and RTO requirements. Secondly, assess the provider's data center locations, as geographical diversity contributes to better disaster recovery resilience. Thirdly, review the provider's Service Level Agreements (SLAs) to ensure they align with the organization's recovery objectives. Security measures, compliance with relevant regulations, and the provider's reputation for reliability and customer support are also crucial factors in the decision-making process.

8. Automation is a key component of Cloud DRaaS solutions. Automated failover processes reduce the risk of human errors during disaster recovery operations. By automating the failover to the cloud environment, organizations can ensure swift and reliable recovery, minimizing downtime and potential data loss. Automation also streamlines routine disaster recovery tasks, such as data replication and backup, freeing IT staff to focus on other critical aspects of disaster recovery preparedness. Overall, automation enhances the efficiency, accuracy, and speed of disaster recovery operations, contributing to improved business continuity and reduced recovery times.

9. To ensure continuous improvement, organizations should conduct regular reviews and analysis of disaster recovery tests and failover events. Documenting lessons learned from each test allows for refinement of the disaster recovery plan and future testing scenarios. Additionally, organizations should optimize their cloud-based disaster recovery environment regularly, ensuring it can efficiently handle failover scenarios. Continuous monitoring and alerting mechanisms are vital for promptly detecting potential issues or anomalies in the cloud environment. By incorporating feedback and improving processes based on real-world experiences, organizations can enhance the effectiveness of their Cloud DRaaS environment, achieving robust disaster recovery capabilities.

Chapter 34: Cloud-Based Artificial Intelligence and Machine Learning

34.1 Introduction to Cloud AI and ML Services

Cloud AI and ML services have democratized access to AI and ML capabilities, empowering businesses of all sizes to leverage data-driven insights and intelligent automation. By utilizing pre-built and scalable AI and ML solutions, organizations can accelerate innovation, enhance customer experiences, and gain a competitive edge in today's data-centric world. These cloud-based services offer an accessible pathway to unlock the true potential of AI and ML without the need for extensive resources and expertise.

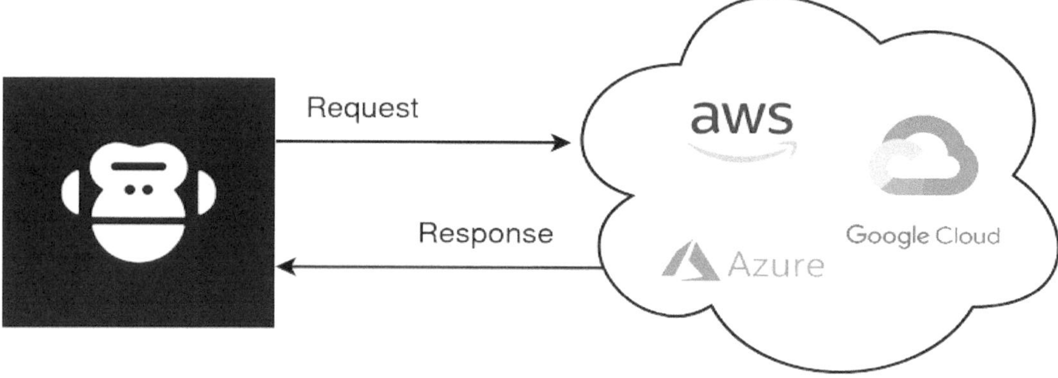

34.1.1. What are Cloud AI and ML Services?

Cloud AI and ML services consist of a suite of pre-built, scalable, and fully managed solutions provided by cloud providers. These services enable businesses to access cutting-edge AI and ML capabilities through simple APIs and interfaces, eliminating the complexities associated with setting up and managing the underlying infrastructure.

34.1.2. Core Components of Cloud AI and ML Services

- **Data Storage and Management:** Cloud AI and ML services often come with storage and management solutions that help organize, store, and process vast amounts of data required for training ML models.

- **Data Preprocessing and Feature Engineering:** These services aid in cleaning, transforming, and engineering data, preparing it for the training of ML models.

- **Model Training and Inference:** Cloud AI and ML services provide facilities for training ML models using various algorithms and frameworks. Once trained, these models can be deployed and used for real-time inference on new data.

- **Automated Machine Learning (AutoML):** AutoML services automate the process of model selection, hyperparameter tuning, and optimization, making it easier for users with limited ML expertise to build effective models.

34.1.3. Benefits of Cloud AI and ML Services

- **Cost-Effective and Scalable** Cloud AI and ML services follow a pay-as-you-go model, enabling organizations to scale their AI and ML operations as needed, without requiring upfront infrastructure investments.

- **Reduced Complexity:** Cloud providers abstract the complexities of AI and ML infrastructure, making these advanced technologies accessible to a broader audience.

- **Time-Efficient:** Cloud AI and ML services accelerate the development and deployment of AI and ML applications, enabling organizations to focus on building solutions rather than managing infrastructure.

- **Integration with Other Cloud Services:** Cloud AI and ML services seamlessly integrate with other cloud services, such as data storage, databases, and analytics, providing a comprehensive ecosystem for AI-powered applications.

34.1.4. Use Cases of Cloud AI and ML Services

- **Natural Language Processing (NLP):** NLP services analyze and understand human language, enabling applications such as sentiment analysis, language translation, chatbots, and voice recognition.

- **Computer Vision:** Computer vision services process and interpret visual information, supporting tasks like image recognition, object detection, facial recognition, and autonomous vehicles.

- **Recommendation Systems:** AI-powered recommendation systems provide personalized suggestions for products, content, and services, enhancing user experiences and driving engagement.

- **Predictive Analytics:** ML services enable predictive analytics, helping organizations forecast trends, make data-driven decisions, and optimize business processes.

34.2 Training and Deployment of ML Models in the Cloud

Training and deploying ML models in the cloud have transformed the way organizations leverage AI and ML capabilities. The cloud's scalability, cost-efficiency, and integration with other services make it an ideal platform for ML model development and deployment. By embracing cloud-based ML solutions, businesses can build powerful AI-driven applications, gain data-driven insights, and stay at the forefront of innovation in today's data-centric world. Cloud-based ML services empower organizations to unleash the full potential of AI and ML without the burden of managing complex infrastructure and resources.

34.2.1 Training ML Models in the Cloud

- **Data Preparation:** The first step in training ML models involves data preparation. Organizations gather, clean, and preprocess data to make it suitable for model training, ensuring high-quality inputs for better results.

- **Cloud Data Storage:** Cloud providers offer scalable and secure data storage solutions that can handle large datasets required for ML model training. These storage services ensure data accessibility and durability during the training process.

- **Model Selection and Architecture:** Choosing the appropriate ML algorithms and model architectures is crucial for the success of the ML application. Based on the specific use case and data characteristics, selecting the right ML approach becomes a critical decision.

- **Model Training:** Cloud-based ML services come into play here, providing the necessary computing resources to train selected ML models using the prepared data. Cloud platforms often offer powerful GPUs and TPUs that accelerate training times, reducing the overall training time.

- **Hyperparameter Tuning:** To optimize model performance, hyperparameter tuning is performed. Cloud platforms may offer automated tools or techniques like Grid Search or Random Search to find the best combination of hyperparameters for the ML model.

34.2.2. Benefits of Training ML Models in the Cloud

- **Scalability:** Cloud platforms provide the resources needed to train ML models at any scale. From small datasets to massive datasets requiring distributed computing, cloud services can handle varying workloads.

- **Cost-Efficiency:** Pay-as-you-go pricing allows organizations to pay only for the compute resources used during model training. This model helps avoid the cost of maintaining dedicated hardware, making ML model training more cost-effective.

- **Performance:** Cloud providers offer access to high-performance hardware, such as GPUs and TPUs, which significantly reduce model training times. This results in faster iterations and quicker deployment of ML models.

- **AutoML:** Some cloud platforms provide AutoML services that automate the model selection and hyperparameter tuning process. This simplifies the ML model training workflow, making it accessible to users with limited ML expertise.

34.2.3. Deploying ML Models in the Cloud

- **Model Serialization:** Once the ML model is trained, it is serialized into a format that can be easily deployed and consumed. Serialization ensures that the model's structure and parameters are saved for future use.

- **Containerization:** To ensure consistency and portability across different environments, the serialized model is packaged into a container. Containers encapsulate the model along with its dependencies, making deployment seamless.

- **Model Hosting:** Cloud-based container services are utilized to deploy the containerized model. This approach allows for scalable and reliable model hosting, enabling the ML model to handle varying workloads.

- **API Development:** APIs are created to enable external applications and services to interact with the hosted ML model for real-time inference. This opens up possibilities for integrating ML-powered capabilities into various applications.

34.2.4. Benefits of Deploying ML Models in the Cloud

- **Scalability and Elasticity:** Cloud-based deployment allows organizations to handle varying workloads and scale the ML model's inference capabilities as needed. This ensures smooth performance during peak times.

- **High Availability:** Cloud providers offer redundancy and failover capabilities, ensuring high availability and reliability of the deployed ML models. This minimizes downtime and enhances the user experience.

- **Global Reach:** Cloud platforms have data centers distributed worldwide, enabling low-latency access to the ML model's inference API from different geographic locations. This improves responsiveness and user experience for global audiences.

- **Real-time Inference:** Cloud-based deployment facilitates real-time inference, making ML-powered applications responsive and interactive. This is especially valuable for applications that require quick and dynamic responses.

34.2.5. Integration with Cloud Services

- **Data Integration:** Cloud-based ML models can seamlessly integrate with other cloud services, such as databases, data lakes, and streaming services, to access and process data. This integration streamlines the entire data pipeline for ML applications.

- **Event-Driven Architectures:** ML model deployments can be integrated into event-driven architectures, allowing for automated responses based on incoming events. This creates dynamic and adaptive ML-powered systems.

34.3 Natural Language Processing and Computer Vision in the Cloud

NLP and Computer Vision are transformative AI capabilities that have reshaped how businesses understand and interact with language and visual data. Cloud service providers have made these capabilities accessible and user-friendly, enabling organizations to leverage NLP and Computer Vision without the need for extensive AI expertise or infrastructure. By integrating these capabilities into their applications, businesses can unlock new opportunities, optimize operations, and deliver innovative solutions that enhance user experiences in an increasingly data-driven and connected world. The future holds even more exciting possibilities as these AI technologies continue to evolve, driving further advancements in various industries and shaping the way we interact with information and our environment.

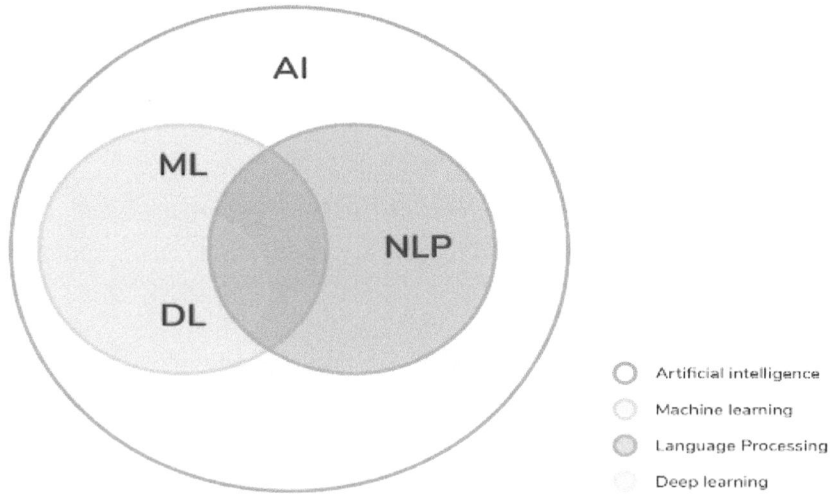

34.3.1. Natural Language Processing (NLP) in the Cloud

- **Sentiment Analysis:** NLP services in the cloud leverage advanced machine learning algorithms to analyze and determine the sentiment expressed in textual content. This can include social media posts, product reviews, customer feedback, and more. By understanding the sentiment as positive, negative, or neutral, businesses can gain valuable insights into customer opinions and brand perception. Sentiment analysis enables organizations to monitor their reputation, identify potential issues, and respond to customer concerns promptly.

- **Language Translation:** Cloud-based NLP services employ state-of-the-art machine translation models to provide real-time language translation. This capability is invaluable for businesses operating in the global market, as it allows them to offer multilingual support to their customers. With cloud-based language translation, companies can break language barriers, expand their reach to a diverse audience, and tailor their content to different regions and language preferences.

- **Named Entity Recognition (NER):** NLP services in the cloud use sophisticated algorithms to identify and extract specific entities from text documents. These entities can include names of people, organizations, locations, dates, and more. Named Entity Recognition enables businesses to automatically recognize and categorize important information from large volumes of textual data. This is particularly useful for tasks like data extraction, entity tagging, and organizing unstructured data.

- **Chatbots and Virtual Assistants:** Cloud-based NLP powers interactive chatbots and virtual assistants, enabling them to understand and respond to natural language queries. Chatbots equipped with NLP capabilities can hold intelligent conversations with users, providing personalized assistance, answering frequently asked s, and resolving customer inquiries. Virtual assistants powered by cloud-based NLP can enhance user experiences by delivering relevant and context-aware responses.

34.3.2. Computer Vision in the Cloud

- **Image Recognition:** Cloud Computer Vision services utilize advanced deep learning models to identify objects, scenes, and patterns within images. Image recognition enables applications like image search and content tagging. Businesses can use this capability to efficiently categorize visual content, making it easier to organize and analyze large collections of images.

- **Object Detection:** Cloud-based Computer Vision can detect and localize multiple objects within an image. This makes it highly valuable in applications like autonomous vehicles, where the technology can identify pedestrians, other vehicles, and obstacles on the road, ensuring safe navigation. Object detection is also widely used in surveillance systems to monitor and analyze activities in real-time.

- **Facial Recognition:** Cloud Computer Vision services offer facial recognition capabilities, enabling applications like user authentication, personalized user experiences, and people counting in crowded areas. Facial recognition can be used for identity verification, access control, and enhancing security measures in various industries.

- **OCR (Optical Character Recognition):** Cloud-based Computer Vision employs OCR algorithms to extract text from images. This facilitates document digitization, enabling businesses to convert physical documents, such as scanned papers or photographs, into searchable and editable digital formats. OCR is particularly useful in digitizing historical records, archiving documents, and facilitating text analysis.

34.3.3. Benefits of NLP and Computer Vision in the Cloud

- **Scalability:** Cloud services provide highly scalable NLP and Computer Vision capabilities, accommodating diverse workloads and processing large datasets efficiently. Businesses can easily scale their AI applications based on demand, ensuring optimal performance and resource utilization.

- **Real-time Inference:** Cloud-based services offer low-latency real-time inference, allowing AI models to process and respond to data with minimal delay. This near-instantaneous response time is crucial for applications requiring immediate feedback, such as real-time chatbots or video analysis.

- **Pre-trained Models:** Cloud providers offer pre-trained NLP and Computer Vision models that have been trained on extensive datasets. These pre-trained models significantly reduce the need for businesses to invest time and resources in training models from scratch. This accelerates application development and enables rapid prototyping of AI-powered solutions.

- **Integration with Other Services:** NLP and Computer Vision services seamlessly integrate with other cloud services. This integration enables businesses to store, process, and analyze data in a unified environment, streamlining their AI-powered workflows. By combining AI capabilities with other cloud services like storage, databases, and analytics, organizations can build comprehensive and robust AI applications.

34.3.4. Use Cases of NLP and Computer Vision in the Cloud

- **Customer Support:** NLP-powered chatbots integrated into cloud-based applications can provide instant and accurate responses to customer queries, improving the efficiency of customer support services. They can handle common queries and issues, allowing human agents to focus on more complex tasks and enhancing overall customer satisfaction.

- **Content Moderation:** Computer Vision services can automatically detect and filter inappropriate or sensitive content in images and videos. For platforms that rely on user-generated content, such as social media and online forums, this is crucial for maintaining a safe and respectful environment for users.

- **Medical Image Analysis:** Cloud-based Computer Vision can assist in medical diagnoses by analyzing medical images, such as X-rays and MRI scans. AI-powered medical image analysis can aid healthcare professionals in detecting anomalies, identifying diseases, and making more accurate and timely diagnoses, potentially improving patient outcomes.

- **Language Translation Services:** NLP services in the cloud facilitate real-time language translation for international communication and localization. Businesses can expand their global presence, reach wider audiences, and adapt their content to different languages and cultures.

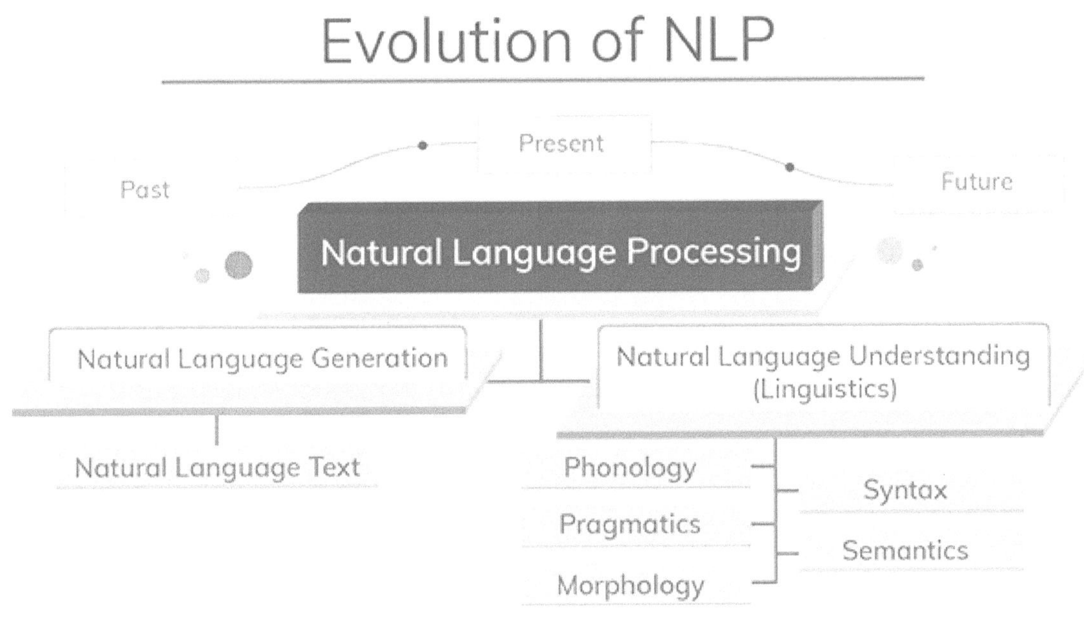

Exercise

Multiple Choice Questions

1. What are Cloud AI and ML Services?

a. Cloud AI and ML services are cloud-based platforms that offer weather forecasting services.

b. Cloud AI and ML services consist of pre-built, scalable, and fully managed solutions provided by cloud providers, enabling businesses to access cutting-edge AI and ML capabilities through simple APIs and interfaces.

c. Cloud AI and ML services are cloud storage solutions offered by cloud providers.

d. Cloud AI and ML services are online gaming platforms.

2. Which of the following is NOT a core component of Cloud AI and ML Services?

a. Data Storage and Management

b. Data Preprocessing and Feature Engineering

c. Model Training and Inference

d. Image Rendering and Animation

3. What benefits do Cloud AI and ML Services offer to businesses?

a. Reduced Complexity, Reduced Scalability, Time-Consuming Deployment

b. Expensive Infrastructure, Limited Integration with Other Services, and Manual Model Training

c. Cost-Effective and Scalable, Reduced Complexity, Time-Efficient, Integration with Other Cloud Services

d. Limited API Support, Manual Data Preprocessing, Limited Use Cases

4. Which use case of Cloud AI and ML Services enables applications such as sentiment analysis, language translation, chatbots, and voice recognition?

a. Natural Language Processing (NLP)

b. Computer Vision

c. Recommendation Systems

d. Predictive Analytics

5. How do Cloud AI and ML services support model selection and hyperparameter tuning for users with limited ML expertise?

a. By providing pre-built machine learning models.

b. By offering cloud storage solutions.

c. By automating the process through AutoML services.

d. By enabling direct access to GPUs and TPUs.

6. Which benefit of training ML models in the cloud allows organizations to handle varying workloads, from small to massive datasets?

a. Cost-Efficiency

b. Performance

c. Scalability

d. AutoML

7. What is the purpose of model serialization when deploying ML models in the cloud?

a. To train the ML model using prepared data.

b. To create APIs for real-time inference.

c. To package the model into a container.

d. To save the model's structure and parameters for future use.

8. Which benefit of deploying ML models in the cloud allows applications to be responsive and interactive?

a. Scalability and Elasticity

b. High Availability

c. Global Reach

d. Real-time Inference

9. What transformative AI capabilities have reshaped how businesses understand and interact with language and visual data?

a. Cloud Computing and Virtual Reality

b. Natural Language Processing (NLP) and Computer Vision

c. Robotic Process Automation (RPA) and IoT Devices

d. Quantum Computing and Blockchain Technology

Review Questions

1. What are Cloud AI and ML Services?
2. How do Cloud AI and ML Services benefit businesses?
3. What are the core components of Cloud AI and ML Services?

4. What are the use cases of Cloud AI and ML Services?
5. What are the benefits of training ML models in the cloud?
6. What is the significance of model serialization in ML model deployment?
7. How does cloud-based deployment benefit ML models?
8. What are the transformative AI capabilities reshaping businesses in the cloud?
9. How do NLP services in the cloud benefit businesses?

Answer Section

Multiple Choice Questions

1. b) Cloud AI and ML services consist of pre-built, scalable, and fully managed solutions provided by cloud providers, enabling businesses to access cutting-edge AI and ML capabilities through simple APIs and interfaces.

2. d) Image Rendering and Animation

3. c) Cost-Effective and Scalable, Reduced Complexity, Time-Efficient, Integration with Other Cloud Services

4. a) Natural Language Processing (NLP)

5. c) By automating the process through AutoML services.

6. c) Scalability

7. d) To save the model's structure and parameters for future use.

8. d) Real-time Inference

9. b) Natural Language Processing (NLP) and Computer Vision

Review Questions

1. Cloud AI and ML services are cloud-based platforms that offer pre-built, scalable, and fully managed solutions for businesses to access cutting-edge AI and ML capabilities. These services provide simple APIs and interfaces, eliminating the complexities of managing infrastructure and enabling organizations of all sizes to leverage data-driven insights and intelligent automation.

2. Cloud AI and ML services offer cost-effective and scalable solutions, allowing organizations to pay-as-they-go and scale their operations as needed. They reduce complexity by abstracting AI and ML infrastructure, making these advanced technologies accessible to a broader audience. Additionally, these services accelerate development and deployment, enabling businesses to focus on building solutions instead of managing infrastructure. Integration with other cloud services provides a comprehensive ecosystem for AI-powered applications.

3. The core components of Cloud AI and ML services include data storage and management solutions to handle vast amounts of training data. Data preprocessing and feature engineering services aid in preparing

data for ML model training. Model training and inference facilities provide computing resources for training ML models using various algorithms and frameworks. Automated Machine Learning (AutoML) services automate model selection, hyperparameter tuning, and optimization for users with limited ML expertise.

4. Cloud AI and ML services find applications in various domains, such as Natural Language Processing (NLP) for sentiment analysis, language translation, chatbots, and voice recognition. Computer Vision enables image recognition, object detection, facial recognition, and autonomous vehicles. AI-powered recommendation systems provide personalized suggestions for products and content. ML services also enable predictive analytics, helping organizations forecast trends, make data-driven decisions, and optimize business processes.

5. Training ML models in the cloud offers scalability, allowing organizations to handle datasets of any size. Pay-as-you-go pricing ensures cost-efficiency, avoiding the need for maintaining dedicated hardware. Access to high-performance hardware like GPUs and TPUs accelerates model training times, enabling faster iterations and quicker deployment. Some cloud platforms offer AutoML services, simplifying the model training workflow for users with limited ML expertise.

6. Model serialization involves saving the trained ML model's structure and parameters in a format that can be easily deployed and consumed. Serialization ensures the model's integrity and allows for future use without the need for retraining. This step is essential for packaging the model into a container and enabling seamless deployment.

7. Cloud-based deployment provides scalability and elasticity, allowing ML models to handle varying workloads and ensuring smooth performance during peak times. Cloud providers offer redundancy and failover capabilities, ensuring high availability and reliability of deployed models, minimizing downtime, and enhancing the user experience. With data centers distributed worldwide, cloud platforms enable low-latency access to ML model inference APIs from different geographic locations, improving responsiveness for global audiences.

8. Natural Language Processing (NLP) and Computer Vision are transformative AI capabilities that have reshaped how businesses understand and interact with language and visual data. Cloud service providers have made these capabilities accessible and user-friendly, empowering organizations to leverage NLP and Computer Vision without extensive AI expertise or infrastructure. Integrating these capabilities into applications unlocks new opportunities, optimizes operations, and delivers innovative solutions that enhance user experiences in today's data-driven and connected world.

9. NLP services in the cloud leverage advanced machine learning algorithms to analyze and determine sentiment expressed in textual content, such as social media posts, product reviews, and customer feedback. Understanding sentiment as positive, negative, or neutral, businesses gain valuable insights into customer opinions and brand perception. This enables monitoring of reputation, identifying potential issues, and responding to customer concerns promptly. Cloud-based NLP also facilitates real-time language translation, breaking language barriers, and expanding businesses' global reach by offering multilingual support to customers, tailoring content to different regions and language preferences.

Chapter 35: Cloud-Native Governance and Policy Management

35.1: Implementing Governance Policies in Cloud Native Environments

Governance policies are essential for maintaining control, security, and compliance in cloud native environments. By implementing best practices and integrating governance into CI/CD pipelines, organizations can effectively address the unique challenges of cloud native technologies and ensure a well-governed, secure, and cost-efficient cloud native environment. Effective governance policies empower organizations to fully leverage the benefits of cloud native technologies while maintaining control and reducing potential risks.

35.1.1. The Significance of Governance in Cloud Native Environments

- **Security and Compliance:** Governance policies play a vital role in enforcing security best practices and ensuring compliance with industry regulations and data protection standards. As cloud-native applications and infrastructure are exposed to various threats, governance measures help safeguard sensitive data and maintain the integrity of the systems.

- **Resource Management:** Effective governance ensures proper allocation and utilization of cloud resources. By establishing governance policies for resource management, organizations can prevent wastage, optimize costs, and efficiently scale resources as needed.

- **Risk Mitigation:** Governance measures help identify and mitigate potential risks and vulnerabilities in cloud native applications and infrastructure. By proactively addressing security concerns and adhering to best practices, organizations can reduce the likelihood of security breaches and operational disruptions.

- **Consistency and Standardization:** Governance policies promote consistency and standardization across cloud native projects. By establishing standardized guidelines and practices, managing cloud resources and collaborating on projects becomes more efficient and less error-prone.

35.1.2. Best Practices for Implementing Governance Policies

- **Cloud Resource Tagging:** Enforce a standardized tagging policy to categorize and label cloud resources. Tags help with resource identification, cost allocation, and management, enabling better organization and tracking of resources.

- **Access Control and Identity Management:** Implement robust identity and access management (IAM) controls to ensure appropriate access levels for users and applications. This ensures that only authorized personnel can access sensitive resources and data.

- **Automated Compliance Checks:** Utilize automated tools to regularly assess the cloud native environment's compliance status. This includes checks for security configurations and adherence to regulatory standards. Automation helps organizations detect and address compliance issues promptly.

- **Policy as Code:** Implement policies as code using tools like Infrastructure as Code (IaC) and configuration management. This approach allows governance policies to be treated like code, enabling versioning, tracking changes, and ensuring reproducibility.

- **Monitoring and Auditing:** Implement comprehensive monitoring and auditing capabilities to track changes, detect security incidents, and monitor resource usage. Continuous monitoring provides insights into the environment's health and helps identify potential issues or anomalies.

- **Lifecycle Management:** Define policies for resource lifecycle management, including automated resource termination and archiving to prevent unnecessary costs. By automating resource cleanup and management, organizations can optimize their cloud spend.

35.1.3. Governance Challenges in Cloud Native Environments

- **Dynamic Infrastructure:** The dynamic nature of cloud native environments can pose challenges in maintaining consistent governance policies across rapidly changing resources. Governance policies need to be adaptable and able to keep pace with the dynamic nature of cloud native infrastructures.

- **Distributed Architecture:** Cloud native applications are often distributed across multiple services, making governance and visibility more complex. Organizations need to establish governance practices that span multiple services and ensure a centralized view of the cloud environment.

- **Container Orchestration:** Containerized environments and orchestration platforms introduce unique governance requirements for container security and resource allocation. Organizations need to implement specific governance measures to secure containers and manage their resources efficiently.

- **Microservices Complexity:** The adoption of microservices adds complexity to governance, as each microservice may have its own specific requirements and policies. Organizations must tailor their governance approach to accommodate the diverse needs of microservices while maintaining consistency.

35.1.4. Integrating Governance into CI/CD Pipelines

- **Infrastructure as Code (IaC):** Incorporate governance policies directly into IaC templates to ensure consistency during resource provisioning. By including governance policies in the code used to create cloud resources, organizations can enforce standardized configurations from the outset.

- **Continuous Compliance Checks:** Integrate automated compliance checks into continuous integration and continuous deployment (CI/CD) pipelines to catch policy violations early. This proactive approach helps identify and address governance issues during the development and deployment process.

- **Automated Remediation:** Implement automated remediation steps to correct policy violations automatically when they are detected. By automating remediation, organizations can quickly rectify any non-compliant resources or configurations, reducing the risk of security incidents

35.2: Policy as Code and Infrastructure Governance

Policy as Code offers a modern and efficient approach to infrastructure governance in cloud native environments. By expressing governance policies as code, organizations can achieve consistency, automation, and version control, leading to more efficient and secure cloud native deployments. Embracing Policy as Code empowers teams to manage and enforce governance policies effectively, ensuring compliance, security, and cost optimization in cloud native environments. This approach fosters collaboration and agility, making it easier for organizations to adapt to the ever-changing demands of the cloud landscape while maintaining robust governance practices.

35.2.1. Understanding Policy as Code (PaC)

Policy as Code allows organizations to define, manage, and enforce governance policies using code. The policies are written in a language that computers can interpret, and they are stored in version-controlled repositories. By applying PaC to cloud native environments, organizations benefit from the following:

- **Consistency:** PaC ensures that governance policies are consistently applied across all cloud resources, environments, and deployments. This reduces the risk of misconfigurations and ensures a uniform approach to governance.

- **Automation:** Policy as Code enables automated enforcement of policies. By integrating PaC into deployment processes, organizations can automatically verify if resources adhere to governance rules, reducing the need for manual checks and interventions.

- **Version Control:** Storing policies as code allows for versioning, tracking changes, and maintaining a history of policy revisions. Teams can review and roll back changes if necessary, providing better control over policy updates.

35.2.2. Implementing Policy as Code for Infrastructure Governance

- **Infrastructure as Code (IaC):** Policy as Code and Infrastructure as Code (IaC) are closely linked. Organizations can integrate PaC policies directly into IaC templates to define governance requirements for cloud resources. This ensures that policies are applied from the moment resources are provisioned.

- **Domain-Specific Language:** To make it easier for teams to write and maintain governance policies, a domain-specific language tailored for policy definition can be used. Such a language provides a more intuitive way to express complex governance requirements.

- **Policy Evaluation:** Continuous monitoring and evaluation are essential for enforcing PaC policies. By continuously monitoring the cloud environment, organizations can detect policy violations and trigger automated corrective actions.

35.2.3. Benefits of Policy as Code for Infrastructure Governance

- **Scalability:** Policy as Code allows governance policies to scale effortlessly as the cloud infrastructure and resources grow. The automated nature of PaC ensures that policies can handle increased complexity without hindering operations.

- **Agility:** PaC allows for rapid updates and changes to governance policies. This agility is vital as cloud native environments often require quick adjustments to accommodate changing business needs and security requirements.

- **Collaboration:** Storing policies as code fosters collaboration among teams. Policies can be reviewed, discussed, and revised using standard version control practices, ensuring that all stakeholders have a say in governance decisions.

- **Auditability and Compliance:** PaC provides a clear audit trail, making it easier to demonstrate compliance with industry regulations and security standards. Organizations can trace the history of policy changes and demonstrate adherence to best practices.

35.2.4. Challenges and Considerations

- **Policy Complexity:** Complex governance policies may require specialized knowledge and skill to implement as code. Organizations should invest in training and support for teams working on intricate governance requirements.

- **Integration with CI/CD Pipelines:** Integrating PaC into CI/CD pipelines requires careful planning and validation to avoid potential conflicts and disruptions. Organizations should thoroughly test policy updates to prevent unintended consequences.

- **Policy Updates and Rollbacks:** Changes to policies should undergo proper testing and validation before being rolled out to production. Proper testing ensures that policy updates do not inadvertently introduce issues or conflicts.

35.2.5. Popular Policy as Code Tools

- **Open Policy Agent (OPA):** OPA is an open-source project that provides a flexible policy language and an engine for policy evaluation and enforcement. It is widely used in cloud native environments for policy enforcement.

- **Terraform Sentinel:** Terraform Sentinel is a policy-as-code framework integrated with HashiCorp Terraform. It enables organizations to define and enforce governance policies related to infrastructure provisioning.

- **Kubernetes Policy Controllers:** Kubernetes supports Policy Controllers that use Policy as Code to define custom policies for resource configurations and security. These controllers help ensure compliance with governance requirements in Kubernetes environments.

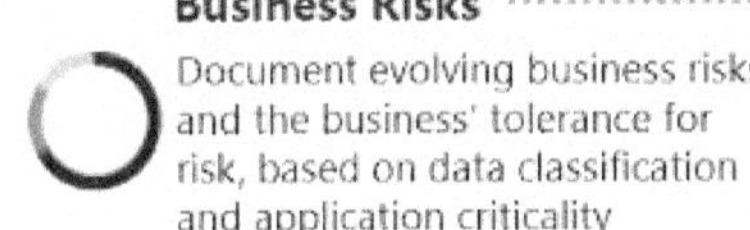
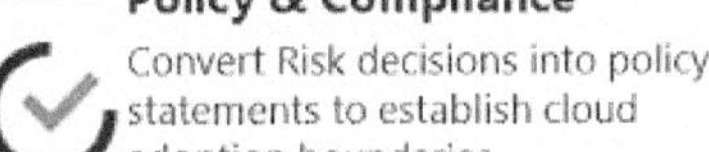
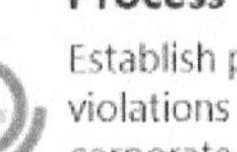

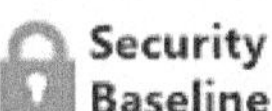

35.3: Managing Access and Permissions in Cloud Native Applications

Managing access and permissions in cloud native applications is fundamental to maintaining security, data integrity, and compliance. By implementing best practices for access management, including the principle of least privilege, RBAC, and multi-factor authentication, organizations can create a secure and efficient access control framework for their cloud native environments. Regular review and auditing of access, along with educating users and developers about security best practices, further strengthens the overall security posture of cloud native applications, ensuring protection against potential threats and unauthorized access. With strong access management practices in place, organizations can confidently leverage the benefits of cloud native technologies while minimizing security risks.

35.3.1. Importance of Access Management in Cloud Native Applications

- **Data Security:** Proper access management ensures that only authorized users and applications have access to sensitive data, safeguarding data confidentiality and integrity.

- **Infrastructure Protection:** Effective access controls prevent unauthorized configuration changes or data exposure in cloud resources, protecting the underlying infrastructure from potential security breaches.

- **Compliance:** Access management is essential for meeting regulatory requirements and industry standards related to data privacy and security. Organizations must demonstrate that access to sensitive resources is appropriately restricted and audited.

35.3.2. Best Practices for Access and Permission Management

- **Least Privilege Principle:** Follow the principle of least privilege, granting users and applications only the minimum access required to perform their tasks. This practice minimizes the risk of potential misuse of privileges.

- **Role-Based Access Control (RBAC):** Implement RBAC to group permissions into roles and assign these roles to users based on their responsibilities. RBAC simplifies access management by associating permissions with defined roles, making it easier to manage access at scale.

- **Multi-Factor Authentication (MFA):** Enforce MFA for user authentication to add an extra layer of security. MFA requires users to provide multiple forms of identification, such as a password and a one-time code sent to their mobile device, reducing the risk of unauthorized access even if a password is compromised.

- **Centralized IAM Policy Management:** Use centralized IAM policy management to maintain consistency and simplify access control administration. Centralization ensures that access policies are consistently applied across various cloud resources and environments.

- **Resource Tagging:** Utilize resource tagging to categorize and organize cloud resources. Tags enable more granular access controls based on specific resource attributes, streamlining permission management.

35.3.3. Implementing Access Management in Cloud Native Environments

- **IAM Services:** Leverage IAM services provided by cloud providers to manage users, roles, and permissions effectively. Cloud-native IAM services offer various features to control access to cloud resources.

- **Service Accounts:** Use service accounts for applications and services to grant them the necessary permissions to interact with cloud resources securely. Service accounts are a safer alternative to using individual user accounts for application access.

- **Kubernetes RBAC:** Implement Kubernetes Role-Based Access Control (RBAC) to manage access to Kubernetes resources within containerized applications. Kubernetes RBAC ensures that only authorized users and services can perform specific actions in the cluster.

- **Secret Management:** Use secure secret management solutions to handle sensitive information, such as passwords, API keys, and encryption keys. Secrets should be stored securely and accessed only by authorized entities.

35.3.4. Regular Review and Auditing

- **Access Reviews:** Conduct regular access reviews to ensure that user permissions align with their current responsibilities and remove unnecessary access. Periodic reviews help prevent overprivileged accounts and unauthorized access.

- **Auditing and Logging:** Enable comprehensive auditing and logging of access events to detect suspicious activities and potential security breaches. Detailed logs provide valuable insights for forensic analysis and incident response.

35.3.5. Handling Third-Party Access

- **Vendor Access Management:** If third-party vendors require access to your cloud resources, establish strict controls and monitor their activity. Vendor access should be granted on a need-to-know basis and revoked when no longer required.

- **Temporary Access:** Provide temporary access to external parties with a well-defined scope and expiration date. Temporary access helps limit exposure to third-party entities and reduces the risk of unauthorized access.

35.3.6. Educating Users and Developers

- **Security Awareness Training:** Educate users and developers about security best practices, including the importance of access management and the risks of sharing credentials. Security awareness training enhances the security posture of the organization by making all stakeholders aware of their roles in maintaining security.

- **Secure Coding Practices:** Train developers to follow secure coding practices, avoiding hardcoding credentials and using secure authentication methods. Secure coding practices prevent common vulnerabilities that could lead to unauthorized access.

Exercise

Multiple Choice Questions

1. What is the significance of governance policies in cloud native environments?

a. Ensuring efficient resource allocation

b. Reducing the complexity of microservices

c. Improving collaboration among teams

d. Maintaining control, security, and compliance

2. Which benefit is associated with implementing governance policies in the cloud?

7a Real-time data analysis

b. Integration with legacy systems

c. Standardization and consistency

d. Multi-factor authentication for users

3. What is a best practice for implementing governance policies in cloud native environments?

s. Manual compliance checks

b. Human-driven resource management

c. Continuous monitoring and auditing

d. Isolating governance from CI/CD pipelines

4. Which challenge is specific to cloud native environments in terms of governance?

a. Static infrastructure configuration

b. Centralized access control management

c. Distributed architecture complexity

d. Limited use of containers

5. How can Policy as Code (PaC) benefit infrastructure governance in cloud native environments?

a. Increasing manual intervention for policy enforcement

b. Ensuring consistent and automated governance policy enforcement

c. Reducing the need for version control in cloud native applications

d. Eliminating the need for access management in CI/CD pipelines

6. Which benefit does Multi-Factor Authentication (MFA) provide for access management in cloud native applications?

a. Simplified user authentication process

b. Increased risk of unauthorized access

c. Additional layers of security for user authentication

d. Elimination of the need for Role-Based Access Control (RBAC)

7. What is the main advantage of implementing Role-Based Access Control (RBAC) in cloud native environments?

a. Simplifying the management of cloud resources

b. Allowing unlimited access for all users

c. Implementing an open policy for access control

d. Associating permissions with defined roles for users

8. What is the primary purpose of conducting regular access reviews in cloud native environments?

a. Identifying new cloud-native resources

b. Ensuring compliance with industry standards

c. Removing unnecessary access and privileges

d. Automatically enforcing governance policies

9. How does education about security best practices benefit access management in cloud native environments?

a. Decreasing the need for auditing and logging

b. Enhancing the security posture of the organization

c. Reducing the complexity of IAM services

d. Exempting users from following the principle of least privilege

REVIEW QUESTIONS

1. What is the significance of governance policies in cloud native environments?

2. How do governance policies benefit cloud native environments?

3. What are some best practices for implementing governance policies in cloud native environments?

4. What are the primary challenges in implementing governance policies in cloud native environments?

5. How does Policy as Code (PaC) help in infrastructure governance for cloud native environments?

6. What are the benefits of Role-Based Access Control (RBAC) for access management in cloud native environments?

7. How does Multi-Factor Authentication (MFA) enhance access management in cloud native applications?

8. How can organizations improve access management through regular review and auditing?

9. How does educating users and developers about security best practices enhance access management in cloud native environments?

Answer Section

Multiple Choice Questions

1. d) Maintaining control, security, and compliance

2. c) Standardization and consistency

3. c) Continuous monitoring and auditing

4. c) Distributed architecture complexity

5. b) Ensuring consistent and automated governance policy enforcement

6. c) Additional layers of security for user authentication

7. d) Associating permissions with defined roles for users

8. c) Removing unnecessary access and privileges

9. b) Enhancing the security posture of the organization

Review Questions

1. Governance policies are crucial in cloud native environments to maintain control, security, and compliance. They ensure that the organization adheres to best practices, industry regulations, and data protection standards. With cloud-native technologies exposed to various threats, governance measures safeguard sensitive data and maintain system integrity.

2. Governance policies provide several benefits, including enhanced security, optimized resource management, risk mitigation, and standardized practices. They enable organizations to manage cloud resources efficiently, reduce potential security breaches, and foster collaboration among teams.

3. To implement governance policies effectively, organizations should enforce cloud resource tagging, implement access control and identity management, use automated compliance checks, and treat policies as code. Additionally, comprehensive monitoring, auditing, and proper lifecycle management are crucial for maintaining governance.

4. The dynamic nature of cloud-native infrastructures, distributed architecture, container orchestration, and complexities introduced by microservices pose significant challenges in maintaining consistent governance policies. Organizations must adapt their governance approaches to suit the unique requirements of cloud native technologies.

5. Policy as Code (PaC) allows organizations to define, manage, and enforce governance policies using code, ensuring consistency and automation. Storing policies as code enables version control, simplifies policy administration, and supports rapid updates to accommodate changing business needs.

6. RBAC simplifies access management by grouping permissions into roles and associating them with users based on their responsibilities. This minimizes the risk of unauthorized access and ensures that users have the necessary privileges to perform their tasks without unnecessary permissions.

7. MFA adds an extra layer of security by requiring users to provide multiple forms of identification during authentication, such as a password and a one-time code. This reduces the risk of unauthorized access, even if a password is compromised, as attackers would need additional authentication factors.

8. Regular access reviews help ensure that user permissions align with their current roles and responsibilities, reducing overprivileged accounts and unauthorized access. Comprehensive auditing and logging of access events help detect suspicious activities, enabling prompt responses to potential security breaches.

9. Security awareness training and promoting secure coding practices help users and developers understand their roles in maintaining security. Educated stakeholders are more aware of potential risks, follow best practices, and contribute to a stronger security posture, reducing the likelihood of unauthorized access and security incidents.

Chapter 36: Cloud Security Operations and Incident Response

36.1 Security Operations in Cloud Environments

Security operations in cloud environments play a pivotal role in safeguarding data, applications, and cloud resources from a multitude of threats. By adopting best practices, leveraging security tools and services, and fostering a security-aware culture, organizations can enhance their security posture in the cloud. Proactive security operations enable organizations to detect and respond to security incidents promptly, ensuring the confidentiality, integrity, and availability of critical data and applications, while meeting regulatory compliance requirements. A robust security operations framework is essential to maintain trust with customers and stakeholders, protect sensitive data, and defend against evolving cyber threats in the dynamic cloud landscape.

36.1.1. Importance of Security Operations in the Cloud

- **Threat Landscape:** Cloud environments face a diverse range of threats, including data breaches, DDoS attacks, and insider threats. Security operations are crucial to identify and address these threats effectively.

- **Data Protection:** Security operations ensure the confidentiality, integrity, and availability of data stored and processed in the cloud. By implementing security controls and best practices, organizations can protect sensitive data from unauthorized access or modifications.

- **Compliance Requirements:** Many industries have strict compliance regulations regarding data security and privacy. Security operations are essential for meeting these requirements and demonstrating adherence to industry standards.

- **Proactive Detection and Response:** Security operations help identify security incidents promptly and respond proactively to minimize potential damages. A swift and effective response can prevent security breaches from escalating into major incidents.

36.1.2. Best Practices for Security Operations in Cloud Environments

- **Cloud Security Architecture:** Design a secure cloud architecture following defense-in-depth principles. This involves separating different layers of the architecture and applying security controls at each level to create multiple layers of protection.

- **Identity and Access Management (IAM):** Implement strong IAM practices, including multi-factor authentication (MFA) and least privilege, to control access to cloud resources. IAM ensures that only authorized users and applications can interact with sensitive data and resources.

- **Encryption:** Utilize encryption to protect data at rest and in transit. This ensures that even if data is compromised, it remains unreadable and unusable to unauthorized entities.

- **Continuous Monitoring:** Implement continuous monitoring of cloud resources to detect suspicious activities and potential security breaches in real-time. Continuous monitoring enhances the organization's ability to respond swiftly to emerging threats.

- **Security Incident Response Plan:** Develop a comprehensive incident response plan that outlines the procedures and actions to be taken in the event of a security incident. A well-defined plan ensures a coordinated and efficient response to security breaches.

- **Security Automation and Orchestration:** Use automation and orchestration to streamline security operations. Automating repetitive tasks and responses allows security teams to focus on more critical security issues and reduces the risk of human errors.

36.1.3. Cloud Security Tools and Services

- **Cloud-Native Security Services:** Leverage cloud providers' security services, such as AWS Security Hub, Azure Security Center, or Google Cloud Security Command Center, to gain centralized visibility and monitoring of security events across the cloud environment.

- **Security Information and Event Management (SIEM):** Employ SIEM solutions to aggregate and analyze security logs from various cloud services and infrastructure components. SIEM tools help identify patterns indicative of security threats.

- **Vulnerability Management:** Utilize vulnerability scanning and management tools to identify and remediate security weaknesses in cloud resources. Regular vulnerability assessments help prevent potential exploits.

- **Threat Intelligence:** Integrate threat intelligence feeds to stay informed about emerging threats and enhance security monitoring. Access to real-time threat intelligence helps security teams proactively defend against evolving threats.

36.1.4. Incident Detection and Response

- **Security Analytics:** Utilize security analytics tools to detect anomalies and potential threats in real-time. security analytics helps identify abnormal behavior and suspicious patterns that may indicate an ongoing security incident.

- **Automated Response:** Implement automated incident response mechanisms to take immediate action against known threats. Automated response actions can block malicious activities and prevent further damage.

- **Forensics and Investigation:** Develop procedures for conducting post-incident forensics and investigations to understand the root cause of security incidents fully. These investigations provide insights to improve security measures and prevent similar incidents in the future.

36.1.5. Employee Training and Awareness

- **Security Awareness Training:** Conduct regular security awareness training for employees to educate them about security best practices and potential threats. Educated employees are a crucial line of defense against social engineering attacks and other security risks.

- **Social Engineering Awareness:** Train employees to recognize and report social engineering attempts, such as phishing attacks. Social engineering awareness helps reduce the likelihood of successful social engineering attacks.

36.2 Threat Detection and Incident Response in the Cloud

Threat detection and incident response are critical components of a robust cloud security strategy. By implementing continuous monitoring, leveraging security analytics, and adopting automated incident response mechanisms, organizations can proactively detect and respond to security threats in cloud environments. Incident response readiness, including incident response plans, forensics, and training, is essential for minimizing the impact of security incidents and ensuring business continuity. Embracing cloud-native security services and tools further enhances the security posture, enabling organizations to protect sensitive data, maintain compliance, and stay resilient against evolving cyber threats in the cloud. A proactive and well-prepared security approach is essential to maintain trust with customers and stakeholders and safeguard critical assets in the dynamic cloud landscape

.

36.2.1. Importance of Threat Detection and Incident Response in the Cloud

- **Rapidly Evolving Threats:** The cloud is a prime target for cyber threats due to the vast amount of valuable data stored in cloud environments. As threats continue to evolve, proactive detection and response are crucial to stay ahead of potential attackers.

- **Data Breach Prevention:** Swift detection and response help prevent data breaches and limit the exposure of sensitive information. Timely action can prevent attackers from exfiltrating data or exploiting vulnerabilities.

- **Compliance and Risk Management:** Effective threat detection and incident response are crucial for maintaining compliance with data protection regulations and managing security risks. Organizations must demonstrate their ability to detect and respond to security incidents to comply with industry standards.

- **Business Continuity:** Quick incident response ensures minimal disruption to cloud services and business continuity. A rapid response can prevent attackers from causing prolonged downtime or service disruptions.

36.2.2. Best Practices for Threat Detection in the Cloud

- **Continuous Monitoring:** Implement continuous monitoring of cloud resources, networks, and user activities to detect suspicious behavior. Continuous monitoring provides real-time insights into security events, enabling swift response.

- **Security Analytics and AI/ML:** Leverage security analytics and AI/ML-powered tools to identify anomalies and potential threats in real-time. These technologies can help security teams identify patterns indicative of malicious activities.

- **Log Analysis:** Analyze security logs from various cloud services and infrastructure components to detect security incidents and patterns. Comprehensive log analysis can provide valuable information for incident investigation and response.

- **Threat Intelligence:** Integrate threat intelligence feeds to stay informed about emerging threats and enhance security monitoring. Access to up-to-date threat intelligence helps security teams proactively defend against evolving threats.

36.2.3. Best Practices for Incident Response in the Cloud

- **Incident Response Plan:** Develop a comprehensive incident response plan tailored to cloud environments, including roles, responsibilities, and escalation procedures. An incident response plan ensures a structured and coordinated response to security incidents.

- **Automated Incident Response:** Implement automated incident response mechanisms to react swiftly to known threats and apply predefined remediation actions. Automation allows for faster response times, reducing the time attackers have to operate.

- **Isolation and Containment:** If an incident occurs, promptly isolate affected resources to contain the threat and prevent further damage. Isolation helps limit the impact of the incident on other parts of the cloud environment.

- **Forensics and Investigation:** After an incident, conduct post-incident forensics and investigation to understand the root cause and prevent similar incidents in the future. Forensics provides insights into the attack vector and weaknesses that need improvement.

36.2.4. Cloud-Native Security Services and Tools

- **Cloud Provider Security Services:** Utilize cloud provider security services like AWS GuardDuty, Azure Sentinel, or Google Cloud Security Command Center for centralized threat detection. These services offer native cloud integrations and provide valuable security insights.

- **Security Information and Event Management (SIEM):** Employ SIEM solutions to aggregate and analyze security logs from cloud and on-premises infrastructure. SIEM tools provide a unified view of security events, enabling better threat detection and correlation.

- **Intrusion Detection and Prevention Systems (IDS/IPS):** Deploy IDS/IPS systems to detect and block potential threats in real-time. These systems monitor network traffic and can take automated actions to thwart attacks.

36.2.5. Incident Response Readiness

- **Tabletop Exercises:** Conduct regular tabletop exercises to simulate security incidents and test the effectiveness of incident response plans. Tabletop exercises help improve incident response capabilities and identify areas for improvement.

- **Training and Awareness:** Regularly train employees and stakeholders on incident response procedures and cybersecurity best practices. Educated staff can recognize and report security incidents promptly, enhancing incident response effectiveness.

36.3 Security Automation and Orchestration in Cloud Security Operations Centers (SOCs)

Security Automation and Orchestration is a game-changer for cloud SOCs, enhancing their capabilities to detect, respond, and mitigate security threats effectively. By implementing SAO, cloud security teams can streamline incident response, optimize resource usage, and maintain consistent security practices in dynamic cloud environments. Embracing cloud-native automation tools and platforms further strengthens SOC operations, enabling organizations to stay ahead of evolving threats and protect their cloud assets and data with speed, accuracy, and scalability. Combining automation with human expertise ensures a well-rounded security approach that effectively safeguards cloud environments against a myriad of security risks. The integration of SAO into cloud SOCs is essential to enhance threat detection, incident response, and overall security resilience in the rapidly evolving cloud landscape.

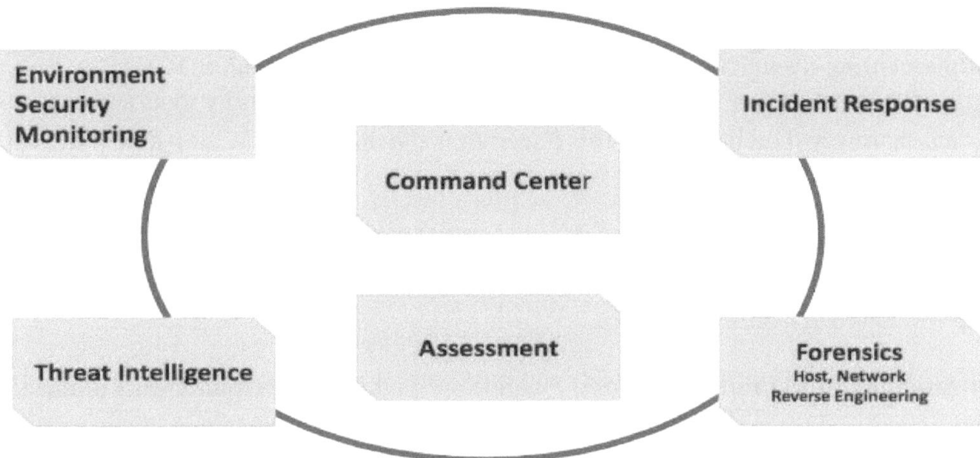

36.3.1. The Role of Security Automation and Orchestration in Cloud SOCs

- **Efficiency and Speed:** SAO accelerates incident response by automating manual tasks, reducing response times, and enabling real-time threat detection. SOC analysts can focus on critical tasks while routine activities are handled by automation.

- **Consistency:** Automation ensures consistent application of security processes and policies, minimizing human errors and improving the overall security posture. Security best practices are consistently followed, enhancing the organization's security readiness.

- **Scalability:** In cloud environments, automation enables SOC teams to handle a large volume of security events and incidents efficiently. As cloud environments scale, automation becomes indispensable for managing security operations effectively.

- **Resource Optimization:** Automation allows SOC analysts to focus on high-value tasks, maximizing the utilization of human expertise. Repetitive and time-consuming tasks are offloaded to automation, freeing up analysts for more strategic activities.

36.3.2. Use Cases of Security Automation and Orchestration in Cloud SOCs

- **Automated Incident Triage:** SAO can analyze and categorize incoming security alerts, prioritizing critical incidents for immediate attention. This triage process helps SOC analysts quickly identify and respond to high-priority threats.

- **Automated Threat Hunting:** Automation can be used to proactively search for potential threats and vulnerabilities in cloud environments. Automated threat hunting tools can detect suspicious activities and emerging threats.

- **Automated Playbooks:** Predefined playbooks automate response actions for specific security incidents, such as malware infections or unauthorized access attempts. These playbooks enable consistent and swift responses to known threats.

- **Security Incident Enrichment:** Automation can enrich security incidents with additional context and threat intelligence to aid SOC analysts in their investigations. Enriched incidents provide analysts with valuable insights for effective decision-making.

36.3.3. Implementing Security Automation and Orchestration in Cloud SOCs

- **Integrating Security Tools:** SAO platforms integrate with various security tools and systems, enabling seamless data sharing and orchestration. This integration enhances the SOC's visibility into security events across the cloud environment.

- **Defining Workflows and Playbooks:** Develop workflows and playbooks that align with cloud-specific security use cases, ensuring efficient automation. Well-defined playbooks ensure consistent and appropriate responses to security incidents.

- **Customization and Flexibility:** Tailor SAO workflows to the unique requirements of the organization's cloud environment and security policies. Customization ensures that automation aligns with specific business needs.

- **Security Policy Compliance:** Automate security policy enforcement to ensure compliance with industry standards and regulatory requirements. Automation helps enforce security policies consistently and in real-time.

36.3.4. Cloud Native Automation Tools and Services

- **Cloud Provider Security Services:** Leverage cloud provider-specific automation tools for security, such as AWS Lambda, Azure Functions, or Google Cloud Functions. These cloud-native services are well-integrated and offer seamless automation capabilities.

- **Security Automation Platforms:** Adopt specialized security automation platforms that offer integration with various security tools and customizable playbooks. These platforms centralize automation efforts and enhance collaboration among SOC teams.

- **Security Orchestration Frameworks:** Use open-source security orchestration frameworks like TheHive, Demisto, or Phantom, tailored for SOC automation. These frameworks provide a foundation for building sophisticated automation workflows.

36.3.5. Continuous Improvement and Human Oversight

- **Ongoing Optimization:** Continuously evaluate and optimize SAO workflows to improve efficiency and effectiveness. Regular review and refinement ensure that automation remains up-to-date and aligned with emerging threats.

- **Human Oversight:** While automation is beneficial, human expertise remains crucial for decision-making and complex incident analysis. SOC analysts play a key role in interpreting automation results and making strategic decisions.

Exercise

Multiple Choice Questions

1. In cloud environments, security operations are essential for:

a. Enhancing resource utilization.

b. Enforcing data sharing policies.

c. Preventing unauthorized resource access.

d. Optimizing cloud cost management.

2. What is the primary purpose of continuous monitoring in cloud security operations?

a. Ensuring 100% uptime of cloud resources.

b. Detecting and mitigating DDoS attacks.

c. Providing real-time insights into security events.

d. Automating resource provisioning and deprovisioning.

3. How can organizations improve incident response in the cloud?

a. Conducting regular security awareness training.

b. Deploying intrusion detection systems.

c. Implementing automated incident response mechanisms.

d. Utilizing continuous vulnerability scanning.

4. Which tool aggregates and analyzes security logs from various cloud services and infrastructure components to detect security incidents and patterns?

a. Security Information and Event Management (SIEM).

b. Intrusion Detection and Prevention Systems (IDS/IPS).

c. Vulnerability Management Platform.

d. Cloud Provider Security Hub.

5. Security Automation and Orchestration (SAO) in cloud SOCs primarily aims to:

a. Reduce the need for skilled security analysts.

b. Maximize the utilization of human expertise.

c. Replace all manual security operations tasks.

d. Ensure absolute consistency in incident response.

6. What is one benefit of automating incident triage in cloud security operations?

a. Minimizing the need for human oversight.

b. Eliminating the need for threat hunting.

c. Streamlining the analysis of security logs.

d. Automatically blocking all incoming threats.

7. Which aspect of security operations is essential for meeting industry compliance requirements?

a. Continuous vulnerability scanning.

b. Real-time threat intelligence feeds.

c. Automated threat hunting.

d. Effective threat detection and response.

8. How can security automation and orchestration benefit cloud SOCs during incident response?

a. Identifying cloud service vulnerabilities proactively.

b. Ensuring 100% detection accuracy of security incidents.

c. Streamlining manual tasks, reducing response times.

d. Eliminating the need for security analysts altogether.

9. Why is threat intelligence integration crucial in security operations?

a. To automate incident triage based on threat severity.

b. To provide security logs from various cloud services.

c. To ensure continuous monitoring of cloud resources.

d. To stay informed about emerging threats for proactive defense.

Review Questions

1. What are the primary benefits of implementing security operations in cloud environments?
2. How does continuous monitoring improve cloud security?
3. What role does automation play in incident response in cloud security operations?
4. How do security analytics and AI/ML-powered tools enhance threat detection in cloud SOCs?
5. What are the best practices for incident response readiness in cloud environments?

6. How does cloud-native automation enhance security operations?
7. What is the significance of threat intelligence integration in cloud security operations?
8. How can organizations maximize the benefits of security automation and orchestration (SAO)?
9. Why is a proactive approach to threat detection and incident response crucial in cloud security?

Answer Section

Multiple Choice Questions

1. c) Preventing unauthorized resource access.
2. c) Providing real-time insights into security events.
3. c) Implementing automated incident response mechanisms.
4. a) Security Information and Event Management (SIEM).
5. b) Maximize the utilization of human expertise.
6. c) Streamlining the analysis of security logs.
7. d) Effective threat detection and response.
8. c) Streamlining manual tasks, reducing response times.
9. d) To stay informed about emerging threats for proactive defense.

Review Questions

1. Implementing security operations in cloud environments offers multiple benefits, including safeguarding data, applications, and cloud resources from diverse threats, ensuring data protection, meeting compliance requirements, and enabling proactive detection and response to security incidents. It enhances the security posture, instills trust with customers and stakeholders, and defends against evolving cyber threats.

2. Continuous monitoring provides real-time insights into security events, network activities, and user behavior in cloud environments. It enables swift detection of suspicious behavior, potential threats, and security incidents, allowing security teams to respond proactively. Continuous monitoring enhances incident response readiness and reduces the time between detection and response, minimizing the impact of security breaches and maintaining business continuity.

3. Automation streamlines incident response by automating manual tasks and predefined response actions through playbooks. It accelerates incident triage, categorizes and prioritizes alerts, and enables swift remediation of known threats. Automation helps SOC analysts focus on critical tasks, optimize resource usage, and respond faster to security incidents, ultimately improving the overall security posture in cloud environments.

4. Security analytics and AI/ML-powered tools analyze vast amounts of security data to identify patterns and anomalies indicative of potential threats. These technologies can detect sophisticated attacks and

emerging threats that traditional methods might miss. They provide deeper insights into security events and improve the accuracy and speed of threat detection in cloud security operations.

5. Incident response readiness in cloud environments involves developing comprehensive incident response plans, implementing automated incident response mechanisms, conducting regular tabletop exercises, and providing continuous training and awareness to employees. It also includes performing post-incident forensics and investigations to understand the root cause of security incidents and enhance future incident response.

6. Cloud-native automation tools and platforms, such as AWS Lambda, Azure Functions, and Google Cloud Functions, seamlessly integrate with cloud environments and security services. They offer scalable and efficient automation capabilities that improve incident response, resource utilization, and overall security operations in dynamic cloud landscapes.

7. Threat intelligence integration keeps security teams informed about emerging threats, attack vectors, and malicious activities in the cloud. Real-time access to threat intelligence feeds enables proactive defense and better decision-making during incident response. It helps security operations stay ahead of evolving cyber threats and enhances the organization's overall security resilience.

8. To maximize the benefits of SAO, organizations should integrate security tools and services, define custom workflows and playbooks, ensure security policy compliance, and regularly optimize automation workflows. They should also balance automation with human oversight to leverage the expertise of SOC analysts in decision-making and complex incident analysis.

9. A proactive approach allows organizations to detect and respond to security threats before they escalate into major incidents. It minimizes the impact of security breaches, prevents data exfiltration, and ensures business continuity. Proactive threat detection and incident response instill confidence in customers, regulators, and stakeholders and demonstrate a strong commitment to maintaining a secure and resilient cloud environment.

Chapter 37: Cloud Identity and Access Management (IAM) Best Practices

37.1: IAM Fundamentals and Concepts in the Cloud

IAM is a foundational pillar of cloud security, controlling access to cloud resources and ensuring data protection. Understanding IAM basics, such as identities, authentication, and authorization, is essential for secure cloud deployments. By following IAM best practices and leveraging IAM features provided by cloud providers, organizations can establish robust access controls, enforce the principle of least privilege, and protect their cloud environments from unauthorized access and potential security risks. A well-implemented IAM strategy enhances cloud security, contributes to regulatory compliance.

37.1.1. IAM Basics in Cloud Environments

- **Identity:** In IAM, an identity represents a unique entity, which could be a user, a group of users, or an application. Each identity is assigned a unique identifier and is associated with a set of credentials used for authentication, such as a username and password.

- **Authentication:** Authentication verifies the identity of a user or application attempting to access cloud resources. Common authentication methods include passwords, where users provide a secret passphrase, and multi-factor authentication (MFA), which requires users to provide additional authentication factors, such as a one-time code from their mobile device, in addition to their passwords. MFA adds an extra layer of security and reduces the risk of unauthorized access even if a user's password is compromised.

- **Authorization:** Authorization determines the level of access a user or application has to specific cloud resources based on their identity and assigned permissions. Once a user's identity is authenticated, the IAM system checks the associated policies to determine what actions the user is allowed or denied to perform. These policies define the specific permissions that dictate what resources the user can access and what operations they can perform on those resources.

37.1.2. IAM Components in Cloud Providers

- **Users:** Users are individuals who have been granted access to the cloud environment. Each user has a unique set of credentials used for authentication. Cloud administrators can create, manage, and delete users, controlling their access to various cloud resources.

- **Groups:** Groups are collections of users with similar roles or access requirements. By assigning permissions to a group, administrators can manage access for multiple users at once. This simplifies access management and ensures consistent permissions for users in similar roles. For example, all members of the "Development Team" group may have access to the cloud-based development environment.

- **Roles:** Roles define a set of permissions that can be assumed by users or applications. Roles are associated with policies that dictate what actions are allowed or denied. By assigning roles to users or groups, administrators can easily manage access controls and apply the principle of least privilege. For instance, a "Read-Only" role may grant users the ability to view data but not modify or delete it.

- **Policies:** Policies are documents defining permissions. They specify which actions are permitted or denied for specific cloud resources. Policies are attached to roles or directly to users, determining what actions they can take within the cloud environment. Policies are written using a specific syntax that defines the allowed or denied actions and the resources to which they apply.

37.1.3. IAM Best Practices in Cloud Environments

- **Principle of Least Privilege:** Follow the principle of least privilege, granting users and applications only the minimum access necessary to perform their tasks. Avoid granting excessive permissions to reduce the risk of accidental or intentional misuse of resources.

- **Use Groups and Roles:** Assign permissions to groups and roles rather than individual users to simplify access management and maintain consistency. This makes it easier to manage access controls as users change roles or leave the organization.

- **Multi-Factor Authentication (MFA):** Enable MFA for enhanced security, requiring users to provide additional authentication factors beyond their passwords. MFA significantly reduces the risk of unauthorized access due to compromised passwords.

- **Regular Reviews:** Conduct regular access reviews to ensure permissions align with users' current roles and responsibilities. Periodic reviews help identify and address any unnecessary or excessive permissions, reducing potential security risks.

37.1.4. IAM in Cloud-Native Services

- **IAM for Compute Services:** Cloud providers offer IAM capabilities for services like virtual machines, containers, and serverless computing platforms. IAM controls determine who can create, modify, and access these computing resources. For example, IAM can restrict users' ability to launch specific instances or manage containers based on their roles.

- **IAM for Storage Services:** IAM controls access to cloud storage services, such as object storage and databases. Administrators can define which users or applications have read, write, or delete access to specific data stored in these services. IAM policies can restrict access to sensitive data stored in cloud databases.

- **IAM for Networking Services:** IAM can be applied to networking resources, such as virtual networks, load balancers, and firewalls. IAM controls can restrict which users or applications can modify network configurations and access network resources. For example, only authorized network administrators should have the ability to modify firewall rules.

37.1.5. IAM and Cloud Security

- **Data Protection:** IAM ensures that only authorized users and applications can access sensitive data, enhancing data protection in the cloud. By controlling access to cloud resources, IAM helps prevent unauthorized data exposure and data breaches.

- **Security Compliance:** IAM plays a crucial role in meeting regulatory compliance requirements, especially regarding data access and authorization. Implementing IAM best practices helps organizations demonstrate compliance with industry standards and regulations.

- **Incident Response:** IAM can help contain security incidents by promptly revoking access for compromised or unauthorized accounts. When a security incident occurs, disabling the affected identity's access can prevent further damage and unauthorized activities.

37.2: Role-Based Access Control (RBAC) in Cloud Environments

Role-Based Access Control is a powerful access control model for cloud environments, offering granular control over user permissions and improving overall security. By implementing RBAC, organizations can enforce the principle of least privilege, streamline access management, and mitigate the risk of unauthorized access to sensitive cloud resources. Regular reviews and adherence to RBAC best practices ensure that access rights remain aligned with user roles and responsibilities, contributing to a more secure and efficient cloud environment. RBAC is an essential component of an organization's IAM strategy, providing a structured and organized approach to access management in dynamic and distributed cloud environments.

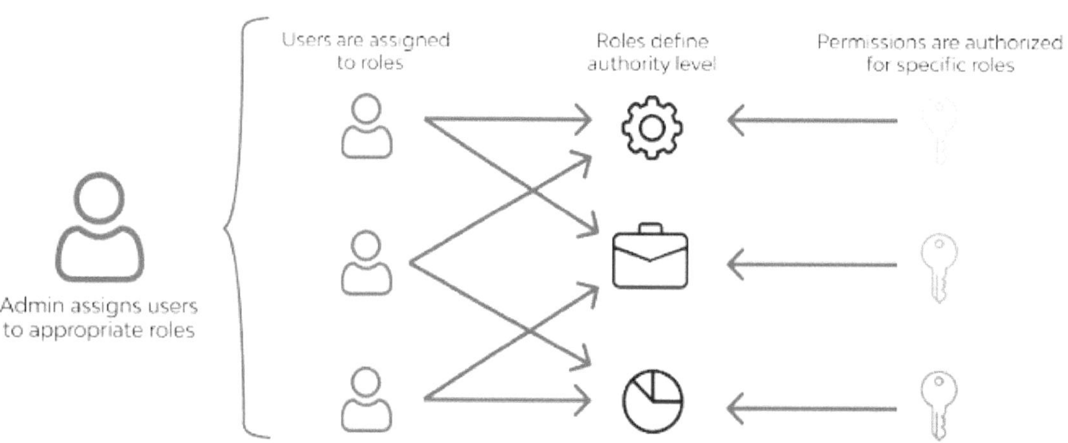

37.2.1. Understanding Role-Based Access Control (RBAC)

- **Roles:** Roles define a set of permissions associated with specific tasks or responsibilities. They represent job functions or categories of users in an organization. For example, roles could be "Administrator," "Developer," "Read-Only User," et Each role is associated with a specific set of permissions that dictate what actions users with that role can perform on cloud resources.

- **Permissions:** Permissions are actions that users can perform on cloud resources, such as read, write, delete, or manage. These permissions are associated with roles and determine the level of access a user has to specific resources within the cloud environment.

- **Users:** Users are individuals who are assigned specific roles and, based on these roles, have permissions to interact with cloud resources. Each user can be associated with one or more roles, allowing them to perform various tasks based on their responsibilities.

37.2.2. Benefits of Role-Based Access Control in Cloud Environments

- **Granular Access Control:** RBAC enables granular control over access, allowing organizations to assign fine-grained permissions based on job functions. This ensures that users have access only to the resources necessary to perform their specific tasks, reducing the risk of unauthorized access.

- **Scalability:** RBAC is scalable, making it suitable for managing access for a large number of users and cloud resources. As organizations grow and more users are added, RBAC provides a structured and organized approach to access management.

- **Simplified Access Management:** By associating permissions with roles rather than individual users, RBAC simplifies access management and reduces administrative overhead. When a new user joins the organization or an existing user changes roles, the access management process becomes more efficient and less error-prone.

- **Improved Security:** RBAC enforces the principle of least privilege, which means users are granted only the permissions they require to perform their duties. This minimizes the potential impact of security breaches and insider threats. In case a user's credentials are compromised, the scope of potential damage is limited to the permissions associated with their role.

37.2.3. Implementing RBAC in Cloud Environments

- **Identify Roles and Responsibilities:** The first step in implementing RBAC is to define roles that align with different job functions or responsibilities in the organization. Roles should be well-defined and mapped to specific tasks or access requirements.

- **Role Assignment:** Once roles are defined, administrators assign appropriate roles to users based on their job roles or responsibilities. Users may have one or more roles, depending on their duties.

- **Role Permissions:** After roles are assigned, administrators define role permissions to specify the actions users with each role can perform on cloud resources. Role permissions should be carefully configured to ensure that users have the necessary access without unnecessary privileges.

- **Regular Reviews:** Regular access reviews are essential to ensure roles and permissions align with users' current roles and responsibilities. Periodic reviews help identify and address any unnecessary or excessive permissions, reducing potential security risks.

37.2.4. RBAC and Cloud-Native Services

- **IAM Services:** Cloud providers offer built-in IAM services that support RBAC, allowing organizations to create and manage roles and permissions. IAM services provide a centralized platform to control access across various cloud services and resources.

- **Resource-Specific RBAC:** Some cloud services, like databases and storage, have their own RBAC models to manage access to specific resources. In these cases, organizations may need to configure resource-specific RBAC in addition to the overarching IAM RBA

37.2.5. Limitations and Considerations

- **Role Proliferation:** While RBAC provides granular access control, creating too many roles can lead to complexity and administrative overhead. Strive for a balance between granularity and simplicity, creating roles that cover common access scenarios without excessive fragmentation.

- **Permission Inheritance:** Administrators should ensure that role permissions are well-defined to avoid unintentional access to resources. In some cases, permissions may be inherited from higher-level roles, leading to unintended access if not properly managed.

37.2.6. RBAC Best Practices

- **Least Privilege Principle:** RBAC aligns well with the principle of least privilege, where administrators assign roles with only the permissions necessary for users to perform their duties. Avoid granting broad, all-encompassing permissions to users.

- **Separation of Duties:** To prevent potential conflicts of interest and enhance security, avoid assigning conflicting roles to a single user. Separating duties ensures that no single user has too much control over critical resources.

- **Regular Auditing:** Conduct regular audits and reviews of role assignments and permissions to ensure adherence to security policies. Regularly review access rights and adjust them as needed based on changes in user roles or responsibilities.

37.3: Identity Federation and Single Sign-On (SSO) in the Cloud

Identity Federation and Single Sign-On are powerful tools for enhancing cloud security and user experience. By enabling seamless and secure access to multiple cloud services and applications, these technologies simplify authentication processes and improve overall security. Implementing Identity Federation and SSO in cloud environments streamlines identity management, centralizes access control, and reduces the risk of password-related vulnerabilities.

Organizations can achieve a balance between user convenience and enhanced security by integrating compatible Identity Providers, enforcing MFA, and adhering to best practices for secure token exchange and user lifecycle management. Identity Federation and Single Sign-On are essential components of an organization's cloud security strategy, providing a structured and organized approach to access management in dynamic and distributed cloud environments. By embracing these technologies, organizations can enhance their security posture while offering a seamless and user-friendly experience to their users across various cloud services and applications.

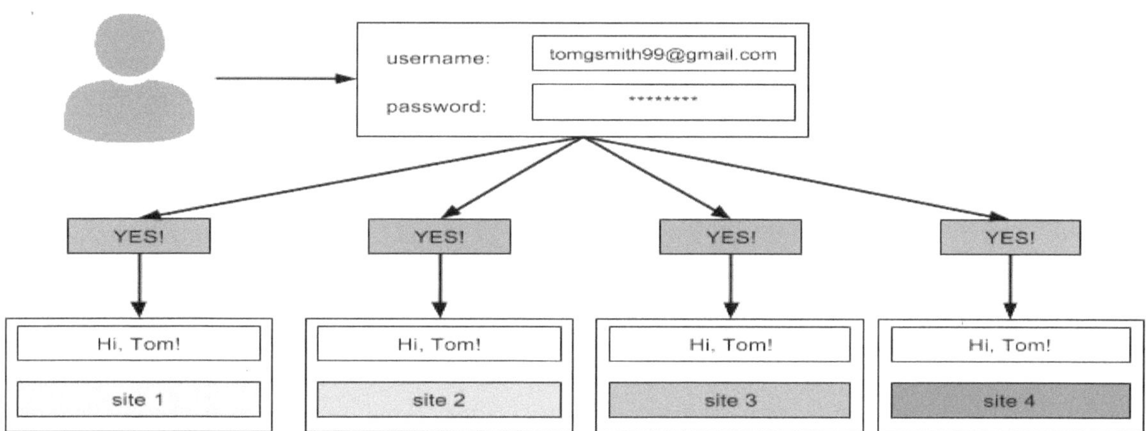

37.3.1. Understanding Identity Federation

- **Identity Providers (IdP):** Identity Providers are trusted systems that authenticate users and issue identity tokens, such as Security Assertion Markup Language (SAML) or OpenID Connect (OIDC) tokens.

- **Service Providers (SP):** Service Providers are applications or services that rely on Identity Providers for user authentication and access control.

- **Identity Tokens:** Identity tokens contain information about the user's identity and authentication status, allowing Service Providers to trust the user's identity.

37.3.2. Benefits of Identity Federation in Cloud Environments

- **Single Identity Across Services:** One of the primary benefits of Identity Federation is that users can access multiple cloud services and applications using a single set of credentials. This reduces password fatigue and improves user experience, as they don't have to remember multiple login credentials for different services.

- **Centralized Identity Management:** Identity Federation centralizes identity management, making it easier to revoke access and manage user privileges. When a user's access needs to be revoked, it can be done centrally through the Identity Provider, ensuring that access is immediately terminated across all connected services.

- **Enhanced Security:** Identity Federation reduces the number of passwords users need to remember, decreasing the risk of weak or reused passwords. This enhances security as users are less likely to use easily guessable passwords or write them down.

37.3.3. Understanding Single Sign-On (SSO)

- **SSO Process:** Single Sign-On allows users to log in once using their credentials, and subsequent access to other applications and services is granted without the need for reauthentication. Once a user is authenticated by the Identity Provider, they can access multiple Service Providers without having to enter their credentials again.

- **SSO Protocols:** SAML and OpenID Connect (OIDC) are common SSO protocols used in cloud environments. SAML is an XML-based standard, while OIDC is built on top of OAuth 2.0 and uses JSON web tokens (JWTs) for identity information.

37.3.4. Benefits of Single Sign-On in Cloud Environments

- **User Convenience:** SSO eliminates the need for users to log in multiple times, enhancing user productivity and reducing frustration. Users can seamlessly move between different applications and services without interruption.

- **Enhanced Security:** SSO simplifies authentication, making it easier for users to comply with security policies. With fewer passwords to remember, users are more likely to use stronger and unique passwords, reducing the risk of password-related vulnerabilities.

- **Centralized Access Control:** SSO enables centralized access control and revocation of user privileges. If a user's access needs to be revoked, it can be done at the Identity Provider level, immediately denying access to all connected Service Providers.

37.3.5. Implementing Identity Federation and Single Sign-On in Cloud Environments

- **Integration with Identity Providers:** Cloud services and applications need to be integrated with compatible Identity Providers supporting SAML or OID This integration establishes a trust relationship between the Identity Provider and Service Provider for federated identity management.

- **Federated Identity Management:** During the integration process, organizations configure the Identity Provider and Service Provider to establish a trusted relationship for federated identity management. The Identity Provider authenticates users and issues identity tokens, while the Service Provider relies on these tokens for user access.

- **Multi-Factor Authentication (MFA):** To enhance security when accessing cloud resources through SSO, organizations should enforce Multi-Factor Authentication (MFA). MFA requires users to provide additional authentication factors beyond their passwords, adding an extra layer of security.

37.3.6. Identity Federation and SSO for Cloud-Native Services

- **Cloud Identity Services:** Many cloud providers offer their own identity and access management services that support Identity Federation and SSO. Organizations can leverage these built-in services for managing access to cloud resources.

- **Kubernetes SSO Integration:** Organizations can integrate Kubernetes clusters with SSO solutions to manage access to containerized applications. This ensures that users accessing Kubernetes resources also benefit from the streamlined authentication provided by SSO.

37.3.7. Considerations and Security Best Practices

- **User Onboarding and Offboarding:** Organizations should implement efficient user onboarding and offboarding processes to ensure smooth identity management. When employees join or leave the organization, their access should be provisioned or revoked promptly.

- **Secure Token Exchange:** To maintain security, organizations should ensure the secure exchange of identity tokens between Identity Providers and Service Providers. Proper token validation and encryption mechanisms should be in place to prevent token tampering or interception.

Exercise

Multiple Choice Questions

1. What is the primary purpose of Identity and Access Management (IAM) in cloud environments?

a. To manage cloud providers' infrastructure and network settings.

b. To optimize cloud resource utilization and cost efficiency.

c. To control access to cloud resources and ensure data protection.

d. To automate cloud service deployments and configurations.

2. What is the role of "Identity Providers" in the context of Identity Federation?

a. They are applications that rely on Service Providers for user authentication.

b. They are unique identifiers assigned to cloud resources.

c. They are trusted systems that authenticate users and issue identity tokens.

d. They are groups of users with similar access requirements.

3. Which authentication method provides an extra layer of security by requiring users to provide additional factors beyond their passwords?

a. Password-based authentication.

b. Single Sign-On (SSO).

c. Role-Based Access Control (RBAC).

d. Multi-Factor Authentication (MFA).

4. What is the benefit of implementing the principle of least privilege in IAM?

a. It simplifies access management and reduces administrative overhead.

b. It allows users to access multiple cloud services using a single set of credentials.

c. It centralizes identity management and access control.

d. It reduces the risk of unauthorized access and potential security breaches.

5. In IAM, what do "Roles" represent?

a. They are sets of permissions associated with specific tasks or responsibilities.

b. They are actions that users can perform on cloud resources.

c. They are individuals who have been granted access to the cloud environment.

d. They are collections of users with similar roles or access requirements.

6. What is the primary benefit of Single Sign-On (SSO) in cloud environments?

a. It centralizes identity management and access control.

b. It enhances user productivity and reduces password fatigue.

c. It establishes a trusted relationship between users and cloud providers.

d. It provides granular control over user permissions.

7. How does Identity Federation simplify user access to cloud services?

a. It enables users to log in once and access multiple services without reauthentication.

b. It grants users full administrative access to all cloud resources.

c. It automatically provisions user access to new cloud resources.

d. It enforces Multi-Factor Authentication (MFA) for every login attempt.

8. What is the primary purpose of regular access reviews in IAM?

a. To ensure compliance with industry standards and regulations.

b. To identify and address any unnecessary or excessive permissions.

c. To enable Single Sign-On (SSO) integration with cloud services.

d. To manage cloud users, groups, and roles.

9. Which IAM concept ensures that users have access only to the resources necessary to perform their specific tasks?

a. Role-Based Access Control (RBAC).

b. Multi-Factor Authentication (MFA).

c. Identity Federation.

d. Single Sign-On (SSO).

Review Questions

1. What are the key components of IAM in cloud environments, and how do they contribute to access control?

2. How does IAM contribute to data protection in cloud environments, and what role does it play in regulatory compliance?

3. What are the main benefits of implementing Role-Based Access Control (RBAC) in cloud environments?

4. How does Identity Federation simplify user access to cloud services, and what are the benefits of Single Sign-On (SSO) in cloud environments?

5. What are the main steps involved in implementing Identity Federation and Single Sign-On (SSO) in cloud environments?

6. How do cloud-native IAM services contribute to access control and security in cloud environments?

7. What are some best practices for IAM implementation in cloud environments to ensure optimal security and compliance?

8. How can IAM be leveraged to enhance incident response and mitigate the impact of security incidents in cloud environments?

Answer Section

Multiple Choice Questions

1. c) To control access to cloud resources and ensure data protection.

2. c) They are trusted systems that authenticate users and issue identity tokens.

3. d) Multi-Factor Authentication (MFA).

4. d) It reduces the risk of unauthorized access and potential security breaches.

5. a) They are sets of permissions associated with specific tasks or responsibilities.

6. b) It enhances user productivity and reduces password fatigue.

7. a) It enables users to log in once and access multiple services without reauthentication.

8. b) To identify and address any unnecessary or excessive permissions.

9. a) Role-Based Access Control (RBAC).

Review Questions

1. IAM in cloud environments comprises identities, authentication, and authorization. Identities represent unique entities such as users or applications. Authentication verifies their identity, often using passwords or MFA. Once authenticated, IAM checks policies to determine authorized actions based on assigned roles and permissions. Users, organized in groups, are assigned roles with specific permissions. These roles enforce the principle of least privilege, allowing users only necessary access. By combining identities, authentication, and authorization, IAM controls access to cloud resources, enhancing security by preventing unauthorized access and ensuring data protection.

2. IAM plays a vital role in data protection by ensuring that only authorized users and applications can access sensitive data stored in cloud environments. By enforcing authentication and authorization mechanisms, IAM prevents unauthorized access, reducing the risk of data breaches. IAM also supports Multi-Factor Authentication (MFA), enhancing data security. Additionally, IAM's centralized access management facilitates swift user revocation, crucial in case of security incidents or employee turnover. In terms of regulatory compliance, IAM enables organizations to demonstrate adherence to data

protection regulations by enforcing the principle of least privilege and maintaining granular control over access.

3. RBAC offers several benefits in cloud environments. First, it enables granular access control, assigning fine-grained permissions based on user roles. This reduces the risk of unauthorized access and potential security breaches. RBAC also simplifies access management by assigning permissions to roles, rather than individual users, streamlining administrative tasks. Scalability is another advantage, making RBAC suitable for large organizations with numerous users and cloud resources. By adhering to the principle of least privilege, RBAC enhances security, ensuring users only have necessary access. Lastly, regular reviews help ensure roles and permissions remain aligned with users' current roles and responsibilities.

4. Identity Federation simplifies user access by allowing users to log in once through their Identity Provider (IdP) and access multiple cloud services without reauthentication. This eliminates the need for users to remember multiple login credentials, enhancing user productivity. The IdP issues identity tokens, which are trusted by Service Providers (SP), streamlining access to various services. Additionally, centralized access control at the IdP ensures swift revocation of user privileges. SSO in cloud environments offers similar benefits by enabling seamless access to multiple applications after the initial login. SSO enhances security by reducing the number of passwords, encouraging stronger and unique credentials.

5. Implementing Identity Federation and SSO involves several key steps. Firstly, organizations need to integrate their cloud services and applications with compatible Identity Providers (IdP) supporting SAML or OIDC protocols. This integration establishes a trust relationship between the IdP and Service Providers (SP). During the process, federated identity management is configured, allowing the IdP to authenticate users and issue identity tokens, which the SP relies on for access control. To enhance security, Multi-Factor Authentication (MFA) should be enforced. Lastly, organizations need to ensure secure token exchange to prevent token tampering and interception.

6. Cloud-native IAM services, provided by cloud providers, enhance access control and security in cloud environments. These services offer centralized and integrated identity and access management, simplifying user and resource provisioning, authentication, and authorization. IAM services support features like Role-Based Access Control (RBAC), allowing organizations to enforce the principle of least privilege and streamline access management. Integration with cloud-native services, such as virtual machines, containers, and databases, extends IAM controls to specific cloud resources, granting administrators granular control. Leveraging these native services enables organizations to maintain consistent security practices and access control across their cloud infrastructure.

7. To ensure optimal security and compliance, organizations should follow several best practices for IAM implementation in cloud environments. Firstly, they should implement the principle of least privilege, granting users and applications only the minimum access necessary. Regular access reviews help identify and address excessive permissions. Enabling Multi-Factor Authentication (MFA) enhances security by adding an extra layer of protection. IAM roles and permissions should be carefully defined and assigned to users and groups to ensure consistent access control. Additionally, integrating cloud-native IAM services and adhering to regulatory requirements ensure secure access management and compliance with industry standards.

8. IAM plays a significant role in enhancing incident response and mitigating the impact of security incidents in cloud environments. When a security incident occurs, IAM can promptly revoke access for compromised or unauthorized accounts, preventing further damage and unauthorized activities. By employing automated incident response mechanisms tied to IAM roles and permissions, organizations can swiftly block malicious activities. Post-incident forensics and investigations can be conducted using IAM logs and data, aiding in understanding the root cause and improving security measures. IAM's centralized access control ensures that immediate action can be taken during incidents, limiting the scope and minimizing the potential damage to cloud resources.

Chapter 38: Cloud Compliance and Auditing Strategies

38.1: Cloud Compliance Frameworks and Standards

Compliance with cloud security frameworks and standards is crucial for organizations to demonstrate their commitment to data protection, privacy, and governance. These frameworks provide guidelines and best practices for securing cloud environments and ensuring that sensitive data is handled responsibly. Organizations should assess their specific compliance needs based on their industry, geographic location, and the types of data they handle.

By adhering to relevant cloud compliance frameworks and standards, organizations can build trust with their customers, partners, and regulators, and establish a strong foundation for secure and compliant cloud deployments. Cloud compliance is an ongoing process, and organizations must regularly review and update their security measures to adapt to the evolving threat landscape and changing regulatory requirements.

38.1.1. General Data Protection Regulation (GDPR)

GDPR is a comprehensive data protection regulation that applies to organizations handling the personal data of EU citizens. It sets out specific requirements for data protection, privacy, and consent, and imposes strict penalties for non-compliance. GDPR places an emphasis on transparency, accountability, and user consent regarding the collection and processing of personal data.

38.1.2. Health Insurance Portability and Accountability Act (HIPAA)

HIPAA is a US law that governs the security and privacy of healthcare data. Organizations that handle Protected Health Information (PHI) must comply with HIPAA's strict security and privacy standards. HIPAA requires organizations to implement administrative, physical, and technical safeguards to protect the confidentiality and integrity of PHI.

38.1.3. Payment Card Industry Data Security Standard (PCI DSS)

PCI DSS is a set of security standards designed to protect cardholder data and ensure secure payment card transactions. It applies to organizations that process, store, or transmit cardholder data. PCI DSS requires strict controls for the handling of cardholder data, including encryption, access controls, and regular security testing.

38.1.4. ISO/IEC 27001

ISO/IEC 27001 is an international standard for Information Security Management Systems (ISMS). It provides a framework for managing information security risks and implementing security controls. Organizations seeking ISO/IEC 27001 certification must conduct risk assessments, establish security policies, and implement a robust set of security controls to protect information assets.

38.1.5. NIST Cybersecurity Framework

Developed by the National Institute of Standards and Technology (NIST), the Cybersecurity Framework provides guidelines for organizations to manage and reduce cybersecurity risks. It consists of a set of standards, guidelines, and best practices to improve the cybersecurity posture of organizations. The framework includes five core functions: Identify, Protect, Detect, Respond, and Recover.

38.1.6. FedRAMP (Federal Risk and Authorization Management Program)

FedRAMP is a US government program that provides a standardized approach to security assessment, authorization, and continuous monitoring for cloud services used by federal agencies. Cloud service providers seeking to serve federal agencies must undergo a rigorous authorization process to demonstrate compliance with FedRAMP requirements.

38.1.7. SOC 2 (Service Organization Control 2)

SOC 2 is an auditing standard that assesses the security, availability, processing integrity, confidentiality, and privacy of cloud service providers. It focuses on the controls and processes used by service organizations to protect customer data and systems. SOC 2 reports are often requested by customers as part of vendor risk management assessments.

38.1.8. CIS (Center for Internet Security) Controls

CIS Controls are a set of cybersecurity best practices developed by the Center for Internet Security. They provide a prioritized approach to improve an organization's cybersecurity posture. The CIS Controls cover a wide range of security areas, including asset management, access control, and incident response.

38.1.9. CSA (Cloud Security Alliance) Cloud Controls Matrix

The CSA Cloud Controls Matrix is a framework that provides a detailed mapping of cloud security controls to various industry compliance standards and regulations. It helps organizations understand how cloud services align with different compliance requirements and assists in selecting compliant cloud service providers.

38.1.10. GDPR and CCPA

The California Consumer Privacy Act (CCPA) is a data protection law that grants California residents specific privacy rights. Organizations that handle personal data of California residents must comply with CCPA requirements, which are similar to GDPR. Both GDPR and CCPA emphasize the protection of individual rights, including the right to access, delete, and opt-out of data collection.

38.2: Implementing Compliance Controls in Cloud Environments

Implementing compliance controls in cloud environments requires a comprehensive and proactive approach to ensure data protection and adherence to relevant regulations and standards. By identifying applicable regulations, defining robust policies, and implementing technical controls, organizations can create a secure and compliant cloud environment. Regular auditing, incident response planning, and employee training contribute to a culture of continuous improvement and commitment to compliance.

With the right strategies and practices in place, organizations can confidently operate in the cloud while meeting industry-specific requirements and building trust with customers and partners. Cloud compliance is an ongoing process, and organizations must regularly review and update their security measures to adapt to the evolving threat landscape and changing regulatory requirements. By prioritizing compliance, organizations can safeguard sensitive data, maintain customer trust, and demonstrate a commitment to data protection and privacy in the cloud.

38.2.1. Identify Applicable Regulations and Standards

- **Assessment:** Begin by identifying the relevant regulations and standards that apply to your organization based on the industry, geographic location, and type of data processed. This assessment is crucial for understanding the compliance landscape and the specific requirements that need to be met.

- **Engage Experts:** Involve legal experts and compliance professionals to understand the specific requirements and implications of the identified regulations and standards. These experts can provide valuable insights and guidance throughout the compliance implementation process.

38.2.2. Define Cloud Compliance Policies

- **Policy Development:** Develop comprehensive cloud compliance policies that align with the identified regulations and standards. These policies should cover all aspects of data protection, privacy, access controls, incident response, and more. Tailor the policies to the unique requirements of your organization.

- **Roles and Responsibilities:** Clearly define roles and responsibilities for enforcing compliance policies, ensuring accountability throughout the organization. Designate individuals or teams responsible for implementing and monitoring compliance controls.

38.2.3. Data Protection and Encryption

- **Data Classification:** Classify data based on its sensitivity and implement appropriate controls to protect each category. Ensure that sensitive data is handled with extra care and subjected to heightened security measures.

- **Encryption:** Utilize encryption for data at rest and data in transit to safeguard sensitive information. Encryption provides an additional layer of protection, ensuring that even if data is compromised, it remains unreadable without the proper decryption keys.

- **Key Management:** Implement robust key management practices to ensure the security of encryption keys. Proper key management is essential for maintaining the confidentiality and integrity of encrypted data.

38.2.4. Access Controls

- **Identity and Access Management (IAM):** Implement strong IAM practices, including role-based access control (RBAC), to manage user access and permissions. This ensures that users have the necessary permissions based on their roles and responsibilities.

- **Multi-Factor Authentication (MFA):** Enforce MFA for user authentication to add an extra layer of security. MFA requires users to provide multiple forms of verification before gaining access, reducing the risk of unauthorized access.

38.2.5. Logging and Monitoring
- **Centralized Logging:** Set up centralized logging to capture and analyze security-related events from various cloud services. Centralized logging enables a comprehensive view of activities across the cloud environment, facilitating threat detection and incident response.

- **Real-Time Monitoring:** Implement real-time monitoring to detect and respond to security incidents promptly. Real-time monitoring allows for immediate action in the event of suspicious or anomalous activities.

38.2.6. Incident Response and Reporting
- **Incident Response Plan:** Develop a comprehensive incident response plan that outlines the procedures to follow in the event of a security incident. The plan should include steps for containment, investigation, resolution, and reporting.

- **Data Breach Notification:** Ensure compliance with data breach notification requirements, if applicable. Promptly notify relevant parties, such as regulatory authorities and affected individuals, in the event of a data breach.

38.2.7. Vendor Management
- **Due Diligence:** Conduct due diligence on cloud service providers to ensure they comply with relevant regulations and standards. Choose reputable and compliant vendors to reduce compliance risks.

- **Contractual Agreements:** Establish clear contractual agreements with cloud service providers regarding data protection and compliance responsibilities. Define the roles and responsibilities of both parties in maintaining compliance.

38.2.8. Regular Audits and Assessments
- **Internal Audits:** Conduct regular internal audits to assess compliance with established policies and controls. Internal audits help identify potential gaps and ensure ongoing adherence to compliance requirements.

- **Third-Party Audits:** Engage third-party auditors to conduct independent assessments of compliance. External audits provide unbiased evaluations and enhance the credibility of your compliance efforts.

38.2.9. Training and Awareness
- **Employee Training:** Provide regular training to employees to educate them about compliance policies and best practices. Training ensures that employees understand their roles in maintaining compliance and adhere to the established policies.

- **Security Awareness:** Foster a security-aware culture to ensure employees understand the importance of compliance and their role in protecting sensitive data.

38.2.10. Continuous Improvement

- Feedback Mechanisms: Establish feedback mechanisms to gather insights from employees and stakeholders on compliance practices. Feedback can identify areas for improvement and inform future compliance initiatives.

- Adaptation: Continuously adapt and improve compliance controls based on changing regulations and emerging threats. Stay informed about evolving compliance requirements and adjust your strategies accordingly.

38.3: Cloud Auditing and Assurance Services

Cloud auditing and assurance services provide valuable insights into the security, compliance, and overall effectiveness of cloud environments. By engaging independent auditors and leveraging standardized frameworks, organizations can gain a comprehensive understanding of their cloud security posture. Audit results and assurance services contribute to continuous improvement, enabling organizations to address risks, strengthen cloud security controls, and maintain compliance with relevant regulations and standards.

With a proactive approach to cloud governance and security, organizations can build trust with their customers, partners, and stakeholders, ensuring a secure and resilient cloud infrastructure. Cloud compliance is an ongoing process, and organizations must regularly review and update their security measures to adapt to the evolving threat landscape and changing regulatory requirements. By prioritizing compliance, organizations can safeguard sensitive data, maintain customer trust, and demonstrate a commitment to data protection and privacy in the cloud.

38.3.1. Understanding Cloud Auditing and Assurance

- Cloud Auditing: Cloud auditing involves evaluating cloud resources, configurations, and security controls to assess the effectiveness of security measures and compliance with policies and standards. It aims to identify vulnerabilities, misconfigurations, and areas of improvement within the cloud environment.

- Assurance Services: Assurance services provide independent assessments of cloud security and compliance to build confidence in the cloud environment. These assessments are conducted by qualified auditors or third-party organizations specializing in cloud security.

38.3.2. Benefits of Cloud Auditing and Assurance Services

- Risk Identification: Auditing services help identify potential security risks and vulnerabilities in the cloud environment, enabling timely remediation. By identifying weak points in the cloud infrastructure, organizations can proactively strengthen their security posture.

- Compliance Validation: Assurance services validate compliance with industry regulations, data protection laws, and security standards. This validation is essential for organizations that handle sensitive data or operate in highly regulated industries.

- Third-Party Validation: Independent audits provide third-party validation of cloud security and compliance. This transparency builds trust with stakeholders, including customers, partners, and regulatory authorities.

- Continuous Improvement: Auditing results and recommendations drive continuous improvement in cloud security and governance practices. Organizations can use the insights gained from audits to enhance their security measures and address emerging threats.

3. Types of Cloud Audits and Assurance Services

- Security Audits*:* Evaluate cloud security controls, data protection practices, access controls, and encryption measures. Security audits help assess the overall security posture of the cloud environment.

- Compliance Audits: Ensure adherence to specific industry regulations, such as GDPR, HIPAA, or PCI DSS, relevant to the organization's operations. Compliance audits verify that the cloud environment meets the required legal and regulatory obligations.

- Risk Assessments: Identify and assess potential risks in the cloud environment, helping organizations prioritize security efforts. Risk assessments are valuable for understanding the potential impact of security incidents and guiding risk management strategies.

- Performance Audits: Evaluate the efficiency and effectiveness of cloud service providers in meeting service level agreements (SLAs). Performance audits ensure that cloud services deliver the expected performance and availability.

4. Cloud Audit Standards and Frameworks

- Cloud Security Alliance (CSA) Security Trust Assurance and Risk (STAR) Registry: Provides a registry of cloud service providers and their security assessment results. Organizations can use the STAR Registry to evaluate the security practices of various cloud vendors.

- American Institute of Certified Public Accountants (AICPA) SOC Reports: Includes SOC 1, SOC 2, and SOC 3 reports, which provide assurance on the security, availability, processing integrity, confidentiality, and privacy of cloud services. These reports are valuable for understanding the controls in place at cloud service providers.

- ISO/IEC 27017: Specifies cloud-specific security controls and guidelines for cloud service providers and cloud customers. This standard helps organizations address cloud-specific security challenges.

5. Engaging Cloud Auditing and Assurance Providers

- Qualified Auditors: Engage qualified and reputable auditors with expertise in cloud security and compliance. Choose auditors who have experience in assessing cloud environments and are familiar with relevant regulations.

- Scope Definition: Define the scope of the audit or assurance engagement, covering specific cloud services and compliance requirements. Clearly communicate the objectives of the audit to the auditors.

- Assessment Methodology: Understand the auditing methodology and how the assessment will be conducted. This includes the tools, techniques, and procedures used during the audit.

- **Remediation Recommendations:** Ensure the auditors provide actionable recommendations for improving cloud security and compliance. These recommendations should be prioritized based on risk and impact.

6. Leveraging Audit Results for Continuous Improvement
- **Actionable Insights:** Use audit results to identify areas for improvement and prioritize security enhancements. Address any weaknesses or gaps identified during the audit process.

- **Continuous Monitoring:** Implement continuous monitoring practices to proactively identify and address security issues. Continuous monitoring helps organizations detect and respond to security incidents in real-time.

- **Response to Findings:** Address and remediate identified weaknesses and vulnerabilities based on audit recommendations. Develop a plan for improving security measures and implement necessary changes.

Exercise

Multiple Choice Questions

1. Which cloud compliance framework focuses on the protection of cardholder data and secure payment card transactions?

a. GDPR

b. HIPAA

c. PCI DSS

d. NIST Cybersecurity Framework

2. ISO/IEC 27001 is an international standard for managing:

a. Personal data of EU citizens

b. Healthcare data

c. Information security

d. Cloud service providers' performance

3. The NIST Cybersecurity Framework consists of how many core functions?

a. 3

b. 4

c. 5

d. 6

4. FedRAMP is a US government program that provides a standardized approach to security assessment for:

a. Cloud service providers

b. Financial institutions

c. Retailers

d. Educational institutions

5. Which audit standard assesses the security, availability, processing integrity, confidentiality, and privacy of cloud service providers?

a. SOC 1

b. SOC 2

c. SOC 3

d. ISO/IEC 27017

6. The CIS Controls cover a wide range of security areas, including all of the following except:

a. Asset management

b. Access control

c. Incident response

d. Vendor management

7. What does the CSA Cloud Controls Matrix help organizations understand?

a. Cloud service providers' performance

b. How cloud services align with compliance requirements

c. Best practices for cloud data encryption

d. How to improve cloud governance

8. What is the primary purpose of engaging independent auditors for cloud environments?

a. Ensuring data classification is accurate

b. Assessing the performance of cloud service providers

c. Validating compliance with regulations and standards

d. Identifying potential security risks

9. How can organizations leverage audit results for continuous improvement?

a. Prioritizing security enhancements and addressing weaknesses

b. Implementing continuous monitoring practices

c. Developing a security awareness program

d. Conducting third-party vendor assessments

Review Questions

1. What Is The General Data Protection Regulation (GDPR), And Who Does It Apply To?

2. How Does The Health Insurance Portability And Accountability Act (HIPAA) Protect Healthcare Data?

3. What Are The Core Functions Of The NIST Cybersecurity Framework?

4. How Does The Payment Card Industry Data Security Standard (PCI DSS) Ensure Secure Payment Card Transactions?

5. What Is ISO/IEC 27001, And How Does It Help Organizations Manage Information Security Risks?

6. How Does Fedramp (Federal Risk And Authorization Management Program) Benefit Cloud Service Providers?

7. What Is SOC 2 (Service Organization Control 2), And How Does It Assess Cloud Service Providers?

8. How Do CIS (Center For Internet Security) Controls Help Organizations Improve Their Cybersecurity Posture?

9. How Does The CSA (Cloud Security Alliance) Cloud Controls Matrix Assist Organizations In Selecting Cloud Service Providers?

10. How Can Organizations Ensure Continuous Improvement In Cloud Compliance And Security?

11. Why Is Cloud Compliance An Ongoing Process, And How Does It Adapt To Changing Regulatory Requirements And Threats?

Answer Section
Multiple Choice Questions

1. c) PCI DSS

2. c) Information security

3. c) 5

4. a) Cloud service providers

5. b) SOC 2

6. d) Vendor management

7. b) How cloud services align with compliance requirements

8. c) Validating compliance with regulations and standards

9. a) Prioritizing security enhancements and addressing weaknesses

Review Questions

1. GDPR is a comprehensive data protection regulation that applies to organizations handling the personal data of EU citizens, regardless of where the organization is located. It sets out specific requirements for data protection, privacy, and consent, and imposes strict penalties for non-compliance. GDPR places an emphasis on transparency, accountability, and user consent regarding the collection and processing of personal data. Organizations subject to GDPR must implement measures to protect personal data, obtain valid consent, provide data breach notifications, and allow individuals to exercise their data rights.

2. HIPAA is a US law that governs the security and privacy of healthcare data, specifically Protected Health Information (PHI). Organizations that handle PHI must comply with HIPAA's strict security and privacy standards. HIPAA requires the implementation of administrative, physical, and technical safeguards to protect the confidentiality and integrity of PHI. It also mandates the appointment of a Privacy Officer and a Security Officer to oversee compliance efforts and conduct risk assessments. Additionally, HIPAA requires the development of policies and procedures for data access, disclosure, and breach notification.

3. The NIST Cybersecurity Framework consists of five core functions: Identify, Protect, Detect, Respond, and Recover. "Identify" involves understanding and managing cybersecurity risks by conducting asset management, risk assessments, and vulnerability assessments. "Protect" focuses on implementing safeguards to ensure data security, such as access controls, data encryption, and security awareness training. "Detect" involves continuous monitoring and detection of cybersecurity events and incidents. "Respond" emphasizes the development of incident response plans and effective response and recovery activities. "Recover" involves planning and implementing strategies to restore operations and services after a cybersecurity incident.

4. PCI DSS is a set of security standards designed to protect cardholder data and ensure secure payment card transactions. It applies to organizations that process, store, or transmit cardholder data. PCI DSS requires strict controls for the handling of cardholder data, including encryption, access controls, and regular security testing. Compliance with PCI DSS helps organizations prevent data breaches and unauthorized access to payment card information. By implementing the necessary security measures, organizations can ensure the protection of sensitive data and maintain customer trust in their ability to conduct secure transactions.

5. ISO/IEC 27001 is an international standard for Information Security Management Systems (ISMS). It provides a framework for managing information security risks and implementing security controls. Organizations seeking ISO/IEC 27001 certification must conduct risk assessments, establish security policies, and implement a robust set of security controls to protect information assets. The standard focuses on a systematic approach to information security, covering areas such as risk management, asset management, access control, and incident response. By following ISO/IEC 27001 guidelines, organizations can identify and address potential security threats and ensure the confidentiality, integrity, and availability of their information assets.

6. FedRAMP is a US government program that provides a standardized approach to security assessment, authorization, and continuous monitoring for cloud services used by federal agencies. Cloud service providers (CSPs) seeking to serve federal agencies must undergo a rigorous authorization process to demonstrate compliance with FedRAMP requirements. Achieving FedRAMP authorization allows CSPs to offer their cloud services to federal customers, expanding their market opportunities and establishing trust with government agencies. FedRAMP authorization also streamlines the procurement process for federal agencies, as they can rely on the standardized security assessment performed by the FedRAMP program.

7. SOC 2 is an auditing standard that assesses the security, availability, processing integrity, confidentiality, and privacy of cloud service providers. It focuses on the controls and processes used by service organizations to protect customer data and systems. SOC 2 reports are often requested by customers as part of vendor risk management assessments. The audit evaluates the design and effectiveness of security controls based on the trust services criteria defined by the American Institute of Certified Public Accountants (AICPA). SOC 2 reports provide valuable insights into the security practices of cloud service providers and help customers make informed decisions about the security of their data in the cloud.

8. CIS Controls are a set of cybersecurity best practices developed by the Center for Internet Security. They provide a prioritized approach to improving an organization's cybersecurity posture. The CIS Controls cover a wide range of security areas, including asset management, access control, and incident response. By implementing the CIS Controls, organizations can identify and address critical security vulnerabilities, reduce the risk of cyberattacks, and enhance their overall security resilience. The controls are regularly updated to reflect the evolving threat landscape, ensuring that organizations stay up-to-date with the latest security best practices.

9. The CSA Cloud Controls Matrix is a framework that provides a detailed mapping of cloud security controls to various industry compliance standards and regulations. It helps organizations understand how cloud services align with different compliance requirements, making it easier to select cloud service providers that meet specific security and compliance needs. The Cloud Controls Matrix allows organizations to assess the security posture of cloud service providers and compare their capabilities against industry standards. By leveraging the Cloud Controls Matrix, organizations can make informed decisions about the security and compliance of cloud service providers and ensure that their cloud deployments adhere to industry best practices.

10. Continuous improvement in cloud compliance and security can be achieved through several strategies. Regular audits and assessments help identify areas for improvement and highlight potential vulnerabilities. Organizations should conduct internal audits to assess compliance with established policies and controls and engage third-party auditors for independent assessments. Feedback mechanisms from employees and stakeholders can provide insights into compliance practices and identify areas for enhancement. Continuous monitoring allows organizations to proactively detect and respond to security incidents in real-time. Additionally, employee training and security awareness programs foster a security-aware culture, ensuring that employees understand the importance of compliance and their role in protecting sensitive data.

11. Cloud compliance is an ongoing process because the regulatory landscape and cybersecurity threats are constantly evolving. New regulations may be introduced, existing ones may be updated, and the threat landscape may change with the emergence of new cybersecurity risks. As a result, organizations must regularly review and update their security measures to stay in compliance with the latest regulations and mitigate emerging threats. By continuously monitoring for changes in the regulatory environment and conducting regular risk assessments, organizations can adapt their cloud compliance strategies and security controls to address new challenges. Ongoing compliance efforts demonstrate an organization's commitment to data protection and privacy in the cloud and contribute to building trust with customers, partners, and stakeholders.

Chapter 39: Cloud-Based Internet of Things (IoT) Solutions

39.1 Overview of Cloud Internet of Things (IoT) Services and Platforms

Cloud IoT services and platforms are essential components of the IoT ecosystem, providing the necessary infrastructure and capabilities to manage, process, and analyze the vast amounts of data generated by connected devices. With their scalability, cost-effectiveness, and real-time data processing capabilities, these services enable organizations to unlock the full potential of IoT, powering a wide range of applications in industries such as home automation, healthcare, manufacturing, and smart cities. As the IoT landscape continues to grow, cloud IoT services will play an increasingly critical role in supporting innovative and transformative IoT solutions. Organizations that leverage cloud IoT services can derive actionable insights from IoT data, improve operational efficiency, and enhance customer experiences, positioning themselves for success in the digital age.

39.1.1. Understanding Cloud IoT Services

- **Data Management:** Cloud IoT services manage the influx of data from connected devices, storing, processing, and analyzing the data in real-time. These services provide a centralized repository for storing the vast amounts of data generated by IoT devices.

- **Device Connectivity:** These services facilitate device registration, authentication, and secure communication between IoT devices and the cloud. By providing secure communication channels, cloud IoT services ensure that data transmitted between devices and the cloud remains confidential and protected from unauthorized access.

- **Scalability:** Cloud IoT services are designed to handle large-scale IoT deployments, ensuring seamless operation even with a vast number of devices. They offer the flexibility to accommodate the exponential growth of connected devices and the data they generate.

39.1.2. Cloud IoT Platform Features

- **Data Ingestion:** Cloud IoT platforms allow devices to send data to the cloud, providing a centralized location for data storage and management. This feature is essential as IoT devices generate massive amounts of data that need to be efficiently processed and analyzed.

- **Data Processing:** Real-time data processing and analytics enable actionable insights and quick decision-making based on IoT-generated data. Cloud IoT platforms leverage sophisticated data processing capabilities to derive meaningful information from the raw data generated by IoT devices.

- **Device Management:** These platforms offer functionalities for device registration, provisioning, and over-the-air updates, simplifying device lifecycle management. Device management features ensure that devices remain updated and function optimally throughout their operational life.

- **Security and Authentication:** Robust security mechanisms, such as device authentication and data encryption, ensure data privacy and protect against potential threats. Cloud IoT platforms employ various security measures to safeguard the integrity and confidentiality of data transmitted between devices and the cloud.

- **Integration:** Cloud IoT platforms integrate with other cloud services, such as data storage, machine learning, and business intelligence tools, to leverage their capabilities. This integration allows organizations to build comprehensive IoT solutions that utilize various cloud services in conjunction.

39.1.3. Major Cloud IoT Service Providers

- **AWS IoT Core:** Amazon Web Services' IoT Core provides scalable and secure IoT services, including device management, data processing, and cloud integration. AWS IoT Core is widely adopted and offers a wide range of features to support IoT deployments.

- **Azure IoT Hub:** Microsoft's Azure IoT Hub enables seamless device connectivity, data ingestion, and integration with Azure's suite of cloud services. Azure IoT Hub is part of Microsoft's robust IoT ecosystem.

- **Google Cloud IoT Core:** Google Cloud IoT Core offers a managed service for IoT device management, data processing, and analytics on Google Cloud Platform. Google Cloud IoT Core leverages Google's infrastructure and data analytics capabilities.

39.1.4. Advantages of Cloud IoT Services and Platforms

- **Scalability:** Cloud IoT services can scale to accommodate the exponential growth of connected devices and the data they generate. Organizations can expand their IoT deployments without worrying about infrastructure limitations.

- **Cost-Effectiveness:** With pay-as-you-go pricing models, organizations can avoid high upfront costs and only pay for the resources they consume. This cost-effectiveness makes cloud IoT services accessible to businesses of all sizes.

- **Rapid Deployment:** Cloud IoT platforms provide pre-built functionalities, enabling organizations to deploy IoT solutions quickly and efficiently. This accelerated deployment allows businesses to capitalize on IoT opportunities without significant development efforts.

- **Real-Time Insights:** Real-time data processing and analytics facilitate quick decision-making and enable the automation of processes based on IoT data Organizations can respond rapidly to changes and events based on real-time insights.

39.1.5. Use Cases for Cloud IoT Services

- **Smart Home Automation:** Cloud IoT services power smart home devices and applications, enabling remote control and automation of appliances, lighting, and security systems. Smart home solutions improve convenience and energy efficiency for homeowners.

- **Industrial IoT (IIoT):** In industrial settings, cloud IoT services collect and analyze data from sensors and machines to optimize manufacturing processes and maintenance. IIoT enhances operational efficiency and reduces downtime.

- **Connected Healthcare:** Cloud IoT platforms support remote patient monitoring, wearable health devices, and data analysis for personalized healthcare services. Connected healthcare solutions improve patient outcomes and healthcare delivery.

- **Smart Cities:** Cloud IoT services contribute to the development of smart city initiatives, such as smart lighting, waste management, and transportation systems. Smart city projects aim to enhance urban living and sustainability.

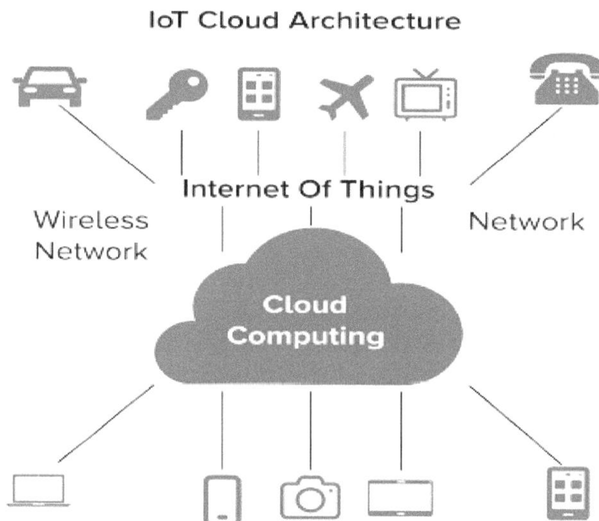

39.2 Device Provisioning and Management in the Cloud

Device provisioning and management in the cloud are integral to successful and secure IoT implementations. Cloud-based solutions offer scalability, flexibility, and cost-effectiveness, making them an ideal choice for managing IoT devices at scale. With device provisioning, secure authentication, and encrypted communication, cloud IoT platforms ensure that only authorized devices can connect and interact with the cloud. Effective device management capabilities allow organizations to monitor, control, and update devices remotely, optimizing performance and maintaining the security of the entire IoT ecosystem. By leveraging cloud-based solutions for device provisioning and management, organizations can harness the full potential of IoT and build resilient and efficient IoT deployments. Proper security measures, such as device authentication and data encryption, play a crucial role in protecting IoT data and ensuring the overall security of the IoT infrastructure. As the IoT landscape continues to grow, cloud IoT platforms will continue to evolve, providing more sophisticated features and further enhancing IoT capabilities for various industries and use cases.

39.2.1. Device Provisioning in the Cloud

- **Device Onboarding:** Device provisioning involves the initial onboarding of IoT devices to the cloud platform. During this process, devices are registered with the cloud service, and secure connections are established to facilitate data transmission.

- **Authentication and Identity:** Cloud IoT platforms use various authentication methods to verify the identity of devices, ensuring only authorized devices can connect to the cloud. This authentication is essential to prevent unauthorized access and potential security breaches.

- **Secure Communication:** Cloud services facilitate encrypted communication between IoT devices and the cloud to protect data from unauthorized access. Secure communication protocols, such as TLS, ensure data integrity and confidentiality during transit.

39.2.2. Device Management in the Cloud

- **Remote Monitoring and Control:** Cloud IoT platforms enable real-time monitoring and control of IoT devices, allowing users to manage devices remotely from anywhere with an internet connection. This capability empowers users to monitor device status and make necessary adjustments or take action in response to changing conditions.

- **Firmware Updates and Configuration:** Cloud-based device management facilitates over-the-air (OTA) firmware updates and configuration changes. OTA updates ensure that devices remain up-to-date with the latest software and security patches, reducing the need for manual updates.

- **Device Diagnostics:** Cloud platforms offer diagnostics and reporting capabilities, allowing users to monitor the health and performance of IoT devices. These diagnostics can help identify potential issues and enable predictive maintenance.

39.2.3. Advantages of Cloud-Based Device Provisioning and Management

- **Scalability:** Cloud solutions can easily scale to accommodate a vast number of IoT devices, supporting large-scale IoT deployments. As the number of connected devices grows, cloud platforms can dynamically allocate resources to handle the increased load.

- **Flexibility and Agility:** Cloud-based provisioning and management allow organizations to adapt quickly to changing IoT requirements and integrate new devices seamlessly. Organizations can easily add or remove devices as needed, enabling greater flexibility in their IoT ecosystem.

- **Cost-Effectiveness:** Cloud services offer pay-as-you-go pricing models, allowing organizations to avoid upfront hardware costs and pay only for the resources they consume. This cost-effectiveness makes cloud IoT solutions accessible to businesses of all sizes.

39.2.4. Device Lifecycle Management

- **Registration and Enrollment:** Devices are registered with the cloud platform during provisioning, and unique identifiers are assigned to each device. These identifiers enable the cloud platform to recognize and manage each device uniquely.

- **Configuration Management:** Cloud platforms facilitate device configuration, ensuring devices operate optimally in the IoT ecosystem. Configuration settings can be remotely adjusted and tailored to specific use cases.

- **Monitoring and Analytics:** Throughout the device lifecycle, cloud platforms monitor device performance and generate analytics to identify potential issues and optimize device usage. Monitoring data and analytics enable organizations to make data-driven decisions for performance improvements and optimization.

- **Decommissioning and Retirement:** When a device reaches the end of its useful life, cloud-based management facilitates decommissioning and proper retirement. This process ensures that decommissioned devices are removed from the IoT network, preventing any security vulnerabilities.

39.2.5. Cloud IoT Platforms and Device Management Services

- **AWS IoT Core:** Amazon Web Services' IoT Core provides device provisioning and management services, supporting large-scale IoT deployments. It offers a comprehensive set of features, including device registration, data processing, and integration with other AWS services.

- **Azure IoT Hub:** Microsoft's Azure IoT Hub offers robust device management capabilities, including firmware updates and diagnostics. Azure IoT Hub is part of Microsoft's extensive IoT ecosystem, providing seamless integration with Azure services.

- **Google Cloud IoT Core:** Google Cloud IoT Core provides secure and scalable device management services, ensuring seamless device connectivity and control. Leveraging Google's infrastructure and data analytics capabilities, Google Cloud IoT Core supports a wide range of IoT applications.

39.2.6. Security Considerations

- **Device Authentication:** Strong device authentication is crucial to prevent unauthorized devices from connecting to the cloud. Proper authentication mechanisms, such as X.509 certificates or API keys, ensure that only legitimate devices can access cloud services.

- **Data Encryption:** Implementing end-to-end data encryption ensures data security during communication between devices and the cloud. Encryption safeguards sensitive data and prevents unauthorized interception.

- **Access Control:** Enforce access control policies to limit device privileges and protect sensitive operations. Implementing role-based access control (RBAC) ensures that devices have appropriate permissions for their intended functions.

39.3 Real-Time Data Processing and Analytics in Cloud IoT Applications

Real-time data processing and analytics are indispensable in Cloud IoT applications, enabling organizations to make timely decisions, respond immediately to events, and gain actionable insights from IoT-generated data. Cloud IoT platforms offer the necessary tools and capabilities to ingest, process, and analyze real-time data from connected devices, empowering organizations to optimize operations, enhance customer experiences, and gain a competitive edge. Leveraging real-time data analytics in use cases such as smart manufacturing, smart grids, and connected vehicles drives efficiency, sustainability, and innovation. However, addressing challenges related to data latency, volume, and quality is crucial to ensure the effectiveness of real-time data processing in Cloud IoT applications. With a well-implemented real-time data processing strategy, organizations can unlock the full potential of IoT data and drive transformative changes in their operations and services. Proper security measures, such as device authentication and data encryption, play a crucial role in protecting IoT data and ensuring the overall security of the IoT infrastructure. As the IoT landscape continues to grow, cloud IoT platforms will continue to evolve, providing more sophisticated features and further enhancing IoT capabilities for various industries and use cases.

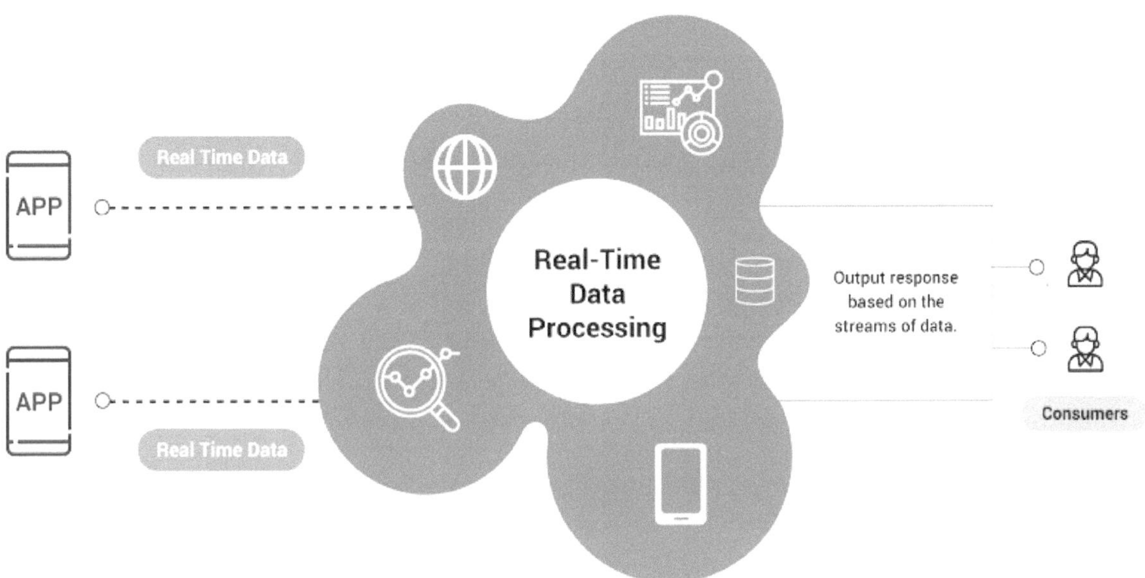

39.3.1. Importance of Real-Time Data Processing in Cloud IoT

- Timely Decision-Making: Real-time data processing enables organizations to make timely decisions based on up-to-date information from IoT devices. This capability is crucial for time-sensitive applications and industries where quick responses are essential.

- Immediate Responses: Cloud IoT applications can trigger automated responses or alerts in real-time, improving operational efficiency and responsiveness. For example, real-time alerts can help detect and address potential issues before they escalate.

- Anomaly Detection: Real-time data processing helps detect anomalies or patterns of interest immediately, reducing potential downtime or critical issues. Early detection of anomalies can lead to proactive maintenance and prevent system failures.

39.3.2. Real-Time Data Processing in Cloud IoT Platforms

- Data Ingestion: Cloud IoT platforms facilitate the ingestion of streaming data from IoT devices, ensuring continuous data flow. Data is ingested from devices as they generate it, without the need for manual intervention.

- Stream Processing: Real-time data is processed as streams, allowing for immediate data transformations and analysis. Stream processing engines enable data to be processed as it arrives, enabling rapid insights.

- Complex Event Processing (CEP): CEP engines analyze streams of data to detect patterns, trends, and significant events in real-time. This technology is valuable for identifying critical events or situations that require immediate attention.

39.3.3. Real-Time Analytics in Cloud IoT Applications

- Data Visualization: Real-time analytics enable the visualization of data through dashboards and charts, providing insights at a glance. Visualization tools help users quickly understand the current state of the IoT ecosystem.

- **Predictive Analytics:** Cloud IoT platforms use real-time data to power predictive analytics, forecasting future trends and potential issues. Predictive models can anticipate maintenance needs, demand patterns, and more.

- **Prescriptive Analytics:** Real-time data analysis enables prescriptive analytics, suggesting optimal actions to address specific situations. Prescriptive analytics can recommend the best course of action based on real-time data.

39.3.4. Benefits of Real-Time Data Processing and Analytics

- **Actionable Insights:** Real-time analytics offer immediate insights, allowing organizations to take proactive actions based on current data. This capability is especially valuable in fast-paced and dynamic environments.

- **Efficient Resource Allocation:** Organizations can optimize resource allocation by analyzing real-time data to match demand and supply effectively. This optimization leads to cost savings and improved resource utilization.

- **Improved Customer Experience:** Real-time data processing enables personalized and context-aware services, enhancing the overall customer experience. Real-time data can be used to tailor services to individual customer preferences and behaviors.

39.3.5. Use Cases for Real-Time Data Processing in Cloud IoT

- **Smart Manufacturing:** Real-time data analytics optimize production processes, predict machine failures, and improve overall efficiency. Manufacturers can respond to real-time production line data to minimize downtime and maximize output.

- **Smart Grids:** Real-time data processing in smart grids helps balance power generation and consumption, ensuring stable energy supply. It enables utility companies to react to fluctuations in energy demand and supply.

- **Connected Vehicles:** Real-time analytics in connected vehicles monitor performance, provide driver assistance, and enable predictive maintenance. This enhances vehicle safety, efficiency, and the overall driving experience.

39.3.6. Challenges and Considerations

- **Data Latency:** Ensuring minimal data latency is crucial for real-time analytics to provide timely insights. Data must be processed and analyzed without significant delays to remain actionable.

- **Data Volume:** Handling massive data volumes in real-time requires robust cloud infrastructure and scalability. Cloud platforms must be able to process and analyze data at high speeds, even with large amounts of incoming data.

- **Data Quality:** Real-time analytics depend on accurate and reliable data; data quality must be maintained throughout the process. Data cleansing and validation techniques are essential to ensure the accuracy of real-time insights.

Exercise

Multiple Choice Questions

1. Which of the following is NOT a characteristic of Cloud IoT services?

a. Scalability

b. Cost-effectiveness

c. Real-time data processing capabilities

d. Data storage in connected devices

2. What is the primary purpose of Cloud IoT services' data management?

a. Facilitating device registration

b. Enabling secure communication channels

c. Storing, processing, and analyzing data from IoT devices

d. Ensuring scalability of IoT deployments

3. Which cloud service provider offers Azure IoT Hub for device management?

a. Google Cloud IoT Core

b. Amazon Web Services (AWS) IoT Core

c. Microsoft Azure

d. IBM Cloud

4. What advantage do Cloud IoT services offer regarding cost?

a. Free services for small businesses

b. High upfront costs for large-scale deployments

c. Pay-as-you-go pricing models

d. Fixed pricing regardless of resource usage

5. Which use case involves Cloud IoT services enabling remote control and automation of appliances?

a. Industrial IoT (IIoT)

b. Connected Healthcare

c. Smart Home Automation

d. Smart Cities

6. What is the primary purpose of device provisioning in the Cloud IoT ecosystem?

a. Monitoring device performance

b. Handling massive data volumes

c. Initial onboarding of IoT devices to the cloud platform

d. Analyzing real-time data

7. How do Cloud IoT platforms ensure that only authorized devices can connect and interact with the cloud?

a. Through complex event processing

b. With secure authentication methods

c. By enabling data visualization

d. Through real-time data processing

8. What is the benefit of real-time data processing in Cloud IoT applications?

a. Timely decision-making

b. Cost-effective cloud solutions

c. Offline data storage for IoT devices

d. Real-time visualization of data

9. Which type of analytics uses real-time data to forecast future trends and potential issues?

a. Data visualization

b. Predictive analytics

c. Stream processing

d. Complex Event Processing (CEP)

10. In Cloud IoT, what does real-time data processing allow organizations to optimize?

a. Firmware updates and configuration

b. Resource allocation and customer experiences

c. Data storage and encryption

d. Device authentication and access control

11. What is a significant challenge in real-time data processing for Cloud IoT applications?

a. Ensuring minimal data latency

b. Handling data encryption during transmission

c. Managing device firmware updates

d. Balancing power generation and consumption

Review Questions

1. What are Cloud IoT services, and why are they crucial in the IoT ecosystem?

2. What are the primary features of Cloud IoT platforms, and how do they enhance IoT deployments?

3. Name three major Cloud IoT service providers and outline their key offerings.

4. What advantages do Cloud IoT services and platforms offer for IoT deployments?

5. How do Cloud IoT services contribute to the development of smart cities?

6. What are the primary security considerations for Cloud IoT implementations?

7. How does real-time data processing in Cloud IoT applications benefit various industries?

8. What are the primary challenges in implementing real-time data processing for Cloud IoT applications?

Answer Section

Multiple Choice Questions

1. d) Data storage in connected devices

2. c) Storing, processing, and analyzing data from IoT devices

3. c) Microsoft Azure

4. c) Pay-as-you-go pricing models

5. c) Smart Home Automation

6. c) Initial onboarding of IoT devices to the cloud platform

7. b) With secure authentication methods

8. a) Timely decision-making

9. b) Predictive analytics

10. b) Resource allocation and customer experiences

11. a) Ensuring minimal data latency

Review Questions

1. Cloud IoT services are essential components that provide the infrastructure and capabilities to manage, process, and analyze vast amounts of data from connected devices. They enable organizations to unlock

the full potential of IoT by offering scalability, cost-effectiveness, and real-time data processing capabilities. Cloud IoT services play a critical role in supporting innovative and transformative IoT solutions, powering applications in various industries like home automation, healthcare, manufacturing, and smart cities. They allow organizations to derive actionable insights from IoT data, enhance operational efficiency, and improve customer experiences, positioning them for success in the digital age.

2. Cloud IoT platforms offer several key features that enhance IoT deployments. These include data ingestion, enabling devices to send data to the cloud for centralized storage and management. Real-time data processing and analytics provide actionable insights and quick decision-making based on IoT-generated data. Device management functionalities allow easy device registration, provisioning, and over-the-air updates, simplifying device lifecycle management. Security and authentication mechanisms, such as data encryption and device authentication, safeguard data privacy and protect against potential threats. Integration with other cloud services empowers organizations to build comprehensive IoT solutions that leverage various cloud capabilities, making the entire ecosystem more powerful and interconnected.

3. Three major Cloud IoT service providers are:

4. AWS IoT Core: Amazon Web Services' IoT Core offers scalable and secure IoT services, including device management, data processing, and cloud integration.

1. Azure IoT Hub: Microsoft's Azure IoT Hub provides seamless device connectivity, data ingestion, and integration with Azure's suite of cloud services.

1. Google Cloud IoT Core: Google's IoT Core offers managed services for IoT device management, data processing, and analytics on Google Cloud Platform, leveraging Google's infrastructure and data analytics capabilities.

2. Cloud IoT services and platforms provide several advantages for IoT deployments. They offer scalability, accommodating the exponential growth of connected devices and data generation. Cost-effectiveness is achieved through pay-as-you-go pricing models, enabling businesses of all sizes to access IoT services without high upfront costs. Cloud IoT platforms provide pre-built functionalities, leading to rapid deployment of IoT solutions without extensive development efforts. Real-time insights from data processing and analytics enable quick decision-making and automation of processes based on real-time IoT data, enhancing operational efficiency. Overall, these advantages make Cloud IoT services integral for organizations seeking to maximize the potential of IoT in various industries.

3. Cloud IoT services play a significant role in the development of smart cities. They contribute to initiatives such as smart lighting, waste management, and transportation systems. With cloud-powered IoT solutions, cities can optimize energy consumption through intelligent lighting systems, reducing costs and promoting sustainability. Waste management becomes more efficient through smart waste bins that alert authorities when they need emptying, minimizing overflow and improving cleanliness. Cloud IoT services also enable intelligent transportation systems, optimizing traffic flow, and reducing congestion. Overall, these initiatives enhance urban living, sustainability, and the overall quality of life in smart cities.

4. Security is a crucial aspect of Cloud IoT implementations. Strong device authentication mechanisms, such as X.509 certificates or API keys, ensure that only authorized devices can connect to the cloud, preventing unauthorized access. Implementing end-to-end data encryption ensures data security during

communication between devices and the cloud, safeguarding sensitive information from unauthorized interception. Enforcing access control policies based on role-based access control (RBAC) limits device privileges and protects sensitive operations from unauthorized access. A comprehensive security strategy is essential to safeguard IoT data and ensure the overall security of the IoT infrastructure, mitigating potential risks and threats.

5. Real-time data processing in Cloud IoT applications provides significant benefits across various industries. In smart manufacturing, it optimizes production processes, predicts machine failures, and improves overall efficiency by responding to real-time production line data. In smart grids, real-time data processing balances power generation and consumption, ensuring stable energy supply and enabling utility companies to respond to fluctuations in energy demand. In connected vehicles, it monitors performance, provides driver assistance, and enables predictive maintenance, enhancing vehicle safety and efficiency. These applications of real-time data processing drive efficiency, sustainability, and innovation in respective industries, creating transformative changes and enhancing customer experiences.

6. Implementing real-time data processing for Cloud IoT applications comes with several challenges. Ensuring minimal data latency is crucial to provide timely insights, as delays in processing can hinder actionable decision-making. Handling massive data volumes in real-time requires robust cloud infrastructure and scalability to process and analyze data at high speeds. Maintaining data quality throughout the process is essential for accurate real-time insights, requiring data cleansing and validation techniques. Addressing these challenges effectively is crucial to maximize the benefits of real-time data processing in Cloud IoT applications and create a seamless and responsive IoT ecosystem.

Chapter 40: Cloud Governance and Ethical Considerations

40.1 Ethical Challenges in Cloud Computing

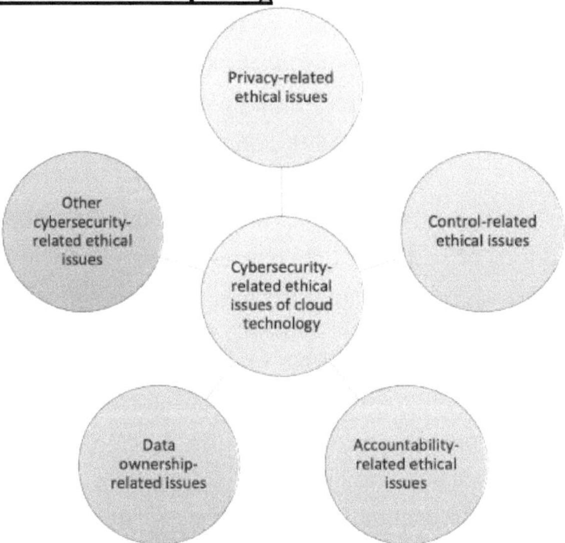

Cloud computing has revolutionized the way data is stored, processed, and accessed, but it also introduces several ethical challenges that organizations and society must address. As cloud technology continues to evolve and become more pervasive, it is crucial to recognize and navigate these ethical issues to ensure responsible and sustainable cloud computing practices Ethical challenges in cloud computing are multifaceted and require a comprehensive approach from cloud service providers, organizations, and policymakers. Addressing data privacy, security, and ownership concerns, as well as promoting transparency and accountability, are crucial steps in building trust and confidence in cloud services. Policymakers should work towards harmonizing data protection laws and ensuring appropriate regulations to safeguard data sovereignty and individual rights. Additionally, promoting digital inclusion and ensuring ethical AI and IoT data use can mitigate the negative impact of cloud computing on vulnerable populations. With a thoughtful and ethical approach, cloud computing can continue to drive innovation and benefit society while respecting privacy, fairness, and sustainability principles. Responsible cloud computing practices can lead to a more secure, equitable, and sustainable digital future.

40.1.1. Data Privacy and Security

- **Data Breaches:** Cloud providers store vast amounts of sensitive data, making them attractive targets for cyberattacks and data breaches. Organizations must ensure robust security measures to protect data from unauthorized access.

- **Data Ownership:** Determining ownership and control of data stored in the cloud can raise ethical concerns, particularly when data is stored across multiple jurisdictions. Clear agreements and policies should be in place to address data ownership.

- **Surveillance and Government Access:** The potential for unauthorized surveillance and government access to cloud-stored data raises s about individual privacy and civil liberties. Transparency and adherence to lawful access procedures are essential.

40.1.2. Data Sovereignty and Jurisdiction

- **Cross-Border Data Flows:** Data stored in the cloud may be subject to different laws and regulations in various countries, raising challenges related to data sovereignty and jurisdiction. Organizations should be mindful of the legal implications of storing data in different regions.

- **Data Residency:** Organizations and individuals must consider where their data is physically stored and ensure compliance with local data protection laws. Understanding data residency requirements is crucial to meet legal and ethical obligations.

40.1.3. Vendor Lock-In and Interoperability

- **Vendor Dependence:** Organizations may face difficulties in migrating from one cloud provider to another due to proprietary formats and services, leading to vendor lock-in. Interoperable standards can mitigate this concern.

- **Interoperability:** Lack of interoperability standards between cloud platforms can limit data portability and hinder competition. Promoting open standards and interoperability is essential to avoid monopolistic practices.

40.1.4. Environmental Impact

- **Energy Consumption:** Cloud data centers consume significant amounts of energy, contributing to environmental concerns such as greenhouse gas emissions. Efforts to improve energy efficiency and adopt renewable energy sources can address this challenge.

- **E-Waste:** The rapid evolution of cloud technology may lead to a higher turnover of hardware, potentially contributing to electronic waste. Responsible e-waste management and recycling practices are necessary to mitigate this impact.

40.1.5. Bias and Fairness in AI and Machine Learning

- **Algorithmic Bias:** Cloud-based AI and machine learning systems can exhibit bias if the training data is not diverse or representative. Ethical AI development involves identifying and mitigating biases in algorithms.

- **Discrimination:** Cloud-driven AI systems could inadvertently perpetuate discrimination if they are not designed and monitored carefully. Organizations must implement fairness and anti-discrimination measures in AI systems.

40.1.6. Digital Divide

- **Access Disparities:** The digital divide between regions and communities can exacerbate existing inequalities, as some may lack access to cloud services and technologies. Efforts to bridge the digital divide through infrastructure development and digital literacy programs are necessary.

- **Skills Gap:** The divide can also manifest in the form of a skills gap, where certain populations lack the necessary expertise to leverage cloud technologies effectively. Promoting digital skills and training programs can address this gap.

40.1.7. Cloud Service Providers' Responsibilities

- **Transparency:** Cloud service providers must be transparent about their practices, data handling, and security measures. Users should be fully informed about how their data is processed and used.

- **Accountability:** Providers should take responsibility for the security and privacy of customer data and be accountable for any breaches. Clear service-level agreements (SLAs) can help establish accountability.

40.1.8. Ethical Use of AI and IoT Data

- **Informed Consent:** The ethical use of AI and IoT data requires obtaining informed consent from individuals whose data is collected. Users should have the ability to control how their data is used.

- **Anonymization and Aggregation:** Ensuring data is anonymized and aggregated when used for AI and IoT analysis can protect individual privacy. Personal data should be processed in a manner that minimizes identification.

40.2 Ensuring Privacy and Data Protection in the Cloud

Privacy and data protection are paramount concerns in cloud computing, as cloud environments handle vast amounts of sensitive data from individuals and organizations. To build trust and maintain compliance with data protection laws, it is crucial to implement robust measures to ensure the privacy and security of data in the cloud. Ensuring privacy and data protection in the cloud is a shared responsibility between cloud service providers and their customers. Implementing data encryption, access controls, and data minimization practices are essential steps to safeguard sensitive information. Regular audits, employee training, and compliance with data protection regulations play critical roles in maintaining the security and privacy of data stored and processed in the cloud. By adopting a proactive approach to privacy and data protection, organizations can build trust with their customers and stakeholders while demonstrating their commitment to responsible and ethical cloud computing practices. Responsible cloud computing practices can lead to a more secure, equitable, and sustainable digital future.

40.2.1. Data Encryption

- **Data at Rest:** Encrypt data stored in the cloud to protect it from unauthorized access in case of data breaches or physical theft. Encryption ensures that even if data is accessed, it remains unreadable without the appropriate decryption keys.

- **Data in Transit:** Use encryption protocols such as TLS (Transport Layer Security) to secure data during transmission between the user's device and the cloud. This protects data while it is being sent over networks, preventing interception and unauthorized access.

40.2.2. Access Control and Authentication

- **Role-Based Access Control (RBAC):** Implement RBAC to ensure that users and applications have appropriate permissions to access specific data and resources in the cloud. RBAC ensures that only authorized users can access sensitive data.

- **Multi-Factor Authentication (MFA):** Enforce MFA to add an extra layer of security and reduce the risk of unauthorized access to cloud accounts. MFA requires users to provide additional forms of verification, such as a one-time code sent to their mobile device, in addition to a password.

40.2.3. Data Minimization

- **Collect Only Necessary Data:** Minimize data collection to retain only the information required to fulfill the intended purpose, reducing the risk of data exposure. Avoid storing excessive or unnecessary personal information.

- **Pseudonymization and Anonymization:** Anonymize or pseudonymize data whenever possible to protect the identity of individuals. By removing or obfuscating personal identifiers, the risk of reidentification is reduced.

40.2.4. Data Residency and Jurisdiction

- **Choose Data Center Locations Wisely:** Select cloud providers with data centers in regions that align with data residency requirements and privacy laws. Ensuring data is stored in jurisdictions with strong data protection regulations can enhance data privacy.

- **Comply with Jurisdictional Regulations:** Ensure compliance with relevant data protection laws in the jurisdictions where the data is processed and stored. Being aware of and adhering to local regulations is essential to avoid legal issues.

40.2.5. Regular Auditing and Monitoring

- **Security Audits:** Conduct regular security audits to identify vulnerabilities and ensure that security measures are up-to-date. Auditing helps detect and address potential weaknesses in the cloud infrastructure.

- **Real-Time Monitoring:** Implement real-time monitoring to detect unusual activities and potential security breaches. Real-time monitoring enables prompt response to security incidents.

40.2.6. Vendor Due Diligence

- **Cloud Service Provider (CSP) Selection:** Conduct thorough due diligence when selecting a cloud service provider, ensuring they meet privacy and security requirements. Choose reputable providers with a track record of strong security practices.

- **Service Level Agreements (SLAs):** Include specific privacy and data protection clauses in SLAs to ensure the CSP's commitment to data security. SLAs should clearly outline the responsibilities of the CSP regarding data protection.

40.2.7. Data Backup and Disaster Recovery

- **Regular Backups:** Implement regular data backups to ensure data integrity and availability in case of data loss or system failures. Backups help restore data to a previous state in the event of a disaster.

- **Disaster Recovery Plans:** Establish disaster recovery plans to minimize the impact of unexpected incidents on data and services. Disaster recovery strategies ensure business continuity and data restoration.

40.2.8. Employee Training and Awareness

- **Security Training:** Educate employees about data protection best practices and potential security risks to prevent inadvertent data breaches. Well-informed employees are better equipped to protect data.

- **Privacy Policies:** Ensure employees understand and adhere to the organization's privacy policies and procedures. Employee compliance with privacy policies is essential for maintaining data security.

40.2.9. Compliance with Data Protection Regulations

- **GDPR Compliance:** If applicable, comply with the General Data Protection Regulation (GDPR) requirements when handling personal data of EU citizens. GDPR sets strict standards for data privacy and protection.

- **Other Data Protection Laws:** Familiarize yourself with and adhere to data protection laws in other relevant jurisdictions. Complying with local regulations ensures that data privacy is upheld worldwide.

40.3 Responsible AI and Ethical Decision-Making in Cloud-Based Systems

As cloud-based systems increasingly incorporate Artificial Intelligence (AI) and machine learning technologies, it becomes crucial to ensure responsible and ethical AI practices. Responsible AI entails developing AI models and algorithms that prioritize fairness, transparency, and accountability. Responsible AI and ethical decision-making in cloud-based systems are essential for building trust and ensuring the positive impact of AI technologies. By prioritizing fairness, transparency, and accountability, organizations can avoid biased and discriminatory AI outcomes. Protecting data privacy and providing human oversight are critical steps to ensure that AI is used responsibly and ethically. Compliance with relevant regulations and continuous improvement through feedback and model updates contribute to the long-term success of responsible AI in cloud-based systems. As AI becomes increasingly integrated into cloud computing, embracing responsible AI practices is a shared responsibility that aligns with societal values and the ethical use of technology. Responsible AI not only safeguards users but also ensures the sustainable and equitable development of AI technologies in the cloud.

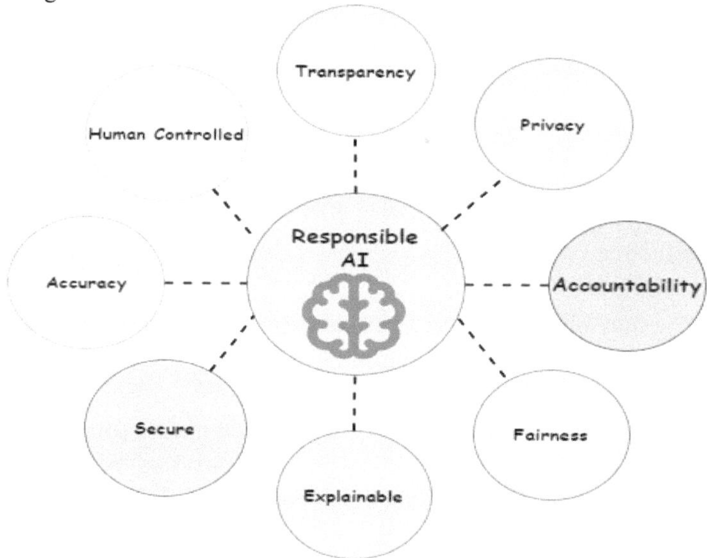

40.3.1. Fairness and Bias Mitigation

- **Data Bias:** Identify and address biases in training data to prevent AI models from producing unfair or discriminatory outcomes. Biases in data can lead to biased decisions, perpetuating existing inequalities.

- **Algorithmic Fairness:** Develop algorithms that provide equitable outcomes across different demographic groups. Ensuring fairness in AI decisions is vital to avoid marginalizing certain populations.

40.3.2. Explainability and Transparency

- **Model Interpretability:** Ensure AI models are interpretable, allowing stakeholders to understand how decisions are made. Transparent models enhance trust and enable better auditing.

- **Transparent Algorithms:** Deploy transparent algorithms that provide clear insights into decision-making processes. This helps users and stakeholders comprehend and validate AI-driven decisions.

40.3.3. Data Privacy and Protection

- **Privacy-Preserving Techniques:** Implement privacy-preserving techniques, such as differential privacy, to protect sensitive data. Preserving data privacy is crucial in AI applications that involve personal or sensitive information.

- **Data Anonymization:** Anonymize personal data to prevent the identification of individuals. Anonymization helps protect the privacy of individuals while still enabling valuable insights from the data.

40.3.4. Accountability and Traceability
- **Audit Trails:** Maintain comprehensive audit trails to trace the decision-making process of AI models. Audit trails enable accountability and facilitate understanding of AI model behavior.

- **Model Monitoring:** Continuously monitor AI models to detect any deviations from expected behavior. Monitoring ensures that models remain accurate and unbiased over time.

40.3.5. Human Oversight and Control
- **Human-in-the-Loop:** Incorporate human oversight and control in critical decision-making processes. Human intervention can prevent AI models from making harmful or erroneous decisions.

- **Human Review:** Establish mechanisms for human review in cases where AI decisions may have significant consequences. Human review ensures that AI outcomes align with ethical standards.

40.3.6. Ethical Use of AI
- **Clear Use Cases:** Define clear and ethical use cases for AI to ensure it aligns with organizational values. Understanding the intended purpose of AI deployment helps avoid unintended and potentially harmful applications.

- **Avoiding Harm:** Assess potential harm or negative impacts of AI deployment and take measures to avoid or mitigate them. Ethical AI should prioritize the well-being of individuals and society.

40.3.7. Compliance with Regulations
- **GDPR and Data Protection Laws:** Comply with data protection laws and regulations, such as the General Data Protection Regulation (GDPR), when handling personal data. Adhering to legal requirements is essential for data privacy and protection.

- **Ethics Guidelines:** Adhere to industry-specific AI ethics guidelines and principles. Following ethical guidelines ensures that AI is used responsibly and transparently.

40.3.8. Continuous Improvement
- **Feedback Mechanisms:** Establish feedback mechanisms to gather insights and concerns from stakeholders. Feedback helps identify areas of improvement and potential ethical issues.

- **Model Updates:** Regularly update AI models to reflect changes in data and to address any identified issues. Keeping models up-to-date is vital for maintaining their accuracy and ethical performance.

Exercise

Multiple Choice Questions

1. What are some of the ethical challenges introduced by cloud computing?

a. Data efficiency and reliability

b. Energy consumption and e-waste management

c. Security audits and data encryption

d. Data breaches and surveillance

2. How can organizations address the issue of data ownership in cloud computing?

a. Storing data in multiple cloud providers simultaneously

b. Creating backup copies of data in different jurisdictions

c. Implementing data minimization practices

d. Establishing clear agreements and policies

3. What is one potential concern related to cross-border data flows in cloud computing?

a. Limited access to cloud services in certain regions

b. Challenges in migrating from one cloud provider to another

c. Diverse data protection laws in different countries

d. The risk of data breaches during data transmission

4. What can organizations do to minimize the environmental impact of cloud data centers?

a. Reduce data residency requirements

b. Increase data collection for better analysis

c. Adopt renewable energy sources

d. Improve data center hardware turnover

5. Why is algorithmic fairness essential in cloud-based AI systems?

a. To ensure optimal data encryption

b. To prevent vendor lock-in

c. To avoid data breaches

d. To avoid biased decision-making

6. How can organizations bridge the digital divide in cloud computing?

a. By limiting access to cloud services

b. By promoting digital literacy programs

c. By increasing data collection practices

d. By avoiding data anonymization

7. What is one way to ensure responsible AI in cloud-based systems?

a. Implementing data ownership agreements

b. Conducting regular security audits

c. Focusing on vendor lock-in strategies

d. Reducing data center energy consumption

8. What does "Human-in-the-Loop" refer to in the context of responsible AI?

a. Incorporating human oversight and control in AI decision-making

b. Using human operators to manage cloud data centers

c. Adopting a data-centric approach to AI deployment

d. Creating data backups to ensure data integrity

9. Why is compliance with data protection laws crucial in cloud computing?

a. To promote data residency and jurisdiction concerns

b. To minimize data encryption requirements

c. To enhance data privacy and protection

d. To increase vendor dependence for better data security

Review Questions

1. What are some of the ethical challenges introduced by cloud computing, and why is it crucial to address them?

2. How can organizations address the issue of data ownership in cloud computing, particularly when data is stored across multiple jurisdictions?

3. What is one potential concern related to cross-border data flows in cloud computing, and how can organizations navigate data sovereignty and jurisdiction challenges?

4. What actions can organizations take to minimize the environmental impact of cloud data centers and promote sustainability?

5. Why is algorithmic fairness essential in cloud-based AI systems, and how can biases in AI models be addressed?

6. How can organizations bridge the digital divide in cloud computing and ensure equitable access to cloud services?

7. What measures can organizations take to ensure responsible AI and ethical decision-making in cloud-based systems?

8. In the context of responsible AI, what does "Human-in-the-Loop" refer to, and why is it important?

9. Why is compliance with data protection laws crucial in cloud computing, and what are some of the key regulations organizations should be aware of?

10. How can organizations implement data encryption and access controls to ensure privacy and data protection in cloud computing?

11. What is the role of regular audits, employee training, and compliance in maintaining the privacy and security of data in the cloud?

Answer Section

Multiple Choice Questions

1. d) Data breaches and surveillance

2. d) Establishing clear agreements and policies

3. c) Diverse data protection laws in different countries

4. c) Adopt renewable energy sources

5. d) To avoid biased decision-making

6. b) By promoting digital literacy programs

7. b) Conducting regular security audits

8. a) Incorporating human oversight and control in AI decision-making

9. c) To enhance data privacy and protection

Review Questions

1. Ethical challenges in cloud computing include data breaches, data ownership ambiguity, government surveillance, and environmental impact. Addressing these challenges is crucial to protect data privacy, ensure security, and build trust in cloud services. Data breaches can lead to unauthorized access and potential misuse of sensitive information. Data ownership ambiguity can result in legal disputes and affect user trust. Government surveillance raises concerns about individual privacy. Environmental impact, such as energy consumption and e-waste, affects sustainability. Addressing these challenges is essential for responsible cloud computing and safeguarding user rights.

2. Organizations can address data ownership challenges in cloud computing by establishing clear agreements and policies defining data ownership and control. Contracts should outline data ownership during collection, storage, and processing stages. When data is stored across multiple jurisdictions, compliance with relevant data protection laws is crucial to protect data ownership rights. Organizations must ensure responsible data handling and privacy protection in the cloud to maintain user trust and adhere to legal requirements.

3. One potential concern with cross-border data flows in cloud computing is the varying laws and regulations across countries, affecting data sovereignty and jurisdiction. Organizations can navigate these challenges by selecting cloud providers with data centers in jurisdictions aligned with data protection

regulations. Complying with local laws ensures data privacy and protects organizations from legal issues related to cross-border data storage and processing.

4. Organizations can minimize the environmental impact of cloud data centers by adopting renewable energy sources, improving energy efficiency, and practicing responsible e-waste management. Reducing greenhouse gas emissions and responsibly handling hardware turnover contributes to sustainability and environmental conservation. Implementing eco-friendly practices in cloud infrastructure supports a more sustainable digital future.

5. Algorithmic fairness is crucial in cloud-based AI systems to avoid biased decision-making. Organizations can address biases in AI models by using diverse and representative training data, applying fairness-aware algorithms, and conducting regular bias audits. Ethical AI development involves identifying and mitigating biases to ensure equitable outcomes and prevent discrimination in AI-driven decisions.

6. Organizations can bridge the digital divide in cloud computing by promoting digital literacy programs and infrastructure development. Ensuring equitable access to cloud services helps reduce disparities between regions and communities. By empowering underserved populations with digital skills and resources, organizations can foster inclusivity and promote equal opportunities in cloud computing.

7. Ensuring responsible AI and ethical decision-making in cloud-based systems involve prioritizing fairness, transparency, and accountability. Regular audits, human oversight, and adherence to AI ethics guidelines help maintain AI model accuracy and ethical performance. Organizations must adopt data anonymization techniques, obtain informed consent, and implement privacy-preserving practices to protect user data and privacy in AI applications.

8. "Human-in-the-Loop" refers to incorporating human oversight and control in critical AI decision-making processes. Human intervention can prevent harmful or biased outcomes by providing context, ethical considerations, and addressing unforeseen circumstances. Including human review in AI systems enhances accountability, mitigates risks, and aligns AI outcomes with ethical standards.

9. Compliance with data protection laws is vital in cloud computing to uphold data privacy and security. Organizations must be aware of regulations such as the General Data Protection Regulation (GDPR) when handling personal data of EU citizens. Adhering to relevant data protection laws ensures responsible data handling, protects user privacy, and avoids potential legal and reputational risks.

10. Organizations can ensure privacy and data protection in cloud computing through data encryption and access controls. Data encryption secures data at rest and during transmission, preventing unauthorized access and ensuring confidentiality. Implementing role-based access control (RBAC) ensures that users and applications have appropriate permissions to access specific data and resources, reducing the risk of data breaches.

11. Regular audits help identify vulnerabilities and weaknesses in cloud infrastructure, ensuring data privacy and security. Employee training on data protection best practices prevents inadvertent data breaches and supports a culture of responsible data handling. Compliance with data protection regulations ensures that organizations meet legal obligations and maintain data privacy and security standards in the cloud.